Compliance and the Law

Compliance and the Law

A MULTI-DISCIPLINARY APPROACH

EDITED BY

SAMUEL KRISLOV, KEITH O. BOYUM,

JERRY N. CLARK, ROGER C. SHAEFER,

and SUSAN O. WHITE

University of Minnesota

Published in cooperation with the

LAW AND SOCIETY ASSOCIATION

SAGE PUBLICATIONS / Beverly Hills · London

Portions of this volume have previously appeared in issues of the *Law and Society Review.*

For information address:

SAGE PUBLICATIONS, INC.
275 South Beverly Drive
Beverly Hills, California 90212

SAGE PUBLICATIONS LTD
St. George's House
44 Hatton Garden, London E C 1

Printed in the United States of America

International Standard Book Number 0-8039-0119-4

Library of Congress Catalog Card No. 73-151670

First Printing

Contents

Compliance and the Law

Compliance, Obedience, and Revolt

An Overview

JERRY N. CLARK, KEITH O. BOYUM,

SAMUEL KRISLOV, and ROGER C. SHAEFER

University of Minnesota

This volume was planned and developed on the assumption that the phenomena of compliance, obedience, and revolt are being treated in parallel, never-intersecting lines by different professions. It was our assumption that the existence of such needlessly discrete approaches—one often not known to its nearest neighbor—has contributed to a lack of development of both theory and accumulated data.

In conception and in execution, this volume has the strengths and weaknesses of such a showcase effort to familiarize across fields, even though focused on a common theme. The quip that cross-disciplinary research leads to cross-sterilization unfortunately has real-life referents, but it is not the rule, nor should it become our guide. All approaches suffer from inherent problems and from the human weakness involved, but "the efficacy of the sacrament is not altered by the unworthiness of the priest."

Originally, much of this volume was planned and published as two integrated issues of the *Law and Society Review.* Our concept was to include two types of articles: (1) review essays with theoretical thrusts, and (2) paradigmatic efforts, often with significant data contributions. The response to those issues has encouraged us to project this volume. That transmutation has impelled us to take on the task not asked of any single contributor to the original effort, but which we feel must be confronted in such a book—the attempt to provide an overall view, a multidisciplinary, integrative effort. Our apprehension at such a task is mitigated slightly by our sense of having lived with the general problem for at least two years, and even more by a fatalistic sense that the task must be attempted, come what may.

A concern for conditions of and propensity to obedience is hardly the exclusive province of any field or any era. It is a fundamental problem of any coherent political philosophy, including (perhaps especially) an anarchist view. It is explicit in such sociological work as, for example, social control, and implicit in work on recidivism. It is in large measure integrated as a nonstated primitive assumption in economic theory, and is the major topic (though in nonlegal, nonglobal language) in organizational theory. Similarly, a huge body of psychological literature has been talking compliance for decades without the authors being aware of it.

The thrust of modern concern, however, seems to have centered in law, sociology, and political science, with actual and usually Supreme Court cases as well as general societal needs providing rather clear incitement to better and more concerted work. These cases seem to us to have been primarily the following:

(1) The desegregation decision, with its demonstration of the possibilities for resistance on the one hand, and potential for social change on the other. A great, natural, and dramatic quasi-experiment, Brown v. Board of Education (1954) sensitized social scientists to the potential of such instances.

(2) The religious cases, Baker v. Carr (1962) and reapportionment, Miranda (1966), and other criminal decisions all contributed to this development.

(3) The quest for simplified criminal laws in recent years has produced strong efforts to eliminate from the domain of criminality a number of practices—adultery, homosexuality, drug use, prostitution, obscenity, drunkenness, and so on; this can be argued in philosophical terms—"consenting adults in private" can be seen as being outside the proper domain of social control as per H. L. A. Hart. It can also be argued in terms of pure social utility—the police can be freed to handle significant matters, while those who cannot resist the attractions of these "crimes without victims" do not create a black market because of their willingness to pay an additional "crime tariff" as suggested by Herbert Packer. In any event, criminal laws lend themselves to argumentation from "before and after" evidence as localities shift their policies under the impetus of uncertain and changing dominant opinion on such matters.

(4) The concern over nation-building. The commitment to creation of new states in the 1950s and 1960s was paralleled by studies in the nature of civic commitment, obligation, and mutual trust. The literature of political socialization and the newly burgeoning legal socialization literature are by-products of that concern.

(5) The crisis of loyalty and obligation. The problem of obedience provoked a small but pregnant literature, which has grown in light of the external

crisis of confidence over the Far Eastern policy and the internal crisis over race. Extensive normative discussions have been matched by numerous empirical studies, e.g., the concomitants of violence.

It may be noted that this broad domain includes a good deal of the most sophisticated and prestigious behavioral research of the past quarter-century. The necessary conclusion that the work of that period has closely reflected major long-range social problems cuts both ways in the perennial, often tedious argument between advocates of "scientific" versus those of "relevant" research.

Nevertheless, the sum total of these efforts is not apparent. Thus, when Thomas Schelling set out some years ago to develop a strategy of conflict, he expected that "Legislators, jurists, lawyers, and legal scholars might be supposed to have subjected the concept [deterrence] to rigorous and systematic scrutiny for many generations" (Schelling, 1960: 10). Instead, he found that neither in law nor in sociology was there a well-developed theory of deterrence that could be utilized in the analysis of international affairs. Subsequent developments, though yet to fully jell, promised to disappoint Schelling less.

In attempting to order this mass of different materials, we—like others—have been struck by the terminology of "impact" and "compliance," generally used interchangeably, but with rather different connotations. We would suggest the two can be defined more sharply to distinguish different though interrelated problems, and the difference utilized to organize our discussion. Briefly put, impact studies are seen as result-oriented, while compliance studies are process-oriented. It is not a matter of one term being more or less exclusive, but rather of overlap and difference. More specifically, "impact" involves the consequent ensuing upon a decision or policy, including all consequences, not merely obedience, while "compliance" is concerned with the process of acceptance, largely prior to the point of "impact." The two then are largely complementary and overlap only slightly. The feedback effects of impact upon compliance are obvious, as are the screening of consequences of propensity to compliance (or lack thereof) in affecting impact.

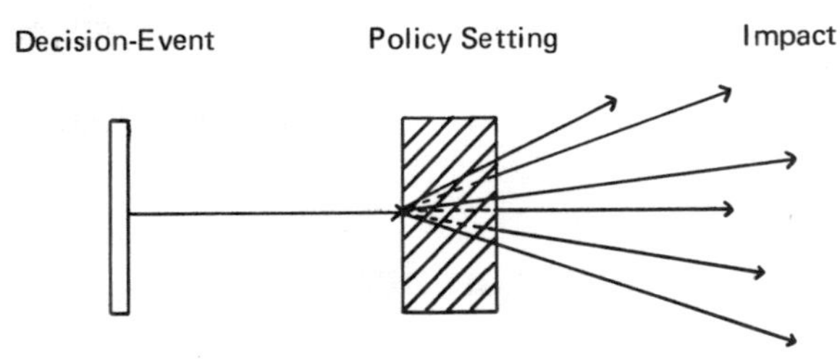

The impact model focuses on the policy responses of decision-makers to events or decisions at other levels, and the general consequences of those responses in terms of compliance and change.

Figure 1: IMPACT MODEL

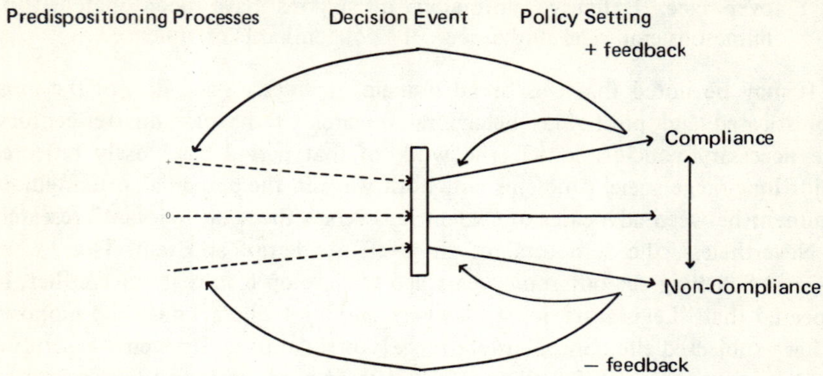

The compliance model is more elaborate than the impact model in its attention to socialization processes and psychological factors that account for predispositions to adopt differing policies and to obey or disobey, and to feedback effects of consequent compliance or non-compliance.

Figure 2: COMPLIANCE MODEL

We would further suggest that a continuum of interest from process to concrete impact can be arrived at with philosophy at the process polar area of concern, and law at the other pole. Although some overlap is to be expected, the perceived ordering is as follows:

(1) philosophy;
(2) psychology;
(3) economics;
(4) sociology;
(5) political science;
(6) law.

It will be noted that the distinction is virtually synonymous with concern with immediate policy effects versus broader processial concern, and that, for many of the fields, we are encompassing broad efforts to combine and maximize the axes of concern.

PHILOSOPHY

In recent years, the philosophical contribution to our topic seems to have concentrated in two major areas. The first is the elaboration of the H. L. A. Hart (itself a variant of Kelsen's approach) position, which derives law as from a system of primary and secondary rules prevailing within the social order (see,

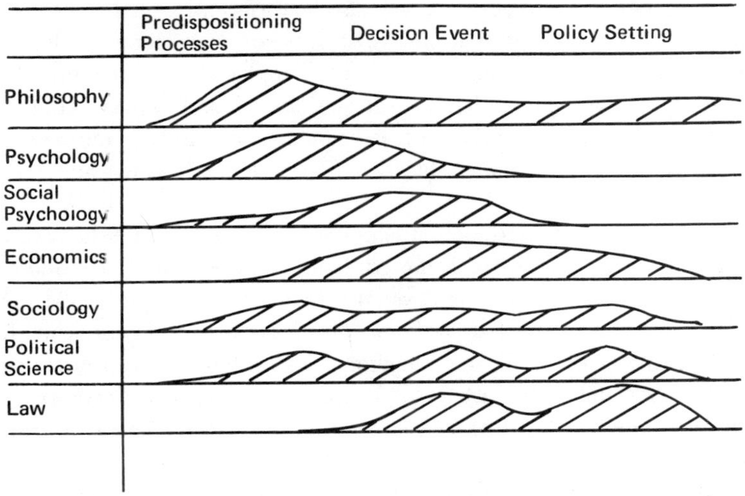

Figure 3: THE COMPLIANCE MODEL AND A HYPOTHETICAL CONTINUUM OF OVERLAPPING DISCIPLINARY INTEREST

e.g., Dworkin, 1967; Sartorius, 1968). Closely related are efforts to define not a perfect state but rather rules for testing movement from one imperfect state to another (Rawls, 1958). Here the critical literature is large (see, e.g., Wolff, 1965, and Rempel, 1969). The Lockean (and therefore Ricardo-like) treatment in turn parallels the discussion of economists on political issues (compare, e.g., Gottlieb, 1968, with Buchanan and Tullock, 1962).

The second major concern has been the overt question of disobedience. Extensive discussion of the normative conditions under which one is freed from the obligation to obey (e.g., Sibley, 1970; Walzer, 1970) and obligation generally (e.g., Flathman, forthcoming) is supplemented by anarchist and nonobligation arguments (e.g., Wolff).

PSYCHOLOGY

Psychology as a field apparently makes no use of the concept of compliance; this is not because psychologists have no interest in the notion, but rather the reverse. Since psychology has dealt with the general problem as a central one for some time, several basic concepts have emerged. The fact that psychology is probably the most advanced of the social sciences seems related to this point as well. As the study of human behavior becomes more sophisticated, more closely defined concepts will be developed to facilitate understanding as regards some segment of the general problem. This is not necessarily a criticism of compliance as a concept: it may prove appropriate for scholars whose concern is with law as a means of social control. Where scholarly concerns differ, it is likely that the set of appropriately employed concepts will also be different.

The whole domain of learning theory is an area, long of interest to psychologists, which bears on the idea of compliance, as Underhill Moore's famous parking experiment demonstrates. Classical or Pavlovian conditioning falls under the general rubric, but does not seem directly relevant to our concerns. Of more interest are the areas of avoidance learning and reinforcement.

The basic notion of instrumental learning is that the previously experienced consequences of a response to some stimulus condition the likelihood of that response recurring. This paradigm can be made to fit a very wide range of behavior—from dogs trained to walk on two legs to a professor who, finding himself locked out of his office, telephones a maintenance man instead of the police who were unhelpful last week. The paradigm's utility, however, is more generally conceded in the former case than in the latter. That is, instrumental learning has been advanced as an effective analytical approach primarily in the instance of infrahuman animals. As Skinner, among others, fervently argues, the more complex motivations of men might be more fruitfully analyzed via some more elaborate conceptions or conceptual schemes.

The concept of reinforcement suggests that behavioral consequences, where serving to increase the likelihood of recurrence, can be conceived as positive reinforcement. In like manner, where those consequences make it less likely that the behavior will be repeated, we may think of them as negative reinforcement. In the example cited above, the professor's call to the police resulted in negative reinforcement, so the behavior was not repeated.

Reinforcement can be taken as an extemely pervasive phenomenon. We can say that Pavlov's dogs learned to salivate at the bell because the food reward reinforced that behavior. We can also say that a student works hard in a course because his teacher's approbation, or that of his peer group, reinforces his behavior. Or the reinforcement might straightforwardly come from the satisfaction of his desire to do well for doing well's sake.

In the case of men, it is very difficult indeed to know exactly what item or items are the reinforcers. Most, if not all, laboratory experiments have been performed on animals. An interesting result is that, for animals higher on the phylogenetic scale, deprivation-independent reinforcers are important and useful. For example, the subject animal need not be hungry, for food is not the only possible reward. Novelty of situation may reinforce the exploratory behavior of rats. It would not seem appropriate to expect less capacity on the part of our hypothetical professor. Reinforcers there may well be, and they may be extremely important in conditioning the behavior of men. At the same time, it is probably true that reinforcement for human beings is so varied that, even under controlled experimental conditions, prediction is at best hazardous. We might say that Hawthorne effects plague the investigator of human learning.

The results of research in avoidance learning are both interesting and suggestive. The area may be dichotomized into active avoidance learning and passive avoidance learning. The former basically entails learning *what* to do (e.g., rats learning to avoid pain); the latter entails learning what *not* to do (e.g., learning to avoid punishment). Passive avoidance learning invites an analogy to rule systems, and seems worthy of a closer look.

Following Solomon's (1968) synopsis of the subfield, we can briefly point to some relevant variables. Where punishment is the consequence of an instrumental response previously established by rewards, the outcome or effect is dependent upon (1) duration, (2) intensity, and (3) repeated exposure of the punishment. In experiments with rats, an increase in these factors tends to hasten a change from the old response. (4) Delay of some length between response and punishment has the opposite effect. A phenomenon of (5) reward-punishment habituation is relevant: simultaneous rewarding and punishing of the response, where the punishment is neither intense nor of long duration, can result not only in a failure to suppress the response, but can actually lead to a situation wherein the punishment serves as a reward in its own right. The presence of (6) a rewarded alternative hastens the suppression of the learned response. The presence of a (7) temporal discriminative alternative—disallowing the act at time and situation A but permitting it at B—is useful. Having B makes disallowing A easier. The (8) temporal order of reward and punishment is important: where a reward-punishment sequence follows the response, the response tends to be extinguished. But a punishment-reward sequence may lead to a strengthening of the response, the subject actually seeking out the punishment, as it were. (9) Species-specific characteristics condition the effectiveness of the punishment. And finally, the (10) natural resistance to extinction of the response is a factor. Punishing the dog for walking on its hind legs will end that response more quickly than punishing him for barking will end his noises.[1]

A quite different thrust in psychology, but one which seems to bear on compliance, is developmental psychology. The acquisition of social norms is clearly related to compliance, and psychologists' contributions are not limited to the socialization literature explicitly developed as such. The focus here is primarily upon cognitive process in relationship to capacity, and the relationship over time and through maturation and other changes.

Some psychologists, notably Jean Piaget (1952; 1955; 1962; 1965) have developed and elaborated a stage theory of intellectual development. The general idea is that children cannot handle certain kinds of thought processes until they are old enough; that is, until they have reached an appropriate stage in the development of their intellectual capacities. The notion is not surprising, in that we commonly expect more from older children than we do from younger, but Piaget's formulation has some unexpected and powerful implications. Although the question remains open, eventually a formal theory of distinct stages may be discarded or modified in the direction of a more continuous conception of intellectual development (compare with Bandura and McDonald, 1963). Yet the basic idea seems likely to retain its viability: the child undergoes qualitative, organizational changes in his cognitive functions.

The maturing child's changing reaction to rules is one application of the theory which is of direct relevance to compliance with the law. At an early stage, the child is what Piaget calls heteronomous, that is, completely subject to the authority of others. He is incapable of being otherwise. Later his conceptions of and reactions to rules change, because the child has acquired a capacity for more elaborate conceptions.

Related work in the area of developmental psychology has focused on moral development rather than cognitive maturation. Lawrence Kohlberg (1964: 405) makes the following fundamental distinction: "Intellectual development, then, is an important condition for development of moral thought, but level of moral thought can be clearly distinguished from general intellectual level." Moral development as such is not taken to be synonymous with social adjustment or socialization. Kohlberg conceives the latter two as essentially outward, as being behavioral phenomena. Moral development is the internal aspect of socialization, the sphere of psychological research.

Evidence for the existence of internalized norms varies by theoretical scheme, according to Kohlberg. There is a behavioral criterion–resistance to temptation; an emotional criterion–measured in terms of guilt feelings; and a judgmental criterion. Judgment as the standard entails discovering a capacity to use the moral criterion to measure worth or rightness of conduct of the self and others. The latter is independent of whether the temptation, for example, was successfully withstood (a classic pitfall in using the subject's behavior as the criterion).

Sophisticated ability to employ complex judgmental criteria apparently comes only with adolescence. Thus there is an apparent correlation with the development of cognitive capacity. There is a body of theoretical work which employs a stage theory in analyzing the progression of children from simple ideas about morality to complex ones, and the intellectual roots are again traceable to Piaget. Exact delineation of the stages and the ages at which children move from one to another, are a matter of some scholarly disagreement, and in any event need not detain us here. Perhaps more suggestive is research which indicates that at least some juvenile delinquents are at a "premoral" stage of judgment, at an age where such would not be expected or normal (compare with Kohlberg, 1964). This proposition does not ignore situational factors influencing actual behavior. In fact, the reverse seems more likely: such things as probability of being caught and dominant peer group ideology have been identified as much *more* proximate and important behavioral determinants than level of moral development. Yet two things seem to stand out. First, where situation is controlled, the independent effects of conscience are evident.

Second, rehabilitation efforts are much more difficult where situational factors are virtually the only behavioral regulators—as is the case with a premoral delinquent.

Recent empirical work on the psychological antecedents of compliance seems to have been predicated on theory which does not have explicit Freudian roots. While Freud is not forgotten, neither are psychoanalytic concepts easily operationalized for the laboratory situation. Freud's contributions, from this historical vantage, are apparent but take indirect form. Bronfenbrenner (1963: 531), in a review of developmental theory, asserts that the influence of Freudian thinking is evidenced by selection of phenomena for study and the formulation of hypotheses. But he notes that Freud himself would have difficulty recognizing modern ideas as having been originally his own.

We turn our attention now to research on aggression, some of which is closer to Freudian ideas than the research reported to this point. Bandura and Walters (1963a) trace a line of intellectual influence to Dollard, Doob, Miller, Mowrer, and Sears, at Yale in 1939. They proposed, in *Frustration and Aggression,* the classic hypothesis: aggression is a natural and inevitable consequence of frustration. For some theorists, the hypothesis quickly underwent some modification; yet frustration was commonly held to be an inevitable antecedent of aggression. The difference, of course, is in the willingness to posit a one-to-one relationship, one instance of aggression for every instance of frustration. The reverse is a more modest claim.

Frustration can be fruitfully taken as "all operations or conditions that prevent or delay reinforcement" (Bandura and Walters, 1963a: 367). Aggression is not as easily pinned down, but it has generally been taken to involve intentionality, behavior *meant* to injure, even though intentionality is extremely difficult to ascertain. Sex differences, socialization, the behavior of models, and differential reinforcement in general are some of the variables which have been found relevant in understanding differential rates of aggressive behavior.

Displacement and projection, and catharsis are processes which are conceptually related to aggression. In the case of the former (really two variables in Freud's scheme, but which have proven difficult to distinguish in empirical studies of fantasy aggression), the concepts apparently have not proven useful, or at any rate have not been convincingly employed as operationally defined. Displacement as currently employed seems unsatisfactory: scapegoats are probably real enough, but the phenomenon of their generation is probably amenable to more useful conceptualization. Thus Freud's contribution seems likely destined for a somewhat more indirect status. Catharsis, the purging of aggressive tendencies through vicarious participation in aggressive activity, is very poorly supported. While there is some evidence that angered adults may be less aggressive following vicarious participation in aggressive activity, the tendency is not evidenced for either children or for nonangered adults in any clear way. Again the most reasonable conclusion may be that Freud pointed to critical phenomena and offered grand hypotheses, heuristically useful in the fullest sense of the term, but we may be well advised not to press further than that in any attempt to employ his conceptual schema in an empirical fashion.

The work of a few psychologists is more concerned with resulting behavior–impact analysis in our terms. Milgram (1965b) has studied obedience to authority in a laboratory situation where the experimenter, a person exercising legitimate authority, ordered naive subjects to administer what they believed to be very severe electrical shock to a "victim." Under many different conditions, where factors such as proximity (experimenter to subject, victim to subject), setting (campus or noncampus), and subject group (students or nonstudents) were varied, a surprising degree of obedience was obtained. Under experimenter orders, many subjects acted harshly toward the victim, even where doing so caused the victim much apparent distress.

Milgram (1965a) also has studied the effects of a group on individual behavior in similar experiments. Paired with a disobedient confederate, the tendency was to act more in congruence with the subject's own social norms. That is, disobedience to a command ordering the administration of pain was manifest much more often than was blind obedience. Groups have other effects too: Darley and Latané (1968a) have advanced the notion of a diffusion of responsibility where positive action is needed or where another person is in difficulty or trouble. Action on the part of one potential help giver is not as likely where the appeal for help is directed generally to more than one person.

SOCIAL PSYCHOLOGICAL BASES

Social psychologists directly employ the term "compliance"; psychologists do not, insofar as we could ascertain, in any theoretical way. However, compliance has a specific meaning in social psychology:

> Compliance can be said to occur when an individual accepts influence because he hopes to achieve a favorable reaction from another person or group. He adopts the induced behavior not because he believes in its content but because he expects to gain specific rewards or approval and avoid specific punishments or disapproval by conforming. Thus the satisfaction derived from compliance is due to the *social effect* of accepting influence [Kelman, 1958: 53].

In Kelman's scheme, compliance comes close to, but is distinguishable from, identification and internalization. He (1963: 440) defines identification as the acceptance of influence by a self-definition anchored in a desired relationship to another. The identifying individual classically takes on all or part of the role of another, a consequence of a wish to be, or at least to be like, the other person. Internalization occurs when influence is accepted "because the induced behavior is congruent with his value system" (Kelman, 1963: 441).

It follows that, and this seems especially suggestive for the study of compliance generally, conditions of performance vary according to which of these phenomena is controlling. Compliance as Kelman uses the term necessitates surveillance. Identification requires that the relationship to the agent individual be salient; internalization requires that values be relevant to the issue at hand (Kelman, 1963: 443).

Social psychology's focus on groups is a source for instruction on the general problem of compliance. (To say that all human behavior is sited in small groups may be oversimplified by being incomplete—but the idea is not for that wrong or not useful.) Distinctions are necessary between membership groups and reference groups, and between different sorts of reference groups (compare with Shibutani, 1955). Some of the groups of which an individual is a member may not constitute a reference group focus for him. In fact, a reference group may be a group to which an individual does not belong: according to Shibutani, the original concept meant nothing more than a group serving as a point of comparison in evaluating one's own status. The term may also apply to a group to which an individual aspires. And perhaps the most useful theoretical meaning constitutes a third use for the term: a group whose perspective is assumed by the actor. All three sorts of groups can affect behavior. Perhaps most relevant for a concern for compliance are groups which mold perspectives and aspirations. Knowing something about a reference group and its salience, we can make some comments about likely behaviors.

Allport (1954: 97) deals generally with conformity in groups, and explains the logic of his "*J*-curve" idea in this way: "Whenever there is a strongly prescribed action for members of an in-group they will, by virtue of their membership, tend to conform." Of course they do not, each one of them, conform completely (a very large group is the reference here). Instead, they conform in a way such that their behaviors can be plotted on a curve which looks more or less like a *J*. Very few won't conform at all; a few conform in an incomplete way; by far the most of the in-group members conform virtually completely to the demand for the behavior. The steepness of the *J*-curve provides some indication of the strength of the demand, and somewhat more indirectly the vitality of the group.

Some other studies have focused on intragroup processes which bring about conformity. Festinger's (1950) landmark article on informal social communication sets out two bases of pressures toward uniformity in a group: the grounding of social reality therein, essentially a matter of gaining agreement and support on how to deal with the world; and what Festinger calls group locomotion, uniformity as instrumental to achieving some goal. Group norms more generally have also been a topic for study. Identifiable behavioral prescriptions arising from group interaction are accompanied by a set of potential sanctions against deviance. But in order for group pressures to be effective, the individual must belong to the "psychological group"—that is, he must have a real tie in his own mind, considering the group and his membership in it important. That qualification highlights the importance of reference groups: psychological groups are almost by definition reference groups and have substantial influence over individual members.

The group can have a dramatic effect even on judgments pertaining to physical phenomena. As Asch discovered, "majority effect" can persuade at least some laboratory subjects to regard what their senses tell them is false. Where the topic is valuational (and the stimulus likely more ambiguous), the effect of a majority opinion is enhanced. It is still further enhanced where the majority is composed of close friends–a situation likely in the real world.

Attitudes constitute another topic, though related to the idea of group influence. Since attitudes are usually conceived as being grounded in groups, it follows that, to effect attitude change, some account must be taken of the group. Antisocial attitudes held by a delinquent are easier to change if he is psychologically removed from the group constituting a base of support for the attitude. There are, however, other bases for attitudes than peer approbation. Katz (1960) points to a set of four functions that attitudes perform for the individual: instrumental, ego-defense, value-expressive, and knowledge. Where attitudes are conceived as important mediators of behavior, they naturally come to the fore in a concern for compliance. Some concern with function seems appropriate where noncompliant attitudes must be changed (e.g., in rehabilitative work with convicts).

The whole notion of influence has led some social psychologists to address a problem which has classically been in the domain of political science–power, influence, and the bases thereof. French and Raven (1959) define reward, coercive, legitimate, referent, and expert power, each having a distinct base and being appropriate to distinct situations. Though the phenomenon is surely real enough, the concept of power as such is probably not as useful as it may seem to be at the outset. That is, many of the social relationships which exhibit the presence and use of "power" can probably be more precisely and fruitfully dealt with by using other concepts. The basic difficulty lies in the use of "power" in a variety of different models, thus making it mean different things at different times. And directly related to that is the problem of measurement. March (1966) seems persuasive that other models of social choice should be used in many situations where "power" seems in evidence.

We have not exhausted social psychological theories and perspectives which may prove useful in a study of compliance. Topics such as leadership, culture generally, role, and various others are probably relevant, though likely in a less direct way. Socialization also remains, however, and seems very much in point. The acquisition of social norms is an area in which psychologists, social psychologists, sociologists, anthropologists, political scientists, and others have all had something to say. Briefly we may note that most research has been done on children, though the process is generalizable to any age group. The idea of resocialization–bringing about changes in the accepted patterns of behavior–becomes relevant for noninfants. The perspective lends itself to problems of deviant behavior, and as well to the generation of accepted modes of behavior. The latter has been the focus of more research and is probably more important: close understanding of how individuals are socialized should lend a great deal to the problem of modifying inappropriate behaviors. The reader is referred to the article by Koeppen in this volume and to Clausen (1968) for further discussion.

Sociology is concerned with studying and analyzing interactions among members of a social system. Since the discipline casts such a wide net, we felt it appropriate for purposes of this analysis to break it down whenever possible by recognized subfields of specialization. Such an analytical categorization is, of course, somewhat arbitrary. However, the areas with which we shall be concerned, and which deal directly or indirectly with the question of compliance are, broadly speaking, sociology of law, social control, socialization, and deviant behavior.

Although sociology's interest in the law can be traced back at least to Durkheim (Davis et al., 1962: 14-25), with few exceptions American sociologists evinced little interest in the area until quite recently. Scholarly texts that dealt with the topic of sociology of law were few in number and nonempirical (Evan, 1962; Davis et al., 1962). As Skolnick (1965: 5-7) points out, questions pertaining to the intersection of law and the social system were addressed primarily by sociologically oriented law professors such as Pound. However, in a special summer edition of *Social Problems* in 1965, Richard Schwartz argued that sociology must begin to rigorously examine the relationship of law and society. In a follow-up article, Skolnick (1965: 5), while discussing possible trends in this "new" field, noted that empirically "the sociology of law is a brand new specialty, only just emerging at the turn of the sixties." Thus it is hardly surprising that Skolnick's (1965) overview of this new field should cite only one empirical study (Ball, 1960) which dealt directly with compliance with the law.

On the other hand, sociologists have empirically examined the question of the deterrent effects of legal sanctions. Much of the research in this area has been directed toward determining what effect, if any, capital punishment has on homicide rates (Schuessler, 1952; Savitz, 1958; Gibbs, 1968a; Osborne, 1968). Other recent studies have examined the influence of legal sanctions in such diverse areas as income tax payments (Schwartz and Orleans, 1967), parking violations (Chambliss, 1966), crackdown in speed violations (Campbell and Ross, 1968), and the effect of the "breathalyser" test in deterring drunk driving (Ross et al., 1970).

Unfortunately, as Schelling's (1960: 10) comment suggests, there appears to be little theoretical work in the area of sanctions and deterrence. The studies to date seem to be limited to dealing with specific problems or answering specific questions (e.g., whether Connecticut's crackdown on speeders decreased highway deaths in that state; Campbell and Ross, 1968). Recently, however, there has been movement toward development of theoretical schemes concerned with sanctions, deterrence, and crime (Chambliss, 1967; Gibbs, 1966c).

One suggested reason for the discipline's apparent neglect of law-related questions is the fact that American sociologists have generally been more concerned with informal methods of social control than with formal mechanisms such as law (Broom and Selznick, 1968: 384; Schur, 1968: 7). This assertion gains support from a quick look at several introductory sociology texts. That is, sociologists refer to such informal mechanisms as religion, marriage, public esteem, ceremony, and so forth, while precious little discussion is given to law as a tool of social control (Rose, 1965; Bennett and Tumin, 1948; Roucek, 1956). However, one aspect of social control which touches on the area under consideration is the problem of how to gain compliance within organizations. This subject has been a topic for sociologists for some time (Weber, 1947; Etzioni, 1961; Blau and Scott, 1962; Litwak and Meyer, 1966), although it has been a concern for management and administrative specialists in a more intensive way for probably an even longer time (Gulick and Urwick 1937; Barnard, 1938).

For our purposes, however, the works of Etzioni (1961), Simon (1956), and Litwak and Meyer (1966), are probably most germane. Etzioni, for example, has developed a scheme for classifying organizations based on the type and level of control used to gain compliance. Simon presents an interesting scheme in which he argues that most human behavior is rational or goal-oriented. Consequently, where noncompliance is a function of such rational calculation, strategies for compliance would involve changing the perceived reward structures associated with various alternative behavior patterns. Litwak and Meyer, on the other hand, take a slightly different tack, examining how two seemingly divergent forms of organization–bureaucratic and external primary groups–coordinate and integrate their activities in patterned and meaningful ways.

Although the notion of social control has enjoyed wide currency since its popularization by the American sociologist Ross in 1901, the concept is nonetheless basically ambiguous (Clark and Gibbs, 1965). The concept is falling into disuse as more and more of the areas once subsumed under it–sociology of religion, sociology of law, penology, and the like–become important independent specialties in their own right.

Sociology's interest in the socialization process has obvious implications for the question of compliance. Studies in this area have been concerned mainly with the way in which children become acquainted with and learn social norms. Variations in child-rearing practices have been noted and analyzed–with emphasis on the quality of interpersonal relationships–by Clausen and Williams (1963), Bronfenbrenner (1958), and Brim (1957), among others. Cross-cultural studies on the socialization process of children have also been done by Whiting (1963), Sears et al. (1957), Bronfenbrenner, (1963), and others.

Deviant or noncompliant behavior–on both its theoretical and empirical levels–has been the focus of extensive work by sociologists. While there have been diverse theories about these phenomena, we will limit ourselves to a discussion of the two most prominent schools or traditions that have developed. Although these two traditions are not necessarily mutually exclusive–indeed, there is a large area of commonality–they nevertheless offer two rather different perspectives from which to analyze noncompliance.

The first school, or the so-called "social structure" tradition, finds its historical antecedents in Durkheim's (1951) work on suicide–especially his notion of *suicide anomique.* But it was not until 1938 that Merton drew out many of the implications and assumptions in Durkheim's work and made them theoretically applicable to the field of deviant behavior. Merton's theory is essentially concerned with the relationship between culture goals and institutionalized means. Culture goals are the wants or desires that the culture holds out as legitimate objectives toward which the individual should strive. For example, he points out that one of the more prominent culture goals in America is wealth. Society, on the other hand, has certain rules and regulations which prescribe the legitimate methods or avenues of attaining these desired culture goals. Merton (1957: 134) asserts that as long as individuals realize "satisfactions from the achievement of goals and satisfactions emerging directly from the institutionally canalized modes of striving to attain them," conformity and hence societal stability will result. However, when there is discrepancy or disjunction between culture goals and avenues for attaining them, the resultant strain is likely to lead to deviant behavior. By way of illustration, he points out that when a culture emphasizes certain goals without an equal emphasis upon institutionalized procedures, "The technically most efficient procedure, whether culturally legitimate or not, becomes typically preferred to institutionally prescribed conduct" (1957: 135). Continued strain as a result of the disassociation between goals and means, coupled with the aberrant behavior generated by this disjunction, leads ultimately to a state of normlessness (*anomie*) and system instability.

An individual can adapt to this strain by either accepting or rejecting the goals themselves; he can likewise accept or reject the institutionalized means. From this basic dichotomy, Merton (1957: 140) generates a typology of adaptation. The first of these modes of adjustment is conformity, or acceptance of both goals and means. The other four modes are all varieties of deviant behavior.

> *Innovators* (e.g., professional thieves, white-collar criminals, cheaters in examinations) adhere to the goals but reject the normatively prescribed means. *Ritualists* (e.g., bureaucrats who slavishly follow the rules without regard for the ends for which they were designed) make a virtue of overconformity to the institutionalized norms at the price of underconformity to the culturally prescribed goals. *Retreatists* (e.g., tramps, chronic drunkards, and drug addicts) withdraw from the "rat race" by abandoning both

> goals and means. *Rebels* (e.g., members of revolutionary movements) withdraw allegiance to a culture and social system they deem unjust and seek to reconstitute the society anew, with a new set of goals and prescriptions for attaining them [Cohen, 1966: 77; italics added].

A number of empirical studies have utilized Merton's theory of deviant behavior. Rosenthal's (1954) study of a Jewish community in a small Polish town prior to World War II, although based on rather sketchy data, found that members of the lower class were the first to deviate from Orthodox religious ways when they were prevented from reaching culturally defined success standards. In a more recent study, Faia (1967) reports that the relationship between alienation and political deviance in the academic community could be accounted for in terms of structural inadequacies or strains which the deviants felt were a result of certain structural norms in the academic community itself. Also of note is a study by Quinney (1963) of retail prescription violations by druggists in New York State. According to the author, prescription violations (deviant behavior) depend upon which of several occupational role expectations a pharmacist chooses to adopt. These various role alternatives are part of the total occupational structure of retail pharmacy. Finally, Kai Erikson (1962), utilizing a structural approach, suggests that noncompliance patterns are stable and predictable.

The structural tradition, then, rather than focusing on characteristics of the individual per se, looks instead at the position (occupation, social class, and so forth) that the individual occupies in a given social system. It is largely concerned with psychological tensions or strains that are generated by discrepancies between goals and means, and the various modes of adjustment that are made to combat these strains. (The structures of society are seen as patterning forms of deviance.) Various critics have pointed out some of the shortcomings of this approach and possible pitfalls in its utilization (Lindesmith and Strauss, 1968: 395-397; Clinard, 1964: 55-56).

The second school the so-called symbolic interactionists, can be traced back to the writings of George Herbert Mead, Florian Znaniecki and W. I. Thomas, among others. Although within this tradition there are somewhat divergent ways of looking at deviant behavior, theories nevertheless deemphasize the study of deviance as an adaptation to strain caused by social structures. Rather, by utilizing such concepts as role, reference group, and self, those in the symbolic interactionist tradition focus on deviance as a culturally patterned system of behavior, emphasizing the *process* of socialization into such culture patterns.

In an attempt to explicate a general theory of criminal behavior, Sutherland (1961) developed his culture transmission theory of differential association. He emphasized, unlike previous theories of criminal behavior, the learned nature of deviance. That is, the individual is socialized into criminal behavior by his association with persons who define the appropriate attitudes and reactions to legal rules. The principle of differential association asserts that "a person becomes delinquent because of an excess of definitions favorable to violations of the law over definitions unfavorable to the violation of the law" (Sutherland and Cressey, 1960: 78).

Glaser (1955) reformulated Sutherland's notion when he argued that since groups are usually made up of diverse elements, interaction and participation in such groups do not in themselves provide an adequate explanation of deviant behavior. Thus Glaser asserts that such behavior could more adequately be accounted for by investigating the role model the deviant chooses to emulate and with whom he voluntarily interacts and identifies. This reformulated theory Glaser called differential identification.

Stratton (1967), who has attempted to test empirically Glaser's theory, found that criminal identification and associational preferences correlated with attitude toward law violations. In a similar study, Matthews (1968) demonstrates that the level of delinquent behavior of an individual is directly related to the level of delinquency reported by his "best friend," and that such an identification among friends is more "intense" than unilateral identification.

A slightly different approach is taken by Becker, Goffman, and others, who draw heavily upon the work of Mead—especially his notions of self and role. The self is seen as a social object which, through a process of communication and interaction, is engaged in the continuing process of building and rebuilding itself out of the vast congerie of roles available in the social milieu. Among these possible roles, of course, are some which society has labeled deviant—roles which may perform important systemic boundary-setting functions (Erikson, 1962). Thus, according to Becker (1963: 9),

> from this point of view, deviance is not a quality of the act a person commits, but rather a consequence of the application by others of rules and sanctions to an "offender." The deviant is one to whom that label has successfully been applied; deviant behavior is behavior that people so label.

The stigma attached to a person because of the "labeling process" serves, in short, to validate an individual's claim to the role of a deviant. For this reason, scholarly interest focuses on the "labeler" as well as on the "labeled."

There have been numerous empirical studies utilizing this theoretical approach (Rubington and Weinberg, 1968). Goffman (1968), for example, demonstrates the modes of adaptation made by mental patients after outside defining agents had labeled them as such. The most frequently cited work based upon this approach is Becker's (1963) study of marijuana users. Another interesting study of the effects of the labeling process is Schwartz and Skolnick's (1962) empirical attempt to determine the impact of a criminal record (legal stigma) on an individual's future employment chances.

In sum, sociology has only recently begun to empirically examine the question of compliance or noncompliance with the law. In the subfield of sociology of law, studies are beginning to emerge which directly tackle the compliance question (Schwartz and Orleans, 1967), while others are concerned with what we have called "impact." That is, sociologists have looked at the effects of laws in terms of whether or not the particular sanctions actually deter or alter behavior.

An attempt to clarify political science perspectives on the study of compliance seems an appropriate way to approach that discipline. A survey of the substantive findings would be an undertaking of far greater magnitude (see Wasby, 1970).

It has been observed before that Brown v. Board of Education appears to have been the stimulus to most of what is now variously called compliance and impact research. A brief glance at the publication dates of empirical studies in the discipline affords some plausibility for this proposition. Whether it is in fact valid, however, seems less important than to weight it together with two other factors: (1) the numerous expressions in the traditional literature of the importance of compliance as a desideratum in Supreme Court decisions–to say nothing of the fundamental concern of political philosophy with the dilemmas of change and stability, order and liberty, and so forth; and (2) the influence on the profession of the so-called behavioral revolution, with its emphasis on the study of actual behavior, as well as a renewed quest for global, integrative theories of politics. On the first point, it is perhaps sufficient to mention the names of a few of the leading critics who either pointed to the problem of potential noncompliance as a major reason for judicial self-restraint or at least as a factor to be weighed in the decision to undertake controversial changes. Robert McCloskey (1960) has dealt with the question of the political costs and benefits of institutional activism. Somewhat earlier, John P. Frank (1958) attempted a similar task. Though there may have been a few expressions of frustration over the lack of data on the policy effects of decisions by the Court or by Congress, the central concern of virtually the entire literature seems to have been with the potential damage to the Court of disobedience to its orders.

The second consideration, the effect of the so-called behavioral revolution on the study of compliance, is more interesting. It soon became apparent that armchair speculation was simply unsatisfactory now that techniques for the study of actual behavior were increasingly available. Thus, by utilizing survey research, intensive interview data, and aggregate data analysis, one might penetrate the surface of generalized behavior to ascertain how people respond to Court decisions and legislative acts and to weigh the effects of demographic, attitudinal, and socioeconomic variables. Interest in grand theory á la Parsons and Easton is at least consistent with the need for empirically based studies which attempt to define or to determine the feedback effects of judicial decisions. Similarly, the emergence of comparative and developmental studies forces the scholar to inquire more generally into the dynamics of political behavior and political change.

A none too clear dichotomy emerges from these considerations. On the one hand are those studies which concern themselves with the immediate consequences of decisions (particularly of appellate courts), and which attempt to understand when and under what circumstances the Court may expect conformity to its decisions. The focus of these studies is short-term, generally specific to a particular decision or issue, and primarily concerned with noncompliance. On the other hand, there are studies which emphasize less the effects of institutional decisions than the determinants of supportive or nonsupportive behavior that make possible (or difficult) the ongoing political-governmental process. At some point, of course, these studies must also concern themselves with the feedback effects of institutional decisions. In this sense, they are as much interested in long-range effects of decisions as the others are in short-run effects. These studies deal with long-run, developmental components of behavior, the long-range effects of institutional decisions; they are seldom specific to a particular issue; and they are equally concerned with compliance and noncompliance.

To put all of this into some historical perspective, it might be argued that the first group, those dealing with short-term effects, are a logical outgrowth of traditional (if not conventional) dispositions to study the Supreme Court in terms of conflicts over legal policy issues. Though not uninfluenced by the behavioral revolution, particularly in method, they are still more policy- than theory-oriented, and they grow out of an established tradition in political science. The second group, those concerned with the determinants of compliant behavior and long-range effects, would seem to be a development more consistent with the thrust of the behavioral revolution. Their emphasis is preeminently theory development, they deal with fundamental elements of behavioral orientations rather than with specific reactions, and they borrow heavily from other social sciences, particularly psychology and social psychology.

Though there are notable exceptions (Peltason, 1955 and 1961; Murphy, 1959b; Vines, 1964; Wasby, 1965; Dolbeare, 1967), the focus of studies has been on the appellate rather than on the trial or local levels. This is not surprising if only because the written opinions of appellate courts are usually more accessible and "newsworthy"; there is furthermore the generally accepted canon that judicial legal doctrine is to be changed, if at all, by higher courts. To the extent, however, that this may reflect the still operative fiction that trial courts are neither sources of policy change nor of much interest for their impact on community behavior, it is unfortunate. In reality, the explanation is probably twofold: appellate decisions and courts are easier to study; and noncompliance with their decisions, because of the wider audience, is more likely to flow and become visible. Whatever the case, it is encouraging to see that trial courts are under increasing scrutiny.

Not only have appellate courts been preferred to trial courts, but the federal courts have taken precedence over state courts. Few studies deal expressly with the impact of state appellate courts. (Some exceptions include Vines, 1965; Levine, 1967; and Beiser, 1968.) And even within the sphere of Supreme Court policy-making, relatively limited policy issues have been studied. An exhaustive treatment may be found elsewhere (Wasby, 1970); suffice it to say that the major areas are the school prayer and related religious issues (Patric, 1957; Sorauf, 1959; Beaney and Beiser, 1964; Katz, 1965; Birkby, 1966; Johnson, 1967; Muir, 1967; Reich, 1968; Way, 1968; and Dolbeare and Hammond, 1969), obscenity (Wasby, 1965, 1968; Levine, 1967; and Barth, 1968), the desegregation cases and race relations in the South (Peltason, 1955, 1961; Blaustein and Ferguson, 1957; Krislov, 1959; and Vines, 1964, 1965), criminal procedure (Nagel, 1965a; Manwaring, 1968; and Milner, 1968, and the chapter in this volume), reapportionment (Landau, 1965; Hofferbert, 1966; Dixon, 1968; and Jewell, 1968), and loyalty-security cases (Murphy, 1962; Mollan, 1965; and Stumpf, 1966). Beyond these are the studies that deal with Court interactions with Congress and with the Executive (Rossiter, 1951; Schmidhauser, 1958; Murphy, 1962; Beaney and Beiser, 1964; Stumpf, 1965, 1966; Nagel, 1965b; and Shapiro, 1968), and with lower federal courts (Murphy, 1959b; Vines, 1964).

Typically, studies are based on a survey research design. That is, the level of impact or compliance is gauged largely by questionnaire data. Dolbeare and Hammond's Wisconsin study (1969) of Supreme Court impact relied on observation as well, and Johnson (1967) is an example of a more intensive case study using a battery of methods to detect both compliance and impact. As Dolbeare and Hammond point out, however, there is considerable basis for doubt as to the reliability of the results of survey research in this area, and "close to the ground" techniques may be necessary. The traditional case study may be an interim alternative, but it is often unappealing due to its usual limitation with respect to inferences to other times and places. Muir's (1967) in-depth observation of a few subjects on the one hand, and Lempert's suggestions for quasi-experimental designs (see his chapter in this volume), drawn largely from Campbell and Stanley (1963) on the other, might be helpful in the development of designs that allow over-time and comparative analysis, with some forethought to the problem of control.

The kind of research design in vogue is limited to a series of socioeconomic and demographic variables. It is not that region, religion, sex, race, urbanization, and the like are unimportant, but there remain attitudinal variables as well as interaction effects of setting and attitude. Krislov (1959) is an early exception to this, as are the more recent studies by Johnson (1967), Muir (1967), Barth (1968), Dolbeare and Hammond (1969), Jacob (1969), and perhaps Kessel (1966).

Despite the earlier suggestion that policy is the orientation of these short-range studies, it is clear from all of this that little in the way of prescription can be distilled from the available research. One explicit attempt to do so emerges as premature (Levine and Becker, 1970) and suggests that we need much more knowledge before this can be attempted. Specifically, more needs to be known about the effects of different structural arrangements, alternative ways of implementing decisions, and feedback effects on institutions and their legitimacy.

Having said all this, two things become increasingly clear: (1) whatever may be said about short-run impact and whatever recommendations we may make about mitigating negative results, the search must continue for answers to the more fundamental behavioral questions of why people obey or disobey and under what circumstances. And (2) we must focus more attention on the feedback effects of decisions and responses: what happens to institutions and their legitimacy and how are relevant practices affected over the long run by the decisions of courts, legislatures, and administrative bodies.

In recent years increased attention has been paid to what Easton (1965) calls support inputs as key variables in the study of the political system (see Koeppen's chapter in this volume). In a brief decade, a substantial body of literature has developed, beginning with Herbert Hyman's (1959) pioneering effort. The most fundamental meaning of socialization studies is what Dennis (1968)[2] refers to as system relevance. From either a systems or a functional vantage, there is an implicit linkage hypothesis that says the context and processes by which one adopts affective, cognitive, and evaluational norms or dispositions have consequences for the political system. Naturally, this has led to concern with learning processes. Hess, as cited in Dennis (1968), suggests that "unit accretion" provides the most common means of gathering information about the political system, interpersonal transfer for developing attitudes toward authority, and cognitive development for acquiring information and dispositions toward specific institutions such as the Supreme Court.

Socialization studies are also concerned with the time element in the sense that the questions of when and where learning begins, the agencies of learning, and differences between generations are suggestive as to the sources of greatest influence and the dynamics of socialization patterns over time. Cross-cultural and subcultural studies (particularly the latter) have increasingly drawn attention to the variations in the orientations of groups to their society and some possible implications of this for political systems. Finally, studies of the extent of socialization (politicization) and of specialized socialization again draw our attention to important elite groups in society.

Perhaps the Murphy and Tanenhaus study (1968) together with that by Dolbeare and Hammond (1969) are most relevant at this point, as attempts to assess the relative importance of diffuse and specific supportive attitudes as ingredients in the Supreme Court's role of legitimizing regime changes (to use the Murphy and Tanenhaus terminology). Whatever the difficulty with the dependent variable, the focus is of interest. The same may be said of studies of sense of efficacy (Jacob, 1969), or civic competence (Almond and Verba, 1963) as ingredients in democratic adjustment.

In this sense, then, compliance is in part the study of the psychological and social bases of dispositions toward regimes and their rules. As such, it is logically and temporally prior to impact and is, in fact, an ingredient of impact. Although normally these dispositions are studied as dependent variables, it seems clear that ultimately they may be used as part of one's list of potential explanatory variables in attempting to account for patterns of compliance.

The studies of violence by Gurr (1967, 1968, and 1970), the Feierabends (1966 and the chapter in this volume), and Flanigan and Fogelman (1970) provide us with still another aspect of the overall problem, that of the feedback effects of the institutions and decisions in which we are interested. In general they are interested in both the causes and the consequences of violence, though typically more so with the former than with the latter. But whether they deal with violence in terms of socioeconomic (Flanigan and Fogelman) or psychological (Gurr) variables, or institutional variables in a psychological framework (Feierabends), they are suggesting that the way in which the systems respond to their environments and to the demands placed upon them will account at least in part for their relative stability, instability, or violence-proneness. Although violence may beget violence, the most important inference for our purposes deals with violence as outcome rather than as input.

In all of the above discussions, political scientists have looked at some form of compliance as the dependent variable, with the "law" as such in a rather ambiguous position. Some have attempted, albeit not very rigorously, to use law as an independent variable. Massell (1968), for example, looks at Soviet use of law as an instrument of social change. The interesting thing about this is that although some consider the distinction between approaches to the study of law to be that between law as dependent and law as independent variable, almost none of these studies really concerns itself with the policy dimensions of law (Wells and Grossman, 1966).

At a more abstract level of analysis are those who are interested in formal models as a means to more careful conceptualization and hypothesis development. As Feeley points out in this volume, the economic models literature may provide the basis for a rational choice approach to the study of the coercive function of sanctioning.

TRADITIONAL LEGAL LITERATURE

Much of the traditional legal literature on compliance is concerned with two questions: the morality of punishment, and the appropriate objects of the criminal sanction. Austin and Bentham, and Kant and Hegel essentially establish the boundaries for the modern debate, while the contemporary works of Andenaes (1952), Wootton (1963), F. A. Allen (1964), and H. L. A. Hart (1968) have contributed further to an understanding of and skepticism toward both deterrence and rehabilitation as justifications for punishment. Lord Devlin (1965), Hart (1963), and Fuller (1964) have been leading exponents of positions with regard to the objects of the criminal penalty, while Packer's (1968) recent major work is perhaps the most useful overview of the debate.

Obviously, the debate on these two questions is highly relevant to any discussion of law as a means of social control. The empirical dimension may be found in studies of the death penalty, recidivism, marijuana and narcotics use, homosexuality, prohibition, and prostitution. In addition to the philosophical discussion of the uses of sanctions, one must also consider the literature on legal obligation to complete the normative-theoretical aspects of law's concern with compliance. The recent compilation of essays in Pennock and Chapman (1970) is a good starting point.

It is useful to begin with a look at the more philosophical literature in law, because, even in the most mundane empirical studies by lawyers, a recurring phenomenon is the juxtaposition of the world as it is with the world as it is supposed to be—the latter measured by the manifest intent of the written law. That is, the typical study deals with a topic of some controversiality and, after an exegesis of the law and the policy behind it, compares this indication of what practices ought to be with what in fact happens. Usually the reality departs sufficiently from the ideal so that one of two policy recommendations seems dictated: either we change the law to make it conform with apparently accepted social mores (the law is "unjust"), or more stringent enforcement of the law is deemed necessary (the law is "just," the conduct immoral). This points up the singular emphasis of lawyers on empirical study for the purposes of policy change. They tend to focus on research problems of high recommendative potential, rather than on the theoretical problems of obtaining compliance (except as a philosophical question), or the impact of the law as an institution for social change (exceptions: Stone, 1950, 1966; Hurst, 1964; Friedman, 1965; and Macauley, 1966), or even to comparative research on the effects of different legal policies.

Some examples of better studies illustrating this point are Blumrosen (1965), desegregation; Foote (1966), bail; Goldstein (1960), police discretion; Griffith and Ayres (1967) and Medalie et al. (1968), *Miranda;* Paulsen (1950), due process; Rabin (1967), conscientious objectors; UCLA Law Review (1966), homosexuality; Goldstein (1967), insanity defense; and Newman (1966) and Blumberg (1967), plea bargaining. Of general importance are the studies for the American Law Institute's Model Penal Code, and the President's Commission on Law Enforcement and Administration of Justice (1967), *The Challenge of Crime in a Free Society.*

Equally important but conforming less to the above pattern are a series of descriptive studies that, although providing the basis for possible recommendation, do not appear to have this as their sole or primary mission. Among these are the works by Barrett (1962), the American Bar Foundation surveys, and a few others.

Although Pound's "jurisprudence of consequences" is of evident influence in the orientation of legal empirical studies, it should be mentioned in connection with another genre of scholarship: the more conventional criticism of the Court in terms of the likely effects (or noneffects) of its recent decisions. Though rigorous empirical study is not characteristic, the reapportionment, right to counsel, exclusionary rule, school prayer, desegregation decisions, among others, have been particularly productive of this sort of criticism. In the judgment of these critics, either the Court has gone too far, overreaching its authority and endangering its future effectiveness or the balance of the system, or it has been insufficiently acute in sensing the political tides, essentially a charge of naivete.

Most of the above has reference to either criminal law and procedure, or to fundamental Constitutional issues. A few additional words should be said about the empirical work of lawyers and law professors in other areas. The structure and procedures of the civil process have received attention in the works of Kalven and Zeisel (1966) on the jury, and Zeisel et al. (1959) on delay; Rosenberg (1959), delay, and (1958), discovery; and Hunting and Neuwirth (1962), litigiousness. More substantive studies include Rosenberg (1959), comparative negligence; Macauley (1966), contractual relations; and Countryman (1964), bankruptcy.

Finally, the pioneering work of Underhill Moore should be mentioned. As Ernest Jones (1966) implies, more sophisticated designs of an experimental variety are probably needed in impact research. Moore would appear to have been ahead of his time. Still another direction, that of formal models for decision-making, is suggested in Mayo and Jones (1965). Perhaps together these two tendencies in legal research will bring lawyers and social scientists in closer contact on problems of impact and compliance.

NOTES

1. There are many extended treatments of learning theory, including Solomon (1968) and Pliskoff and Ferster (1968), both in the International Encyclopedia of the Social Sciences. Honig's (1966) collection is also available; special reference should be made to the article by Azrin and Holtz (1966) in that volume. And Skinner's *Science and Human Behavior* (1953) is an important work in the field.

2. The following discussion of political socialization follows closely that by Dennis in his useful article.

REFERENCES

References to this chapter are included in the volume's bibliography.

Part One

ALTERNATIVE APPROACHES

Chapter 1

The Practice of Fidelity to Law

ROBERT S. GERSTEIN
University of California, Los Angeles

What is it that sets legal systems apart from other kinds of systems of social control? Traditionally, legal philosophers have tried to answer the question in terms of some uniquely essential quality which distinguishes law from everything else. It now seems clear that the concept of law is best understood, not in terms of any single feature to be taken as the essence of law, but as a whole set of family resemblances between the various things we call legal systems (Hart, 1961: 1-17, 234). What I propose to do here is to deal with one particular facet of the concept which, I think, has not been given sufficient attention by the currently dominant positivist school of legal philosophy.

I will argue that an important part of the concept of law involves the notion of a society in which each person governs his own conduct by applying to himself the rules which have been laid down by society for everyone. There are two central points to be made here. First, I wish to claim that a society with a legal system is one in which people apply rules to their own conduct, not one in which people are manipulated by officials who act in accordance with the rules. Second, I want to make the point that it is a society in which people have made a commitment to follow uniformly applicable societal rules when their conduct affects the interests of others, not one in which they make such decisions on the basis of their own unfettered discretion.

A consideration of this aspect of the concept of law is, I believe, of special importance because it makes clear the close connection between the concept of law and a particular view of man in society: a view in which each man is seen as a free, responsible agent who owes to each other man in society a duty to respect his equal status as a free responsible agent.

TWO KINDS OF RULES

It is Hans Kelsen who has most clearly stated the view that the chief characteristic of a legal system is that officials exercise coercive control over people under the authorization of a system of rules which justifies such coercion. For Kelsen (1967: 47-48) the crucial difference between the order of a thief and the order of a policeman is that the policeman is authorized to give his order by a rule which is part of a generally effective system of rules, while the thief's order is not. Kelsen centers his attention almost entirely on those rules which authorize official coercion. They are the only proper objects for legal analysis. A legal system is a system of rules governing the use of force by officials. All other sorts of legal standards can be and ought to be reduced to rules of this sort for purposes of analysis. The notice, "No Smoking," for example, is not really an independent part of the legal system. It is merely a crude and incomplete (though, for its purpose, useful) way of restating the norm, "If the court finds that a person has been smoking, it is authorized to visit a sanction upon him." The first form (addressed to the citizen) is entirely "dependent" on the second (addressed to the official) and is "superfluous from the point of view of legislative technique" (Kelsen, 1967: 55; 1945: 61).[1] It is quite natural that, having taken such a view, Kelsen does not give much attention to the way in which the average man understands and conforms to the rules of law which apply to his conduct. Kelsen (1967: 48) in fact concerns himself with this facet of legal experience only in that he requires that a legal system be effective in the territory in which it applies. But this tells us very little. One would assume that the condition of effectiveness would be satisfied so long as the official action authorized by it was being carried on regularly and without serious opposition. The only thing that follows from this in relation to the conduct of the average man is that he is relatively acquiescent. We know nothing more about the way he relates to the legal system.

H. L. A. Hart criticizes Kelsen from precisely this point of view; Kelsen's reductionism achieves uniformity only at the price of serious distortion in that it misses precisely that crucial aspect of the legal means of social control which I am emphasizing here:

> What is distinctive of this [legal] technique . . . is that the members of society are left to discover the rules and conform their behavior to them; in this sense they "apply" the rules themselves to themselves, though they are provided with a motive for conformity in the sanction added to the rule. Plainly we shall conceal the characteristic way in which such rules function if we concentrate on, or make primary, the

> rules requiring courts to impose the sanctions in the event of disobedience; for these latter rules make provision for the breakdown or failure of the primary purpose of the sanction. [Hart, 1961: 38]

Hart's way of escaping this distortion is to look upon law as a union of two sorts of rules: primary and secondary. The primary rules are the prohibitory rules addressed to the populace as a whole; the secondary rules are not prohibitory but authorizing or facilitating rules, rules which authorize the creation, change, interpretation, and enforcement of the primary rules. The rules governing official conduct are of course secondary rules, as are the rules governing the conduct of the private citizen when he makes a contract or executes a will (Hart, 1961: 89-96).

Hart's corrections of Kelsen's analysis have added greatly to the richness of the positivist model of the legal system. It accommodates all of Kelsen's insights into the importance of the rules authorizing official action, while opening up the possibility of a much richer appraisal of the role of the rules which govern the average man's everyday conduct as well.

Hart also makes us aware of the importance of a consideration of the "internal point of view" in the understanding of legal phenomena. He makes it clear that one who takes the strictly external point of view—one who considers only the external behavior of people and does not take their understanding of that behavior into account—will never understand all that it is important to understand about what it is that goes into making a legal system (Hart, 1961: 55-56, 86-88). But Hart is disappointing in his statement of the insights which are to be gained from the internal point of view.

No objection will be raised with regard to Hart's account of the way in which officials must look upon the conduct of their offices in relation to the secondary rules which govern them in a legal system. He effectively makes the point that the officials must not only conform their conduct to the standards set by the secondary rules, but that they must also regard them as "common public standards for behavior." They must use them to criticize their own and other official conduct on the basis of commonly accepted rules if the "characteristic unity and continuity" of the legal system is not to be lost (Hart, 1961: 112-113).

When it comes to a consideration of the internal aspect of the primary rules to be obeyed by the people as a whole, however, Hart's analysis is deficient. It does not effectively elucidate the legal means of control as ones in which people apply "the rules themselves to themselves," as the passage quoted above seemed to promise it would.

Hart is right in asserting that the people as a whole need not look upon each of the primary norms in the way that the officials must look upon each of the secondary norms. This is to a large extent simply because secondary rules have a very different nature from primary rules. It is in the nature of a primary rule, a rule of obligation that deviation will be a violation of it, and not an exception to it, even if unpunished; even, indeed, if such deviation is very widespread. Only the general failure to abide by the set of primary rules of the legal system as a whole would be inconsistent with its existence as a legal system. An unpunished murder is still a crime even though unpunished, so long as there is in the legal system a law against murder which is generally enforced. But secondary rules are different in this respect. The existence of the secondary rules which delineate official action consists of the very practice of the officials itself.[2] A deviation from what has been regarded as the rule, if such deviation is not met with an effective response, will be in effect an exception to the rule, not a violation of it. What originally seemed to be unauthorized action is established as authorized by official acceptance. Thus the decision of a court may appear to be a clear violation of a rule of law, but it will stand as the law of the case in which it was handed down if not effectively challenged on appeal. If it is upheld on appeal, or not appealed at all, then it will stand as an exception to or modification of the rule, not as a violation of it.

But while this shows that the citizenry need not have the same attitudes toward the primary rules that the officials have toward secondary rules, it does not establish what attitudes the citizenry must have, and it surely does not prove that they need not have any attitudes at all.

Hart does indeed assert that the strictly external point of view does not reveal all there is to know about the way the average man relates to the law, any more than it reveals all there is to know about how officials relate to it. At a minimum then, Hart's insistence on the need to see that all of the rules of the legal system, primary and secondary, have an internal aspect, would apparently lead him to agree that the citizenry at large must have some concern for the rules of the legal system.

HYPOTHETICAL CASE: DISREGARD OF PRIMARY RULES

It is useful to imagine what it might be like to have a system of primary and secondary rules in a society where the people as a whole simply had no attitude at all toward the primary rules, where they simply disregarded them. It is possible to conceive of a society in which people disregard the primary rules, and yet, when seen from the strictly external point of view, people seem to conform their conduct to them. We might imagine a situation in which a group of people are guided in their conduct by a religious morality, the primary rules of which are very similar to the primary rules of the legal system. They are wholly ignorant of the law. When they conform their conduct to the rules, they never have in mind the legal rules; only the moral rules mean anything to them. When they consider the possible imposition of sanctions in planning their conduct, it is the supernatural sanctions of their religion which concern them, never the legal sanctions. The officials continue to create, change, interpret, and enforce the primary rules in accordance with the secondary rules, but their actions are generally disregarded by the public at large. Yet it still might be said that this is an effective legal system because the primary rules are generally obeyed, or at least not in general disobeyed.[3]

In such a case one who took what Hart (1961: 87) calls the "extreme external point of view" would see all there was to see about the relation of the public to the primary rules. Their conduct happens to conform to the rules; the rules read as if they were descriptions of their conduct, and might be used as a basis for predicting what they are likely to do in the future, but that is all. We need not go further and ask about their internal point of view with regard to the rules of the legal system because they have none.

The peculiarity of this case is of course that the legal system has no apparent function. We have officials treating the people in particular ways in accordance with secondary rules, and judging their conduct on the basis of the primary rules. But it is difficult to see why they are doing this, unless they happen to derive some peculiar satisfaction from it, because they are not effectively guiding anyone's conduct.

Further, one wonders whether this would be a system of primary *and* secondary rules. Clearly there are secondary rules which guide official action, but are there really primary rules? There are such rules on the books, but they do not guide the conduct of the people to whom they are directed. This is a situation where it makes perfect sense to say that they are merely aspects of the secondary rules, that they "are superfluous from the point of view of legislative technique," as Kelsen suggests (1967: 47-48). As Hart (1961: 38) points out, Kelsen's approach on this point is misleading because it distracts us from the point that the rules of obligation are indeed in the normal case primary in their function of guiding everyday conduct, while the secondary rules come into play only when there has been a breakdown in the normal functioning of the primary rules. But in the case we are imagining, Kelsen's approach would be quite appropriate.

The problem is, of course, that we would have great difficulty in saying in such a case that there was a legal system. Of course, there may be and probably are some people in every society who take up this stance toward the legal system, and many of us do part of the time; but if people in general took this position all of the time we would have strong reason for saying that there was no legal system in existence. Surely it seems questionable to call any system of rules an effective legal system if it has no function in controlling the conduct of the people to which it purports to apply.

Once it has been established that people must, at a minimum, have some attitude toward a system of rules if we are to be satisfied that it is a legal system, it must then be asked just what specific attitudes might or might not be appropriate to a legal system.

HYPOTHETICAL CASE: MINIMAL CONCERN WITH RULES

The next hypothetical situation I would like to consider is one in which the people do take the rules of the system into account in deciding what to do and what not to do, but where their concern with them is so minimal that, as Hart (1961: 87-88) suggests, it could be "very nearly" reproduced from the strictly external point of view.

I am hypothesizing a situation in which people do take the rules into account only when in the particular case they have reason to fear the imposition of a sanction if they do not. In such a situation, assuming that the enforcement mechanism is sufficiently effective to put people in fear of sanctions in the great majority of cases, it would be perfectly reasonable to say that the primary rules were generally obeyed and that the system was therefore effective.

But some of the problems which led us to feel that we might not be dealing with a legal system in the first case are still present here, though in a different form. It is true that in the present case the legal system does have a function. It may properly be called a means of social control. We may still ask, however, whether this control is of a kind which has the major features which we would generally connect with the concept of law. Specifically, we may ask whether this is really a case of social control achieved through compliance with rules by people who regard such rules as applicable to themselves.

This is a case in which the legal rules come into the average citizen's calculations only in the following way: whenever he considers carefully whether to take a particular course of action, he asks, among other things, whether the authorities are likely to stop him or punish him for it. Of course, he will realize that the authorities will probably decide whether to interfere with his actions on the basis of their consistency with the rules under which they operate. But his interest in the rules goes no further than considering them as a factor to be taken into account in predicting whether official action will be taken against him. He will want to know whether the officials will regard his particular actions as violations, whether they can be bribed to think otherwise, whether they are likely to find out about them, and whether they are likely to bother to take action against him anyway. The primary rules form a part of this calculation only because he knows they embody those parts of the secondary rules which will be important factors in determining possible official action against him.

If this is so, then the people do not look upon the primary rules as rules for themselves. They have no sort of commitment to act in general in accordance with them. They have, as Hart (1961: 87-88) says, "rejected" them, and are concerned with them when, and only when, "it is judged that unpleasant consequences are likely to follow violation." They are seen as rules for the officials, one of the bases on which to predict official action, rather than as rules for the people themselves to follow. In fact, then, they remain no more than aspects of the secondary rules. They are still without existence independent from the rules which govern official action. If no primary rules were promulgated, the only difference it would make would be in the greater difficulty which the citizens would have in making judgments about when officials might take action against them. They would have to work this out from a study of the secondary rules or practical observation of the officials in action. Beyond this, it would make no difference that there were no primary rules. A functioning set of secondary rules conditioning official action with regard to citizens on the previous actions of those citizens, if generally known, would be sufficient to achieve general uniformity in the behavior of the citizenry, under the conditions we have established in this case; this is the only consequence which flows from having primary rules. It is true that this case differs from the first case in that the citizens are seen as taking the rules into account in deciding what to do. But they do not take the existence of the rules as legal rules as in itself a reason for acting or not acting in a particular way. They are simply facts about an aspect of the situation in which the citizen will be acting which may make it dangerous for him to act in a particular way. To the extent that they are rules at all *to* the citizen, they are rules *for* the official, not *for* the citizen. The primary rules are simply an indirect though handy means of finding out whether officials are likely to react unfavorably if they catch you doing certain things. They say, "Don't do this, don't do that," but are taken to mean no more than "We'll deal with you in ways you don't like if we find out you are doing this or that."

It would appear then that the "primary rules" are under such circumstances pretty clearly secondary in relation to what Hart calls the "secondary rules," and, further, that they do not function as rules for the very people to whom they are addressed. The problem might be expressed in terms of saying that mere general obedience to the primary rules is insufficient to bring them to life in the full sense in which they are necessary to an effective legal system. Their internal aspect remains insufficiently developed in that no one looks upon them as standards for their conduct.

Hart (1961: 197) is clearly aware that all of these things would be true of a system in which this attitude (which he himself characterizes as "rejection" of the rules) was general. But while admitting that a system of social control under such circumstances might be abnormal and unstable, he has little doubt that it would be a legal system. Hart (1961: 88) assumes that a society living under a legal system will normally include both people who reject the system and people who accept it, people for whom "the violation of a rule is not merely a basis for the prediction that a hostile reaction will follow but a *reason* for hostility." He also assumes that the health and stability of the legal system will depend to a considerable degree on the proportion of one to the other (Hart, 1961: 197). But he quite clearly envisions the possibility of a system which is rejected by the great majority of the citizenry, but which he would still call a legal system. "The society in which this was so might be deplorably sheeplike; the sheep might end in the slaughterhouse. But there is little reason for thinking that it could not exist or for denying it the title of a legal system" (Hart, 1961: 114). In a primitive, prelegal society, each of the rules of obligation relating to the basic societal need for security must have very general acceptance in order to keep the society together. But for Hart, the peculiar virtue of a legal system is that it allows for the replacement of this general acceptance of rules of obligation with the acceptance of the secondary rules by a small circle of officials, who could then use coercion in order to achieve obedience.

It is surely worth pointing out that there are significant differences between the type and extent of general acceptance necessary to the existence of the rules of obligation in a prelegal community and that which is necessary for the existence of a legal system. But as I have tried to show, it very much overstates the import of the difference to contrast the need for general acceptance in the prelegal case with the possibility of general rejection in the case of a legal system.

OBLIGATION: RULES OF THUMB

Some of the objections which have been made to the hypothetical society which we have been discussing as a model for a legal system might be met by a relatively minor but crucial modification.

The modification is based on the realization that it is indeed unrealistic to set up a model for a legal system in which people generally decide to obey the law only after going through a calculation of the risk involved in each particular case. It would involve changing this hypothetical society into one in which most people have made the long-range decision to obey the law out of fear of the punishment which can generally be expected to follow disobedience. They do not have to calculate in every case in order to decide whether to obey the law or not; they have come to the conclusion that it would in general be better to do so.

It might be thought that in such a situation the primary rules do in fact function as rules for the people. This is not a case in which the decision to obey or not is open in every instance, and the rules might therefore seem to be rules *for* the citizens though they obey out of fear. But even this does not seem to be sufficient. If there is any sense in which the citizens truly regard the primary rules as rules, it is still only as "rules of thumb" (Rawls, 1955: 23), only as shorthand summations of the practical experience which has led them to believe that the consequences of obeying the law in any particular case are likely to be more favorable than the consequences of disobeying the law. The point becomes clearer when we think about the possibility that people with such an attitude might become convinced in a particular case that there was no real likelihood of punishment for disobedience. In such a case they would regard themselves as having no reason to continue to obey the law. This makes it clear that the status of a rule as part of the legal system is not for them in itself a reason for obeying it. The rules of law do not really function as rules for them. They are not taken to be responsible agents who apply rules to themselves, but rather to be people who respond to the stimulus of fear in accordance with the pattern set by official action regularized by rules.

Of course, there are people under any system who have this attitude. But what would be our reaction to a system in which everyone–including the officials when acting in their roles as private citizens–took this attitude?[4] It would be a system in which no person looked upon the primary rules as rules for himself. It is, for our purposes, not fundamentally different from the model as originally stated. It is still true that the primary rules are only resorted to by the citizens as indications of official action. They guide conduct, but not as genuine standards; they are no more than rules of thumb to be followed generally if you want to keep out of trouble, and to be disregarded in those cases where you have reason to believe that you are unlikely to get into trouble anyway.

Would there be an argument against calling a system of rules an effective legal system under such conditions? It would be a system in which such common expressions as "respect for law" and "fidelity to law" would be inappropriate. It would be a system in which the concept "legal obligation," as I would understand it, would be out of place. I would argue for a notion of obligation which would be applicable only where the existence of rules as established rules of whatever sort (legal or moral or otherwise) is in itself regarded as a reason for obeying them. Seen in this light, the concept is appropriate to those cases in which the individual is seen as a responsible agent who applies standards to his own conduct. But in the case we are considering, even the officials, who are presumed conscientiously to apply the secondary rules in their capacity as officials, regard it as perfectly acceptable to get around the primary rules in their private lives, whenever it is prudent to do so.

It may be preferable, then, to talk about this as a case in which the citizens are in general obliged to obey the legal rules (except of course in those cases where they were convinced that they could disobey with impunity), rather than obligated to do so.[5] We would also want some new terminology to describe the impact of these hypothetical conditions on the meaning of the officials' commitment to apply sanctions to violations of the primary rules by the citizenry. It again seems not wholly appropriate to use the language of obligation about the application of rules to people who are looked upon in this way. We could better express the significance of the relationship by talking simply about people as being liable or not to the application of sanctions, depending upon whether they conformed their conduct to the rules.

The language of obligation would be unnecessary and misleading in this case. But the notion of obligation is generally understood to be inextricably bound up with the notion of legal system. It therefore appears that a system of rules in such circumstances, for which the notion of obligation would not be appropriate, would have some difficulty in establishing its credentials as a legal system.

DISCUSSION OF CASES

What is missing in all of the cases so far considered is a full development of the internal aspect of the primary rules. It is true that in the last two cases the primary rules did enter into the calculations of the people at large, but not as rules to be followed by them, any more than statistical generalizations which might be formulated about when people are likely to take raincoats because there are signs of rain could be regarded as rules to be followed by the people involved. They give us no sense of a society living under a legal system as one in which each person is assumed to have given up some measure of his absolute discretion to do as he chooses so that the burdens of maintaining the conditions necessary for a common life may be borne equally by all. The internal aspect of the primary rules can be supplied, and the rules themselves given independent existence, only where the existence of the primary rules as rules of the legal system is taken by the vast majority of people as a reason for obeying them.

When this is the case there can no longer be any question about the primary rules being no more than aspects of the secondary rules. They take on a meaning of their own, and become genuinely primary in their function of guiding the everyday conduct of the people, each of whom undertakes the responsibility of applying them to himself.

Such a system might be described as one in which there is a general practice of fidelity or obedience to the law. It is important to make clear just what this would mean and what it would not mean. It would mean that people in general would always have a reason for obeying the law. A practice which would allow for the existence of the duty in some circumstances but not in others would not do.

The problem with the cases previously considered was not simply that they involved no other motivation than the fear of sanctions. The thing which was important was that the sole motivating factor was that they were examples of a more general category of cases in which the legal system is operated essentially by officials who direct the actions of private citizens, rather than being mainly a matter of private citizens committing themselves to regulate their own actions in accordance with rules. All of the hypotheticals so far considered failed as models for the legal system because in none of them did compliance with the law depend upon a general commitment on the part of the private citizen to obey the law. In each of them the citizens regarded themselves as having a reason to obey the law only under certain circumstances. In the first case (that of the group who shared a moral code by which they regulated their actions but utterly disregarded the legal system) the fact that certain conduct was required by a legal rule was not even among the considerations regarded as relevant by those deciding how they were going to act. In the second and third cases, the fact that conduct was required by the legal system was relevant only to the extent that the individual involved was convinced he would be punished if he disobeyed (or at least was not convinced that he was unlikely to be punished). In each of them a commitment to obey the law was lacking.

This can obviously continue to be a problem even where there are motivations other than the fear of sanctions, even where people are "positively" motivated to obey the law. We might imagine, for example, a society of careful utilitarians. Each of them always tries to do that which seems to him likely to produce the best consequences under the circumstances. Such people would, in a broad range of cases, not take the law into account as a significant factor. This is because they would presumably find that the law required them to do what they would have done in any case, that which seems the best thing to do under the circumstances. There would be other cases in which they would take account of the law just because they would be concerned about the sanction, which might persuade them not to do what would otherwise have seemed to be the best thing to do. So far they resemble the people in the models we have already considered to some extent (as we all do to some extent) either disregarding the law or being concerned with it only out of the fear of the sanctions. But, being careful utilitarians, they would be concerned about the usefulness of obeying the law in ways in which the rather cruder thinkers of the previous cases would not. They would, for example, be aware of the fact that the law sets up public standards which they can rely upon each other to follow in those areas where chaos would result from an absence of some such common basis for reliance. The obvious case would be that of the traffic laws, where we constantly rely upon each other to follow the regularized patterns established by the law. The people in the model we are considering would take such laws into account before acting, both in making their estimate of what other people are likely to do and in deciding what other people are likely to expect them to do.

But the mere fact that these people do take some of the rules of the legal system into account for reasons other than the fear of sanctions does not in itself mean that they are participating in the practice of fidelity to the law, nor should it remove all doubt about this as a good model for a society with a legal system. There is still no general commitment to obey the law. The legal rule enters into consideration only indirectly. It is a fact on the basis of which they can assume that people will act in a particular way and rely upon them to do the same, unless there is evidence to the contrary. The crucial point is that evidence to the contrary, evidence to the effect that people will not be relying on them to obey the law in a particular case, will be sufficient to wipe out any reason they had for obeying the law (except of course fear of the sanction). Legal rules still function for them as no more than rules of thumb, to be disregarded when other evidence shows they are not useful guides for the prediction of what people are likely to do. Any talk of an obligation to obey the rules still seems inappropriate.

Such a society would not, I think, display the kind of mutual trust and confidence in the willingness of each to bear an equal share of the burden of maintaining order and working toward justice which is characteristic of a legal system. Given the diversity of individual capacities for judgment and self-control, the only sound foundation for such confidence is, I believe, the general commitment of each to obey the law. It should be made clear again that this is not to assert that the citizenry under a legal system has the same attitude toward the primary rules as the officials have to the secondary rules. Each particular secondary rule must be looked upon by all of the officials as a common standard. If a particular rule is not so regarded by all officials, then doubts arise as to whether it is in fact one of the secondary rules of the system, and the "characteristic unity" of the system begins to break down (Hart, 1961: 113). But this would clearly not be the case with the primary rules of the system. The fact that a particular rule may be disobeyed in a substantial number of cases does not raise doubts as to whether it is a legal rule, at least so long as it continues to be enforced by the officials. Nor does the fact that there are a number of such rules which are frequently disobeyed give rise to doubts as to whether the system is an effective legal system, so long as the great majority of its rules are generally obeyed. What I am arguing for is a far more modest view, a view in which some degree of disobedience would be compatible with the existence of the system, and, indeed, even expected.

What is important is that the attitudes of the great majority of the people would be such that they could be described as part of a general practice of fidelity to the law. This is not a practice which is to be defined by the whole body of the primary rules of the legal system as such (as would be the case with the official's practice of fidelity to the secondary rules). It is not realistic to think of the majority of the citizenry as having adopted each of these rules as a rule to live by. But it is realistic to think of the adoption of a practice which is defined by the single rule: obey the law. It is a practice which relates not to the particular rules of the system, but to the system as a whole.

In this respect it would differ significantly from the kind of attitude necessary to hold together a prelegal society, where "the rules by which the group lives will not form a system, but will simply be a set of separate standards, without any identifying or common mark." (Hart, 1961: 90) In such a situation each separate rule must be accepted as a common standard. The very fact that the rules of obligation in a legal system do form a *system* of rules to be identified on the basis of the secondary rules makes possible its support by a practice which relates to the system as a whole rather than particular rules. Disobedience to a particular rule whether out of ignorance or on the basis of the conscious decision that the reasons for obedience are overborne by the reasons for disobedience in the particular case is not necessarily conduct incónsistent with such a practice. Nor need it involve either moral approval of the rules by the people as a whole,[6] or their constant attention to them at every moment of their working lives. The only attitude which would be inconsistent with the practice of fidelity to the law would be one which would allow for a decision in a particular case that there was no reason at all to obey what is clearly known to be the law.

If there is such a general practice, it does seem appropriate to talk of legal obligation, as it did not in the cases previously discussed. It seems quite natural to speak of obligation in relation to a system of rules which people in general have a reason for obeying just because it is the established legal system. This does not mean that the attitude should be confused with legal obligation as such. It is by no means suggested that a person has a legal obligation to obey a particular rule only if he has this attitude toward it. A person is under a legal obligation whenever a rule of the legal system of which he is a subject says he is. The point being made here is one which relates to the question of whether the system is indeed a legal system. If it is not supported by this practice, then there is some reason to be doubtful on that question. To put the point in another form, it is not the intention here to identify legal obligation with the obligation to obey the law, but only to suggest that the notion of legal obligation would be a very peculiar one if people in general did not regard themselves as being under an obligation to obey the law.[7]

CONCLUSION

I have considered a number of hypothetical models of society in order to illuminate the point that a society living under a legal system is one in which social control is achieved through each person's application of common rules to his own conduct. In particular I have tried to represent this aspect of the concept of law more clearly by developing the model of a society in which the practice of fidelity to law has been generally adopted.

Hart sums up his position on the problems with which we have been dealing by stating two minimum conditions for the existence of a legal system: the secondary rules must be accepted as "common public standards of official behavior" by the officials, and the primary rules must be "generally obeyed" by private citizens.

One way to make the point here would be to suggest a modification of the necessary and sufficient conditions set out by Hart. The requirement that "those rules of behaviour which are valid according to the system's ultimate criteria of validity must be generally obeyed" might be altered into a requirement that "there be a general practice of fidelity to those rules of behaviour which are valid, etc." But it is not my purpose to establish a new set of necessary and sufficient conditions. I only wish to cast some light on an area of our understanding of the nature of law (an understanding which has been greatly enriched by Hart's book) which is left in partial obscurity by Hart's set of conditions. This purpose will have been served sufficiently well if I have in fact established that the absence of the practice of fidelity to law would throw some doubt on our determination to say that what in other respects appeared to be a legal system was in fact a legal system.[8]

NOTES

1. For the view that Hart makes the opposite error of reducing the secondary rules to aspects of the primary rules, see Jonathan Cohen (1962: 403).

2. Practice is here intended to include not only official action but the justifications which officials would give for it and judgments they would make about it as well.

3. The case is similar to that used by Woozley (1967: 68) to make much the same point.

4. Hart (1961: 113) seems to contemplate such a case when he says that even the officials "need only obey" the primary rules which apply to them in their personal capacity.

5. See Hart (1961: 88). The classical positivist view is, of course, that obligation consists in nothing more than being obliged. See Austin (1832: 14).

6. Thus, I would agree with Hart that it is possible for people to "accept the authority" of the system even though their consciences tell them they ought not to (Hart, 1961: 198-199). See also Woozley (1967: 76).

7. Of course, not enough has been said here to establish the existence of the moral obligation to obey the law, but it should be apparent that the general view of the relation of society to the legal system which is developed here is one from which a general duty to obey the law would arise. See Morris (1965) and Rawls (1958 and 1963). For a critique of this view, see Wasserstrom (1963).

8. The approach is that developed by Morris (1965: 365-368).

REFERENCES

AUSTIN, J. (1832) The Province of Jurisprudence Determined. London: J. Murray.

COHEN, L. J. (1962) "The concept of law." Mind 71 (July): 395-412.

HART, H. L. A. (1961) The Concept of Law. Oxford: Clarendon Press.

KELSEN, H. (1967) The Pure Theory of Law. Berkeley: Univ. of California Press.

--- (1945) General Theory of Law and State. Cambridge: Harvard Univ. Press.

MORRIS, H. (1965) "Punishment for thoughts." Monist 49 (July): 342-376.

RAWLS, J. (1963) "The sense of justice." Philosophical Rev. 72 (July): 281-305.

--- (1958) "Justice as fairness." Philosophical Rev. 67 (April): 164-194.

--- (1955) "Two concepts of rules." Philosophical Rev. 64 (January): 3-32.

WASSERSTROM, R. A. (1963) "The obligation to obey the law." UCLA Law Rev. 10 (May): 780-807.

WOOZLEY, A. D. (1967) "The existence of rules." Nous 1 (March): 63-79.

Chapter 2

Coercion and Compliance

A New Look at an Old Problem

MALCOLM FEELEY – *New York University*

Despite the general recognition of its importance, it has been noted that there is a paucity of theoretical treatment of the problems of compliance to law (Krislov, 1966). While there is a vast literature dealing with rule-specified behavior, a direct focus on the peculiarities of *legal* rules and compliance to them seems to have been skirted in favor of more general treatments of social norms, less-structured rule and compliance systems, and basic or constitutional rules. And when law and the problems of compliance have received specific attention, it has usually been in terms of a broad, societal level, relating legal norms to cultural norms or focusing on "trouble cases" and instances of noncompliance. Detailed empirical studies in sociology have tended to focus on deviant behavior and its correlates, while in political science the approach has tended towards even less-general descriptions and case studies of the impact and consequences of legislative and judicial policy-making.

On the other hand an impressive body of literature with its roots in economics has begun to develop theoretical formulations of individual and collective decision-making in a variety of social and political situations which has direct relevance to the study of law and legal choice (Blau, 1964; Thibaut and Kelley, 1959; Arrow, 1951; Buchanan and Tullock, 1962; Olson, 1965; Coleman, 1966a, b, c). There are a number of compelling reasons why the application of this general orientation and concern for formal theory ought to be particularly useful in the development of a theoretical characterization of laws, the problems of compliance and noncompliance, and the functions of formal, legal sanctions. First is the strict insistence on the adherence to the individualistic postulate, the characterization of collectivities in terms of their individual, constituent members. Such a requirement would seem particularly desirable in the study of law and society, where so often analysts have been guilty of both reification and assigning "purpose" to vaguely defined collectivities. Another is the nature of the legal system itself: it is a highly formalized system of rules which are usually selected by and operate under definite and clearly determined social mechanisms. Thus while laws are promulgated in a host of ways and deal with a wide variety of types of human behavior, on a more abstract level the legal system can be conceptualized as a rather formal, well-defined system of social choice and interaction, the elements of which are specifiable. All this leads me to think that the more formal approaches and orientation of recent social choice theorists might have particular significance for the study of law and the problems of compliance. In particular, there are several impressive discussions which deal with theories of constitution-making. Obviously such theories of basic norms, to adhere to Kelsen's terminology, have direct implications for the structure and consequences of substantive, primary norms which form the daily stuff of the law. Consequently, these particular studies provide a convenient point to begin the attempt to develop a theory of compliance.

FOUNDATIONS FOR AN ECONOMIC THEORY OF COMPLIANCE

Among this literature James Buchanan and Gordon Tullock's *The Calculus of Consent* (1962), subtitled "The Logical Foundations of Constitutional Democracy," offers the most directly relevant place to begin the task. The focus of their examination is quite simple: "to analyze the calculus of the rational individual when he is faced with the questions of constitutional choice" in order to answer the question, "when will an individual member of the group find it advantageous to enter into a 'political' relationship with his fellows?" (See Buchanan and Tullock, 1962: 43.) They then proceed to examine the strategies, calculations, and consequences of the rational individual engaging in constitutional construction, and introduce several mechanisms which, they argue, will allow individuals to reach unanimous agreement on a constitution. The foremost device is a set of variable decision-rules. Thus for example, provisions involving basic civil liberties and property rights can only be altered by a rule approaching unanimity of consent, while less important concerns can be adopted by less stringent decision-rules. This set of variable decision-rules allows decision-making costs to be minimized in proportion to the amount of externalities imposed by the particular collective decisions. Buchanan and Tullock also argue that the mechanisms of log-rolling, side-payments, and vote-trading can be incorporated into a set of institutions which implement this conception of a unanimous consent-based system. Realizing that each particular decision or decision-rule will probably result in a net benefit for each individual, there is a tendency to support a personally nonbeneficial decision-rule (or decision under it) only in turn for some type of compensation through one of these adjustment mechanisms. Furthermore, they argue that these devices, plus the desire to minimize decision-making costs of purely voluntary action, can be utilized to insure that each individual will benefit from collective governmental action in the long run, and hence will voluntarily support all its activities and programs. Any net costs incurred in a particular instance must be viewed as exchanges for future benefits.

Thus, by adopting a market model of voluntary and mutually beneficial exchange as the basis of a unanimously agreed upon constitutional system, it is argued that each individual will maximize his utility in the long run, and that a stable equilibrium will be achieved. On a general level this notion of mutual benefit seems to be a reasonable conception of political life, particularly in the actions of formal representative bodies. But can we expect this voluntary conception of social and political life to hold on a societal level in all cases? Are particular operational or substantive policies always adopted and accepted on a purely voluntary basis?

The appropriateness of this reliance on a market model and purely voluntary political organization to provide social wants should be carefully scrutinized. Traditionally a basic characteristic of a market system is that the products be exclusive and divisible, since the basis of the exchange relationship is that individuals can maximize their personal utility and attain a state of marginal equilibrium through *quid pro quo* and self-policing transactions. On the other hand many of the basic and traditional functions of government are not of this nature. Rather they often tend to be "public" in nature; that is, once they are produced they are available to all whether they want them or pay for them. Such goods are not feasibly exchanged in *quid pro quo* transactions. Consequently it does not seem to always be the case that even unanimous desire for these goods would result in the spontaneous and voluntary decision to adopt them, whether by government or through private actions, even when the decision-making costs are ignored. When a large group is involved, it is questionable whether there is sufficient incentive for individuals to contribute voluntarily toward or voluntarily accept the costs of producing such a desired goal. And if they are drawn into action, there is a tendency for them to understate their preferences in order to minimize thieir costs. Since they receive the benefits anyway, and their contributions make no difference to the amount of the good produced, the incentive of the market place is lacking.

Buchanan and Tullock (1962: 68-85) have attempted to overcome this problem by introducing the practices of compensation, logrolling, side-payments, and vote-trading over time. Coleman (1966b, c) has presented similar arguments in at least two articles. The gist of this very interesting argument is that with the opportunity for a large number of decisions of varying importance to be made over an extended period of time, individuals can achieve a state of marginal equilibrium by exchanging their votes on particular issues for others' support on other issues. That is, these numerous votes, of varying importance to the individual, have the same function as goods in the market, and can be bartered in a manner to express precisely his interest on each one. A "vote market" has thus been created by considering numerous collective decisions through time, rather than conceiving each collective decision as a distinct and isolated event.

Let us examine in more detail the implications of this argument since it has important consequences for the explanation of "the most difficult of all intellectual problems in the functioning of society: how individuals, each acting in his own self-interest, can nevertheless make collective decisions, function as an on-going society, and survive together without a 'war of all against all' " (Coleman, 1966a: 66). This vote-market system does seem to handle the problem of revealing preferences and arriving at decisions in an institutional setting where votes can clearly and openly be traded and collected. But it is still not clear that this purely voluntary characterization of collective action would be successful in a broader social setting, particularly at the policy implementation and enforcement level. If indeed, it is to begin to offer a theory of social action, and not just decision, this problem must be resolved. In a sense this problem of implementation is the most fundamental of questions in social interaction and cohesion, and must be considered concurrently with any theory of collective choice which purports to explain social cohesion. An examination of the nature of public goods will point out some of the problems of a purely voluntaristic conception of social exchanges and cohesion.

THE THEORY OF PUBLIC GOODS

While the notion of public, collective, or social goods is an old and important concept, it is not the most well-developed concept in economic theory. There is at best only the most general agreement on the precise characteristics of "pure" public goods. Despite this lack of theoretical development and clarity, the concept persists as an important one in political economy, and in the instance of Baumol's, *Welfare Economics and the Theory of the State* (1952), and Olson's, *Logic of Collective Action* (1965), has begun to make a place for itself in contemporary political science. In this paper I am suggesting its significance for the development of a framework for characterizing a legal system, or at least a good number of laws within one, and examining the attendant problems of compliance. Let us briefly examine the fundamentals of the concept.

Samuelson (1954: 387) has distinguished between two ideal types of goods: "private consumption goods" and "collective consumption goods." The former are goods

> $(X_1, \text{---}, X_n)$ which can be parcelled out among different individuals $(1,2, \ldots, i, \ldots, s)$ according to the relations, $X_j = \sum_{1}^{s} X_j^i$, and collective consumption goods $(X_{n+1}, \ldots, X_{n+m})$ which all enjoy in common, in the sense that each individual's consumption of such a good leads to no subtraction from any other individual's consumption of that good, so that $X_{n+j} = X_{n+j}^i$ simultaneously for each and every i^{th} individual and each collective consumptive good.

Thus the public consumption good "differs from a private consumption good in that each man's consumption of it . . . is related to the total by a condition of equality rather than summation" (Samuelson, 1955: 350).

Head, in elaborating on the theory, points out two distinct elements of public or collective goods: (1) jointness of supply, lumpiness or indivisibility of the product, and (2) the nature of external economies, or the problem of exclusion. Jointness of supply is the characteristic of a good so that "once produced, any given unit of the good can be made equally available to all" (Head, 1962: 201). That is, if a good is made available to one individual or group, it can easily be supplied to an additional person without a corresponding loss to the others. The problem of external economies is the infeasibility or impracticality of excluding potential users of the good. The reasons for these external economies (or diseconomies) are described as the divorce of scarcity from effective ownership. That is, the satisfaction derived from such public goods by any individual is independent of his own contribution, because there is no feasible (or efficient) means of "exchanging" the product on a *quid pro quo* basis as there is with private goods in the market. The benefits from public goods accrue to all, and are independent of any individual's particular contribution. Head (1962: 202-203) notes that the effect of all this is

> to create divergencies between private and social costs and benefits, and thus to prevent the satisfaction of the optimum conditions. Some economic units can enjoy some of the benefits without having to pay for them, and it would, of course, be grossly unrealistic to expect them to contribute voluntarily . . . [and] similarly where the full social costs cannot be charged to an economic unit through the pricing process, again voluntary contributions by way of compensation or expenditures to reduce the costs in question cannot reasonably be expected.

How then, and by what criteria, are these types of goods to be provided? This is, of course, one of the central debates in public finance, and there is no simple, agreed-upon answer. The problem arises in seeking a mechanism for accurately ascertaining the preferences of individuals for the goods, since for any single issue the ideal arragement of the market is not operative. Regardless of the type of political system—including a system in which policies are decided by unanimous agreement—each person will be reluctant to contribute voluntarily to the cost of providing the good. Two interrelated factors contribute to this:

> Any one person can hope to snatch some selfish benefit in a way not possible under the self-policing competitive pricing of private goods. It is in the selfish interest of each person to give false signals, to pretend to have less interest in a collective consumption activity than he really has. [Samuelson, 1954: 388-389]

Assuming that there is some attempt to allocate costs proportionate to use or to intensity of preference, the person would thus save on payments. Second, the tendency is not to want to contribute anything since the benefit can be enjoyed anyway, and the failure of a single individual to contribute will not affect the overall policy. No small amount of effort has gone into resolving these tendencies, often characterized as the problem of contingency of the "free-rider."

Early writers on the subject, perhaps more in terms of justification than explanation, suggested that "the tax tends to take away from each and all that quantity of wealth which they would have voluntarily yielded to the state for the satisfaction of their purely collective wants" (A. Graziani, quoted in Colm, 1936: 4). Here Graziani attempts to solve both the problem of ascertaining true preferences and the insignificance of the individual's contribution to the whole by simply assuming that a person's tax was clearly an accurate assessment of the value of the benefits he enjoyed from the government, and that recognizing this he would gladly and voluntarily surrender his money. The discussion of the nature of public goods in the previous section clearly exposes the weaknesses of this argument.

More recently in traditional public finance, such practical devices as compensation, multiple pricing systems, variable voting rules, plurality voting, point voting, and administrative units with homogeneous characteristics have been suggested as means of indirectly ascertaining individual preferences and allocating costs proportionately. In Buchanan and Tullock's and Coleman's more sophisticated approach, they suggested that some of the above provisions, coupled with the numerous voting opportunities and provisions for logrolling and vote-trading over time, will result in true expression of individual preferences and voluntary acceptance of the costs and collective policies.

However, even with all these provisions there is no guarantee that the costs for each decision will be voluntarily accepted if the policy in question has the characteristics of a public good. The problem of the free rider in the implementation stage has not been solved. Thus it appears that coercion is necessary to secure payment of costs whether or not individuals actually register their true preferences either in the immediate situation or in the long run. In the case of public goods, argreement is distinct from implementation and long-run benefits from immediate costs; the spontaneity and immediacy of the self-policing traditional market transaction are lacking. Even when a particular policy was agreed to by a unanimous vote of the entire collectivity, there would still be a desire *not* to pay the costs. Each person's realization that the benefits are divorced from individual payments of costs would be sufficient to cause the failure to procure the unanimously desired policy.[1]

It is primarily for this reason that a purely voluntary consent system for financing public projects by government is infeasible. Indeed, history has not recorded any nation that has supported its national defense purely from contributions. Recognizing this tendency, then, how would a polity of rational men react? Since each would be as likely as the next to refuse to pay his costs, in an early agreement they would no doubt agree to make their subsequent decisions binding upon all of them. In other words, they would agree among themselves to act under a system of coercive sanctions, so that each of them could be assured that the others would contribute their fair share (to be determined) of the costs. It would, then, be rational for each person to agree to be coerced in order to assure that all others would contribute their costs to the collectively shared benefits. Ideally one would want all others to be placed in this coercive system, while he himself remained free of the coercive constraints, thus minimizing his collectively imposed costs and increasing his benefits. Needless to say, since each person would be just as likely as the next to want this, it would not tend to come about. The important condition to note in this discussion is that the element of coercion would be accepted even in a system which operated by unanimous consent on each decision. Even the rule of unanimity and the true expression of preferences would not negate the desire and need for coercion. And as decisions began to be decided by less than unanimous consent, and through representatives, the need for coercion would tend to increase as the chances for undesirable enactments increased. Given this characterization of public goods and its implications, how is it to be related to law and the problems of compliance?

LAWS AS PUBLIC GOODS

The concept of public goods will be useful in characterizing some types of laws, examining the functions of sanctions, and in dealing with the problems of compliance. But first, what precisely is meant by characterizing laws as public goods? Can all laws be regarded as such? What are the problems arising from such a characterization? What are the implications? These are the questions to be discussed in this section.

Two different types of laws might be considered as "public goods." I will briefly mention the first and most obvious type and then focus the remainder of the discussion on the more tentative type. First, those parts of the budget which specify expenditures for public projects, and are coupled with corresponding taxes and provisions for coercive sanctions to be applied in the case of nonpayment, might be regarded as public goods. These projects are precisely the public goods with which economists deal. The collective benefits flowing from budget expenditures then can be regarded as public goods. Or stated another way, the laws specifying the benefits—the state of being—(and also specifying the costs, i.e., amount of taxes and sanctions for noncompliance) can be regarded as public goods. Here the costs are, of course, stated in monetary units surrendered in taxation; in other societies they might be in terms of property or service. Thus, I have simply taken certain traditional public goods and called them laws. It is obvious that the discussion of the need for and importance of coercion, raised in the last section above, is also applicable to them. While this might be regarded as simply semantic sleight of hand, it is important to note. The point is that a good portion of any government's laws are these types of budgetary provisions, and that it has been primarily political economists—almost alone among social theorists—who have emphasized the importance of coercive sanctions in securing them and in gaining compliance. As will be seen more clearly, this in itself is quite important. But first, can the characterization be expanded beyond the confines of the official budget-enabling legislation? I think it can.

Here I want to expand the notion of public goods beyond those items provided for in the budget and "purchased" through compulsory taxation. Many other types of laws provide for a state of being, or benefits, that also share the distinguishing characteristics of traditional public goods, but in a different context. Many traffic regulations, laws regulating public behavior, laws against theft, and the like seem to fall within this category. Once enacted and operative, they tend (in principle at any rate) to apply to everyone equally, and the benefits cannot be feasibly withheld from anyone. The burglar's property is protected as well as the good burgher's; the speeder has benefit of the safe highway as well as the slow driver. What I am suggesting is that the state of being or social condition that laws specify and secure are to be regarded as the collective benefits—the public goods—and that the costs, rather than being in the more traditional form of money, goods, or services, be in terms of the constrained or regulated behavior also specified by the law. To extend an example given above, the thief has benefit of the same protection of his property as do other people, despite the fact that he is not paying his prescribed share of the cost of producing the collective benefits. Furthermore, if everyone decided to burgle his neighbor, the protection offered against theft would soon disappear. This however, is not part of the concern of the individual thief who calculates only for himself in the immediate situation; he enjoys the full public benefits without paying his prescribed share of the costs. Since costs and benefits are divorced from each other and not "exchanged," he is able to successfully burn his candle at both ends in the absence of an efficacious coercive element.

It is this type of law—having as its *purpose* a general state of being which is available to everyone and is achieved only when a large proportion of people "contribute" to the cost—that I want to characterize as a "public good." Stated in another way, public goods laws are those laws which specify a particular pattern of behavior (or lack of it) to be performed by all those within the polity, and which is achieved only when there is some high degree of compliance to the specifications. All laws obviously do not begin to possess these characteristics. An act recognizing a foreign government could not be considered a "public goods law" in this sense, nor would a law specifying the municipal boundaries of Minneapolis, nor would a law specifying the procedures to obtain a valid marriage certificate. None of these laws requires compliance or widespread consent in order to be efficacious, or to provide for the public benefit. While it is impossible to precisely establish the boundaries, public goods laws, as I have characterized them, would tend to take the form of criminal laws, though even here there are exceptions.

Returning to the definition, a public good was seen to be any good which, if consumed by any person in a group, cannot feasibly be withheld from the others in that group. What I have suggested, then, is that some laws—beyond purely budgetary provisions—share these characteristics: whenever they are enacted and made operative, the general benefits are made available to everyone and cannot feasibly be withheld from anyone. That is, some laws tend to possess the same distinctive problems of "jointness of supply" and exclusion possessed by the traditional types of public goods. The benefits of some laws (as I have characterized them) can easily be supplied to an additional person without a corresponding loss to others. It is rather infeasible to exclude potential users of the good since there is no feasible (or efficient) means of "exchanging" the product on a *quid pro quo* basis. The benefits from the public laws accrue to all and are independent of any individual's particular contribution.

Now that I have established a correspondence between the traditional notion of public goods and the notion that some laws might also be considered public goods, I will extend the analogy in order to make use of the theory of public goods and examine some of its implications. Here the "pricing" mechanism, the distribution of costs, and the laws as public goods will be examined. As discussed earlier, one of the distinguishing and most difficult features of public goods in the determination of an acceptable mechanism to distribute costs in some proportionate relation to the received benefits. The self-policing, *quid pro quo* arrangement which results in optimal allocations in each transaction is not present and a mechanism producing something less must be utilized. In the case of the traditional public goods, this results in the needs and desire for a coercive system in order to avoid the nonpayment or underpayment of the "free rider" on a given policy enactment.

Likewise, in the case of laws as public goods, does this free rider problem emerge? Will the individual seek to enjoy the benefits without wanting to pay his share of the costs? The analogy seems to hold, though here the direct comparison with the characteristics of traditional public goods becomes a bit more complicated. It is useful here to distinguish among "types" of laws. Those types of laws which are direct enabling and enforcing provisions of the budget would, of course, be subject to all the pricing and compliance problems to which traditional public goods are subject, since the costs are levied in the form of taxes. However, where costs are conceived in terms of limited or constrained behavior, some differences are noted. Primarily, the tendency to understate preferences would not be so great since the costs for each individual are fixed and cannot easily be decreased by successfully understating one's preferences. That is, it is not so clear that there would be a strong tendency to understate one's preferences, since the basic cost—in terms of compliant behavior—tends to be an either/or alternative. The same costs—constrained behavior—must be paid regardless of how much or how little the benefits are desired.[2]

The more fundamental need for the provision of coercive sanctions in public goods theory centers around the tendency not to want to pay at all, since the benefits are forthcoming anyway. This is at the heart of the problem of the free rider in the theory of public economy and in the analogous situations in public law. As with traditional public goods, it would appear that a collectivity of rational men, under whatever decision-rule they were operating, would be able to agree to undertake the production of a public policy whose costs were financed through constrained or limited behavior *only if* there was a set of coercive sanctions to act as an additional incentive to contribute to the good and guarantee that it would be produced. As in the provision of traditional public goods, they would agree among themselves to adopt a system of sanctions so that each of them could be assured that the others would contribute their share of the costs, in order that there should be a guarantee that collective benefits would be forthcoming in adequate quantity. It would be rational for each person to agree to be placed in the coercive system in order to assure that all others would likewise contribute their share of the costs (constrained behavior) to the collectively shared benefits.

This is not to argue that all persons obey these types of laws solely from fear of legal sanctions. What are high costs in terms of constrained behavior for some, might be negligible costs or even positive benefits for others, and hence the importance of the sanctions in securing compliance would vary. Certainly in regard to many forms of human conduct, many persons' patterns of behavior would be the same whether specified by a legal rule and sanction or not. However, the collectivity is not assured of a general state of being, i.e., the securing of the collective benefits, in the absence of such a system of efficacious sanctions. The divorce of the cost from the benefit is the source of this problem.

It should be emphasized that here too the need and desire for a system including coercive elements would be forthcoming under any type of operating rules. It would be desired and needed even in a situation requiring unanimous consent in which everyone perceived the law as beneficial. That is, in order to protect against the actions of a person who earnestly wanted the benefits, but who also earnestly disliked paying the costs, it would be rational for everyone to agree to institute a penalty for noncompliance. Given this conception, coercive sanctions take on an important and seemingly paradoxical function in even the most homogeneous of groups: they serve as incentives to get people to contribute to the collective goal that they support. The ubiquity of systems of coercive sanctions, even in highly homogeneous and seemingly consensual societies tends to add some support to this proposition.[3]

And as a group's decision-rules depart from unanimity (e.g., simple majority rule of the entire group, representative assemblies, administrative rule-making), the possibility of particular laws being regarded as "public bads," i.e., undesirable collective "benefits," would increase for some individuals and subgroups. It would be expected here that for some groups the need for a coercive system would increase as the value of the collective benefits decreased. Here individuals would be expected to pay costs for a "benefit" they regarded as negative, hence there would be a two-fold basis for not wanting to comply. This outlook could become particularly significant if a homogeneous and concentrated subgroup in a population refused to view the collectively produced object of the law as a truly public "good." Such an example is seen in the various civil rights provisions aimed at overcoming racial segregation in the South. Here, "outsiders" have forced laws down the throats of unwilling southern whites and, needless to say, have met with strong opposition.

In the above discussion a fundamental point was argued: because of the public goods nature of some laws, it cannot be expected that individuals will achieve a state of marginal equilibrium at the adoption of each law, even operating under decision-rules requiring unanimous consent. Furthermore, the public goods nature of these laws precludes the possibility of the voluntary procurement of the collective policy even if unanimously desired. Consequently, there is the need and rational desire for a system of coercive sanctions. An examination of the implications of this argument will produce some interesting results. Perhaps foremost is the fact that if we can conceive of a law as a public good, then sanctions will not be designed primarily to "convince" or "oblige" the reluctant recipient of the legal benefits bestowed upon him. Nor will they be designed primarily to protect society from those few irrational, anomic individuals who seek to wreak havoc on others and themselves. While it is certainly the case that coercive sanctions are used to secure compliance from both of these types, its main function is more general. It is to help compel rational, maximizing individuals who want and enjoy the benefits of the law to contribute to the costs of providing those benefits by obeying the law. A primary function of these coercive sanctions then is directed not at the irrational, but the rational; not at the deviant, but the normal; not at the dissenter, but the proponent.

Formal, legal sanctions in this formulation, then, take on a considerably broader and more important position in the explanation of compliance to legal rules than they are usually given, and go some way toward reviving the Austinian conception of law, albeit in a more limited and radically different form. Even those theorists who have postulated individual self-interest as an axiom have tended to ignore the problem of compliance or have tended to develop some type of "exchange" theory of compliance by ignoring the discrete characteristics of each public goods type law. Still other discussions of law emphasize the irrational, deviant, and anomic characteristics of convicted noncompliants, and fail to adequately consider the motives and characteristics of the more numerous and more skillful unconvicted noncompliants and compliants.[4] The implicit presumption of these approaches seems to be that it is normal and expected that one would voluntarily comply, and thus the problem is solely to explain the "deviance." This paper has attempted to begin to examine the other side of this problem and to explore what I think is the prior, more basic and infinitely more difficult question, why people comply with the law.

SUMMARY

What this discussion has tried to do is to conceptualize the double-edged problem of compliance and noncompliance to laws in terms of rational choice applied to a set of individual-choice situations. Each situation involving behavior governed by a legal norm can be regarded as a choice situation in which the rational actor must undertake a process of calculation to determine his course of behavior. What particularly distinguishes choices involving legally prescribed behavior from choices of other social actions are the *legally prescribed sanctions* attached to the law. This introduces an additional element into the decision process, though its importance would, of course, vary widely among individuals depending upon their intensities of preference, estimates, perceptions, and values.

In the discussion above, it has been suggested that the coercive element in law might play a larger part in the securing of compliance than it is frequently given. In particular, an "exchange" model accounting for the acceptance of and compliance to laws has been briefly explored and rejected. The public goods nature of at least some (particularly criminal) laws caused the rejection of such an explanation of compliance. By pursuing an "economic" approach to the problem, albeit not an "exchange" or market model, it was suggested that coercive sanctions would take on an additional importance beyond what most models of compliance and noncompliance afford them. It was seen that for some situations, even where everyone regarded the law as beneficial, not even the consensus on the goals would necessarily result in compliance in the pursuit of the goals. This "free rider" phenomenon helps, I think, explain why so many seemingly "well-adjusted" and upright citizens, who appear to share the legally institutionalized norms and values of their communities, frequently violate those norms. The attainment of the desired goal and a particular individual's behavior are not necessarily dependent upon each other. Thus the function of the coercive element of law is not only to curb the behavior of those who do not subscribe to the purpose or goal of the legal rule, but is much broader–to curb *all* those who do not want to pay a particular set of costs, and who *may* or *may not* support or accept the collective goal the legal rule seeks to obtain. This interpretation or approach, then, goes a long way toward resolving the classical paradox faced by students of law: "If a law is not supported by the mores of the community, it is ineffectual; if it is, the law is unnecessary."

While this discussion has not produced a "model" or "theory" of compliance and noncompliance, it has, I think begun to suggest some considerations which any such theory must deal with, namely, the function of the coercive element attached to the law. It has suggested a broader function of the coercive element than most discussions of compliance and noncompliance and "deviant behavior" attribute to it. Furthermore, this discussion has suggested a framework for conceptualizing the twin problems of compliance and noncompliance. A type of cost-benefit or rational-choice analysis has been suggested, in which individuals are assumed to make social choices on specific, substantive matters in order to maximize utility. In this framework, then, the coercive provisions of law are regarded as "cost factors" in the calculus of decisions affecting behavior governed by legal rules. The decision to comply or not to comply (or some degree in between) to a law would entail a consideration of the likelihood and magnitude of the application of a coercive sanction as a cost to be weighed against the possible benefits accruing through some course of action.

While most economic theories of choice have dealt with discussions to adopt consititutional or fundamental rules for a polity (i.e., rules of the game rather than specific decisions under a particular rule), a few theorists have begun to extend the analysis to particular or substantive social-choice situations as has been the case in this discussion. For instance, Professor Coleman (1966a) has briefly discussed alternatives to the acceptance of a system of constitutional rules, revolt, and emigration. Professor Ireland (1967: 50) has attempted to raise and formalize the problem about the "point at which the individual will resort to revolution and what factors will he take into consideration." In this paper I have discussed and suggested a similar rational choice approach, but have applied it to a much less grand set of alternatives than those of revolution and emigration. Here the focus has been on the functions of the coercive sanctions in law and the calculus of the rational individual in his decisions to comply with or violate the laws selectively in a political system of which he himself may well approve. It is probably this concern for the less dramatic types of social-choice situations that will eventually lead to the most fruitful insights and theories of social cohesion.

NOTES

1. Olson (1965: 22-65) has developed this point in the context of interest group formation, and it seems appropriately raised here in regard to the individual decision to participate in the implementation of a particular policy enactment.

2. This might be challenged, however. Consider a situation where individuals argue that they will benefit only slightly from a public goods law. Since the costs are not subject to reduction, by convincingly understating their preferences, they might successfully hold out for some other type of compensation above the public goods benefits. Some have tended to characterize the OEO payment to Chicago's Blackstone Rangers in these terms. But even here the compensation is distinct from the decision to comply or not. And since the effect of attempts to induce increased compliance by forms of compensation is not crucial to the present argument, it will not be pursued further here.

3. For a neo-Austinian conception of law, which emphasizes the coercive element, see the discussions and analyses of several primitive legal systems by E. A. Hoebel (1954).

4. Richard Schwartz (Schwartz and Orleans, 1967) has begun to make a small step to correct this misbalance of investigation. His findings in a recent study attest to the importance of legal sanctions in securing widespread compliance to tax law among supposedly well-adjusted and prosperous members of the middle class. Such evidence, while sketchy and tentative, adds some support to the theoretical formulation of the importance of sanctions presented in this paper.

REFERENCES

ARROW, K. (1951) Social Choice and Individual Values. New York: John Wiley.

BAUMOL, W. (1952) Welfare Economics and the Theory of the State. Cambridge: Harvard Univ. Press.

BLAU, P. (1964) Exchange and Power in Social Life. New York: John Wiley.

BUCHANAN, J. and G. TULLOCK (1962) The Calculus of Consent. Ann Arbor: Univ. of Michigan Press.

COLEMAN, J. S. (1966a) "Individual interests and collective action." Papers in Non-Market Decision-Making, I. Charlottesville, Va.: University of Virginia Center of Political Economy.

--- (1966b) "Foundations for a theory of collective decision." Amer. J. of Sociology 71 (May): 615-627.

--- (1966c) "The possibility of a social welfare function." Amer. Economic Rev. 61 (December): 1105-1122.

COLM, G. (1936) "Theory of public expenditures." Annals of the Amer. Academy of Pol. and Social Sci. 183 (January): 1-11.

DOWNS, A. (1957) An Economic Theory of Democracy. New York: Harper & Row.

HEAD, J. G. (1962) "Public goods and public policy." Public Finance 27, 3: 197-219.

HOEBEL, E. A. (1954) The Law of Primitive Man. Cambridge: Harvard Univ. Press.

HOMANS, G. (1961) Social Behavior: Its Elementary Forms. New York: Harcourt, Brace & World.

IRELAND, T. (1967) "The rationale of revolt." Papers on Non-Market Decision-Making, III. Charlottesville Va.: University of Virginia Center of Political Economy.

KRISLOV, S. (1966) "The perimeters of power: the concept of compliance as an approach to the study of the legal and political process." Delivered at the Annual Meeting of the American Polical Science Association, New York.

MUSGRAVE, R. (1959) The Theory of Public Finance. New York: McGraw-Hill.

OLSON, M. (1965) The Logic of Collective Action. Cambridge: Harvard Univ. Press.

SAMUELSON, P. (1955) "Diagrammatic exposition of a theory of public expenditure." Rev. of Economics and Statistics 37 (November): 350-356.

--- (1954) "The pure theory of public expenditure." Rev. of Economics and Statistics 36 (November): 387-389.

SCHWARTZ, R. and S. ORLEANS (1967) "On legal sanctions." Univ. of Chicago Law Rev. 34 (Winter): 274-300.

THIBAUT, J. and H. KELLEY (1959) The Social Psychology of Groups. New York: John Wiley.

Chapter 3

Strategies of Research Design in the Legal Impact Study

The Control of Plausible Rival Hypotheses

RICHARD LEMPERT – *University of Michigan*

A legal impact study represents an attempt to ascertain how a particular law affects the conduct and attitudes of those individuals, groups, or other relevant units located in jurisdictions where that law is in force. By its very nature, such a study involves one essential comparison; the comparison between actual behavior patterns in jurisdictions having the law in question and the behavior patterns which would have existed in those same jurisdictions had the law in question never been enacted. Since this comparison is one which by definition cannot actually be made, the problem for the legal impact theorist is how to estimate best what the behavior patterns would have been in a certain jurisdiction had the law in question never existed there. The legislator or court seeking to determine the actual or probable effects of a law faces a similar problem.

There are three ways in which this comparison can be achieved. One is by comparing the same jurisdiction before and after the passage of the law in

AUTHOR'S NOTE: *This work is supported by a grant from the Cooperative Research Branch of the Social Security Administration and the Welfare Administration under SSA Grant 201, Department of Health, Education, and Welfare, Washington, D.C., and from funds of the Public Affairs Committee of Oberlin College under a Ford Foundation Grant. Research facilities were provided by the Social Science Research Institute, University of Hawaii.*

The writer would like to express his special thanks to Professors Kiyoshi Ikeda, Donald T. Campbell, and Harry V. Ball for the general encouragement they have given him and for their helpful criticism of earlier drafts of this paper.

question and noting any behavioral changes which seem to have followed as a result of the passage of the law. The second is by comparing jurisdictions which have a particular law with those that do not and assuming that, if not for the law, behavior in the two sets of jurisdictions would have been the same. The third method is by combining the two approaches. This involves examining behavior patterns in a particular set of jurisdictions both before and after they passed the law in question and comparing these patterns with those found over the same period of time in a set of jurisdictions not having the law in question.

Each of these basic ways of approaching the comparison problem can be broken down further into a variety of comparative approaches, each of which can be evaluated on the basis of how well it controls for "plausible rival hypotheses." A plausible rival hypothesis in this case is a nonexperimental variable which could reasonably explain the behavioral change which the investigator would like to be able to attribute to the existence of the law. The problem of controlling for such plausible rival hypotheses is vital for effective legal impact research.

Perhaps we can better grasp the nature of this problem if we look first at a concrete example of legal impact research and at the efforts which have to be made to control for plausible rival hypotheses in the field situation. One study which serves our purposes well is the Kiyoshi Ikeda-Douglas Yamamura study of public housing on the island of Oahu, Hawaii (see Ikeda et al., 1964; Ikeda et al., 1966). This three-year investigation sought, as a major goal, to discover the effects which different types of housing regulations have on mobility patterns among housing project families.

Initial investigation clearly showed that mobility (as measured by income increases over time and moves from project tenancy directly into home ownership) was higher among families that lived in projects without income limits (Navy lease) than it was among families that lived in projects having low (federal) or moderate (state) income limits. While this finding was in line with theoretical considerations, a number of plausible rival hypotheses had to be dealt with before one could begin to determine exactly what effects could be traced to the impact of the different legal-administrative regulations.

For example, it was possible that the tenants of the Navy lease projects had started from a higher income base than had the tenants of the state or federal projects. To check this, it was necessary to go to the records of the Hawaiian Housing Authority and examine the initial incomes of sample families applying for public housing on Oahu during the time periods under study.[1] Initial income for Navy lease families was found to fall somewhere between the initial income of federal housing families and that of state housing families (Ikeda et al., 1964: Table 2, Appendix).

A second possibility was that families entered into the different projects at different points in their life cycle. If this were true, it might be that the very young and the very old entered the projects with income limits, while those in the most mobile age brackets usually applied for Navy lease housing. This was also checked by resort to the running records.[2] In general, a higher percentage of the residents of the Navy lease project were under thirty when they applied for public housing than were residents of the other two projects, but they were similar to the state housing families in number of children, and the difference was not enough to explain the different outcomes (Ikeda et al., 1964: Tables 3-5, Appendix).

A third and more subtle threat to the hypothesis that the law had an effect in this area was the possibility that, while the three housing groups were similar with respect to easily operationalized characteristics such as initial income, they differed significantly on such hard-to-measure social-psychological characteristics as their general outlook on life, the relative weights which they gave to income, residential, and familial values, and on the network of significant others to whom they could turn for moral and financial support. In order to properly assess the factors which came to play in this area, it was decided to interview members of some six hundred families.[3] To increase the validity of the study, the sample of families interviewed included a number of families who applied for public housing and who met the requirements for the particular projects, but who were forced to turn to the private rental market because of a lack of space in public housing. The data from the interviews and from this latter group of families are only now being processed. But early results indicate that, even after controlling for the above social-psychological factors, a legal impact will be demonstrable.

This is not to say that the above sketch exhausts the number of plausible rival hypotheses which threaten the validity of the Ikeda-Yamamura study. Others exist, and efforts have been made to control for them. It does give one an idea, however, of some of the major threats which can be encountered when one is doing actual legal impact work. The length and intensity of the study indicate one type of work which is needed in the area. But this does not mean that the only type of legal impact work which can be valuable must be as lengthy or as extensive. Many valuable but simpler studies have been done with much smaller expenditures of both time and money.[4] Enough remains to be learned in the legal impact area to indicate a need for both long-term and short-run research.

The basic plan of this paper is to consider certain preexperimental and quasi-experimental designs which Professors Donald Campbell and Julian Stanley set forth in a chapter from the *Handbook of Research on Teaching* entitled "Experimental and Quasi-Experimental Designs for Research on Teaching" and see how these design considerations can be helpful when dealing with sociolegal problems of the type described above.[5] For the purpose of this paper, we shall follow the numbering and the illustrative systems which Campbell and Stanley set forth in their work.

In this illustrative system, X equals the experimental variable which for purposes of this paper will always be the particular law whose impact is being studied; O delineates each point at which an observation of the relevant behavior is taken, and a dashed line (– – – –) is used to equate two observational units (Campbell and Stanley, 1963: 176). For the purpose of this paper, the observational units (jurisdictions) will always be states of the United States, unless some other unit is specified.

We shall also adopt Campbell and Stanley's basic criterion for the internal validity of an experimental design, namely that a design is more valid internally the better it is able to control for plausible rival hypotheses. In other words the more certain an investigator can be that the experimental variable is causally associated with perceived changes, the more successful his experiment and the more valid the experimental design he has chosen to use (Campbell and Stanley, 1963: 175).

The strengths and weaknesses of experimental designs are usually discussed in the abstract, and to a large extent this procedure will be followed here. However, the relative power or strength of an experimental design is always related to the situation in which it is applied. The power or strength of a design is its ability to rule out the plausible rival hypotheses available. Thus a design which might have many potential weaknesses on paper may not have them when applied in a given legal impact study. Similarly, a design with many potential weaknesses may be just slightly modified in a given legal impact study and many of these weaknesses will disappear. Finally, even when the weaknesses of a particular design cannot be adequately controlled for, it is often the best design available, and it is often preferable that the investigator go ahead with an imperfect design rather than leave an interesting area completely unexplored. The essential requirement in these cases is to note explicitly the potential imperfections in any reports growing out of such studies.

GENERAL CONSIDERATIONS

Before going into the specifics of the various designs, there are several general points which should be discussed. In the first place, the designs as set forth with respect to impact studies might be rightly referred to by the purist as nonexperimental (observational) designs rather than as quasi-experimental ones. As Campbell and Stanley present their quasi-experimental designs, they are quasi-experimental because of the investigator's inability to equate his experimental group with his control group through some sort of random selection technique. But even in this situation, it is still the investigator who introduces the experimental variable into one group and not into the other. In many legal impact studies, the investigator cannot be the experimenter; he is incapable of randomly assigning laws to different populations and is also incapable, for the most part, of playing any part in the introduction of the laws or in any way of controlling the setting in which they are introduced.

This difference, while creating a different set of rival hypotheses which must be controlled, does not mean that the format of the quasi-experimental and preexperimental designs[6] cannot be applied to impact studies. The fact that the investigator himself does not introduce the experimental variable should not force us to call legal impact studies nonexperimental. The perspective toward comparisons is the same, and the rigor with which the design can be followed can also be the same and should be if the "experimental" assessment is to have the highest possible validity (Campbell, 1957).

Campbell and Stanley present eight factors which are potential threats to the internal validity of an experimental design because they provide possible sources of plausible rival hypotheses. They are: history, maturation, testing, instrumentation, regression, selection, mortality,[7] and the interaction of certain of these factors such as selection and maturation,[8] and the like. Because of the quasi-experimental nature of legal impact studies and because of the particular nature of the law, many of these threats may be disregarded by the experimenter in this area, while others pose special problems which would not be present in the normal social-psychological quasi-experimental situation. In discussing the possible influences of these sources of plausible rival hypotheses, and for the purposes of general discussion throughout this paper, we shall assume a standard experimental situation in which the experimenter is interested in assessing the effects of a certain law on the behavior of people living in states of the United States which have that law. In all cases, the experimenter has available to him a sizable group of states which have different laws applying to the same subject or a group which is without any formal regulation of the subject.

Since administrative agencies often keep statistical records concerning the incidence of the behavior which they are supposed to regulate (e.g., crime rates for types of cases reaching court), the effects of a particular law often may be measured by commonly available statistical data. Testing effects should therefore be nonexistent, and instrumentation effects will often be minimal, though there are some threats to validity in this area.

(1) First, an investigator may be attempting to compare two states which use different methods of computing their statistical reports on the same subject. This can be controlled by utilizing data collected by national organizations which prescribe uniform methods of data collection in all states.

(2) The second problem is that a state or subdivision thereof may change its methods of reporting data. In Chicago, for example, when a new police superintendent took office, he publicly announced that he was going to institute a more thorough system for reporting criminal activities and that the crime rate should be expected to increase considerably because of this. By doing this, the superintendent was in effect preventing any real comparison of the work of the police department under his supervision with its work under his predecessor. This type of change,

> while probably infrequent, should always be looked for when one sees a marked change in the statistics he is gathering. This must be done even if the change in the statistics follows shortly after the introduction of the law under study, because a good possibility exists that the method of collecting data was changed in conjunction with the law.

Maturation, mortality, and regression should also present minimal threats to the types of experimental designs which apply in this area, though there are situations when each of these features will have to be examined in detail before they can be disregarded as possible explanations of any perceived changes. For example, if a time-series study were to be made of tort damage awards in two states having different legal norms, a more rapid increase in award size in one of them than in the other might be due to a difference in certain long-range secular trends (maturation effects) such as inflation, rather than to the differences in the laws of the two states.

The major threats to the validity of legal impact designs are three: history; history-selection interaction; and, one peculiar to the sociology of law, the problem of distinguishing the law as it appears on the books from the "law in fact."

Of these, the determination of what the law is in fact should be preliminary to most studies. The law as it appears on the statute books may be only a partial and sometimes misleading guide as to the administered situation which in fact exists. If the law is within the province of a particular administrative agency, the agency's interpretation of the law and its activities in reference to the law must be traced. In many cases, court decisions must be examined to see what "glosses" the judges have placed on the law. In still other cases, there may be differential enforcement by the police, in which case the system must be examined in detail at this level. In each of these cases, there are ways of getting at the character of the law as administered.

History is another potential threat to the internal validity of sociolegal experimental designs, but ordinarily it should not be too difficult to control for. It is an especially plausible rival hypothesis in the "before-and-after" type designs, such as design 2 and design 7 (discussed below). A coincidental historical happening can often explain a perceived behavior change just as well as the experimental variable can. This is why it is always wise to use "before-and-after" type designs in connection with a group of control states which does not have the particular law in question and which has been subject to the same historical influences as the group of affected states. If a geographically well-distributed group of states with a given law can be compared with a similar group of states without the law, history may usually be ruled out as an explanatory cause for the differences in perceived behavior which the experimental hypothesis would suggest is caused by the law under study.

In comparing laws among states, one may often want to focus on the situation in the three or four years before their passage and on the situation in the years immediately after their passage. Unless the date of the passage of the laws is the same, this procedure is almost always to be avoided. Any perceived differences may actually be due to history, but the design itself will have failed to correct for it, and one reading the write-up of the intervention will likewise be unable to correct for it.

The legal impact theorist should also guard against the possibility that the enactment of a particular law may be only one of several similarly directed governmental interventions in the same historical period. In Hawaii, for instance, the legislature recently passed a law setting up a special program to encourage home ownership among public housing familes (Hawaii Session Laws, 1964).[9] Along with this, the local housing authority made an administrative decision to furnish all families participating in the program with certain special services and counseling. If the number of people moving from public housing into their own homes should significantly rise in the projects affected by the law but not rise in those unaffected (or in similar projects in other states not having the particular law), it might be hypothesized that the legal stimulus regarding home ownership had indeed caused the change. However, it is possible that it is the extra services and counseling which are responsible for any rise in home ownership and that the residential mobility rate of the affected housing families would have gone up without the special program if they had only been furnished with the extra counseling and services.

Such changes, stimulated by the law but not required by it or in fact a part of it, must always be looked to by the legal impact theorist as a source of plausible rival hypotheses. Until government officials become more specific in their interventions, the most the legal sociologist can say will often be that a particular law, when coupled with certain other administrative actions, will lead to a certain behavior change.

This is not to say that legal impact research is unwarranted in the situation where the law has been embellished by administrative practice. For while it is impossible to say with certainty that the law produced a specific change, it is often possible to say with a high degree of certainty that a particular legal structure plus a particular series of administrative interventions resulted in a certain change in behavior patterns. Such results are quite satisfying to the practically oriented, who are primarily interested in knowing what agent or agents can produce a certain change. What changes are induced by the law and what by administrative measures depends largely on how much direction the legislature chooses to write into its particular legal mandates. What is administrative policy in one state may be written law in another. Also, as different states adopt different variations of a similar legal-administered intervention package, it may become possible for later investigators to separate out exactly what the most important change agents in the package are, be they legal or otherwise.

Selection is the most severe threat which operates in a manner specific to sociolegal research. This is because a law represents two things–a regulatory device and (especially, but not exclusively, in a democratic political system) an expression of the people's feelings about a particular issue. This variable is especially likely to be a factor where a legal system is being studied in isolation or where a whole nation is being studied. For example, to the best of my knowledge, every state in this nation has a law against incest, and there is very little incest in this country. The mere concurrence of these two facts does not prove that the fact that incest is made criminal is responsible for its lack of prevalence. Indeed, the opposite is probably true. The American people feel incest is such a bad thing that they have made a crime of it. However, America would not be an incestuous nation even if such laws did not exist.

Arnold Rose (1954) points up the fact that the French legal structure has traditionally subjected France's voluntary associations to a variety of hindering regulations. He also points out that the average Frenchman has fewer ties with voluntary associations than does his American counterpart who lives in a society where the right of association is constitutionally protected. Yet these factual congruencies do not necessarily mean that Franco-American differences in voluntary association participation can be explained on the basis of the differing legal structures. The plausible rival hypothesis exists that, for specific cultural reasons, the French and the Americans are differentially motivated to enter voluntary associations and that these differences have been reflected in legal patterns rather than caused by them. Rose (1961) reaches the only safe conclusion on the subject when he says in an article treating the same subject on the Italian scene that it is at least clear that the law has not helped increase participation.

Any research design purporting to deal with the impact of a particular law on the behavior of a populace will have to make certain that the law is indeed more than an expression of the popular will of the people and that the people would be acting differently without the law. There are a variety of ways in which this hypothesis can be ruled out. Harry Ball (1960) used one of them in his study on rent control. In polling landlords as to what they thought of the law, he found that a large proportion of them thought that the law was unfair and (presumably) would have been charging higher rents if it were not on the books. He also found that a majority of those who disapproved of the law were obeying the rules. The techniques he used strongly suggest that rent control laws were a major influence on the level of rent in Hawaii during the period in which they were enforced.

The self-selection weakness also does not enter in too strongly when dealing with some of the more technical aspects of the law. For instance, the rules of evidence vary in certain particulars from state to state. If a study were to be made to see if this affected the direction of jury verdicts in certain types of cases, it would be incorrect to say that any difference that existed occurred because the people in the state, as represented *by the jury* had wanted certain types of cases to go preponderantly in a given direction and so had passed the particular rule of evidence. It is possible, of course, that the laws were passed because a certain pressure group or a majority of state legislators wanted the rule, but since these people are not on the jury, an experimenter can still say, given the proper control conditions and the desired results, that the rule of evidence has influenced the direction of jury verdicts in particular types of cases – e.g., a rule relating to the introduction of insurance liability figures in personal injury cases.

This selection weakness can also be controlled to a large extent by using a group of states spread out over the country in the experimental group–i.e., having the law, and a similarly spread group in the control group. Given the mobility in this country and the broad common grounds between people in neighboring states, if people in twenty-five scattered states having a particular law act one way and people in the other twenty-five act another way with regard to the subject matter of the statute, one can usually be safe in saying that it is the law in its regulative aspect rather than in its expressive aspect which has caused the perceived behavioral difference.

The types of validity threats which affect legal impact experiments are all such as to make the study of only one state with a particular law represent a relatively poor experiment design. Studying one state with a particular law and one state without it is much better and can be quite impressive if a time-linked comparison (design 14 below) shows a sharp effect. However, this design grows less effective the more dissimilar the states are in other explanatory variables.

The best design will always involve a time-linked comparison of a group of states having a particular law with a similar group of states not having that law. This design is more valid the more heterogeneous each set of states is within itself and the more similar the two sets of states when each set is viewed as a whole. For instance, if Mississippi and Alabama have anti-miscegenation statutes coupled with an almost nonexistent rate of interracial marriages while New York and New Jersey lack such statutes and have a much higher rate of interracial marriage, this factual congruence will provide little ground for an investigator saying that anti-miscegenation statutes cut down on the rate of interracial marriage. However, if Mississippi and New York were to have such statutes along with a significantly lower rate of interracial marriages than Alabama and New Jersey, then the investigator would have much more reason to believe that the laws had an impact in this area. The degree of certainty would increase if Alabama and New Jersey had once had such a law and if the rate of interracial marriages had shown a marked increase once the laws were repealed or, conversely, if Mississippi and New York had once lacked such a law and if the rate of interracial marriage had shown a marked decrease after the law was passed.

Strictly speaking, no experimental design is valid outside the particular groups which were measured in the course of the experiment, and, even for those groups, the internal validity would be limited to the extent to which the experimental results are reproducible. But if experimental results could not be generalized, there would be little sense in doing any but the most widely encompassing experiments.

Fortunately, the results of almost all experiments can be generalized to some extent to units not involved in the experimental situation. This generalizability is what Campbell and Stanley refer to as the external validity of the design.[10] By and large, we can say that the greater the external validity of a particular experimental design, the more potential applications it will have and the more it will tell one about "real world" situations. It is in this area of external validity that legal impact designs have a great potential strength. When we study the impact of a law in several states, we are examining what are essentially highly heterogeneous groupings involving millions of individuals. Thus we have a strong basis for generalizing the results of such a study to people in all states across the United States; far stronger, for instance, than we might have for generalizing a study of racial attitudes among students in a sociology course to students in the same university taking an advanced biology course.

THE PREEXPERIMENTAL AND QUASI-EXPERIMENTAL DESIGNS[11]

Design 1: X O–THE ONE-SHOT CASE STUDY

Design 1 to the legal sociologist is a simple descriptive design with observations taken at one point in time. Using a design 1 approach simply involves noting that a society has a particular law (the X factor) and that certain conditions exist in the area which the law is designed to regulate (the O factor). This design is neither experimental nor quasi-experimental, in that, even if one were to know that a particular law existed in a certain society (e.g., a law against incest) and that a particular condition existed in that society (e.g., a lack of incestuous relationships), he would have no way of knowing whether and to what extent the law was responsible for the behavior observed. An observer from another planet during the Prohibition era might have noted the amount of drinking which went on in this country and, if he were to draw conclusions from a design 1 approach, assumed that for Americans a law against drinking encourages the consumption of alcoholic beverages. In fact, alcohol consumption was probably much lower during the Prohibition period than before or after, if for no other reason than that it was less readily available. The incidence of arrests for public drunkenness certainly suggests that this was the case.

Once it is established that design 1 is not *experimental,* it must be pointed out that in a certain sense it can be *scientific;* that is, to the extent that the methods of determining what the law is and what the relevant conditions are follow a scientifically oriented procedure. It also should be pointed out that there is a real need for a taxonomy of diverse legal structures. Those following a simple design 1 pattern of observation are performing a very valuable activity when they report their findings. Such findings, however, have the limitations which inevitably characterize the case study. They cannot, by themselves, provide the basis for testing generalizations.

Design 2: O X O–ONE-GROUP PRETEST POSTTEST DESIGN

This design differs from design 1 in that it calls for an observation of the behavior which the law purports to regulate both before and after the passage of the law in question. In the language of the social-psychologist, the law is the *experimental variable* and the two observations are a *pretest* and a *posttest.* For the social-psychologist, the pretest and posttest are often administered questionnaires designed to measure operationally the behavior which the experimental variable is supposed to affect. For the legal impact theorists, the pretest and posttest equivalents will ordinarily take the form of statistical reports of the behavior which the law is designed to regulate collected at two points in time (before and after the passage of the law under study). It is in this sense that the terms pretest and posttest will be used in this paper.

Design 2 is superior to design 1 in some respects. It would, for example, have given the interplanetary observer mentioned above a more correct picture of the relationship between drinking and the law in the United States. Nevertheless, design 2 is relatively weak in controlling plausible rival hypotheses and should be avoided where possible. Its first weakness is in controlling for independent historical factors. Indeed, it is weaker in this area than it would be when applied to the normal social-psychological situation because the likelihood of independent historical variables entering as causal factors in the perceived change increases as the time lapse between the measurements increases. In the case of social-psychological experimentation, this time lapse may be kept minimal, but, in the case of field experiments where officially collected data are relied upon, there is often at least a year between available observational points. Indeed, if the law is to show any effect, an even longer time period between observations is sometimes needed.

Design 2 is also quite weak in the area of history-selection interaction. Using it does not help the investigator decide whether a particular law caused a perceived behavioral change or whether the change would have occurred anyway, with the law being merely an expression of an intent that such a change should occur. For example, there was a recent case in Hawaii in which a patient with a history of dangerous activities was released from a mental hospital ninety days after being admitted. He bought a gun and shot at cars passing along one of the state's principal highways, killing a policeman and wounding several tourists.

It is quite probable that this incident will result in a change in the Hawaiian insanity statutes regarding criminal and civil commitments to asylums. It is predictable that, if such a law were passed, the pattern of releases from mental hospitals of those who were potentially dangerous to society would change. But even without the passage of such a law, it is predictable that the sniping incident and its repercussions will lead to a change in the pattern of release of such dangerous persons. The design 2 approach cannot determine whether the law being studied caused the change in behavior, whether an intent to change behavior (which would have been carried out, law or no law) was responsible for the passage of the law, or whether the factors of law and intent are related in such a way that both will explain part of any perceived behavior change.

Where several such incidents pile up, there is the added possibility that this will lead to such drastic changes at the administrative level that the whole system of record-keeping will be revamped or that classificatory standards will be revised. In either case, the possibility exists that such administrative changes will lead to pseudo-effects not attributable to the law in question, in that they will disguise changes which the law has brought about. The sniping instance discussed above might lead to a different method of classifying people as dangerously insane, which would lead to a different pattern of release among such individuals whether or not the legislature adopts stricter standards governing their release and whether or not the hospital itself imposes more stringent procedures.

Another reason why design 2 should be avoided is that the use of statistics from only two points in time can be very misleading. Two arbitrarily chosen points in time may not be typical periods at which to measure the incidence of that behavior which is supposed to be affected by the law, and the investigator may well find a seeming change which is actually the result of regression artifacts, i.e., a stochastic probability that extreme phenomena will appear less extreme on remeasurement. For instance, in Connecticut, there was a tightening of the driving regulations after a year with an especially high death toll, and the next year the death toll fell markedly (see Campbell and Ross, 1968). The state officials praised the new law system and gave it much credit for the drop in deaths, which a statistician could have predicted would occur (given the figures for auto deaths in the ten years previous) on the basis of regression artifacts alone.

This type of design is especially dangerous in the sociology of law for two reasons. One is that, because of the responsive-expressive characteristics of the law, there is a higher-than-chance probability that if the year before the passage of the law is chosen as one of the two points, it will have been a year of exceptionally high incidence of the type of the behavior which the law is trying to regulate, since laws often gain their necessary momentum for passage in response to just such out-of-the-ordinary situations.

The second reason is that the design 2 approach tends to be very misleading to the public at large, yet such studies often are publicized widely. Witness the use which politicians make of such "designs." I do not think it is pessimistic to say that the people of Connecticut are much more likely to listen to Ribicoff's "hard facts" concerning the drop in deaths in Connecticut and to attribute this difference to "his" speeding law than they are to listen to the scholarly talk of some social scientists who claim that, when the whole time-series is examined, the decrease in lives lost could be explained on the basis of statistical probabilities. Social scientists, if they cannot correct such political arguments, should at least try to keep their work from adding to the misinformation which the general public may receive.

Design 3: $\frac{X \_ O}{O}$ STATIC-GROUP COMPARISON

Design 3 has been the traditional design of the great generalizers and the creators of much of the early sociology of law theory (see e.g., Durkheim, 1899-1900). Their technique has generally been to note that certain societies have a particular law and that certain conditions exist in those societies, while other societies lacking that law have comparatively different situations. Usually their conclusions have run in the opposite direction from those of the legal impact theorists, and they have tried to equate certain societal changes (as independent variables) with the legal structure of the nation (as dependent variables), rather than vice versa. Such comparisons, when operating in this direction, have been fruitful in stimulating the generation of the more abstract legal theory. But they are basically methods of thought, rather than a systematic research design.

When it comes to actually testing hypotheses, however, and particularly when one is trying to test the hypothesis that a law has a certain influence, design 3 has certain grave weaknesses. The gravest is the self-selection weakness. If one state has a particular law and another lacks it, even if observed conditions in the two states are different, it cannot be stated authoritatively that the law has caused the perceived difference until all the other features which the two states do not share and which could have caused the difference have been examined. This includes the possibility that because of a different history, location, or other factors, the people of the state having the legal variable would have acted in the direction that the law requires if the law had not been passed in the first place.

It seems design 3 can approach true experimental design the more numerous and the more heterogeneous a group of units that can be put in each slot. If twenty-five different states all have a particular law and show a certain type of behavior while twenty-five states without the law possess mutually similar behavior patterns which differ from those of the first set in a systematic way, then the hypothesis that the law is responsible for a particular pattern of behavior becomes much more tenable.

There remains, however, a major threat to validity resulting from the lack of a nonreactive pretest measurement.[12] For it is possible the the two groups of states differed along similar dimensions before the law was adopted by one set of them. The law might be an expression of a belief which for a certain set of reasons is peculiar to twenty-five states of the United States and not to the other twenty-five, or it might be symptomatic of a condition which prevails in the states having the law but is not an important factor in those states without the law. In either case, the design 3 approach, even with a variety of states in each block, would yield only a reflection of differential conditions which prevailed in the states in question before the passage of the particular law rather than the effect brought about by the law. Often the investigator can ascertain if this factor is confounding his results by examining the states in question in some detail. As a rule, the more heterogeneous the "treated" and "nontreated" states, the more likely it is that possible causal beliefs and conditions will be randomly distributed throughout both groups, thereby increasing the probability that design 3 will prove to be a satisfactory design.

Design 7: O O OXO O O TIME-SERIES

The investigator who is using the design 7 approach takes a series of behavioral observations at points in time before and after the enactment of the law being studied. If the behavioral curve shows a sharp change in the predicted direction during the period after the passage of the law, it is hypothesized that the law caused the particular change. As Campbell and Stanley demonstrate, design 7 is considerably better than design 2, since it controls for maturation, regression, and certain selection and interaction effects. If, for example, the Connecticut traffic death statistics discussed above had been plotted over time, the drop in deaths following the tightening of the laws would have been shown to be what it was—a pseudo-effect predictable from statistical regression.

Despite the fact that design 7 is a great improvement over design 2 and is often well worth using, it is still subject to a serious defect—the lack of a control population. The validity of a design 7 approach may be limited because it does not control for independent historical variables, for history-selection interaction effects which are the results of the expressive function of the law, and for the fact that certain nonlegal variables are often associated with the onset of a law. These, rather than the law itself, may be the primary explanatory variables.

As an example of how these three effects may jeopardize the validity of a design 7-type impact study, we shall give a brief description of a hypothetical study of this type and indicate the kinds of factors which would not be controlled within this design. Let us take the law passed by the Hawaiian legislature designed to encourage public housing families to move into their own homes by giving them a special subsidy if they wish to save for their own homes while in public housing. Let us suppose that our observations show that two in every hundred public housing families move into their own homes each year before the passage of the law and that this number goes up to five in a hundred during the several years following the passage of the law. The hypothesis is that housing families have been influenced by the law to increase their rate of home ownership.

Factors which threaten this hypothesis and which would not show up in the design 7 approach include: (1) independent historical variables: e.g., the price of housing in Hawaii might have gone down about the same time that the law was passed; (2) history-selection interaction: e.g., it might be that legislature enacted the program largely because of active lobbying by a group of tenants who are planning to buy their own homes in any case and wanted to see if something could be done to make things easier for them; (3) influence of nonlegal variables: e.g., it might be that a group of special services not required by the law are being administratively provided for these families and are responsible for the rise in home ownership.

Design 10: $\frac{O \; X \; O}{O \; - \; O}$ NONEQUIVALENT CONTROL GROUP DESIGN

Design 10, the nonequivalent control group design, is one which, while often the best available for quasi-experimentation in a social-psychological setting, should not have to be used with great frequency by the legal impact theorist. This design calls for a pretest and a posttest measurement from both the experimental and control populations, and differs from a true experimental design only insofar as membership in the two groups is not determined by a random selection procedure. In the type of problems the legal impact theorist will deal with, the pretest and posttest scores will usually be in the form of statistical data. Where such data are available, they usually exist and should be used for a period of years preceding the introduction of the experimental variable, as well as for a period after the introduction of that variable.

When a design 10 approach is used in a social-psychological setting, the correct procedure is to live with any differences that come to light on the pretest. For example, if an investigator has two classrooms available and can introduce the experimental variable into one of them, he should not be deterred by the fact that the two groups have different mean scores on the pretest. Most importantly, he should not take a subset of the one class with the same mean as the entire set of the other class and use it as his control population. As Campbell has convincingly shown, differences which arise between two such matched groups can often be explained by regression artifacts (Campbell and Clayton, 1961).

Regression can similarly confound the results of a design 10 legal impact study. The danger is especially great in such studies because the investigator is likely to choose as a comparable state one which is similar to the experimental state at the before-point in time in order to make a "better" comparison. Yet there is a definite possibility that the two states chosen are only coincidentally identical in their behavior patterns in the given year and that differential changes in behavior could be expected merely on the basis of differential behavior patterns in the two states over an extended period of time.

Aside from the regression situation in which the behavioral data from one or both states are taken in a year which for that state varies greatly from a relatively stable mean level of behavior, there is also a danger that the study may be confounded by trends which are disguised in the single pretest, single posttest comparison approach.

1 = pretest measurement
2 = posttest measurement
X = point of introduction of experimental variable
No measurement taken at this time

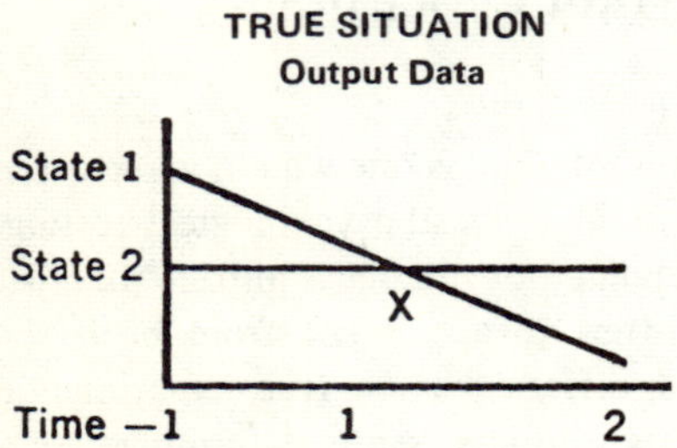

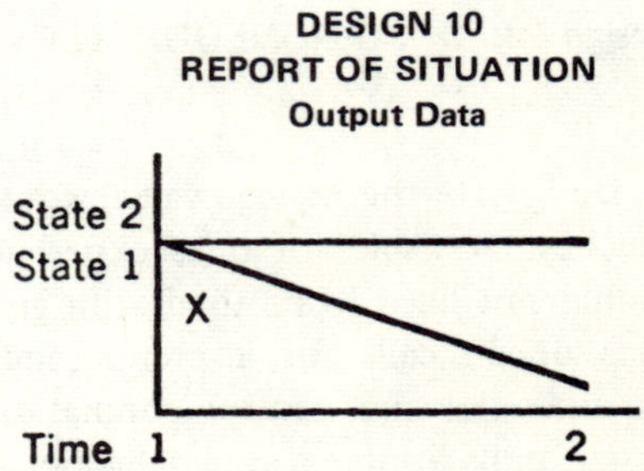

If, for instance, there is a situation like that graphed above, it is obvious that we have no grounds for concluding that the law has created the desired change in the behavior in state 1 and that the addition of state 2 as a control has only served to make the investigator more sure of a false conclusion.

In using design 10, the results are not clearly interpretable, because merely living with differences does not solve the problem of comparing two states. Any single year which is chosen by the investigator may be an unusual year in certain respects for a particular state and, for that state, a subsequent shift in behavioral patterns away from the extreme case may be seen as regression. Similarly, trend patterns may come into play when data from two states are being analyzed, even if the states were chosen randomly rather than because of an initial equality in a certain respect.

The flaws in design 10 are corrected to some extent (and this is one reason why it is a relatively powerful design in the social-psychological setting) as more units figure into the analysis. In other words, if the mean of the data from twenty-five states which had a certain law were to be compared with the mean of similar data from twenty-five states without the law, then a researcher would be in a situation to live with the differences and perhaps interpret them meaningfully. If the original intergroup difference is not great, then the multiple-unit variation of design 10 may be a very successful one. However, the wider the original differences, the more likely it would be that some factor other than the laws was responsible for the subsequent differences in behavior. This is especially so because of the history-selection interaction process which has often been referred to in this paper.

Design 14: O O O OXO O O O MULTIPLE TIME-SERIES
O O O O O O O O

The best way to correct for the flaws of design 10 is to use design 14, the multiple time-series design. This design is the design par excellence for impact theory experimentation, the comparison becoming more valid the larger the number of units which may be fitted into the experimental and control groups and the greater the similarity of the two time-series measurements during the period prior to the introduction of the experimental variable. For example, if a group of states with a certain law and a group of states without that particular law can be compared over time, and if the behavior patterns are similar until the law is introduced in the experimental states, an investigator can attribute subsequent changes over time to the law with a high degree of certainty. It is obvious that this design controls for regression effects, trend effects, and for certain types of history. If only two states are being compared, there is still the chance that the history-selection interaction has been the cause of any resultant change, but is very unlikely that people of two states will be alike for an extended period of years and then undergo a sudden differentiation in their population's activity-linked attitudinal characteristics. If such differentiated behavior is perceived, it is much more likely that the law has caused it than that an underlying attitude difference suddenly developed between the people of the two states. This rival hypothesis becomes less and less plausible with the inclusion of more states which are heterogeneous.

The rival hypothesis, that the extralegal changes are causing the difference in behavior patterns, is still one which must be checked in this design. However, it too becomes less plausible as more and more states fall into the experimental and control categories, since even when laws are similar on the books, extralegal patterns tend to be differentiated. If investigation shows that such extralegal patterns differ in a relatively random fashion among the states in the sample, but that behavior patterns between the experimental and control states are systematically differentiated, then the investigator may again state with a high degree of certainty that the law is causing the observed differences. This design rates very high on the internal validity criteria.

The beauty of design 14 is not only that its internal validity is inherently higher than that of the other quasi-experimental designs but that it is especially well adapted for legal impact studies. The United States federal system of government has furnished the experimenter with fifty states which, in the words of the Supreme Court, are "natural laboratories." Much of the behavioral output of these laboratories with respect to particular laws is reported in relatively available and uniform statistical form. Where such information exists, it is usually available over an extended period of time. Legal sociologists can take advantage of these natural laboratories and, using the design 14 approach, start intensive investigations of exactly how certain laws influence specific behavioral patterns. Once there is more information as to how this occurs, there will be a more reasoned basis for determining "why" the patterns occur as they do.

While the state laboratory approach has been used in most of the examples in this paper, this is not the only situation in which the impact theorist can work. Almost all political subdivisions, from towns through nations, have certain areas of legal variation and other areas of legal symmetry. Certain voluntary organizations have rule structures which lend themselves to the types of experimental study suggested in this paper. As a general rule, comparative studies of organizations which rely upon formal enacted rule-making procedures can also be researched within this frame.[13]

CONCLUSION

In this paper, an attempt has been made to indicate the manner in which some of the experimental designs described by Campbell and Stanley can be applied to the problems which confront the sociologist who wishes to study the effects of laws on behavior. We have tried to demonstrate how legal impact studies confront certain types of plausible rival hypotheses which are peculiar to them or are especially difficult to control for. To the extent that the design 14 approach appears applicable, it should be used since it best disposes of these alternative explanations. If design 14 cannot be used, it is almost always better to use an inferior design than to do no study at all. The important thing is that the experimenter be aware of the potential weaknesses which exist in his materials and examine the empirical situation closely to see if any such weaknesses in design may be confounding his results.

It should be emphasized that this paper has been dealing with only one area of sociology of law research. In other areas, especially where one is trying to discover how extralegal factors affect legal relationships, the experimenter may be able to selectively control the administration of the experimental variable. Often he will be able to randomize the administration of the experimental item and so will be in a position to use a true experimental design. In particular, we think that there is a great deal of room to use true experimentation in any area which might be best called the social-psychology of law, i.e., working with individuals and small groups to see how people react in various law-related situations. Much of the experimentation at this level, such as the Chicago jury study, will not be of a legal impact nature, but it is possible that small group experiments could be set up to test impact-oriented hypotheses. If this were done, many fruitful hypotheses could be generated. Such work would often involve true experimental designs with high internal validity. However, the external validity of any observed results would always be open to question. Here again, the "real world" impact study will become a necessity, and here again the designs discussed above can be put to use.

NOTES

1. The sample was drawn from two complete cohorts of public housing applicants, those who applied between 1953 and 1957 and those who applied between 1960 and 1964.

2. For a general discussion of material which can be gleaned from the running record, see Webb et al. (1966: especially chs. 3 and 4).

3. Actually around 1,000 interviews were administered, because in about 350 cases both the husband and wife were interviewed for each family.

4. For a simpler study using just interview data, see Break (1957). For a less complex study relying mainly on questionnaire data, see Nagel (1965).

5. Quasi-experimental studies, as distinguished from experimental studies, occur when the experimenter is unable to achieve full control over relevant variables (Campbell and Stanley, 1963: 204). Experimental research encompasses "that portion of research in which variables are manipulated and their effects upon other variables observed" (Campbell and Stanley, 1963: 171). On experimentation, see generally Kaplan (1964: 126-170).

6. Research which is scientific in its systematic approach to the data but which lacks the controls necessary for either quasi-experimental or experimental studies.

7. History: "The specific events [other than the introduction of the law] between the first and second measurements."

Maturation: "Processes within the respondents operating as a function of the passage of time" per se (not specific to particular events).

Testing: "The effects of taking a test upon the scores of the second testing."

Instrumentation: "Changes in the calibration of a measuring instrument or changes in the observers or scores used may produce changes in the obtained measurement."

Regression: "[Operates] where groups have been selected on the basis of their extreme scores."

Selection: "Biases resulting in differential selection of respondents for the comparison group."

Mortality: "Differential loss of respondents from the comparison groups" (Campbell and Stanley, 1963: 175).

8. "[The danger arises] in certain of the multiple-group quasi-experimental designs [that] such an interaction effect might be mistaken for the effect of the experimental variable" (Campbell and Stanley, 1963: 175).

9. See Act 22. For a theoretical discussion of this program and of general public housing interventions, see Ikeda et al. (1964).

10. Campbell and Stanley (1963: 176) refer to external validity as "representativeness."

11. Design numbers as employed by Campbell and Stanley have been retained. For a more detailed discussion of these designs and of statistical methods which can be used in connection with them, the reader is referred to Campbell and Stanley (1963: 175-176).

12. A nonreactive pretest occurs when the pretest does not affect the subjects under study, thereby avoiding an effect on subsequent observations.

13. For a discussion of what factors must be considered in conjunction with the formal rule structures and of possible approaches to the study of formal organizations, see Blau (1957).

REFERENCES

BALL, H. V. (1960) "Social structure and rent control violations." Amer. J. of Sociology 65 (May): 598-604.

BLAU, P. (1957) "Formal organizations: dimensions of analysis." Amer. J. of Sociology 63 (July): 58-69.

BREAK, G. F. (1957) "Income taxes and incentives to work." Amer. Economic Rev. 47 (September): 529-549.

CAMPBELL, D. T. (1957) "Factors relevant to the validity of experiments in social settings." Psych. Bull. 54 (July): 297-312.

--- and K. N. CLAYTON (1961) "Avoiding regression effects in panel studies of communication impact." Studies in Public Communication 3:99-118.

CAMPBELL, D. T. and H. L. ROSS (1968) "The Connecticut crackdown on speeding: time-series data in quasi-experimental analysis." Law and Society Rev. 3 (August): 33-53.

CAMPBELL, D. T. and J. C. STANLEY (1963) "Experimental and quasi-experimental designs for research on teaching," pp. 171-246 in N. L. Gage (ed.) Handbook of Research on Teaching. Chicago: Rand McNally.

DURKHEIM, E. (1899-1900) "Deux lois de l'evolution pénale." L'Annee Sociologique 4 (July-June): 65-95.

IKEDA, K., H. V. BALL, and D. YAMAMURA (1964) "Legal interventions, social mobility, and dependence: a study of public assistance in housing for low income families." Presented at the American Sociological Association.

--- and R. LEMPERT (1966) "Regulatory norms and occupational conduct among low income households: a study of public assistance in housing." Presented at the American Sociological Association.

KAPLAN, A. (1964) The Conduct of Inquiry: Methodology for Behavioral Science. San Francisco: Chandler.

NAGEL, S. S. (1965) "Testing the effects of excluding illegally seized evidence." Wisconsin Law Rev. 1965 (Spring): 283-310.

ROSE, A. (1961) "On individualism and social responsibility." European J. of Sociology 2, 1: 163-169.

--- (1954) Theory and Method in the Social Sciences. Minneapolis: Univ. of Minnesota Press.

WEBB, E. J., D. T. CAMPBELL, R. D. SCHWARTZ, and L. SECHREST (1966) Unobtrusive Measures: Nonreactive Research in the Social Sciences. Chicago: Rand McNally.

Chapter 4

Nomotics

The Science of Human Rule Systems

ROBERT HOGAN – *The Johns Hopkins University*

NANCY HENLEY – *University of Maryland*

Several philosophers, psychologists, and sociologists have recently begun to reexamine the problem of explanation in social science.[1] Instead of describing man in terms of organized traits, needs, drive-cathexes, coping and defense mechanisms, or self-actualizing tendencies, the new movement is concerned with "man as rule follower." This paper outlines the essentials of such an approach (*nomotics*–from the Greek *nomos*, "law, convention"–refers to the study of human rule systems), beginning with an examination of four behavior systems which can be conceptualized as networks of rule-governed activities. We describe some key properties of rule systems, point out certain important differences in the manners in which they are used, and suggest methods for studying rule systems in general. We also present an analysis of the topic of obedience, a central factor in the operation and preservation of any given system.

SOME ILLUSTRATIVE RULE SYSTEMS

Even the most unreflective person appreciates the utility of rules for the conduct of human affairs. Somewhat more reflection is necessary, however, to recognize that the careful acting-out of rule-guided activities appeals to something very deep and powerful in the human psyche. The intrinsic reward of ritualized behavior accounts for a variety of seemingly pointless activities: the phenomenon of nonbelievers attending church years after the onset of their apostasy, the stylized and often ludicrous procession of the Christmas season, and indeed, all those activities which the anthropologists describe as "rites of intensification" and "rites of passage." Moreover, this rule dependence apparently begins quite early in life, as parents will attest who have disrupted their children's bedtime rituals.

Games

If one knew nothing about football and watched a game, it would be impossible to understand the players' actions. A reading of the rule book for that sport would make much of the activity comprehensible. Furthermore, access to the coach's game plan would make an even greater amount of behavior predictable. These remarks are obvious; that which makes them so, however, is the power of rules as explanatory concepts.

It is surprising to note how frequently rule systems are referred to as games. Wittgenstein (1953) described language learning as "the original word game," and it has become conventional to refer to one's occupation as a game. Piaget (1965) noted the similarity between morality and games, and began his study of moral judgment in children with an investigation of their attitudes toward the rules of marbles. One reason games are seen as prototypical rule systems may be that their apparent triviality affords us an opportunity for irony—war, social interaction, and one's life work are normally matters of grave seriousness.

Games are important in the study of rule systems and social behavior for two reasons. First, winning frequently depends on the optimal use of game rules, which themselves are usually arbitrary. Thus players often use rules in a highly self-conscious fashion, which in turn tends to make the relevant behavior more visible. Second, certain fundamental themes seem common to all games and may reflect important regularities in our thought processes. Thus, for example, games always involve the concepts of cooperation and opposition, they have clear-cut beginnings and ends with provisions for time-outs, and they are never three-sided.

Games also seem important for human development. Playing with one's peers involves behavior qualitatively different from that typically required for dealing with one's parents (e.g., cooperation and reciprocity replace punishment-based compliance). Playing games also forces a child into a double-contingency relationship (i.e., taking into account the other person's potential reactions to one's own actions and vice versa) in which the cognitive demands are quite complex, and which undoubtedly stimulates intellectual growth. Because a fairly high order of cognitive development is necessary before a child can effectively play a game, there is also a natural interaction between game-playing and intellectual growth.

Social Interaction

Many writers have noted the rule systems underlying interpersonal relations; many have also made use of an analogy to games as an analytical device.[2]

Goffman (1959) has presented a dramaturgical analysis of interpersonal relations from the viewpoint of the rules of good theatre.

Rules governing social interaction seem to fall into two broad categories which are nicely exemplified by the social theories of Freud (1960) and Lévi-Strauss (1968). Starting with approximately the same observations (e.g., the primal horde and the events surrounding the Oedipal crisis), Freud and Lévi-Strauss develop contrasting but complementary theories of society. In highly schematized form, their arguments may be summarized as follows:

According to Freud, rules are basic to society, the basic rule is the rule of obedience, and the basic act of obedience is the renunciation of incestuous desires and the internalization of parental commands. This obedience minimizes interpersonal conflict, thereby bringing stability to society.

According to Lévi-Strauss, rules are basic to society; the basic rule, however, is the rule of reciprocity, and the basic act of reciprocity is the exchange of women. This exchange produces the mutual dependency which causes society to cohere.

Freud emphasizes competitive striving; Lévi-Strauss emphasizes reciprocity. Implicit here is the distinction between the in-group and the out-group, with Freud and Lévi-Strauss representing two extreme points of view. That is, Freud sees all other persons in society as the out-group, whereas Lévi-Strauss regards total societies as in-groups with other cultures as out-groups. But most importantly, the rules for social interaction vary markedly depending on the group with which one is dealing. The in-group/out-group distinction profoundly influences interpersonal relations. The distinction is mirrored in all forms of address (e.g., *ne me tutoyez pas*) and in a large number of social-psychological concepts: solidarity and status; *communitas* and *societas*; altruism and ego-centrism. The distinction reflects a deep, perhaps archetypal cleavage in man's thinking; it is probably no accident that the infant develops attachment for its mother and fear of strangers more or less simultaneously.

Language

Languages are generally recognized as governed by systems of rules known as grammars. The most influential movement in modern linguistics has been the attempt to develop a metatheory which will account for the grammars of all languages. Noam Chomsky (1965: 8) has proposed for this purpose the notion of a generative grammar, "a system of rules that in some explicit and well-defined way assigns structural descriptions to sentences." Chomsky (1965: 56) stresses the implications of linguistic metatheory for psychology:

> The language acquisition device is only one component of the total system of intellectual structures that can be applied to problem solving and concept formation; in other words, the *faculté de langage* is only one of the faculties of the mind.

Linguistic rules are probably the most thoroughly delineated and abstractly stated of any rule system. Consequently, certain concepts from linguistics may possibly extend into other governed areas. Some linguistic concepts which might lend themselves to analogic application are: prescriptive versus descriptive linguistics; diachronic and synchronic investigation; the hierarchy extending from language family to language to dialect, and then to idiolect; isoglosses; and context.

Morality

Hart (1961) has suggested that the basis of a society's morality is a system of rules of conduct which defines a network of reciprocal rights and obligations, and which prohibits at least gross acts of malevolence. Piaget (1965) observed that "all morality consists in a system of rules, and the essence of all morality is to be sought for in the respect which the individual acquires for these rules." Freud maintained that moral development was more or less complete when the child had internalized a set of parental rules and prohibitions. The rule-oriented foundations of morality have perhaps been most explicitly elaborated by the contemporary philosopher, Bernard Gert (1968: 5-6):

> The moral rules are central to morality. And the moral philosopher ought to be concerned only with that code of conduct of which the moral rules form the core. . . . His principal tasks are the following: Discovering if there is a unique set of characteristics which all or most . . . moral rules have in common . . . . The moral philosopher must explain the nature of moral rules, showing their relationship to our conduct and to our judgments, as well as explaining and justifying, if possible, our attitudes toward them.

FORMAL PROPERTIES OF RULE SYSTEMS

Certain formal properties of rule systems can be identified by pointing to common characteristics in different systems, and by noting some distinctions which may be made in their classification. The following list of formal properties is considered suggestive rather than exhaustive or definitive.

Common Characteristics

Codification. A human rule system will normally have a formal, usually a written, code. Examples are Hammurabi's Code, dictionaries and grammars, Hoyle, etiquette books, *The Watch Officer's Guide*, criminal and civil codes, and those books which various trades call their "bibles." There may also be a codifier (God, Emily Post, Congress), and the codification process is never complete in those systems which are responsive to change and evolutionary pressures.

Custodian and exemplar. A human rule system will have a custodian or high priest to make decisions about the rules (the Pope, the umpire, the courts, the French Academy). There may also be an exemplar (Budda, Christ, "Mr. Football," "Mr. Republican") and a custodian may sometimes serve as examplar. Emily Post was at once codifier, custodian, and exemplar.

Deviation from the code. Typically, it is impossible to follow all the rules of a given system. Fortunately there is an esthetic of rule-following related to this; i.e., it is unseemly to observe the rules too scrupulously. One who does so is regarded as a martinet or a Draconian, as punctilious, pedantic, or a prig. This ethic, in combination with the nominal obedience to the rules normally required by one's fellows, suggests that a measure of hypocrisy may be an inevitable by-product of rule-governed behavior.

A distinction should be made between the coded rules and the rules which describe actual behavior. In grammar this is the difference between prescriptive and descriptive grammar; in social interaction, it is the difference between the formal and informal structure of groups; in morality, it is the difference between the Ten Commandments and the Kinsey Report.

Deviation and in-group status. The amount of acceptable deviation differs for the in-group and the out-group in both kind and degree. Members of an in-group are typically allowed more absolute deviation from a code, giving rise to the frequent observation that there is a "different set of rules" for the in-group. Actually the converse might be true; that is, the in-group might be best defined in terms of the rules they are permitted to violate (e.g., the well-known legal immunity of high government officials, businessmen, and movie stars; on the bridge of a ship, only the captain may whistle). Thus, as Roger Downs has observed, the pattern of rule deviation in one sense may define the in-group.

Social consequences of skillful play. As suggested above, expert play is not to be equated with relentless rule-following. Rather, virtuoso performance in the manner of Heifetz, Gandhi, or Shakespeare requires occasional neglect of at least some of the rules. Good play is almost always rewarded. One is tempted to speculate, however, that the magnitude of the reward is an inverse function of the complexity of the rule system (i.e., the simpler the system, the more people who are able to appreciate expert play). Thus football players are much better-paid than poets, painters, or philosophers, and in the case of morality, a virtuoso performance may lead only to martyrdom.

Ethics. In each human rule system there seems to be an overriding ethic, recognized by all mature players, which has its origins in empathy or role-taking ability, and which is variously called sportsmanship, courtesy, justice, reciprocity, or ethical communication. The effect of the ethic is to generate the distinction between the letter and the spirit of the law.

Distinctions

Distinctions may be made among human rule systems in four important ways:

Complexity. Complexity is here defined in terms of the total number of rules of a system and their interrelationships. Primitive children's games represent instances of simple systems; interpersonal relations, moralities, and languages involve a considerable increase in complexity.

Clarity of evaluative critieria. A closely related distinction involves the clarity with which the criteria for evaluating performance have been articulated or are visible. For example, clear-cut competitive standards of excellence are available for all forms of athletic endeavor. However, there is considerable confusion concerning the evaluation of moral behavior, and with regard to language behavior, it seems almost impossible to derive generally accepted standards for determining excellence.

Mode of presentation. A third distinction concerns the process through which the rules are discerned–either deduction or induction. In the deductive mode, general principles are presented and the player must himself derive the rules for particular cases (e.g., "If your opponent comes to the net, keep your passing shot low"). In the inductive mode, instructions are given for each case as it arises, however, the player must discover the general principles himself (e.g., "Say 'I am,' not 'I are.' ").

Freedom to participate. The final distinction to be drawn involves the difference between mandatory and optional participation. Clearly no one is required to play badminton; but we must all at some time converse with another person. One major function of systems of optional play might be to prepare us for systems of mandatory play.

Although these distinctions appear conceptually independent, most naturally occurring rule systems seem empirically to fall into two categories. The first type is relatively simple, with deductive instruction, clear-cut evaluative criteria, and optional play (war, athletic competition, parlor games, symbolic logic). The second type of rule system is relatively complex, with inductive instruction, ambiguous evaluative criteria, and mandatory play (language, social interaction, morality). For the newcomer to one of these latter systems (e.g., the office cocktail party), to be simultaneously aware that certain rules are inviolable and yet uncertain as to their content can be a devastating experience. We are presently unable to account for the preeminence of these two types of systems.

FORMAL PROPERTIES OF RULES

Common Characteristics

There is an inexorable quality about the rules of any given system which may be stated in terms of two general laws. First, rules typically persist long after they have served their original purpose; rules are, in a very real sense, "nonbiodegradable." As a consequence of this, the number of rules in any system typically increases over time. Second, within many systems there seems to be a nomotic equivalent of Gresham's Law, i.e., rules which promote competition tend to replace rules which support sociability and the sense of community. Status considerations almost inevitably take precedence over tendencies toward solidarity.

Classification

Proper study of human rule systems requires a general method for characterizing rules. Symbolic logic has been used as such a system in the study of concept formation (compare with Hunt, 1962). Scandura (1968) has also suggested a research language for the description of rules. Another possible approach is that taken by theorists in linguistics and psychology who have proposed relational rules that define equivalence, superordination, and the like (see especially Deese, 1969a, 1969b).

The dimensions of codification and observation provide what is perhaps a more functional and less abstruse classification system. That is, rules may be classified into three sensible categories according to whether or not they are codified, and whether or not they are observed:

(1) Codified and observed.
(2) Codified, but not observed (as noted above, these are often in-group rules).
(3) Not codified, but observed (such rules are typically learned by being broken).[3]

Finally, rules may be characterized in terms of arbitrariness, equity, and importance.

INDIVIDUAL DIFFERENCES IN RULE-FOLLOWING

Rule systems have an interesting conceptual status—they are closer to traditional sociological than psychological concepts. In general, rules determine the parameters of social action and provide reliable guides to expected conduct. Thus careful specification of the features of rule systems will make predictable much of what people do. However, human action cannot be understood solely in terms of information derived from the study of rules. Specifically, rule systems can't account for variations from the norm (e.g., creative innovation and delinquency), and the variations in human behavior are as interesting as the regularities. A complete explanation of social action (i.e., one that also explains variations) requires taking into account the individual actor's motives, plans, or intentions.

The proper operation of any social system depends on a modicum of compliance from the participants; the question "Why does John Doe pay his income tax?" is a prototypical case in point. The solution to this problem, from a nomotic point of view, requires giving an account of how he personally regards the relevant rules, how he typically reacts to them, how he uses them. In general, an adequate answer to any question concerning compliance requires a description of the actor's position with regard to five cognitive or attitudinal dimensions. These are discussed below. (It should be noted here that we assume that individuals will manifest considerable consistency in their attitudes across rule systems. Thus, for example, if John Doe fudges on his income tax return, he will probably be late for appointments, "doctor" his golf score, and not return library books on time.)

The first dimension has to do with knowledge of the rules; obviously one can only follow rules that he knows. However, social action always occurs within matrices of rules, and we are normally justified in assuming people know them. Generally speaking, ignorance of the law is rarely accepted as a legitimate excuse for its violation. Consequently this first dimension lacks powerful explanatory force.

A second and more important reason for John Doe paying his income tax is that he feels the rules covering taxation are personally obligatory and binding. In Hart's (1961) felicitous phrase, John Doe regards the rules concerning income tax from an "internal point of view," and not merely as an indication of what will befall him at the hands of authorities if he fails to comply. The psychological dimension involved here is conventionally labelled "socialization," where the more socialized person is assumed to consider social rules consistently from an internal point of view. Mounting psychological evidence indicates that parent-child relations characterized by warmth and nurturance, combined with the maintenance of firm limits, produce the most socialized children.

It is clear, however, that many John Does who pay their income tax had parents who were neither warm and nurturant nor consistent in setting behavioral limits. An auxiliary or compensatory function must emerge which somehow induces obedience in persons who have been denied the appropriate early socialization experiences. This compensatory function is the third dimension of individual differences in rule-oriented behavior.

The first author has presented evidence elsewhere (Hogan, 1969) to suggest that a person, under certain conditions, may comply with social rules in spite of regarding them as essentially alien and external. In particular, if the otherwise unsocialized John Doe develops the capacity to adopt "the moral point of view" (i.e., to consider the consequences of his actions for the welfare of others), he may be generally conforming in his behavior. Adopting the moral point of view seems to depend on the capacity for empathy or what G. H. Mead termed "taking the role of the generalized other" (Strauss, 1964: 205-206, 224-226). It is a relatively straightforward process, the rudiments of which are taught when we ask a child, "How would you like to have that done to you?" Although training in the disposition to take the moral point of view may begin at home, its full elaboration probably depends on a moderately high level of cognitive development and on extensive peer group interaction—both of which occur some time after the child enters school (circa age 7-8).

There is a fourth explanation for obedience. Here John Doe's social compliance results not from benevolent tendencies but from cowardice or lack of nerve. Such persons have insufficient force of character to oppose society and consequently conform out of weakness. Conforming behavior of this type, however, requires considerable environmental support in the form of socialized peers; in other surroundings such persons may be only highly conforming delinquents. The opposite end of this dimension is autonomy. High autonomy, in the absence of socialization and a role-taking disposition, leads to what Kierkegaard (1954: 103-111) called a "demonic man." Demonic men (e.g., the Red Baron, Ivan the Terrible, Macbeth) compel our admiration despite their villainy. Conversely, high autonomy combined with high socialization and empathy probably characterized such praiseworthy persons as Socrates, Gandhi, and Martin Luther King.

Any discussion of rule compliance must also deal with the topic of principled disobedience, the subject of our final dimension. Earlier in the paper we noted that there seems to be an ethic, related to the notion of fairness, associated with every rule system. Such ethics are important for two reasons. First, they protect individuals from the tyranny of procrustean or monolithic rule systems. Second, they provide a means for keeping the purposes of the rule system in view and for insuring the continued existence of an avenue for change. Invocation of the ethic, however, almost always disrupts the operation of a system to some degree because a major method for such invocation is principled disobedience.

The first author has shown in earlier research (Hogan, forthcoming) that there are regular and stable differences among people in terms of their disposition to invoke the overriding ethic of a system. Such differences are closely related to personality structure and these differences predispose people to endorse contrasting social and legal philosophies. For example, the most important feature of the tradition of jurisprudence deriving from Thomas Aquinas is a willingness to call the manifest law into moral account. Conversely, in the tradition of legal positivism stemming from John Austin and Hans Kelsen, a firm distinction is maintained between the law as it is and the law as it ought to be.

Persons who are quick to criticize legal systems on moral grounds tend to be intuitive, individualistic, and uncomfortable with schedules and preestablished procedures. Persons who are reluctant to criticize the law in moral terms are typically counterintuitive, tough-minded, and "super-dependable." However, the most important point is that differences in the disposition to call upon the overriding ethic of social systems are related to principled disobedience (Hogan, forthcoming), and a complete explanation of rule compliance requires taking into account this final dimension.

EVALUATION OF RULE SYSTEMS

Some rule systems are regarded as worse than others. A major problem for nomotics is to determine the grounds on which these evaluative judgments are made. Presently we can only offer five relatively speculative observations. First, we may look at the types of rules that exist in a given system. Obviously a preponderance of type 2 and type 3 rules (see section on classification above) would make a rule system cumbersome and even vicious. Second, rule systems tend to be bad when the rules are imposed from the outside, that is, by agents other than the governed. Third, sheer numerosity of rules is undesirable. However, there is no way presently to determine the number of rules that is optimum for a given system. A fourth desideratum of rule systems might be that they permit virtuoso performance, but again, determining how such a quality might be measured is difficult. Finally, the arbitrariness, equity, and importance of the rules within a system obviously must be considered when the system is being evaluated.

CONCLUSION

We hope that the interdisciplinary study of rules will produce a general science of human rule systems. This science would consider such problems as what sort of rules characterize human rule systems, which of these are most easily learned, what instructional methods are best for different rule systems, what typical links exist among rules within a system, and so on. Paradigms for the study of rule systems already exist in experiments on concept formation (compare with Bourne, 1966) and miniature linguistic systems (e.g., Braine, 1963; Esper, 1925), as well as the cross-cultural study of various social systems (e.g., comparative linguistics and comparative law).

Probably the central question in the study of rules concerns the problem of rule acquisition. Opinion tends to divide between empiricist and rationalist answers to the problem. The authors are inclined to doubt that traditional psychological concepts derived from learning theory can account for all the facts about human systems of rules. Chomsky's (1959: 57) statement concerning the acquisition of grammar may well be applied to rule acquisition in general:

> The fact that all normal children acquire essentially comparable grammars of great complexity with remarkable rapidity suggests that human beings are somehow specially designed to to this, with data-handling or "hypothesis-formulating" abilities of unknown character and complexity.

In this paper we have tried to suggest that rule systems (games, languages, morality, law) may be regarded as the warp of society, while individual differences in dealing with the rules constitute society's woof. A complete account of any social act will employ concepts from both domains. A careful elaboration of the important properties of human rule systems combined with precise specification of the manner in which people formulate, use, and modify rules, may ultimately result in a general theory to account for most forms of social behavior.

NOTES

1. See Mace, 1966; Mischel, 1964; Peters, 1958.
2. See Berne, 1964; Coleman, 1968; Potter, 1948.
3. Occasionally these covert rules are "trap rules," i.e., they seem to exist solely to catch people. In many high schools and colleges, for example, there is a rule that the school seal, set in the floor, must not be stepped on. Violation of this rule is punished by upperclassmen or appointed monitors. It is clear, however, that if the seal is not to be stepped on, it should be mounted on the wall.

REFERENCES

BERNE, E. (1964) Games People Play. New York: Grove.
BOURNE, L. (1966) Human Conceptual Behavior. Boston: Allyn & Bacon.
BRAINE, M. D. S. (1963) "On learning the grammatical order of words." Psych. Rev. 70 (July): 323-348.
CHOMSKY, N. (1965) Aspects of the Theory of Syntax. Cambridge: MIT Press.
--- (1959) "Review of Skinner's verbal behavior." Language 35 (January-March): 26-58.
COLEMAN, J. S. (1968) "Games as vehicles for social theory." Center for the Study of Social Organization of Schools. Report 21. Baltimore: Johns Hopkins University.
DEESE, J. (1969a) "Behavior and fact." Amer. Psychologist 24 (May): 515-522.
--- (1969b) "Conceptual categories in the study of content." pp. 39-56 in G. Gerbner et al. (eds.) Analysis of Communication Content. New York: John Wiley.
ESPER, E. A. (1925) "A technique for the experimental investigation of associative interference in artificial linguistic material." Language Monographs 1 (November): 5-47.
FREUD, S. (1960) Group Psychology and the Analysis of the Ego. New York: Bantam.
GERT, B. (1968) The Moral Rules. Unpublished. Department of Philosophy, Dartmouth College.
GOFFMAN, E. (1959) The Presentation of Self in Everyday Life. Garden City, N.Y.: Doubleday.

HART, H. L. A. (1961) The Concept of Law. Oxford, England: Oxford Univ. Press.

HOGAN, R. (forthcoming) "A dimension of moral judgment." J. of Consulting and Clinical Psych.

--- (1969) "The development of an empathy scale." J. of Consulting and Clinical Psych. 33 (June): 307-316.

HUNT, E. B. (1962) Concept Learning. New York: John Wiley.

KIERKEGAARD, S. (1954) Fear and Trembling. Garden City, N.Y. Doubleday.

LEVI-STRAUSS, C. (1968) The Elementary Structure of Kinship. Boston: Beacon.

MACE, C. A. (1966) "Causal explanations in psychology," pp. 22-27 in C. Banks and P. L. Broadhurst (eds.) Studies in Psychology Presented to Cyril Burt. New York: Barnes & Noble.

MISCHEL, T. (1964) "Personal constructs, rules, and the logic of clinical activity." Psych. Rev. 21 (May): 180-192.

PETERS, R. S. (1958) The Concept of Motivation. London: Routledge & Kegan Paul.

PIAGET, J. (1965) The Moral Judgment of the Child. New York: Free Press.

POTTER, S. (1948) Gamesmanship. New York: Holt, Rinehart & Winston.

SCANDURA, J. (1968) "New directions for theory and research on rule learning. I. A set-function language." Acta Psychologica 28 (November): 301-321.

STRAUSS, A. (1964) George Herbert Mead on Social Psychology. Chicago: Univ. of Chicago Press.

WITTGENSTEIN, L. (1953) Philosopical Investigations. New York: Macmillan.

Chapter 5

Methodological Concerns in Studying Supreme Court Efficacy

JAMES P. LEVINE – *University of Oregon*

Only a few years ago it was customary and appropriate to begin an essay on Supreme Court efficacy by lamenting the paucity of empirical studies dealing with this problem. Such an introduction is no longer in order, since we have recently witnessed a flourishing of research on the actual consequences of judicial decisions. Both the appearance of at least one book of readings on Supreme Court impact (Becker, 1969) and the focusing of panels around this topic at political science conventions are indications of the emergence of "legal impact" as a significant field of scholarly inquiry.

Ironically, however, the proliferation of impact studies has muddled our understanding of judicial effectiveness as much as it has clarified it. After surveying the literature reporting the reactions of police, school teachers, draft board members, and the like to various Supreme Court decisions, one is bewildered if he attempts to relate, reconcile, or "propositionalize" the hodgepodge of findings that has accrued. We are left with the common sense truism that patterns of compliance and defiance with the Supreme Court vary—from decision to decision, from community to community, and from individual to individual. Such a trivial conclusion could have been reached by anyone who simply reads *Time Magazine* and notes, say, the continuation of police harassment of minorities and the decline of sex censorship.

My contention is that the low yield of these studies is partially the result of their methodological inadequacy. In scrutinizing conclusions about Supreme Court efficacy, irrelevance, or impotence which are suggested by researchers, we are usually at a loss to understand the meaning or assess the validity of the propositions being advanced. What follows are some ideas for improving the conceptualization, design, and execution of projects intended to ascertain the repercussions of Supreme Court decisions.

A TYPOLOGY OF OUTCOMES

Much dissensus about the extent of Supreme Court efficacy is a result of differences in the range of consequences being investigated. There may be both immediate and long-range effects in the aftermath of decisions, and it is implausible to expect the latter to occur as frequently, or with as great an intensity, as the former. For example, it proves nothing to contrast President Truman's return of the steel mills to private industry directly after Youngstown Sheet and Tube Co. v. Sawyer (1952) with the persistence of intolerance against Jehovah's Witnesses after the flag salutes cases (Minersville School District v. Gobitis, 1940; West Virginia Board of Education v. Barnette, 1943). Certainly presumed effects more proximate to the action of the Supreme Court (such as a President's compliance with a specific court injunction) will have a higher probability of materializing than more remote contingencies (such as significant shifts of public opinion across the nation) which are affected by many other factors.

In order to build up an inventory of empirical propositions which can be meaningfully compared and theoretically integrated, it is essential that we develop a system of classifying diverse kinds of outcomes. In other words, it is important that scholars be more precise in conceptualizing the dependent variable of various impact studies so that we can stop putting apples and oranges in the same basket. To this end I suggest the following primitive typology of effects based on the apparent "causal distance" from the agent of change. This breakdown implies that there are crucial theoretical differences in processes required to effectuate social changes of varying magnitudes. The conditions necessary for Supreme Court efficacy are much more stringent when the people and institutions to be controlled are farther removed from the Court's range of command and less threatened by the force of its sanctions. It is much easier for the Supreme Court to curb a few cantankerous federal judges than to reallocate the fundamental values of the society.

Four major kinds of outcomes may be defined: specific implementation, hierarchical control, political impact, and social consequences. *Specific implementation* is the extent to which the Supreme Court obtains compliance from lower court judges with specific mandates, orders, and directives. We are essentially asking whether parties who win in the Supreme Court wind up reaping the fruits of their victories outside the Court. Speaking to this question is a study conducted by the Harvard Law Review (1954) which traces the fates of cases requiring further litigation in state courts after the Supreme Court has ruled; it shows that half of the winners above wound up as losers when final judgments were rendered. Less systematically, Murphy (1959) has collected some particularly egregious examples of lower court insubordination, including a case in which a conviction excoriated by the Supreme Court because of racial bias in jury selection was allowed to stand by the Georgia Supreme Court—resulting in the electrocution of the hapless defendant. There is also a middle ground between successful and unsuccessful implementation, such as the ability of du Pont to delay divestiture of its General Motors stock for four years following the Supreme Court's ruling that du Pont's holdings violated antitrust laws (Abraham, 1967: 24-25).

The Supreme Court exercises *hierarchical control* of the judiciary when its holdings are considered to be authoritative statements of law by lower court judges dealing with similar issues. This kind of effect is more comprehensive than implementation since it involves the shaping of routine adjudication of cases and not just the righting of individual wrongs and the dispensing of equity among a few litigants. The Supreme Court's difficulty in controlling subordinate judges is documented in Peltason's (1961) study of judicial resistance to Brown v. Board of Education (1954). A more recent study shows that the Court's words in the Gault case (1967) granting substantial procedural rights to juvenile defendants have been largely ignored by lower-court judges in three large cities (Lefstein et al., 1969). Notwithstanding both the norms of the judicial role and oaths of office in support of the Constitution sworn to by judges, there is considerable variance in the deference which rank-and-file judges give to the Supreme Court.

Political impact is the responsiveness of government officials who receive new legal obligations as a result of Supreme Court decisions. It involves voluntary (or self-initiated) changes in behavior which occur in the absence of any court action, i.e., prior to the application of judicial coercion. Since seeking of judicial remedies to secure legal rights is infrequent, the Supreme Court's influence on American life depends largely on the willingness of elites to obey the "Supreme Law of the Land" and alter their behavior accordingly. Ironically, however, numerous studies (Yale Law Journal, 1967) of police interrogation practices show that the precise stipulations of Miranda v. Arizona (1966) have been only partially heeded by the enforcers of "law and order," and it is now clear that many public schools have wantonly ignored the school prayer decisions (Dolbeare and Hammond, 1969). Because many Supreme Court rulings are applicable to literally thousands of uncoordinated individuals and agencies, it is to be expected that the dimensions of noncompliance will be greater than is true of judges whose actions are much more likely to be reviewed and reversed.

Social consequences are the broadest and most diffuse of all effects, but in the final analysis, they are the most important. The term is meant to denote the output of the political system—the authoritative allocation of values to the society. If the Supreme Court's decisions are followed by judges and officials charged with the responsibility of carrying them out, what difference does it make? How, if at all, is the fabric of society affected? What dislocations of social or economic life ensue? Notwithstanding the speculations of pundits, politicians, and professors, the answers to these questions are nowhere in sight due to the almost complete lack of research on the net results of Supreme Court decisions.

At least five types of social consequences can be identified: (1) regulation of behavior, (2) allocation of costs and benefits, (3) symbolic effects, (4) second-order consequences, (5) feedback. Let us examine them in turn.

The Court is a *regulator* of behavior when it effectively sets the parameters of behavior that may be engaged in with impunity. Regulation is positive when the Court constrains individuals by sustaining the use of sanctions against them; it is negative when the use of sanctions is prohibited and individuals are liberated from coercive measures and thus permitted to choose their own course of action. The openness of retail book stores which I found in my study of bookseller self-censorship (Levine, 1970) is an example of successful regulation by the Court, while the Court's growing concern about the protection of individual privacy ("the right to be let alone") has not seemed to stem the pervasive trend toward increased government intrusion into personal lives (Westin, 1967).[1] Although the regulatory function is one of the most significant government activities, we are by and large in the dark as to the Supreme Court's ability to exercise social control and draw the lines of individual freedom.

Directly related to regulation is *allocation:* who gains and who loses (or as Harold Lasswell [1958] put it, who gets what?). If the Court *is* able to manipulate behavior, does a redistribution of economic costs and benefits among various interests and individuals result, and if so, what does the new pattern look like? To the extent that the Court's support of antitrust laws has prevented or retarded industrial concentration, small businesses have gained at the expense of larger ones. If the Court in the 1969 term decides to invalidate welfare laws which set absolute maximum family allowances regardless of the number of dependents (Dandridge v. Williams, 1969) and the decision is followed by the affected states, increased costs will be incurred by taxpayers and increased benefits enjoyed by the families of the unemployed. The significance of the allocation problem is highlighted by the public furor created by the reapportionment decisions which surely raised the specter to many of reconstituted legislatures collecting and dispensing the public purse in radically different ways.

The Court produces *symbolic effects* when its legitimacy and prestige attach to the interests and values it supports. It is often alleged that the Supreme Court's public stature is such that it can alter the balance of political forces by changing or reinforcing public attitudes, mobilizing support for innovative public policies, reassuring concerned publics and thus quelling further demands, or generating new political issues (Levine and Becker, 1969: 8-10). Arguments of this nature are more abundant than empirical findings, but there are inklings of evidence that the Court can indeed be a gadfly in the political process by distributing symbolic goods. The Court's consistency and unanimity in the school desegregation cases (in which there has not been one dissenting vote since 1954) is probably a major factor accounting for the accelerated increase of public acceptance of integration since Brown v. Board of Education (1954). By extending the constitutional rights of the poor (such as in Gideon v. Wainwright [1963] which guaranteed the right to counsel to indigents accused of felonies) the Court may pacify discontent about inequality by giving the illusion of a new order—even though major reforms require pressure on legislative and executive institutions. And the Court's heavy involvement with questions of police practice and due process is undoubtedly one (among many) factors contributing to the emergence of "law and order" as *the* dominant political issue in contemporary American politics. In this secular age, political symbols are fast replacing religion as both the opiate and intoxicant of the masses, and it may well be that the symbolic outcomes of Supreme Court decisions are an important input into other policy-making processes. Since men do *not* live by bread alone, the blessings, damnations, and graces which they receive from the preachers on the bench may be significant in determining how they ultimately feel, think, and act as political animals.

Second-order consequences of Supreme Court decisions are the resulting social changes that are unrelated to (and sometimes inconsistent with) the primary missions or goals of the Court. Although difficult to detect and subject to little research, these unintended consequences are often the basis of intense criticism thrust at the Court. So it is contended that the Warren Court contributed to the increased crime rate by extending the civil rights of defendants and encouraged sexual promiscuity by liberalizing obscenity norms. Sometimes the presumed side effects are deemed positive and are used to justify particular decisions. For example, many clergymen based their praise of the school prayer decisions on the assumption that there would be increased religious observances in the home and parents would assume new responsibility for the spiritual guidance of their children.[2] Since these kinds of assertions are often made by elites with a considerable following, and since they often become the focus of heated controversy about the wisdom of judicial doctrines, one use of information on second-order consequences would be to reduce the public's gullibility for unwarranted conclusions. Furthermore, some second-order consequences inevitably do result from the development of public policies, and a Court with multiple goals and priorities should be able to proceed more rationally if it knows what the by-products of its decisions actually are.

This leads us to the last type of social consequence to be considered. The Supreme Court works under a serious handicap because of the lack of *feedback* which it receives about the consequences of its decisions. Feedback is used in the narrow cybernetic sense and alludes to those communications which enable decision makers to constantly correct and modify their behavior so that goals might be achieved more efficiently (Deutsch, 1966: Ch. 5, 11). To my knowledge, the Court has never attempted to monitor systematically the impact of its decisions so that it could adjust its policies according to the results being accomplished and the problems that are incurred; nor has it inspired other agencies to undertake such tasks. A notable exception is the careful charting of the snail-like pace of Southern school desegregation by both the federal government and civil rights groups which may have led to the abandoning of the "all deliberate speed" doctrine in October 1969, in favor of a flat rule requiring immediate desegregation (Alexander v. Holmes County Board of Education, 1969).

To the extent that the Supreme Court engages in conscious, problem-solving behavior and rationally tries to solve social, economic, and political problems, the development of feedback mechanisms would enable it to function with greater efficacy. And since the Court presently has neither the resources nor (apparently) the inclination to develop this kind of apparatus, it is important to study the circumstances and incentives which impel outsiders to provide such services for the Court. The selective gathering and dissemination of information about particular outcomes of Supreme Court decisions may, in the long run, be the most significant outcome of all—for it determines the extent to which and the areas in which the Court is able to learn from the experience of the past and make the necessary adjustments in devising policies for the future. Studying past failure may be the key to future success.

CLARIFYING CAUSAL RELATIONS

Hans Zetterberg (1965: Ch. 4) has pointed out that one common source of misunderstanding about propositions in social science is vagueness about the causal linkage between determinants and results. Many studies of Supreme Court efficacy have harbored such a weakness in failing to qualify the expected relation between decision and outcomes. It *should* be theoretically obvious that even under optimal conditions the announcement of a rule of law by the Supreme Court does not create the instantaneous and drastic effects of a nuclear explosion, a stock market crash, or even a freeze on federal construction expenditures ordered by the President. Nevertheless many observers of the Court are constantly astonished and enraged when it turns out that the Court's words fail to turn the world inside out overnight. Most social scientists would sneer at the reasoning used in the old story of how a kingdom was lost for want of a nail in a horse's shoe, but it is equally faulty to expect a court decision to change the tide of history. To clear up some of this confusion, I shall now try to specify the logical connection among variables in propositions about the effectiveness of the Supreme Court.

First, the relations between decisions and outcomes are *probabilistic* rather than deterministic. If the Supreme Court acts, then some kinds of changes probably occur, but they do not invariably occur. In political science it is rare when phenomenon Y *always* follows phenomenon X and such relationships usually involve "micro-politics" (individual actions) rather than "macro-politics" (system behavior). The outcomes under study are usually quite complex events occurring in a wide range of contexts (e.g., from local political arenas to the national economy), so it is unreasonable to expect *one independent variable* to explain *all* of the observed variance. Correlations approaching 1.0 (i.e., *absolute* control of lower courts, *total* compliance by bureaucrats) are very unlikely; as we move further from the locus of Supreme Court commands and other social processes intervene, we should anticipate attenuated effects.

Second, the relations are *sequential.* In metaphysical terms, *all* causal relations require the effect to be preceded by the cause, but we can distinguish coextensive propositions where the time gap between cause and effect are minute (e.g., Boyle's Law) from those where it is considerable. Relations between Congressional seniority and influence over legislation are of the former variety in that the two variables change almost simultaneously: *as soon as* one serves x number of years, he *immediately* attains higher ranking committee assignments. Contrariwise, when the Supreme Court acts, outcomes occur *later* (and sometimes much later).

In discussing Supreme Court efficacy we are dealing with an indirect causal relationship in that other factors intervene between the initial cause and the ultimate effect. Decisions must be communicated to lower-court judges (normally by lawyers arguing cases), a process which is extremely slow. Bureaucrats must devise changes in routines and instruct lower-level personnel accordingly. The mass media must digest and diffuse judicial symbols to a generally disinterested audience. In light of all of these (and other) requisite events, it should not be surprising that outcomes are delayed, and it is suggested that researchers should wait for some period of time to transpire before assessing responses.

A good case in point is school desegregation in the Deep South which did not materialize beyond tokenism until ten years after Brown v. Board of Education (1954). Legitimate criticism of this tragic delay should not obfuscate the rather complex chain reaction of social processes triggered by the court decision which can be diagrammed as follows:

(1954)	→	(1955-1964)	→	(1965)	→	(1966-1968)	→	(1969)
Supreme Court Decision		**Political Controversy**		**Legislative Action**		**Administrative Action**		**Social Change**
(Desegregation ordered)		(Civil rights becomes issue)		(Congress prohibits funding segregated schools)		(HEW withholds funds from segregated schools)		(Substantial integration in Deep South)

If it is valid to claim that but for the 1954 decision the subsequent events would not have occurred (or would have been forestalled), then it is proper to consider the Supreme Court's action as a cause of a major social transformation even though much time elapsed between the decision and the outcomes.

Third, the relation is *contingent:* if the Court acts, certain outcomes will follow, but only if other circumstances prevail. A set of what Jones (1966) calls "leverage variables" controls the forcefulness of judicial decisions and determines the scope and intensity of their impact. Enough evidence has now been collected on the imperfect relation between decisions and outcomes ("the banality of noncompliance" [Dolbeare and Hammond, 1969: 6-12]) to spur researchers into a quest for factors which determine the degree of efficacy attained by the Court. The following is a partial list of necessary and/or sufficient conditions for Supreme Court efficacy that have been mentioned in the literature:

REQUISITES OF SUPREME COURT EFFICACY

Internal Supreme Court Processes (attributes of decisions)

(1) Clarity of announced policy (specific doctrines)

(2) Consensus on the Court (lack of dissents or concurring opinions)

(3) Periodic reiteration of rules

(4) Craftsmanship of opinions (persuasiveness of legal argument)

External Governmental Conditions

(1) Accurate communication to elites
(2) Positive reaction by public attorneys
(3) Official lawfulness (commitment to obey laws even when unliked)
(4) Low fiscal costs of compliance
(5) Political invulnerability of elites (security of position)
(6) Structural coordination of affected individuals (hierarchy)

Environment Conditions

(1) Strong public support of decisions
(2) Low intensity of opposition opinion
(3) Sympathetic treatment of decisions by media
(4) Favorable commentary by opinion leaders
(5) Substantial ensuing litigation relating to decision
(6) High ratio between resources of beneficiaries and resources of victims of decision
(7) Legitimacy of Supreme Court as rule-maker

One clear failing of the above hypothesized contingencies is their lack of a parsimonious and coherent theoretical framework. I think that our understanding of the conditions of Supreme Court efficacy would begin increasing cumulatively instead of sporadically if we dared to suggest explanations of fairly high generality to guide our inquiries. Utility theory (analysis of compliance in terms of costs and benefits to various actors) and dissonance theory (examination of alternative ways of reducing cognitive inconsistency between legal norms and contrary behavior) have been advanced to explain outcomes,[3] but these have been presented in rather casual form making it difficult to deduce specific propositions.

Other potentially fruitful bodies of social theory should also be explored while those mentioned above are elaborated. Learning theory would direct attention to the positive and negative reinforcements following reactions to decisions and conditioning certain kinds of responses. Communications theory would ask whether information about judicial doctrines is being rapidly transmitted to receivers and how much is lost (or distorted) as it travels through formal and informal channels of communication. Organization theory would focus on the lines of command within institutions and the conditions under which bureaucratic resistance to innovations such as legal change are broken down.

Building abstract models based on these theories will inevitably mean that we sacrifice realism to gain simplicity in our explanations,[4] but the long-run payoff of this strategy of inquiry may be that we eliminate the necessity of testing many untenable hypotheses and thus wasting scarce research resources. I would hope that as a result of such theory-building we would see fewer studies with totally inconclusive findings such as Birkby's (1966) failure to isolate any factors accounting for the wide variance in compliance with the Bible-reading decisions by the 152 school districts of Tennessee. Perhaps it just makes no sense to investigate various demographic attributes of areas affected by decisions or social background characteristics of individual decision makers (as Birkby did) if there are no sound reasons to expect such factors to make a difference. Students of Supreme Court efficacy should take a lesson from Karl Popper (1959: 11)[5] who reminds us that theories are nets and he who casts will catch.

The Supreme Court, then, is better understood as a *catalyst* of change rather than a singular effector of change. In order to predict when it will produce sociopolitical reactions, it is necessary to bring to bear more general ideas about the workings of political and social systems. But if we at least recognize the tenuous nature of the theoretical relationship between decisions and outcomes, perhaps we will lower our expectations of the Court and suffer less disillusionment when cherished decisions go down the political drain and sink into the lifeless pages of constitutional law tomes. The Supreme Court is *not* a Supreme Being.

COLLECTING VALID DATA

> The Fact is the first thing. Make sure of it. Get it perfectly clear. Polish it till it shines and sparkles like a gem. Then connect it with other facts. Examine it in relation to them, for in that lies its worth and its significance. It is of little use alone. So make it a diamond in the necklace, a stone, perhaps a cornerstone in your building.

The above words uttered by James Bryce (1909: 10) in his presidential address to the American Political Science Association are profoundly relevant to students of Supreme Court efficacy. The law-abidingness of government officials and employees are the outcomes subject to most empirical research, but the data generated often are invalid indicators of the dimensions of conformity to or deviance from the legal obligations imposed upon them by the Supreme Court.

Johnson's (1967) study of compliance with school prayer decision, for example, provides us with the reactions of school administrators and school board members as well as the attitudes of townspeople toward the Supreme

Court's decisions, but it never really ascertains whether religious exercises continued in the classroom. Since high level officials often blind themselves to what is going on below and cognitively screen out realities about illegitimate day-to-day practices (Dolbeare and Hammond, 1969: 10), relying on their reports about what happened is an unjustified act of faith. Furthermore, the study of one school district with only 2,000 residents in rural Illinois precludes any generalization to the larger social world.

The low visibility, high complexity, and multiplicity of many bureaucracies (including school systems) conceals and clouds many official actions, and it behooves us, first and foremost to penetrate this haze and expose the institutions to the light of day. To accomplish this task, imaginative and daring methods of data collection must be used even if they are crude and unsystematic. Probing and snooping in the fashion of a Ralph Nader may turn up more relevant evidence than the more orthodox techniques of social science, and it may be worth giving up some reliability to obtain large gains in validity.[6] To get "clean" data on what are frequently dirty dealings (or at least illegal ones) requires shrewdness, flexibility, tenacity—and guts.

As is true of political science generally, survey research has been the predominant method of studying outcomes of Supreme Court decisions. In addition to the normal sources of error contaminating interview data (e.g., the guinea pig effect, interviewer interaction effects, response sets [Webb et al., 1966: ch. 1]), which are serious in themselves, there are problems peculiar to impact research that reduce the payoff of this approach. Whereas most surveys are attempts to ascertain current opinions, attitudes, or beliefs of those questioned, interviewing individuals about governmental practices is intended to determine *facts about past behavior.* And the same fallibilities of memory and recall (e.g., selective perception and retention) that often invalidate or discredit the testimony of witnesses at trials cast doubt on the accuracy of respondents' descriptions of official conduct or misconduct. For example, in the Georgetown University study of police interrogation in Washington, D.C. following Miranda v. Arizona (Medalie et al., 1968), defendants were asked whether they had been informed of their procedural rights (to remain silent, and the like). However, one must be highly skeptical about the credibility of their recollections of exactly what transpired in the tense and frightening stationhouse atmosphere.

Besides these honest errors stemming from limited human capabilities, respondents often have a vested interest in consciously perverting the truth. If people tend to hesitate in relating unpopular views to interviewers because they fear social disapproval, then *a fortiori* people will be unlikely to admit engaging in illegal or unconstitutional behavior. Assurances of confidentiality made to respondents hardly eliminate apprehension that confessions of impropriety would be disclosed, resulting in censures or sanctions of various kinds. Even if anonymity is preserved in research reports, public attention brought to noncompliance could threaten those who are trying to resist change.

Consequently, asking movie censors (Carmen, 1967) or district attorneys (Barth, 1968) whether they conform to Supreme Court guidelines on obscenity and inquiring of school teachers whether they lead prayers in class (Way, 1968: 204) is not much more revealing than it would be to ask taxpayers whether they declare all their income or fabricate any deductions. It is naive to expect people to incriminate themselves, and it can be assumed that those implicated in unlawful actions will generally take steps to conceal or whitewash them. People will lie to save their skins.

The same principle applies to those who are served or regulated by institutions subject to Court-imposed constraints. These parties may see real benefits to be gained by falsely alleging illegality. Large numbers of convicts interviewed by Trebach (1964) contended that they were denied constitutional rights, but surely many of them must have hoped for new appeals on the basis of such charges. The involved participant who has much at stake is not in a good position to be objective.

Where noncompliant behavior of institutions has been subject to much political controversy and public scrutiny, calculated attempts may be made at high levels of command to deny information to outsiders by ordering subordinates to remain silent when approached by interrogators. This is especially so when the leadership feels that changing practices in the direction of conformity would impede them in carrying out their central responsibilities. My own students were continually rebuffed in their attempts to interview FBI agents in Oregon about wiretapping practices in the aftermath of the Alderman, Ivanov, and Butenko (1969) cases (which require disclosure of electronic surveillance records to defendants whose telephones were tapped). In one instance, a student was told in no uncertain terms to refrain from further investigation.[7] Even if some individuals agree to talk, the small sample thus obtained is likely to be overrepresentative of those who are complying. Refusals to cooperate are common when people are under fire for their professional practices, and "no comment" in large numbers is the death toll for survey studies. As a result, some outcomes of Supreme Court decisions may be totally unresearchable through survey instruments.

But all is not despair. Various "unobtrusive measures" may be employed to gather better social intelligence. Although psychologists would quarrel with the old saying that seeing is believing, observational methods do have the great virtue of eliminating highly unreliable middlemen from the fact-finding process. Similarly, archival data (public and private records) are not ordinarily produced and distorted with the rummaging social scientist in mind; history does not lie (usually). Both of these sources of data come closer to "letting the facts speak for themselves"; they can provide relatively nonreactive and more objective measures of some outcomes of interest to us. Although neither is a panacea, I think greater use of them would herald marked advances in our understanding of Supreme Court efficacy. To demonstrate their potential, I shall now describe some successful studies using unobtrusive measures and suggest other opportunities for their use yet to be seized upon and exploited by social scientists.

A number of studies have made good use of visible observation (where those being studied are aware of the researcher's presence) to examine outcomes. Three juvenile courts were systematically observed by a team of scholars for a period of three months following the 1967 Gault decision (which granted formal procedural rights to youthful defendants whose cases previously could be tried very informally) to discover the degree of hierarchical control maintained by the Supreme Court over lower courts. They found that in two of the courts, children were "frequently and sometimes flagrantly denied their constitutional rights." (Lefstein et al., 1969: 560). In quantitative terms, only 59 out of 148 youths were given full advice of their right to counsel and 101 out of 121 who lacked counsel were not informed about the privilege against self-incrimination. Subtle nuances also came to light by watching the train of events; even those judges who technically complied often recited the defendant's rights rapidly, ritualistically, and incomprehensibly so that the form and not the spirit of Gault was honored. Since judges are probably as self-serving as others, I doubt whether this rather stark portrayal of judicial lawlessness would have resulted from asking them whether they had revised their courtroom procedures to conform to Gault.

Conspicuous observation has also succeeded in documenting police disregard of the Miranda case in a least one urban community. Although police have complained bitterly about being "handcuffed" by the Supreme Court, students at Yale Law School who observed police interrogations around-the-clock in New Haven found that only 25 out of 118 suspects were informed of their rights (Yale Law Journal, 1967). After an initial period of caution, police apparently accustomed themselves to the presence of observers in the station and resumed their normal style of operation—thus exposing wholesale violations of constitutional rules.

It may be argued that in studies of this nature it is never clear whether actors under surveillance temporarily modify their behavior to present a good image to observers or at least to make their malfeasance appear less egregious. If this is what they are willing to reveal on stage, one might say, imagine what is happening when the curtain is drawn. It is a real enough problem, but it is still more difficult to erect and maintain a false front when faced with the pressures of the daily job situation and the necessities of accomplishing certain tasks than it is to mouth high-sounding abstract commitments to legality in the very artificial interview context. Institutionalized work routines (even those contravening legal norms) are not likely to be drastically upset for long periods of time simply because they are being scrutinized by normally innocuous cadres of social scientists.

Nevertheless, validity is increased substantially if observers attach themselves to the organizations they are studying. The subjects of impact research will certainly be more at ease and will put up fewer defenses if they feel they are dealing with sympathetic "insiders" who understand their plights and dilemmas rather than aloof "outsiders" who are coldly judging and perhaps condemning them. After several months of riding with police in squad cars on patrol and occasionally even assisting them with their duties (passing a flashlight, witnessing a confession, and the like), Skolnick (1967) developed such good rapport that he was allowed regularly to witness grossly unlawful raids and searches. True "participant observation" such as this can build strong interpersonal ties and win the confidence of those whose behavior is being examined. The more integrated into the system the social scientist becomes the more likely that he gets an accurate picture of what is going on instead of a "snow-job" tailor-made for his personal viewing.

Of course, obtaining this kind of access initially is a formidable task in itself since cooperation with social scientists generally offers no rewards and is usually perceived as a useless and unnecessary nuisance.[8] Furthermore, even if the observer receives total acceptance from those with whom he is interacting and inconspicuously blends in with the environment, there is always the lurking danger that they are unconsciously adjusting their behavior to meet his expectations. And if the participant observer participates more than he observes, his own objectivity may be impaired because he is co-opted into accepting the norms and perceptions of the group he is serving.

To obviate some of these problems, I propose (with some hesitation due to the ethical dilemmas raised) other observational methods to study outcomes which minimize the risk of reactivity by concealing the identity or presence of the observer. Eyewitness reports by informants who come in contact with those affected by Supreme Court decisions in the normal course of events can be useful if there is some assurance that they lack any strong biases which would prevent neutral observations. So, for example, public school children can be solicited to note and discuss the treatment of religion in their classrooms and telephone company employees might be induced to relate the extent to which telephones are tapped by the government. Because such individuals are alerted in advance to discern whether particular rules and criteria are being followed, it is a more valid technique than the *post hoc* interview. On the other hand, the situations are few where on-the-spot observers who are both disinterested and communicative can be found.

Consequently, a more feasible strategy is one of direct spying ("hidden observation") on or the infiltration of operations about which the Supreme Court has issued regulations and constraints. The only sure way of preventing artificially contrived displays of compliance is to disguise, camouflage, or hide the researcher—so that he becomes almost literally "a fly on the wall." This is axiomatic to law enforcement and national intelligence agencies which constantly infiltrate organizations (such as protest movements and juvenile gangs) to search for illegal or subversive behavior, and I suggest reversing the process to uncover unlawful official conduct.[9] Police officers have been able to conceal successfully their ulterior motives and real allegiances when joining hippie communes and settlements which are very suspicious of newcomers and aliens, so it should not be inordinately difficult for social scientists (especially graduate students) to work their way into various social and political institutions which produce outcomes of interest. Working side by side with unknowing and unsuspecting police officers, Internal Revenue agents, welfare workers, and school administrators is an excellent vantage point from which to find out the day-to-day meaningfulness of Supreme Court decisions.

This mode of attack is quite limited to a highly dedicated and militant breed of researchers. The actual and alternative costs of such infiltration are high, as one must temporarily sever his ties with the academic community and lose the benefits which it offers (e.g., flexible hours, stimulating work, probably higher pay). Also, the strain of adopting the norms of a strange and uncomfortable role requiring the performance of unpleasant tasks and the tension arising from living under false pretenses will deter most individuals. However, those who are willing to bear the strenuous burdens of a dual life may well be justly compensated with rich and exciting data about significant political processes.

A less demanding approach is secret observation of natural situations. The drawbacks of my own study of the effects of the Supreme Court's obscenity decisions on bookseller self-censorship point to the potential of this method (Levine, 1970). To ascertain the openness of the retail book trade, I sent a mail questionnaire to 250 booksellers in twelve states asking them about their book selection policies and whether they stocked ten specific books dealing with sex. Since there are many good reasons why booksellers might falsify their responses, it would have been much better simply to browse through various book stores and take a visual inventory of the "sex books" for sale. Indeed, I must frankly admit that a personal tour which I recently made of the "smut shops" on New York's Forty-Second Street was a better measure of freedom in the urban bookstore than the costly and time-consuming survey which I conducted.

Because the observer is himself unobserved or unnoticed, this kind of surveillance is an excellent way of obtaining valid factual data about behavioral outcomes. So, if we want to find out whether police respect civil liberties or whether protesters abide by restrictions authorized by the Supreme Court during demonstrations, we ought to have "plainclothes" social scientists trailing both groups incognito and recording the actions that take place. And to really boost validity, it makes sense to use devices such as tape recorders and cameras whenever possible to capture indelibly the words and events that occur. Psychologist Gordon Allport once said, if you want to know what people think and how they feel, ask them (Selltiz et al., 1963: 236); I would add, if you want to know what they *do* and how they *behave*, watch them.

All the observational approaches just discussed may involve a high "dross rate," in that the situations in which Supreme Court decisions are relevant to the actor's behavior are rare. A large part of the patrolman's daily duties, for example, involves services to the community (e.g., retrieving cats from trees, filling out traffic accident reports) which have nothing to do with constitutional law. Rather than squander valuable resources scrutinizing such insignificant conduct, it may be more economical to examine some outcomes of Supreme Court decisions by experimentally manipulating the environment so that individuals are forced to decide whether or not to comply.

Data on the social consequences of Jones v. Mayer (1968) (which essentially forged a broad-gauged federal open housing law) might best be obtained by this kind of intervention by the researcher. Black and white observers could make consecutive visits to realtors and landlords to inquire about the purchase or rental of real estate. The extent to which the two races are treated uniformly would be a good measure of racial equality in the housing market. Since the researchers would have no intent to follow through on their requests and consummate any deals, this is clearly a form of entrapment. However, if the subjects remain unaware of the social experiment being performed on them, then their actions should be indicative of their normal *modus operandus* and a valid test of Supreme Court efficacy.

Many of these proposals raise very sticky questions of morality. Fundamental concerns such as invasion of privacy, breach of trust, and social manipulation certainly should be considered seriously prior to engaging in observational research. Individuals differ greatly in their sensitivity about and antagonism to various methods of research on human beings, so that some would find none of these methods distasteful while others would abhor even straightforward survey techniques as an unjustified interference with personal autonomy. The social sciences have barely confronted the question, and a consensus about professional ethics is far off on the horizon.

For myself, I would always ask whether the potential benefits from detecting illegality justify infringing upon the liberty and dignity of those being studied and whether the social values seemingly dependent upon compliance with the Supreme Court (e.g., free speech, due process) are of sufficient importance in my own calculus of preferences to merit tampering with individual lives. Others may disagree with this relativistic framing of the issue and favor absolute prohibitions of certain kinds of research, but suffice it to say that the intent of the present article is to present options which are technically feasible and to leave open questions about the propriety and wisdom of actually putting the various alternatives into practice.

Another source of data on outcomes which has gone largely untapped are the archives and documents of governmental and private institutions. This genre of data can furnish us with motion pictures of events rather than the all-too-frequent snapshots which we get through interviews or isolated observations, so we are in a better position to judge the effects of the Supreme Court over time. From a practical standpoint, written documents are often inexpensive and accessible, enabling the researcher to carry on without mammoth financial support.

The running record, of course, is itself fraught with both systematic and random errors involved in recording aspects of human behavior, and (as any good historian knows) the longevity of what has been written does not correct original mistakes and distortions or fill in crucial omissions. For example, aggregate data on crime which would seem to be ideal for plotting second-order consequences of some Supreme Court decisions on defendants' rights are extremely misleading and unreliable because of the vagaries of crime reporting by the thousands of sundry law enforcement agencies. But at least the original producers of records and the amassers of descriptive statistics, as deceptive as they might be, do not usually orient their work to the visions of social scientists who may later appear on the scene and scrounge through their books. The recording, tabulating, and collecting of factual information is often a job responsibility or a legal burden, and for most individuals the eventual uses to which the data is put is the last thing on their minds.

Accrued records can sometimes provide measures of political impacts of decisions on governmental bodies. Since both federal and state agencies regularly take an accounting of the number of citizens represented in legislative districts, the effects of the reapportionment decisions on the legislatures can be best charted by using such data to construct indices of malapportionment (Schubert and Press, 1964). Similarly, data on actual Southern school desegregation collected by the United States Office of Education and the Southern Regional Council are ideal indicators of whether segregation has been eliminated with "all deliberate speed."

Readily available government budgets also can be rough indicators of political responses to decisions since many policies stipulated by the Supreme Court require substantial fiscal expenditures for broad implementation. So, one might ascertain the funds allocated by the Office of Economic Opportunity, state legislatures, and local councils for legal aid services to determine whether the right-to-counsel decisions have made much difference to indigents accused of crime. Likewise, budgetary data would reveal whether prodigious resources are being directed toward increasing the manpower of the juvenile courts—a clear necessity if the formal procedures intended to protect juvenile defendants ordered by the Supreme Court in the Gault decision are to be operationalized at the local level. When studying outcomes, money talks.

Culling of state legislation can reveal the extent to which Supreme Court legitimation of state laws spurs other states to follow suit. Removing the taint of possible unconstitutionality from proposed laws under debate may be an important factor in securing passage and initiating new programs, so it is important to study this generally neglected "bandwagon effect." A simple search of the law library would show whether a rash of states enacted "stop and frisk" laws after they were sustained in Terry v. Ohio (1967). The statute books would also quickly tell whether the Supreme Court's approval, in Ginsberg v. New York (1968), of the New York law which sets up a specially restrictive obscenity standard for minors has been copied by other states as a means of salvaging their constantly attacked obscenity regulations. The public record is often the best source of those outcomes which are public events.

Finally a wealth of data on social consequences of Supreme Court decisions lies in store for those who would creatively peruse written records and sort out the wheat from very abundant chaff. Indeed, there is a nascent academic field exclusively concerned with the development of adequate "social indicators"–indices to the socially important conditions of society (Bauer, 1966).[10] Recognizing the barriers to obtaining reliable data on the state of the nation ("measuring the unmeasurable"), some scholars are nonetheless beginning to look for the "least worst" measures of the society's health, security, and freedom.[11] Also, data banks are being created to make data from diverse and remote sources conveniently accessible to researchers; we now even have a "Riot Data Clearinghouse" (at Brandeis University) which is a repository for facts about urban disorders and violence. Students of Supreme Court efficacy would do well to seize upon such data as they accumulate and plug them into their own hypotheses about the long-range consequences of decisions.

Even now, records pertinent to a variety of social consequences of a somewhat lesser scale abound. This is especially true of economic effects which are subject to much easier quantification and summation. The efficacy of the Supreme Court's consistent support and extension of anti-trust laws in the last few decades could be tested by looking at data on the concentration of ownership in various industries. Federal income tax law is another area in which the Court continues to make economic policy, and, with the cooperation of the Internal Revenue Service, one could check whether taxpayers are taking heed of the Court's rulings.[12] For example, a sample of returns of the rapidly increasing number of taxpayers involved in divorce litigation might be examined to see whether they have stopped deducting legal fees since the Court declared that such expenses are nondeductible (United States v. Gilmore, 1963). In still another issue area, one might correlate the varying degrees of favoritism shown by the Court to organized labor over the years with the rate at which union membership has risen to examine the Court's effects on labor-management relations. There is a wealth of statistical data available to help judge whether the Supreme Court has had much of a voice on how economic power and resources have been divided and distributed.

The mass media contain partial answers to many questions about outcomes.

Content analysis of crime stories in newspapers might show whether reporters have curtailed and restrained their pretrial coverage since the Supreme Court ruled in Sheppard v. Maxwell (1966) that massive press publicity prejudices the rights of defendants to a fair trial and thus violates due process of law. The consequences of New York Times v. Sullivan (1964), which held that public officials cannot recover libel damages for criticism of their conduct in office unless malice can be proven, could be studied by checking whether political writing has become more hostile, rash, or inflammatory since the decision. One could turn to the entertainment sections of newspapers and scan the advertisements of movie theaters as one way of probing whether the Court's premissiveness toward depictions of sexuality has resulted in more erotic movie fare (i.e., "freedom of the arts") in various localities. Methodically sifting through old newspapers in dusty library rooms may not provide the fun or the glory of "going out into the field," but the dividends of this kind of tedious research may in some cases be far greater.

To summarize this section, I might invoke an old Biblical adage: seek and ye shall find. Indicators of Supreme Court outcomes do not stare us in the face; creative planning and aggressive searching are needed to ferret out the facts. Clearly, some measures will be oblique and tenuous (especially where behavior is being intentionally masked), but these failings can be overcome by using several sets of data to zero in on or "triangulate" our hypotheses about Supreme Court efficacy.[13] Even if interviews are the sole source of data, we can have greater confidence in the findings if the opinions of respondents having very different vantage points and interests are sought.[14] The working rules of the detective, "running down every lead" and "checking all the angles" should be among our cardinal methodological tenets.

INFERRING CAUSATION

A central difficulty in demonstrating Supreme Court efficacy is establishing the causal relation between decisions and subsequent behavioral events. No matter how valid the data which is collected, it will prove little if the basic research design does not permit legitimate inferences about causation. What is necessary is to try to eliminate alternative hypotheses which might explain the outcomes that have been observed.[15] Common sense tells us that an epidemic of armed robberies the week after the announcement of a decision like Miranda v. Arizona (1966) is not likely to have been caused by the Supreme Court, and a decline in the population of some Connecticut towns since 1965 probably did not result from the Court's invalidating of legislative bans on the sale of contraceptives in Griswold v. Connecticut (1965). Although these particular examples of untenable causal links are patently obvious and even ludicrous, many studies of Supreme Court outcomes can be faulted because of just this kind of fallacy.

Sorauf (1959) fell prey to this methodological pitfall when he investigated the repercussions of Zorach v. Clauson (1952) which upheld the constitutionality of "released time" programs. Enrollment statistics were collected showing that attendance in such programs had increased since the 1952 decision, but no steps were taken to control for other factors which might very well have accounted for the surge in participation. The expansion of such programs may have been due to mere population growth or it may have been a side effect of the migration of many parochial school students into public school systems. Or, the increase after Zorach may have simply been a continuation of a trend beginning long before Zorach was ever adjudicated—to be explained as a reaction to the inexorable secularization of American culture. Interpreting the data is sheer guesswork, and we have no way of pinning responsibility for the observed phenomena on the court.

I realize that it is not always easy to build in controls when designing research on Supreme Court efficacy, but some efforts can be made to isolate the effects specifically wrought by the Court. Lempert's excellent article (1966) on strategies of research design in legal impact studies covers much of the same ground, so I will limit myself to considerations peculiar to studies of the Supreme Court. One *caveat* is an order: the subject of causal inference in nonexperimental research opens up a Pandora's Box of tough and complex methodological issues,[16] and the following discussion is only intended to scratch the surface.

At the outset, the inadequacy of "one-shot" case studies must be emphasized. Although research on Supreme Court outcomes is often of this nature, Campbell and Stanley (1966: 6), two sophisticated methodologists, forcefully argue that "such studies have such an absence of control as to be of almost no scientific value." The previously discussed study of the implementation of *In re Gault* by three juvenile courts suffers from this kind of deficiency in that all of the observations were made after the decision. From the data which is presented, it is impossible to determine how much, if any, of the judges' conduct represented Court-induced innovation. One can only suppose, intuit, or recollect on the basis of earlier more casual observations what things were like in the days prior to Gault.

Since comparison is the *sine qua non* of science, the "before and after" design is one remedy for this defect (although a stop-gap one at that). Observation of individual, institutional, or system performance before Supreme Court decisions provides a base line enabling us to gauge the degree of change inaugurated after the Court's rulings. Many schools in border states remained segregated in the years following Brown v. Board of Education, but if this situation is contrasted with the well-nigh universal segregation in some of these states before Brown, the dramatic effects of the decision in this area are made clear.

Docketing of cases occurs up to a full year ahead of final disposition by the Court, so seasoned analysts can often predict decisions well in advance. If divisions on the Court have been infrequent or uneven and conjecture about results can be made with some confidence, then behavior in question can be observed in anticipation of the Court's decision. Thus Muir (1967) interviewed school personnel before and after the Bible reading decision (Abington Township School District v. Schempp, 1963) and was able to get data on how individuals in comfortable routines react when traditional ways are constitutionally undermined. After the decision, psychological processes of attitude change and rationalization were discernible because Muir knew how these people stood before their practices were deemed illegal.

An approximation of this method is to rely on reports of earlier studies to get soundings of predecision behavior. My own study of booksellers examined their policies only after a decade of liberal obscenity decisions starting with Roth v. United States (1957), but I could at least make some crude comparisons with the pre-Roth situation in the retail book industry by alluding to the dire reports of strict censorship noted in several law review articles appearing in the mid-1950s. This is at best a third-rate approach, however, since one must sometimes depend on unreplicable findings of dubious credibility; but it is still better than assuming implicitly what transpired earlier.

The before-and-after design has at least two major drawbacks. First, historical events other than Supreme Court decisions may have intervened and caused any changes that are detected. Undoubtedly, statistical data would show a sharp rise in the number of applications for conscientious objector status received by the Selective Service system between 1964 and 1966, but to attribute this to the Supreme Court's decision in United States v. Seeger (1965), which broadened the grounds for conscientious objection so that atheists and agnostics could qualify, would be to ignore the simultaneously occuring escalation of the Vietnam War and the growing momentum of the protest movement which were probably more significant factors. Similarly, increased marijuana prosecutions following Leary v. United States (1969), in which the conviction of Timothy Leary for failure to register illegal drugs was reversed, are apparently the result of an ongoing radical transformation of youth culture, and it would be preposterous to contend that the Supreme Court's vindication of a leading drug cultist inspired droves of youngsters to experiment with drugs. To show that the Court brought about certain outcomes, the researcher must convincingly reject arguments that other events taking place between the two observation points accounted for the changes that were observed.

A second difficulty relates to what statisticians call "regression effects"—the high probability that extreme occurences of some phenomenon will appear more moderate on subsequent measurements. Campbell and Ross (1968) have shown that the decline in traffic fatalities following the highly publicized

Connecticut speed crackdown would probably have taken place regardless of the state program because the years immediately preceding the crackdown featured an abnormally high accident rate. Likewise, the decrease in prosecution of Communists in the aftermath of Yates v. United States (1958), which narrowly restricted the applicability of the Smith Act, may well have occured even without the Court's decision because Yates came on the heels of one of the most vigorous campaigns in American history against alleged subversives. Actually, it is excesses of this nature that the Court is often trying to counter, and ironically they sometimes will subside without judicial action by the workings of statistical chance. By looking at only two points in time which may be highly atypical, we are unable to discover whether apparent outcomes are merely chance happenings resulting from the laws of probability.

These spurious effects can be somewhat controlled through time-series research in which behavior is plotted at various intervals before and after supreme court decisions. Idiosyncratic and transitory changes in behavior can be discounted if a long time period is examined, and changes effected by the Supreme Court should stand out over and above long-term trends caused by nonlegal factors. This approach is particularly appropriate where a Supreme Court decision marks an abrupt shift in policy, so we can expect to see outcomes which are sharp departures from the past.

This kind of research is most feasible when we are dealing with standardized data on outcomes (such as percentages) which can be meaningfully compared over time. Since national samples of people are often asked the same or similar questions in mass surveys conducted over the years and their responses are now being stored on computer tape in accessible data pools, the potential exists for quantifying and then comparing the state of public opinion on various issues to investigate some symbolic effects of Supreme Court decisions. Hyman and Sheatsley (1964) gathered opinion data from various polls since 1930 to chart changes in attitudes toward desegregation in the South and concluded that Brown v. Board of Education stimulated a rapid acceleration of the previously gradual trend toward acceptance of racial integration.

Other possibilities suggest themselves. By checking state welfare rolls at regular periods, it could be established whether Shapiro v. Thompson (1969), which overturned state laws that required minimum residence within the state to establish welfare eligibility, motivated large numbers of the unemployed to migrate to states paying high benefits from states offering a mere pittance. Longitudinal analysis of legislative roll-call votes could test whether the reapportionment decisions substantially altered the balance among and relative sizes of urban, rural, and suburban blocs in state legislatures. To find out if the famous "switch in time that saved nine" by the Supreme Court in 1937 resulted in more sympathetic treatment of organized labor by trial judges, one could collect yearly data from various jurisdictions on the percentage of strike-breaking suits against unions in which management was successful in getting injunctions issued. My guess is that long-term data will rarely reveal striking differences, but that will only go to prove that the Supreme Court is not as powerful as both its friends and critics often assume.

A reformulation of the research problem makes another strategy viable. If we ask what the consequences of future rules yet to be laid down by the Supreme Court might be, then a straightforward comparison of the outcomes of alternative rules operative in different settings makes sense. Such research could optimize Supreme Court policy-making by giving the Justices a more solid idea of the likely repercussions of their action than their own personal hunches and speculations which are now often the basis (if not the written rationale) of their decisions. At the very least, studies like this might abate their worries about disastrous results which are sometimes envisaged and condemned by opponents of new doctrines under consideration.

The federal system of court organization is an ideal context in which to execute such comparative studies. States that are very similar in many attributes (demography and so on) are often governed by different laws, and this variation ("splits of authority") allows the investigator to track the social consequences of alternative legal policies. The states can be seen as laboratories and the lawmakers (legislatures and appellate courts) as social experimenters who conduct "trial runs" of rules before they are adopted on the national level.[17]

Using this approach, one could study, for example, the effectiveness of capital punishment as a deterrent to crime. States which have given up the death penalty can be compared with those which still maintain it to determine whether the former have had more homicides per capita than the latter. If there are no differences, the Supreme Court might be more willing to categorize this type of sentence as a "cruel and unusual punishment" which is prohibited by the Eighth Amendment.

In an intuitive way the Justices engage in this kind of comparative thinking all the time. In Harper v. Virginia (1966), which declared poll taxes in state elections unconstitutional, the Court must have ruminated on the degree of black disenfranchisement in states with and without taxes on voting.[18] The Court avowedly brought to bear various state experiences in deciding Mapp v. Ohio (1961) and concluded that among alternative means to prevent police from conducting improper searches, only the exclusionary rule (prohibiting the admission of illegally seized evidence in court) seemed to secure compliance with the Fourth Amendment. This empirical mentality is laudable, but it is no substitute for systematic comparisons of carefully collected data.

The above strategies may seem needlessly complex and cumbersome to some, but they represent the bare minimum of controls which must be applied in social research to guard against threats to validity. To be sure, it would be futile to try to emulate the elegant designs employed in experimental sciences since it is virtually impossible to manipulate variables, structure the environment, or randomize subjects in studying outcomes of political processes. What should be done is to control pragmatically for as many extraneous factors as the data permit, and above all to remain constantly alert to the plausible rival hypotheses (other than Supreme Court efficacy) which might account for the observed outcomes.

CONCLUSIONS AND ASPIRATIONS

As the discipline of political science undergoes its "post-behavioral" self-analysis, there is growing sentiment that policy research should be high on the agenda of the profession in the coming years. It is becoming painfully clear in our absurdly unmanageable world that the "science of muddling through" (Lindblom, 1959) is no longer an adequate method of political decision-making, and more rational planning is necessary if we are to cope with the stresses and strains of modern society. Nowhere is this more true than in the cloistered chambers of the Supreme Court where the Justices often stumble blindly and haphazardly in quest of working rules of law that accomplish desired ends (Miller, 1964-1965).

A simple perusal of recent opinions of the Supreme Court attests to the ignorance of social and political realities on which many decisions are based. A good illustration is Williams v. Rhodes (1968) declaring it unconstitutional for Ohio to require fifteen percent of the electorate to sign petitions in order to get a third party on the ballot for the Presidency. A series of specific questions about the effects of electoral and party systems are raised by the Court, and the answers which they give rest on pure speculation. Does the two-party system encourage compromise and political stability? Do third parties frustrate majority will by making it easier for the second choice of a majority to be the winner? Is it easier for disaffected groups to work within the two-party system (if primaries are held) than to organize separate parties? Is multiple party choice helpful or confusing to voters? It is by no means self-evident what political arrangements best guarantee an equal voice for all citizens in the selection of public officials, and unfortunately the discipline of political science which should be vitally concerned with the consequences of constitutional rules has devoted woefully little attention to these kinds of issues.

Many other decisions suffer from a similar lack of information. The Court grants all defendants accused of major crimes the right to trial by jury (Duncan v. Louisiana, 1968), but it is not at all clear whether juries are less prejudiced and more objective than judges in resolving factual disputes. In the absence of an understanding of the psychopathology of alcoholism, conviction of chronic alcoholics for intoxication in public is approved against contentions that such derelicts are powerless to change their behavior due to their irresistible compulsion to drink (Powell v. Texas. 1968). The Court wrestles with the wiretapping issue without sufficient evidence on the value or necessity of electronic eavesdropping to fight organized crime. In lieu of knowledge, the Court turns to past precedents—which are often irrelevant—and the eternal verities—which are often wrong.

A major theme running through modern jurisprudence since Holmes is that judges should look forward to the consequences of decisions instead of backwards toward axiomatic first principles. However, for courts to perform this predictive function, they need sound empirical studies which test prospective courses of action against reality (Mayo and Jones, 1964-1965). Unless these studies have a firm methodological foundation, the sophistry of the lawyers will merely be replaced by the pretentious sham of the social scientist. The urgency of the agonizing problems confronting the Supreme Court should not prompt scholars to present premature diagnoses and remedies based on hasty and ill-founded research.

My hope is that the methodological sensitivity and refinement which I am urging will not only give us a better understanding of the role of the Supreme Court in American life but will also facilitate more effective policy-making by the Court. The two goals are convergent as the ultimate criterion of valid theories, predictability, is the greatest asset of governing institutions. If there is to be any salvation for our troubled and frightened nation it is through rationality, and it is incumbent upon academia to lead the way in providing it.[19]

There is no better way to begin than to insist on intellectual integrity and humility in our capacity as advisors to the throne. The Supreme Court needs us—but only when we have something to say.

NOTES

1. See Westin (1967) for a comprehensive analysis of the cases concerned with the right to privacy.

2. Of the same order but even more broadly sweeping (and less justifiable) is Eldridge Cleaver's interpretation (1968: 192) of the importance of Brown v. Board of Education:

> If separation of the black and white people in America along the color line had the effect, in terms of social imagery, of separating the Mind from the Body—the oppressor whites usurping sovereignty by monopolizing the Mind, abdicating the Body and becoming bodiless Omnipotent Administrators and Ultrafeminines; and the oppressed blacks, divested of sovereignty and therefore of the mind, manifesting the body and becoming mindless Supermasculine Menials and Black Amazons—if this is so, then the 1954 U.S. Supreme Court decision in the case of Brown v. Board of Education, demolishing the principle of segregation of the races in public education

> and striking at the very root of the practice of segregation generally, was a major surgical operation performed by nine men in black robes on the racial Maginot Line which is imbedded as deep as sex or the lust for lucre in the schismatic American psyche. This piece of social surgery . . . is more marvelous than a successful heart transplant would be, for it was meant to graft the nation's Mind onto its Body and vice versa.

3. Utility theory is briefly discussed by Krislov (1965: ch. 6) and Levine and Becker (1969: 6-8). Dissonance theory has been applied by Muir (1967: ch. 4).

4. William Mitchell (1967) argues that this is a choice which social scientists must always make since the goals of simplicity and realism are to some extent antithetical.

5. The comment was originally made by the German poet Novalis.

6. Raymond Bauer (1966: 37) opts for this choice in doing research on impact of government policies by posing a rhetorical question: "Is it better to have a crude measure of the variable you are really interested in, or a precise measure of a variable which is only an approximation of what you are interested in?"

7. In this case the agent turned the interview around and began asking the student questions about *his* draft status and political activities. This intimidation was successful in shutting off further inquiry as the student, who was considering applying for a conscientious objector exemption, thought it would be prudent to select another class project.

8. On rare occasions social scientists do have something to offer (such as expertise) as an inducement to decision makers to open up their quarters. My colleague, Thomas Hovet, Jr., has developed a tacit exchange relationship with United Nations delegates and Secretariat officials whereby he gives them information on voting patterns and advice on strategy in return for close access to the negotiating process.

9. It is a standing joke that the FBI now has majority control of the American Communist Party.

10. A number of essays on this topic can be found in Bauer (1966).

11. A compendium of social indicators has been drawn together by a research team directed by economist Mancur Olsen under the auspices of the federal government. See U.S. Department of Health, Education and Welfare (1969).

12. In a study of the effectiveness of sanctions as a means of inducing compliance with tax laws, Richard Schwartz and Sonya Orleans (1967) received remarkable cooperation from the Internal Revenue Service who made available returns of groups of taxpayers who were the subject of a field experiment (without disclosing the identities of the individuals involved).

13. For a powerful exposition of the argument that multiple measures are necessary to test propositions in the social sciences, see Campbell and Fiske (1959).

14. For example, to reconstruct what transpires at draft board hearings, board members, clerks, and appellants all should be questioned.

15. This is the orientation of Campbell and Stanley (1966) in their rigorous critique of various research designs used in education studies.

16. For a thorough technical treatment of these issues, see Blalock (1961).

17. Where virtually all fifty states have the same policy which the Supreme Court is contemplating overriding, cross-national studies might shed light on the consequences to be expected. Should the Court some day seriously consider overruling Roth v. United States and declaring *all* obscenity laws unconstitutional infringements on the right of free speech, it might find it profitable to compare the social consequences of Denmark's "anything goes" policy on sexual speech with the more restricted situation in America. Of course, all kinds of social and cultural differences for which controls are lacking distinguish nations from each other, so extreme caution must be exercised when findings of this kind are interpreted.

18. I think Justice Douglas is being less than candid when he says, in a footnote, that "we do not stop to determine whether on this record the Virginia tax in its modern setting serves the . . . end [of excluding blacks from the polls]."

19. Karl Deutsch's (1966: 255) words, though overstated, express this notion pointedly: "All studies of politics, and all techniques and models suggested as instruments of political analysis, have this purpose: that men should be more able to act in politics with their eyes open."

CASES

ABINGTON TOWNSHIP SCHOOL DISTRICT v. SCHEMPP 374 U.S. 203 (1963).
ALDERMAN v. UNITED STATES 394 U.S. 165 (1969).
ALEXANDER v. HOLMES COUNTY BOARD OF EDUCATION 24 LEd2d 19 (1969).
BROWN v. BOARD OF EDUCATION 347 U.S. 483 (1954).
BUTENKO v. UNITED STATES 394 U.S. 165 (1969).

DANDRIDGE v. WILLIAMS 90 S. Ct. 149 (1969).
DUNCAN v. LOUISIANA 391 U.S. 145 (1968).
In re GAULT 387 U.S. 1 (1967).
GIDEON v. WAINWRIGHT 372 U.S. 335 (1963).
GINSBERG v. NEW YORK 390 U.S. 629 (1968).

GRISWOLD v. CONNECTICUT 381 U.S. 479 (1965).
HARPER v. VIRGINIA 383 U.S. 663 (1966).
IVANOV v. UNITED STATES 384 U.S. 165 (1969).
JONES v. MAYER 389 U.S. 968 (1968).
LEARY v. UNITED STATES 23 LEd2d 57 (1969).

MAPP v. OHIO 367 U.S. 643 (1961).
MINERSVILLE SCHOOL DISTRICT v. GOBITIS 310 U.S. 586 (1940).
MIRANDA v. ARIZONA 384 U.S. 436 (1966).
NEW YORK TIMES v. SULLIVAN 376 U.S. 254 (1964).
POWELL v. TEXAS 392 U.S. 514 (1968).
ROTH v. UNITED STATES 354 U.S. 476 (1957).

SHAPIRO v. THOMPSON 394 U.S. 618 (1969).
SHEPPARD v. MAXWELL 384 U.S. 333 (1966).
TERRY v. OHIO 387 U.S. 929 (1967).
UNITED STATES v. GILMORE 372 U.S. 39 (1963).
UNITED STATES v. SEEGER 380 U.S. 163 (1965).

WEST VIRGINIA BOARD OF EDUCATION v. BARNETTE 319 U.S. 624 (1943).
WILLIAMS v. RHODES 393 U.S. 23 (1968).
YATES v. UNITED STATES 356 U.S. 363 (1958).
YOUNGSTOWN SHEET AND TUBE COMPANY v. SAWYER 343 U.S. 579 (1952).
ZORACH v. CLAUSON 343 U.S. 306 (1952).

REFERENCES

ABRAHAM, H. (1967) Freedom and the Court. New York: Oxford Univ. Press.

BARTH, T. (1968) "Perception and acceptance of Supreme Court decisions at the state and local level." J. of Public Law 17, 2: 308-350.

BAUER, R. (1966) "Detection and anticipation of impact: the nature of the task," pp. 1-67 in R. Bauer (ed.) Social Indicators. Cambridge: MIT Press.

BECKER, T. [ed.] (1969) The Impact of Supreme Court Decisions. New York: Oxford Univ. Press.

BIRKBY, R. (1966) "The Supreme Court and the Bible Belt: Tennessee reaction to the 'Schempp' decision." Midwest J. of Pol. Sci. 10 (August): 304-319.

BLALOCK, H., Jr. (1961) Causal Inference in Nonexperimental Research. Chapel Hill: Univ. of North Carolina Press.

BRYCE, J. (1909) "The relations of Political science to history and to practice." Amer. Pol. Sci. Rev. 3 (February): 1-19.

CAMPBELL, D. and D. FISKE (1959) "Convergent and discriminant validation by the multitrait-multimethod matrix." Psychological Bull. 56 (March): 81-105.

CAMPBELL, D. and H. L. ROSS (1968) "The Connecticut crackdown on speeding: time-series data in quasi-experimental analysis." Law and Society Rev. 3 (August): 33-53.

CAMPBELL, D. and J. STANLEY (1966) Experimental and Quasi-Experimental Designs for Research. Chicago: Rand-McNally.

CARMEN, I. (1967) Movies, Censorship and the Law. Ann Arbor: Univ. of Michigan Press.

CLEAVER, E. (1968) Soul on Ice. New York: McGraw-Hill.

DEUTSCH, K. (1966) The Nerves of Government. New York: Free Press.

DOLBEARE, K. and P. HAMMOND (1969) "Local elites, the impact of judicial decisions and the process of change." Presented at the 1969 Meeting of the American Political Science Association.

Harvard Law Review (1954) [Note] "Evasion of Supreme Court mandates in cases remanded to state courts since 1941." 67 (May): 1251-1280.

HYMAN, H. and P. SHEATSLEY (1964) "Attitudes toward desegregation." Scientific Amer. 211 (July): 16-23.

JOHNSON, R. (1967) The Dynamics of Compliance: Supreme Court Decision-Making from a New Perspective. Evanston, Ill.: Northwestern Univ. Press.

JONES, E. (1966) "Impact research and sociology of law: some tentative suggestions." Wisconsin Law Rev. 1966 (Spring): 331-339.

KRISLOV, S. (1965) The Supreme Court in the Political Process. New York: Macmillan.

LASSWELL, H. (1958) Politics: Who Gets What, When, How? Cleveland: World Publishing Co.

LEFSTEIN, N., V. STAPLETON, and L. TEITELBAUM (1969) "In search of juvenile justice: *Gault* and its implementations." Law and Society Rev. 3 (May): 491-562.

LEMPERT, R. (1966) "Strategies of research design in the legal impact study." Law and Society Rev. 1 (November): 111-132.

LEVINE, J. (1970) "The Supreme Court and sex censorship: a study of judicial efficacy." forthcoming in J. Fiszman (ed.) The American Political Arena. Boston: Little, Brown.

--- and T. BECKER (1969) "Toward and beyond a theory of Supreme Court impact." Presented at 1969 Meeting of American Political Science Association.

LINDBLOM, C. (1959) "The science of muddling through." Public Administration Rev. 19 (Winter): 79-88.

MAYO, L. and E. JONES (1964-1965) "Legal-policy decision process: alternative thinking and the predictive function." George Washington Law Rev. 33 (October): 318-456.

MEDALIE, R., L. ZEITZ, and P. ALEXANDER (1968) "Custodial police interrogation in our nation's capital: the attempt to implement *Miranda*." Michigan Law Rev. 66 (May): 1347-1422.

MILLER, A. (1964-1965) "On the need for 'impact analysis' of Supreme Court decisions." Georgetown Law J. 53 (Winter): 365-401.

MITCHELL, W. (1967) "The shape of political theory to come: from political sociology to political economy." Amer. Behavioral Scientist 11 (November): 19-20.

MUIR, W., Jr. (1967) Prayer and the Public Schools. Chicago: Univ. of Chicago Press.

MURPHY, W. (1959) "Lower court checks on Supreme Court power." Amer. Pol. Sci. Rev. 53 (December): 1017-1031.

PELTASON, J. W. (1961) Fifty-Eight Lonely Men: Federal Judges and School Desegregation. New York: Harcourt, Brace & World.

POPPER, K. (1959) The Logic of Scientific Discovery. New York: Science Editions.

SCHUBERT, G. and C. PRESS (1964) "Measuring malapportionment." Amer. Pol. Sci. Rev. 58 (June): 303-327 and 58 (December): 966-970.

SCHWARTZ, R. and S. ORLEANS (1967) "On legal sanctions." Univ. of Chicago Law Rev. 34 (Winter): 274-300.

SELLTIZ, C., M. JAHODA, M. DEUTSCH, and S. COOK (1963) Research Methods in Social Relations. New York: Holt, Rinehart & Winston.

SKOLNICK, J. (1967) Justice Without Trial. New York: John Wiley.

SORAUF, F. J. (1959) "*Zorach v. Clauson*: the impact of a Supreme Court decision." Amer. Pol. Sci. Rev. 53 (September): 777-791.

TREBACH, A. (1964) The Rationing of Justice. New Brunswick: Rutgers Univ. Press.

U.S. Department of Health, Education and Welfare (1969) Toward a Social Report. Washington, D.C.: U.S. Government Printing Office.

WAY, H. F., Jr. (1968) "Survey research on judicial decisions: the prayer and Bible reading cases." Western Pol. Q. 21 (June): 189-205.

WEBB, E., D. CAMPBELL, R. SCHWARTZ, and L. SECHREST (1966) Unobtrusive Measures: Nonreactive Research in the Social Sciences. Chicago: Rand McNally.

WESTIN, A. (1967) Privacy and Freedom. New York: Atheneum.

Yale Law Journal (1967) [Note] "Interrogations in New Haven: the impact of *Miranda*." 76 (July): 1521-1648.

ZETTERBERG, H. (1965) On Theory and Verification in Sociology. Totowa, N.J.: Bedminister Press.

Chapter 6

The Supreme Court's Impact

Some Problems of Conceptualization and Measurement

STEPHEN L. WASBY
Southern Illinois University, Carbondale, Illinois

The impact of what judges decide is a crucial part of what is studied by those sharing a political rather than only a legal perspective on the United States Supreme Court. It has become important as we have shifted our attention from "output, which is the decision of the Court including its orders and statement of policy" to consideration of "outcome, which is the final results or impact of output" (Barth, 1968: 315, note). This development is much more recent than the beginnings of the political perspective on the courts. Explicit attention to impact, backed by studies of impacts of particular decisions, is less than twenty years old, dating from the aftermath of Brown v. Board of Education (1954), which made political scientists aware that compliance with decisions of the Supreme Court was neither automatic, immediate, nor uniform. As Krislov (1963: 7) has remarked, from the standpoint of Court process, the decision in Brown v. Board of Education has had its greatest effect in educating "students as to the limits and operations of the court system generally."

Existing Studies of Impact

The plethora of existing studies which has given rise to the current issue of this journal and a recent collection of readings (Becker, 1969) shows that inattention has changed to attention. One reason for the change, in addition to the shock of recognition caused by Brown v. Board, is a more general emphasis in the social sciences on the effects of legal decisions of any sort. "In recent years, a growing call has been heard for emphasis on the empirical consequences of legal decisions—not merely on the theoretical and logical aspects of a self-contained legal system, but also on the impact of the system on a broader society" (Krislov, 1968: 165). Thus there is a relationship between studies of the impact of Supreme Court decisions and studies of the effect of statutes and regulations, within the rubric of the sociology of law (see Jones, 1966; Massell, 1968; Nagel, forthcoming).

The emphasis of political scientists who have become involved in this endeavor has been limited largely to examination of impacts of the United States Supreme Court and, to a far smaller degree, of state supreme courts. While our look at impact shows that the "upper-court myth" has lessened its hold because it is no longer presumed that the only place to look for "the law" is in the doctrine of Supreme Court decisions, the concentration on high appellate bodies indicates that the myth has retained its hold on us; we are not concentrating on the decisions of lower courts where the bulk of cases is decided. Moreover, the appellate court emphasis has brought criticism, such as that "most impact analysis has been conducted as a 'top-down approach' which relies excessively on a hierarchical view of courts" (Barth, 1968: 316). As an alternative, we are told that our focus should be on development of policy at the local level, "with Supreme Court decisions considered as one factor among many in that development" (Barth, 1968: 316), and that "only when we appreciate more fully the totality of the forces impinging on individuals at the level of implementation can we account for the varying responses made to Supreme Court policy and thus see this decisional structure in greater perspective" (Johnson, 1967: 16).[1] In addition to attention to the impact of high appellate courts, or perhaps in part because of that emphasis, we have not studied impact with respect to a large range of law. The concentration has been on what Jacob has called "policy-making" rather than on "norm enforcement," on large public policy issues rather than perhaps more numerous private law controversies, on impacts involving relationships between government agencies or between government agencies and individuals rather than between individuals and individuals (see Wells and Grossman, 1966: 290).

Some Limitations on Impact Study

In their initial work, those studying the effect of the Court's decisions tended to deal with compliance, or rather, with noncompliance. Their initial attention was turned in this direction because they had assumed automatic compliance with the Court's decisions. To the extent the law is thought to be found and declared rather than the product of a political process, one gets the feeling that obedience should be forthcoming; after all, it is "the law" one is obeying, not nine men on the Supreme Court. If, however, one views the Court as part and parcel of the political process, one would be more likely to discount what the judges say. Work on noncompliance was a reflection of, and was reinforced by, values—values embodied, or thought to be embodied, in the American legal system, as well as the values of those conducting the research. According to the "rule of law" supposedly prevailing in America, those affected by decisions of the courts, but most particularly by the decisions of the U.S. Supreme Court as the highest court of the land, are supposed to follow the Court's decisions even if they are unhappy with those decisions. They are, in other words, to comply at least until efforts have been made within other political arenas, like the legislature, to reverse the decision, or within the judiciary itself to bring about reversal. That some individuals, including government officials, made no effort to comply with decisions even while seeking reversal through recognized channels brought attention to the matter of compliance and noncompliance. Because the decisions involved, like the school desegregation cases, were often liberal in thrust, and the values of those studying the court to a large extent were parallel, while the values of the noncompliers were clearly different, the researchers' values reinforced concern with noncompliance.

Their concern with noncompliance led to the study of areas where the phenomenon seemed greatest. Those areas were ones, such as school desegregation, involving much social change, affecting large proportions of public officials—e.g., police procedure—or directly involving important symbolic values, like school prayer. As Barth (1968: 313) has noted, "The opposition generated by unpopular decisions involving symbolic values. . .is usually more diffuse and latent than the opposition generated by unpopular economic decisions like those of the 1930s." Researchers thus probably found more, and more diffuse, noncompliance than if a fuller range of subject-matter areas, including economic policy, had been examined. However, attention to areas of greater noncompliance allowed more ready identification of factors affecting impact, even if providing an incomplete picture of their relative weights.

Another limitation to what we have thus far done in impact analysis is our concentration on the effects of decisions without relating the results to the process by which they occur—even though one might classify impact studies as part of a "process approach" to public law matters. Thus, as Wells and Grossman (1966: 287) comment, "The major emphasis [of impact studies] was upon the problem of implementation, rather than upon relating the process with the resultant policy." In short, although process is recognized in that it is known that what the court does is followed by action elsewhere or that what the courts do follows action in other political arenas, we have concentrated on what comes out of the pipeline rather than dealing in addition with what goes on in the pipeline or how the pipeline affects the product.

Material on impact, explicit and implicit, needs to be pulled together and integrated. Much of what exists is based on case studies of the effect of particular decisions in individual jurisdictions. Although we have been warned to concentrate on the process by which impact occurs and not just on the final result, we still need more case studies. But we need them concerning a wide range of subjects and a variety of affected areas. We particularly need before-and-after studies; the fact that most impact studies have been carried out "after the fact" has contributed to our lack of understanding. If we could conduct before-and-after impact studies, we might be able to obtain a picture of change (or nonchange) less contaminated by reaction to a decision that is possible with after-only studies. Difficulties in carrying out before-and-after studies arise because one is not likely to know a priori where impact will take place, so that one could conduct a survey for the "before" part of a study. If one could find an area where it was not known what the Supreme Court was considering, and if one could determine that people in that area would react to the decision, one might be able to overcome this. Otherwise, some reconstruction is possible from newspapers or from studies undertaken for other reasons, such as the American Bar Foundation studies of police practices (LaFave, 1965; Newman, 1966), community power structures studies, or even constitutional history.[2]

Although some volumes utilizing designs of vastly increased sophistication have recently appeared (for example, Johnson, 1967; Muir, 1967), we are not generally ready for studies based on elaborate, methodologically advanced research designs. The methodological difficulties confronting us are substantial. Before we become too pleased with ourselves for having come this far, we should seriously note Krislov's (1968: 166) warning:

> Impact studies present grave problems in research and require vast resources seldom available. Even conceptually, the problem of impact measurement presents grave difficulties hardly resolved by the usual efforts at studying the immediate aftermath of some dramatic event or decision. (Even the most careful study cannot establish whether alleged changes were not merely coincidentally but actually consequentially related.). . . Normal approaches [such as public opinion surveys], though excellent research strategies, not only provide limited information, but also require extensive and expensive efforts from researchers.

Keeping this in mind, we should seek to improve the quality of our impact studies. But that goal exists primarily as a step toward another more important one—the building of theory concerning the judicial process and the role of courts and law in the political system.

With this history and these strictures in mind, we can proceed to the principal portion of this paper where we deal with conceptualization and measurement problems connected with the study of impact. The intention is to be suggestive of the types of problems which have been encountered; certainly the presentation is not exhaustive, in part because it is expected that many more problems will be encountered as we move beyond our present relatively elementary state and as further studies are carried out.

Problems of Conceptualization and Measurement

"Impact," "compliance," "effect," "aftermath," "evasion"—all are words one hears in discussing the Supreme Court. Despite the number of "impact studies" which have now been carried out, there has been insufficient grappling with the meaning of concepts like compliance and impact. This lack of attention leads directly to confusion and disagreement about the Supreme Court's place in the American political system.

When we begin to talk about what happens after the Supreme Court decides a case, we are initially talking about aftermath—that is, events which occur after the decision. However, we do not wish to examine the entire aftermath of Supreme Court decisions; many constitutional historians have already written about this material, and their work need not be repeated. When we talk about aftermath, we are not necessarily talking about events affected by the decision, although we may leave the incorrect impression that the Supreme Court is in some way a cause of that aftermath, thus committing the fallacy of post hoc ergo propter hoc. We do not want to fall into the trap of claiming that because B follows A, A causes B. For example, after ex parte Bakelite Corp. (1929), in which the Court declared that the Court of Customs Appeals was a legislative rather than a constitutional court, Congress declared it and other legislative courts to be constitutional courts (an action subsequently confirmed by the Supreme Court in Glidden v. Zdanok [1962]). From that bare statement of facts alone, one could *not* assert that it was *because* of Bakelite that Congress so acted, even though that might seem a likely inference. We need more evidence before aftermath becomes impact. For example, the lapse of time (more than twenty years) between Bakelite and congressional action would tend to negate our "likely inference."

If the term aftermath is too broad, what then? Impact and compliance are the two terms most important for our work; evasion is a special term subsidiary to the others. We may begin by asserting that there is a difference between *impact* and *compliance*. Political scientists' concern has been largely with the latter. Perhaps this was in part because some types of compliance, and particularly noncompliance, could be easily seen. However, to separate the impact or effect of a Supreme Court decision from other factors in the political milieu producing the same phenomena was a matter of considerable difficulty. By comparison with impact, compliance narrows our focus, restricting us to finding out to what degree a specific decision is obeyed. ("Decision" might mean the mandate of the Court with respect to specific named individuals, or it might mean the Court's holding in a case.) If we are interested in complaince, we would want to know, for instance, whether the University of Florida Law School ever admitted Virgil Hawkins (Florida ex rel Hawkins v. Board of Control, 1954),[3] or whether schools were desegregated after Brown or legislatures reapportioned on the basis of one man-one vote after Reynolds v. Sims (1964). In dealing with "complaince," we are clearly interested in something narrower than the total impact of the decision, and to use one where we mean the other will not assist our work.

> Supreme Court rulings . . . may invoke a range of responses. To use the term "compliance" to characterize this process is rather unfortunate, for this seems to suggest a single approved response to a court ruling. In certain instances, to be sure, such a view would be entirely satisfactory. [Johnson, 1967: 23]

Compliance brings a narrower focus than does impact, but is not separate from it; compliance is a subset of impact. Using compliance does not, however, provide much relief from the measurement problems which afflict the determination of impact which we shall discuss later. If, as Petrick (1968: 7) argues, "The problem of noncompliance arises from the fact that human groups find it difficult to carry out effectively acts for which they have no underlying beliefs," then attitudes and beliefs, and particularly the matter of intent, must be taken into account in our examination of what happens with Court decisions after their issuance. In talking about impact, we can say that a decision had such-and-such an impact or effect, even on people who had no knowledge of or feeling about the decision; we can try to make judgments about impact on the basis of people's observable behavior. With compliance, however, we need to know whether or not they knew about the case and their intent with respect to it. "Whether the actions of other participants in the political process represent compliance with or evasion of Court decisions can only be determined after it is established that they were cognizant of the judicial policy" (Barth, 1968: 315).

A person's behavior may be congruent with what the Court has ordered, but it may be he is operating parallel to the court's line of action, rather than operating *in order to carry out* that order. Perhaps he was going to do anyway what the Court ordered. In these instances, the behavior is what the Court requires, but it is not carried out because the Court required it. Compliance requires the latter, and implies a feeling that one ought to obey a decision. "An individual may sense that a law is just but violate it nonetheless (i.e., one should not confuse violation of a law with a 'rejection' of it); and individuals may conform to a law even though they view the law as unjust" (Gibbs, 1968: 436-437). Or, as Feest (1968: 448) argues with respect to other types of legal regulations:

> Compliance . . . is more than outward conformity with a regulation. Behavior which externally (objectively) conforms with a certain regulation may not coincide with internal (subjective) intention to conform. . . . The concept of compliance has . . . three essential elements: (a) norm-awareness, (b) intention to conform, and (c) conforming behavior.

Compliance may thus exist even when disrespect for the law or the Court is being expressed, as was the case with most begrudging obedience with Brown v. Board of Education. In fact, the existence of complaints (except insofar as they are a cover-up) coupled with behavior fitting the prescriptions of the Court might be taken as a clear indication that compliance is occurring. We might, however, want to give a specific title to situations where people obey a ruling while trying to change or reverse it. "Reversal behavior" might be an appropriate label.

Supreme Court Authority

Why people comply raises the question of the Court's *authority,* the basis on which people accept its decisions as ones which the Court has a *right* to give, and which they, for that reason, ought to obey. Bases for that authority might include: a formal allocation of power to the Court to decide constitutionality; the Court's expertise; the formal setting in which the Court operates, which evokes respect; charismatic leadership of some judges; people's need for some body or institution which can confine conflict and thus fulfill security needs (Petrick, 1968). The Court's authority is related to the legitimacy people grant it. But using compliance as a measure of legitimacy does not carry our analysis very far. Petrick has recently asserted that the final test of the Supreme Court's legitimacy is compliance with its decisions, particularly important because the Court lacks other legitimating devices like the ballot box. He says that we measure state and local government reaction to Supreme Court decisions in terms of *behavioral* compliance or noncompliance. But how does one know from examining behavior to what extent the Court is considered legitimate? Perhaps a complete failure to attempt compliance would indicate nonlegitimacy, but what about token compliance? Petrick says it may indicate only nonapproval rather than nonlegitimacy. And if noncompliance does not necessarily mean non-legitimacy, but perhaps only nonapproval of a particular decision, has one gone very far?

Petrick (1968: 7) also argues that if "compliance gradually and ultimately replaces non-compliance, it would appear that acceptance of the Court's authority is superseding disapproval of the decision." Perhaps—but perhaps people's views toward the subject matter of the case itself have changed. Does increased compliance with Brown v. Board of Education mean that those people who first resisted the decision now love the Court? Not necessarily, any more than that the same compliance means greater feelings of brotherhood toward members of other races. Perhaps the compliers have accepted the necessity, for political reasons, for reasons of accepting federal funds, of allowing Negroes to attend school with whites; perhaps they are just resigned to the situation. But neither of these latter alternatives means greater legitimacy granted the Court.

Evasion and Instrumental Noncompliance

When we talk about compliance, we know there is noncompliance. But there is also a shadowy something called evasion, somewhere between outright acceptance and outright refusal to comply. How do we identify it? Some forms are relatively easy to distinguish. People attempt to limit the scope of the decision, to avoid its full force, to make sure it doesn't apply to them. They do not say they will not conform or comply but try to avoid a situation where that would become an issue.[4] Sometimes this is made easy by the Court. If there has been a procedural defect which the Court has invalidated, it may be quite possible for affected officials to achieve the same ends by altering their procedures only slightly, thus making the protection which the Court has appeared to give meaningless, other than as a statement of principle. For example, in Gardner v. Broderick (1968), the Court held that a policeman cannot be discharged for refusing to waive immunity. But if he can be discharged for refusal to answer questions concerning his official conduct, does this decision make much difference to him? It does preserve his Fifth Amendment rights, but means being out of a job even without being prosecuted. Similarly, in Garrity v. New Jersey (1967), the Court held that testimony compelled under threat of loss of job was not admissible in criminal proceedings; thus an officer might testify and lose his job, with only the satisfaction, if it can be called that, of not being prosecuted. Again, in terms of employment, there is little effect.

What should we say when we find state officials persisting in trying to develop a statute or regulations which the Supreme Court will uphold, after the Court has struck down earlier regulations? After Freedman v. Maryland (1965), procedures in a number of jurisdictions were revised to bring them under the Court's new requirements; not all such attempts were initially successful, but there were efforts made. Shall we say that this is evasion or avoidance, or that it is compliant behavior because the individuals involved were trying to mesh their interests/goals/values with what the Court will allow, and sincerely want to do something the Court will find acceptable? Or is the only action we can call compliance in such a situation the total absence of laws which do not exactly resemble the procedural requirements established by the Court in the Freedman case? Certainly even unsuccessful attempts to being oneself within the rulings of the Court are different from the situation in which the Louisiana legislature, at the time of the New Orleans school desegregation crisis, modified statutes only slightly after they were struck down, as part of a continuing battle with the courts to avoid the force of school desegregation orders. But how do we judge? Apparently we must examine motive and intent in making our determination.

Another difficulty in interpretation is created by the fact that some noncompliance is meant to be a grounds for bargaining within the larger political system, that is, it is *instrumental.* "The zone of acceptance is a consequence of either tacit or direct bargaining and thus is by no means an independent variable" (Krislov, 1963: 11). Political leaders may feel that if they refuse to grant immediate complaince to the Court's orders, they can gain some ends perhaps not related directly to the subject matter of the cases. The gains they seek may be within the states. Governor Faubus' attempt to prevent desegregation in Little Rock, coming as it did when he was about to face an election contest, may be explained in part as a maneuver for popularity among certain elements in the electorate. The gains may, on the other hand, be at the national level, particularly in Congress. When the national government does not present a united front, instrumental noncompliance is a temptation or meaningful alternative to the state politician. If the person with whom it is hoped a bargain can be struck realizes that the noncomplier must give in eventually, the attempt to bargain by delaying compliance may misfire. On the other hand, if the national official wishes to have the program implemented quickly, he may be willing to compromise or to make concessions in other areas to get his way.

Another Concept: Impact

In recent years, we have seen a shift from concern about the narrower concept, compliance, to the broader one, impact; at least we find the latter studied in addition to the former. The shift in emphasis has not reduced the conceptualization or measurement problems facing students of the judicial process, as we shall soon see, nor has it meant that political scientists have changed their assumptions about what should happen after the Court decides a case. They are still affected by an expectation that decisions of the Supreme Court will have some effect, and find it difficult to accept the possible irrelevance of decisions, or the relatively small role they may play in what occurs after the Court has spoken. If something like school desegregation depends as heavily on the character and structure of the community and on the community's elites as some have suggested (Crain, 1968), the Court's decisions may not mean very much beyond having served as catalysts or sparks for action—but that is a matter for research.

One of the prime difficulties in dealing with impact is that the decisions of the Supreme Court are part of a general milieu in which later events take place and part of a set of multiple causes of such events. If several factors are operating in the same direction, how does one separate the impact the Court's decision has by comparison with other elements of the situation? Schmidhauser (1958: 161) raises the question of how one avoids overstating the influence of a single institution like the Court "upon so complex a social and political development as federal centralization." How does one determine whether companies have taken the Supreme Court's cases on restraint of trade into consideration in determining trade practices, unless corporation officials will talk honestly about the subject? If a proposed merger takes a given form, how does one tell what role economic considerations played as contrasted with consideration of legal matters, including both Supreme Court decisions and advice of counsel as to the likelihood of action by the Department of Justice? When trying to judge the impact of the Court's decisions on government regulation of the economy, how does one separate the effects of those decisions from the "natural" growth of the economy and the existence of economic forms like the corporation? Arthur Miller (1968: 81, 131), writing on the American economy, carries the point further and argues that the Court, "rather than being the *cause* of constitutional change, is the *instrument*" of such change by its updating of the Constitution, enabling the document "to remain relevant and current."[5] Had the Court not done this, he asserts, it would have been swept aside. He thus suggests that the Court's impact on the economy is "in the immortal words of Senator Everett McKinley Dirksen, about like that of 'a snowflake wafting down upon the bosom of the mighty Potomac' " (Miller, 1968: 82).

There is, despite Miller's seeming clarity, considerable difficulty with what he says. How does one distinguish between the Court's being a cause and its being an instrument of social change? Even if one avoids one extreme, of assuming the Court to have a direct, unilateral, independent, and immediate effect, it is difficult to come to the opposite conclusion that the Court simply *reflects* what is going on in the society, economy, or polity. Miller (1968: 82) himself says, "Doubtless [the Court] does have some power and does wield some influence over the shape of events." At a minimum, if the Court is in political interaction with other actors, the influence relationship is reciprocal, with the Court affecting others as well as others affecting the Court. Perhaps we can only arrive at the Scotch verdict, "not proved," rather than Miller's stronger assertions about lack of impact.

In talking about Brown v. Board of Education, how much of what has happened with respect to school desegregation in the South does one attribute to the "changing South," to the economic and social changes which accompanied Brown, and how much to Brown itself? To pursue Brown a bit further, how can one determine if Brown has had an effect on movement of whites from the central cities of metropolitan areas to the suburbs? General population movement occurred during the period of Brown and its aftermath, even in Southern cities where segregation in the schools continued. But can one infer from this that Brown did not have any impact on that movement? How is one to tell whether the movement might have been in anticipation of ultimate compliance with Brown, or whether Brown may have reinforced a preexisting desire to move to the suburbs? In order to provide even a preliminary test, one would need year-by-year mobility rates for the pre-Brown as well as the post-Brown years, with the latter divided into precompliance and postcompliance years by area, as well as data from some cities with long-standing desegregation (or at least pre-Brown desegregation) for control purposes. One can easily see that obtaining this data would pose considerable problems.

Data on Impact

There are some questions of impact about which data may not be as difficult to obtain. For example, to test the effect of Supreme Court decisions on the level of litigation, one could examine lower-court dockets to determine how many cases have been filed dealing with the subject of a Supreme Court case. Or one could determine requests for certiorari dealing with a given subject. One could also look at the records of a particular organization, like the NAACP, to see if its activities in the field of litigation increased after a court victory. Although these would not provide perfect indicators of impact, they would give substantial evidence on the matter.

Perhaps we can identify situations where the Court's actions have had no relevance, and thus decrease the universe of phenomena at which we look. It is important to isolate the proportions of instances where cases do and do not have impact. This is one situation where negative findings–i.e., that there is no impact–are of extreme importance. Thus to study an area in contemplation of possible impact and to find no impact is an important finding in itself. After this sorting-out process, however, we are still left with situations in which it is unclear whether the Court's decisions did have an effect, and with others where it is fairly clear that there was some effect, but how much or of what kind is not certain. In this connection, it may help to look at the matter of relative rates: some activity may persist after a Supreme Court decision, seemingly indicating no impact, but the rate or intensity of activity may be slowed or advanced. The growth of the "positive state" was not prevented by the Court's striking down attempts at economic regulation, but that does not mean the decisions were without effect, at least on the pace of that growth. To consider only instances where behavior or policy is completely reversed after a Court decision is to limit study of impact unnecessarily. But we must be careful, because there is a "discontinuous reception given Supreme Court decisions" (Miller and Scheflin, 1967: 288), reducing the number of possible instances where we might find a test of impact.

Not all impacts of court decisions are direct. We may be able to talk about the direct effect a Supreme Court decision has on a lower-court judge. But if we are talking about the impact on government officials in local communities, or on "the public," we need to consider both direct impact and indirect impact. This latter phenomenon occurs when the Court's decision has an effect on some officials, who have an effect on others, who in turn finally have an effect on the local community, which may or may not even realize that what is occurring is resulting from the Supreme Court's initial action. These second-order effects of a

Court decision—reactions of those affected by government agencies on which the Court's decision may first fall—may be greater or clearer than the decision's direct effects. If an agency adjusts its policy or procedure to comply, some disfavored clients will complain; if an agency persists in the face of directives to change, as apparently has occurred with the Patent Office (Shapiro, 1968: 143-226), those wishing the changes ordered by the Supreme Court will react negatively.

The difficulties of separating the impact of the Court's decisions from other factors influencing a given outcome may mean we can isolate impact effectively only where there is direct and obvious (visible) resistance to a Court decision, and that the only impact we can study precisely is clear noncompliance. Part of the problem of determining impact is that we often do not have a test of whether the Court's decision is having an effect. For example, if the public holds parents to a higher standard with respect to the behavior of their children than does the law, how do we know that the law is even relevant? Would we have to say that the only impact in that situation would be a change in public attitude so that only that which the law allowed was considered acceptable? If we note cases in which the Supreme Court has defined the jurisdiction of certain agencies broadly through statutory interpretation, what can we say when the agencies are cautious and do not utilize the full jurisdiction the courts allow?[6] Do we say there is no impact, or that the impact is that the decision is irrelevant, or that the Court has not been successful in getting others to accept what it says is possible?

The Role of Power in Court Decisions

If we do try to go beyond obvious instances of direct noncompliance, we get into matters involving the concept of power, a concept which, despite its centrality for political science, still lacks clear conceptualization. Power involves one actor moving another actor against his will, from passivity to an act or from one act already intended to another act. It may also involve keeping a person from an intended shift in position. If A wants X done, and B does it, one is tempted to say that A has power with respect to B.[7] But this is not really an adequate operationalization. If A wants something done and B may have done it anyhow, or may already be moving in the direction of doing it, we cannot say that A has power with respect to B. On the other hand, it may not be necessary for A to want something done before we can talk about his having power; if B decided to do something because he *thought* A wanted it done, A might have power even if A had not communicated any orders or suggestions. We see this when actors comply with Court rulings before specific enforcement orders are issued, or when they interpret a case as applying to them in advance of such application. This explains why Cardozo said that the power of the Supreme

Court is not measured solely by the number of times it is exercised. This anticipatory effect also leads to restrictions upon or avoidance of the Court, as well as compliance. Thus, because of rumors the Court would strike down Reconstruction, the House Judiciary Committee reported a bill requiring two-thirds concurrence when a law of Congress was struck down. More recently, the Post Office often mooted cases involving restrictions on receipt of mail when an irate individual threatened to go to court, in order to avoid a Supreme Court ruling on its practices of holding mail.[8]

Some feel we must include in a definition of power the communication of A's desire to B, after which, for power to exist, B would have to do something he would not otherwise have done. However, A may engineer a situation, implied in the term manipulation, so that B does A's bidding without any direct communication or feeling of being coerced. However, the Supreme Court may be less able than other governmental bodies to structure situations in this fashion because it is not able to retain continuous surveillance of cases once they leave the Court's hands. The foregoing implies that, to obtain a clear measurement of power, one must know the intent of actors, at least the intent of those acted upon, just as one must know intent in order to measure compliance as some have defined it.

In measuring the Court's power, one may start with measures which utilize only visible activity. However, even though relatively "hard," such measures are defective because they both go too far and are too limited. They go too far because they include situations in which an actor was already going to do what the Court requires, and they are too limited because they do not include situations in which no behavioral change occurs because the Court has prevented an individual from shifting his position. Therefore, measures of behavioral change or lack of change must be coupled with knowledge of intent, precisely the matter most difficult to uncover. With respect to historical examples, we obviously cannot find many of the actors so that we might inquire about their intent. Even when actors are available, we would be likely to ask them only after a Court decision has occurred, thus allowing them to rationalize their acts and to adjust their responses to what they have already done. Even if we were to ask them before a relevant decision were handed down, their intent might be affected by the expectation of possible rulings and adjustment they had made in their behavior based on anticipation of the Court's ruling in a given direction.

Measuring Impact

If it is so difficult to ascertain intent, are we left without the possibility of studying impact? At least in the short run, the answer would appear to be no, because there is still much we can learn by depicting thoroughly what appears to have occurred in the aftermath of court decisions, in tracing out the consequences of Court action to the best of our ability in a far more systematic way than we have done heretofore. What can we use as measures? Where do we begin to look? For example, do we measure the impact of the school desegregation decisions in terms of the percentage of Negro students attending classes in previously all-white schools? Or in terms of the percentage of school districts with some Negroes in integrated classes? Or in terms of the movement of whites to the suburbs from the core cities of metropolitan areas? In the area of criminal procedure, does one look at impact of decisions in terms of alleged increases in the crime rate? In terms of the number of cases which go to trial? In terms of convictions obtained? In terms of changes in police methods? In terms of the growth of interest groups, e.g., of policemen, which arise in opposition to the decisions? Or in terms of the number of cases brought to the courts to test the applicability of what the Supreme Court has declared? An easy but unsatisfying answer for the present is that perhaps all of these, individually or in combination, might be legitimate operationalizations.

There are additional measures. One might be the frequency with which a court decision is mentioned. "When the constitutionality of policy proposals is under discussion, one may expect frequent references to relevant Supreme Court cases" (Wasby, 1968: 102). Because less frequent mention might be expected from nonlawyer policy makers and by lay members of interested publics than from lawyers, "A possible measure of the scope of the impact of Supreme Court opinions would be the frequency with which the opinions were mentioned outside courts and among nonlawyers, particularly by members of 'attentive publics.' " One type of mention received by certain Court opinions is that they do not provide enough guidance for lower-court judges or lawyers dealing with the subject. What such complaints mean, however, is not clear. While it may simply be an escape to or excuse for policy otherwise preferred, it might also mean that the complainers would comply if given the opportunity and the guidance; one simply cannot tell from the complaints themselves.

One can use numbers of those affected as a measure of impact. But if, with regard to school desegregation, one does use the percentage of Negro students attending classes in previously all-white schools, some questions are still unanswered. The percentage involved is usually quite small and is often cited with dismay by those who see it. Robert Crain (1968: 357), however, points out that those militating for school desegregation often cease their efforts when the numbers of Negro students added to previously all-white schools are quite small, perhaps indicating a preference for a symbolic rather than a numerical gain. This, of course, suggests a different basis for evaluation. One also has the difficulty of ascertaining how many Negro parents want their children going to school in previously all-white schools. Apart from the intimidation of those parents which occurs, there may be some who do not wish their children to be involved, or to be among the first. If one is to include them in figuring the base for percentage of Negro children in desegregated schools, one may not obtain a precise picture of impact—certainly one would not obtain the same picture as if they were excluded from one's count. To be sure, the percentage of all Negro students in desegregated schools (figured on the largest base[9]) is quite important if one wants to know to what extent the *values* discussed by the justices in Brown have been implemented, a crucial matter regardless of the wishes of the parents involved. But even this suggests again that what one means by impact may require asking different questions under different circumstances.

Even if one solves the problem of calculating the percentage of students now in desegregated schools, one might want to know other items concerning compliance with Brown. What, for example, are the problems after desegregation occurs? Is there social segregation within the schools, or does desegregation occur there and perhaps extend to children's activities after school hours? Has there been restriction of faculty and student freedom of speech on the subject? The point is that it is important to know *where* to look in determining measurements.

Some Other Considerations in Measurement

To return to the matter of the proportionate amount of impact, one must recognize that there may be only a few jurisdictions in which a Court decision, even a doctrinally important one, can have a specific effect on individuals. Although we must keep in mind the difference between class actions, on behalf of the plaintiff "and all other similarly situated," and cases brought only on behalf of a single plaintiff, if a case rule can be used in only a small number of cases, the impact is limited. Examples include some of the Supreme Court's criminal procedure rulings of the 1960s, because the procedure involved occurred in only a single state, as was true with both denial of right to jury (Duncan v. Louisiana, 1968) and courtroom television (Estes v. Texas, 1965), or because some states were already in compliance with rules the Supreme Court incorporated in the Fourteenth Amendment. Other cases with a limited effect include the Penn Central Merger and N and W Inclusion Cases (1968), which affected immediately only the railroads involved in the merger. Although the case might also have the more diffuse effect of encouraging mergers, the number of corporations existing which could be covered by the case was relatively small. The Permian Basin Area Rate Cases (1968) directly affected only one major national government agency and a limited number of corporations involved in the rate-setting proceedings, although other possible effects—for example, on administrative proceedings generally—might radiate from the case.

In dealing with the measurement of impact, we must inject the notion of *time* into our study. Where in time does one look for impact? One must be careful. All impact is not immediate. There may be a lag before those affected even know about a decision, much less have time to react to it. One must be careful to distinguish between resistance to the Supreme Court's ruling and the general slowness of the system to respond. Even when officials know of cases and agree that implementation should occur, it may be unrealistic to expect immediate full compliance, particularly where bureaucratic machinery must be altered. The speed of reaction may also depend on how people feel about a decision. Thus, when people approve of a decision, there may be no immediate need for them to act. Follow-up action may be necessary to nail down a decision, but it may await possible voluntary compliance by others. On the other hand, those opposed are more likely to feel compelled to react promptly rather than leave an impression of compliance by nonaction. However, these individuals may change their minds later; that is, we can distinguish between immediate emotional opposition and "sober second thought," as in the case of the Congressman who sponsored, but later withdrew, a resolution opposing the prayer decisions. After time has passed following a decision, the "parade of horribles" which some have felt would come from the decision may not have occurred, and tempers may cool. Thus Murphy (1962: 238) noted, with respect to critics of the Supreme Court's decisions on internal security in the 1950s, that "after several years of living with decisions like *Mallory; Nelson; Yates;* and *Cole v. Young,* a crisis in law enforcement had not developed, nor had packs of Communists descended on the country or infested government employment."

Just as all impact is not immediate, some impact may also continue for a long time, and long-run effects may be greater than short-run effects, although the long-run effects of many decisions are nil, particularly in the economic area, because social forces outrun what the Court has done. Kelly and Harbison (1955: 229) have noted that Marbury v. Madison (1803), which established judicial review, was an example of a case the implications of which were not clear at the time it was decided. "Marshall's argument in favor of the Court's power to declare an act of Congress void was not of major significance at the time he made it." Similarly, the convictions upheld in Gitlow v. New York (1925) had far less importance than the decision's impact through the incorporation of the First Amendment's protections for speech and press in the Fourteenth Amendment.

Time may be important because intervening events may be necessary before a decision is implemented. For example, there was a long lag between decision and action with respect to United States v. Standard Oil Co. (1947), where the Court held there was no recovery by the government under the concept of allocating a cause of action to the master for injury to his servant. The government withdrew a number of suits similar to Standard Oil which were pending at the time of that decision, and Congress did not fill the statutory void left by the case. Only after the General Accounting Office showed in 1960 that substantial sums of money could be recovered and were being recovered by those agencies which were acting under their power to issue regulations to that effect, did Congress respond with the Federal Medical Care Recovery Act of 1963 (Noone, 1969: 259-261).

In dealing with impact in relation to time, one can designate an arbitrary cutoff point or talk in terms of immediate impact, that is, obvious changes clearly resulting from a decision or attributed to it, recognizing that the longer the time after a decision, the broader (in more areas) and thinner (less immediate and powerful) the impact. However, it is useful to consider long-run as well as short-run effects. The range of possible effects can be shown as follows: There are immediate impacts, as of case X at point t_1, indicated by (1). Some decisions have no impact; they are never received or heard of, as noted by (2), and as far as impact is concerned, we may say they have aborted. Some blend in with the political milieu, noted at (3). As we proceed through time, there are other decisions (X' and X") which have their impacts, at points t_2 and t_4, noted at (4) and (6) respectively. Our initial case, X, has some long-range effects, for example, note points t_3 and t_5, at (5) and (7). The further one proceeds in time, the more one encounters a problem in distinguishing the impact of the case from other factors and from the impact of other cases on the political environment.

It should be stressed again that the relationship between the Supreme Court and the political environment is not unidirectional. Thus Supreme Court cases lay the groundwork for later cases, in at least two senses: one, a case will spawn additional cases aimed at clarification or extension; and, two, the impact of a case on the environment perhaps changes the environment in such a way that conflicts resulting in cases are produced. The Supreme Court receives feedback from its decisions (represented by the broken-line arrows), which may affect what the Court subsequently does. Thus the impact *of* the Court has an impact *on* the Court.

There is no conclusion to be reached from what has been presented here. We have looked at the way in which the study of the impact of Supreme Court decisions has progressed and have dealt with a number of conceptual and methodological aspects of the subject. It is hoped that this presentation will provide a jumping-off point for those interested in moving us further along the path toward greater knowledge of impact and the judicial process.

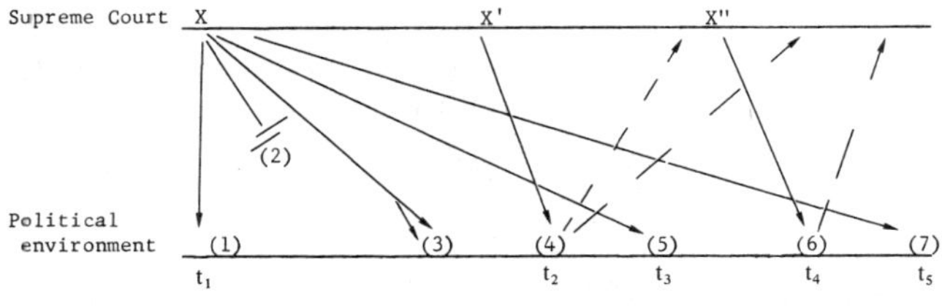

Figure 1.

NOTES

1. This is in line with the "consumer perspective" on the law advocated by the late Edmond Cahn; he contrasted this with an "official perspective" of the "processors" of the law (Cahn, 1966: 21).

2. The amount of material in Warren (1922) is quite substantial. See also Kelly and Harbison (1955).

3. The set of decisions which followed is presented in Murphy and Pritchett, 1961: 606-618.

4. Blaustein and Ferguson distinguish between "avoidance," comparable to "evasion" here, and "evasion," which is noncompliance.

> There are no constitutional limitations to measures of "avoidance." It is perfectly proper–at least as far as the courts are concerned–for an individual or a state full of individuals to attempt to "avoid" the consequences of desegregation. "Evasion," on the other hand, is against the law. [Blaustein and Ferguson, 1957: 240-241]

5. His distinction is like that made by Sidney Hook (1943) between the "Event-Making" and "Event-ful" Man.

6. See Fainsod et al. (1959: 502) for a discussion of the Federal Trade Commission and the Supreme Court's trade regulation cases.

7. The following discussion draws on "On the Operationalization of 'Power' and 'Class' " in Wasby (1970: 81-84).

8. However, the department's regulations were invalidated by the Supreme Court in Lamont v. Postmaster General (1965), in which the Court made clear that such efforts to block a case would not be allowed to prevent a ruling on the relevant regulation.

9. Nagel (1969: 10) reminds us we should use "as a percentage base only those school districts that have some schoolage Negro children and some schoolage white children." However, if districts have been established so as to reinforce segregation, perhaps this suggestion should not be followed.

CASES

Ex parte BAKELITE CORP. (1929) 279 U.S. 438.
BROWN v. BOARD OF EDUCATION OF TOPEKA (1954) 347 U.S. 483; 349 U.S. 294.
COLE v. YOUNG (1956) 351 U.S. 536.
DUNCAN v. LOUISIANA (1968) 391 U.S. 145.
ESTES v. TEXAS (1965) 381 U.S. 532.

FLORIDA ex rel. HAWKINS v. BOARD OF CONTROL (1954) 347 U.S. 971.
FREEDMAN v. MARYLAND (1965) 380 U.S. 51.
GARDNER v. BRODERICK (1968) 392 U.S. 273.
GARRITY v. NEW JERSEY (1967) 385 U.S. 493.
GITLOW v. NEW YORK (1925) 268 U.S. 652.

GLIDDEN v. ZDANOK (1962) 370 U.S. 530.
LAMONT v. POSTMASTER GENERAL (1965) 381 U.S. 301.
MALLORY v. UNITED STATES (1957) 354 U.S. 449.

MARBURY v. MADISON (1803) 1 Cranch 137.
NELSON AND GLOBE v. LOS ANGELES (1960) 362 U.S. 1.
PENN CENTRAL MERGER AND N AND W INCLUSION CASES (1968) 389 U.S. 486.
PERMIAN BASIN AREA RATE CASES (1968) 390 U.S. 747.
REYNOLDS v. SIMS (1964) 377 U.S. 533.

ROTH v. UNITED STATES (1957) 354 U.S. 476.
UNITED STATES v. STANDARD OIL CO. (1947) 332 U.S. 301.
YATES v. UNITED STATES (1957) 354 U.S. 298.

REFERENCES

BARTH, T. (1968) "Perception and acceptance of Supreme Court decisions at the state and local level." J. of Public Law 17 (June): 308-350.

BECKER, T. (1969) The Impact of Supreme Court Decisions: Empirical Studies. New York: Oxford Univ. Press.

BLAUSTEIN, A. and C. C. FERGUSON, Jr. (1957) Desegregation and the Law: The Meaning and Effect of the School Desegregation Cases. New Brunswick, N.J.: Rutgers Univ. Press.

CAHN, E. (1966) "Law in the consumer perspective," in L. Cahn (ed.) Confronting Injustice: The Edmond Cahn Reader. Boston: Little, Brown.

CRAIN, R. (1968) The Politics of School Desegregation: Comparative Case Studies of Community Structure and Policy-making. Chicago: Aldine.

FAINSOD, L., L. GORDON, and J. C. PALAMOUNTAIN, Jr. (1959) Government and the American Economy. New York: W. W. Norton.

FEEST, J. (1968) "Compliance with legal regulations: observation of stop sign behavior." Law and Society Rev. 2 (May): 447-461.

GIBBS, J. P. (1968) "Definitions of law and empirical questions." Law and Society Rev. 2 (May): 429-446.

HOOK, S. (1943) The Hero in History. New York: John Day.

JOHNSON, R. (1967) The Dynamics of Compliance. Evanston: Northwestern Univ. Press.

JONES E. M. (1966) "Impact research and sociology of law: some tentative proposals." Wisconsin Law Rev. 1 (Spring): 331-339.

KELLY, A. and W. HARBISON (1955) The American Constitution: Its Origins and Development. New York: W. W. Norton.

KRISLOV, S. (1968) The Supreme Court and Political Freedom. New York: Free Press.

--- (1963) "The perimeters of power: patterns of compliance and opposition to Supreme Court decisions." Presented to the American Political Science Association.

LaFAVE, W. (1965) Arrest: The Decision to Take a Suspect into Custody. Boston: Little, Brown.

MASSELL, G. (1968) "Law as an instrument of revolutionary change in a traditional milieu: the case of Soviet Central Asia." Law and Society Rev. 2 (February): 179-228.

MILLER, A. S. (1968) The Supreme Court and American Capitalism. New York: Free Press.

--- and A. W. SCHEFLIN (1967) "The power of the Supreme Court in the age of the positive state." Duke Law J. 1967 (April): 273-320.

MUIR, W. K., Jr. (1967) Prayer in the Public Schools: Law and Attitude Change. Chicago: Univ. of Chicago Press.

MURPHY, W. (1962) Congress and the Court. Chicago: Univ. of Chicago Press.

--- and C. H. PRITCHETT [eds.] (1961) Courts, Judges, and Politics: An Introduction to the Judicial Process. New York: Random House.

NAGEL, S. (forthcoming) The Effects of Alternative Legal Policies.

--- (1969) The Legal Process from a Behavioral Perspective. Homewood, Ill.: Dorsey.

NEWMAN, D. (1966) Conviction: The Determination of Guilt or Innocence without Trial. Boston: Little, Brown.

NOONE, M. F. (1969) "Federal Medical Care Recovery Act." Amer. Bar Assn. J. 55 (March): 259-261.

PETRICK, M. J. (1968) "The Supreme Court and authority acceptance." Western Pol. Q. 21 (March): 5-19.

SCHMIDHAUSER, J. (1958) The Supreme Court as Final Arbiter in Federal-State Relations, 1789-1957. Chapel Hill: Univ. of North Carolina Press.

SHAPIRO, M. (1968) The Supreme Court and Administrative Agencies. New York: Free Press.

WARREN, C. (1922) The Supreme Court in United States History. Boston: Little, Brown.

WASBY, S. (1970) Political Science: the Discipline and its Dimensions. New York: Charles Scribner.

--- (1968) "The pure and the prurient: the Supreme Court, obscenity and Oregon policy," in D. Everson (ed.) The Supreme Court as Policy-maker: Three Studies on the Impact of Judicial Decisions. Carbondale: Public Affairs Research Bureau, Southern Illinois University.

WELLS, R. and J. GROSSMAN (1966) "The concept of judicial policy-making." J. of Public Law 15, 2: 286-310.

Part Two

SOCIALIZATION AT THE PERSONAL AND GROUP LEVELS

Chapter 7

Adolescent Perspectives on Law and Government

JOSEPH ADELSON – *University of Michigan*

LYNNETTE BEALL – *University of California, Berkeley*

The research we report here has had as its aim a study of the acquisition of political philosophy during the adolescent years. We have always known, in a rough and general way, that adolescence is marked by a rapid growth in the comprehension of political ideas. At the threshold of adolescence, at eleven or twelve, the youngster has only a dim, diffuse, and incomplete notion of the political order; by the time he has reached eighteen, he will be, more often than not, a fully formed political creature, possessing a stable and coherent understanding of political structures and functions, and in many cases, committing himself to a philosophy of government. How does this transition take place? In particular, how do learning and cognitive maturation interact to produce these sweeping changes? As a first approach to these questions, we undertook a developmental and cross-national study of adolescents. Youngsters of eleven, thirteen, fifteen, and eighteen were interviewed in three countries: the United States, England, and Germany. (German eleven-year-olds were not interviewed because of fund limitations. Hence, the cross-national analysis compares subjects thirteen through eighteen years of age.) By interviewing youngsters from pubescence to late adolescence we hoped to discern the maturation of political perspectives; by comparing youngsters in three countries with rather different political traditions we hoped to get some sense of the differential impact of social ideas.

BACKGROUND

For our interview schedule, we wanted a format which would not prove to be too difficult for younger subjects, and at the same time not be tediously simple-minded for older adolescents. Our pretesting taught us that we should avoid questions tied to current political issues, for these tended to elicit ready-made opinion—that is, slogans, cliches, and catch-phrases. We devised an interview schedule which began with this premise: Imagine that a thousand people leave their country to move to a Pacific island to establish a new community. Once there, they are confronted with the task of developing rules and regulations for governing themselves. The items were open-ended and to some degree projective: We asked simple open-ended questions, such as, "What is the purpose of government?" or "What is the purpose of law?" We also asked dilemma questions—for example, "What should be done about a religious sect which refused to undergo vaccination?" or "Should people without children pay public school taxes?" We also made extensive use of linked sequences of questions which allowed us to explore a political issue as it unfolded. For example, we said that some concern was expressed about cigarette smoking, and we asked the child to comment on a number of proposed solutions, such as forbidding it, raising taxes, prohibiting advertising, and so on. We then said that a prohibition law had been passed, but was being commonly violated. What should be done then? This format allowed us to survey a wide array of topics, many of them traditional issues in political philosophy: the scope and limits of governmental authority; the reciprocal obligations between citizen and community; conceptions of law, freedom, crime, political partisanship, political influence, utopias; and so on.

In selecting the sample, we were primarily concerned about assuring comparability among ages and among countries. At each age level, Ss were matched for sex and IQ; the national samples were matched for age, sex, and IQ. At each age level in each country, we had thirty Ss, equally divided as to sex, two-thirds of whom were of average, and one-third above average intelligence. We did not match for social class, hoping that the IQ matching would produce essential comparability. As it turned out, the American and German samples show roughly equivalent class distributions—the Americans somewhat higher—but the English sample has a greater proportion of working and lower-middle-class subjects. However, our analyses make it quite clear that national differences are not a function of class differences. As a matter of fact, and very much to our surprise, neither sex, nor IQ, nor social class is of much importance in determining the growth of political ideas. To anticipate our findings, what does matter, primarily, is age, and secondarily, nation.

DEVELOPMENTAL RESULTS

Perhaps our most striking finding is the sharp decline in authoritarian conceptions of government and law over the course of adolescence. It is a tendency which is equally visible in the three national samples, though with some variations, as we will see. The purpose of government, for younger adolescents, those thirteen and under, is felt to be the enforcement of law and in turn, the aim of law is to curb wickedness. Whether the topic be law, government, or justice, the young adolescent's attitude is essentially the same: the citizen's duty is to obey authority, and the failure to do so merits punishment. The social contract, so to speak, is unilateral; the citizen is viewed as owing obligations to the state, but not as possessing rights.

Although this often tacit way of formulating the relations of citizen and state is everywhere discernible through the interviews of the younger subjects, it is perhaps most clearly seen in the understanding of the law. Asked the purpose of the law, about seventy percent of those thirteen and under mention restrictive or coercive functions exclusively; at fifteen, the percentage across all countries has dropped to forty-four percent, and at eighteen, to twenty percent. An exclusively beneficial view of law, one which stresses its contribution to the common good, is found in only eight percent of those thirteen and under, and rises to twenty percent and forty-one percent at fifteen and eighteen. For example, a characteristic response of an eleven- or thirteen-year-old, asked the purpose of law, would be: "To help keep us safe and free," or the even more sophisticated, "I think they are a statement of customs and the ideals that people have about how they should live at certain times."

When we inquire more deeply into the younger adolescent's view of the law by questioning him about specific laws, we find that he rarely imagines, on his own, that a law might be absurd, mistaken, or unfair. He assumes authority to be both omniscient and fundamentally benign; hence, law is enacted only for good and proper reasons. The younger child does not possess a functional view of law; he does not, for example, suggest that a law which is inadequate or ineffective might be revised; he does not see law as mutable, as susceptible to amendment. Laws emerge from the empyrean; once there they must be submitted to.

Later in adolescence–the watershed mark is usually, though not always, between thirteen and fifteen–a radically different view of law is evident. It is now understood that law is a human product, and that men are fallible; hence, law is to be treated in the same skeptical spirit we treat other human artifacts. Law is no longer seen as absolute, or as external to the citizen. It is an experiment, a rehearsal. We try out the law and consult the common experience. If trial determines that the law enhances the general welfare, then it is retained; otherwise it can be abandoned or revised.

With the passage of time, we find, in short, that a critical, pragmatic, relativistic view of law emerges and become dominant. In confronting a proposal for a new law, the older adolescent subjects it to several sorts of scrutiny. What are its latent effects? Whose interests are served, whose are damaged? What are the long-range as against the short-term effects of a law? Can the law be enforced, and are the costs of enforcement worth the good gained by the law? Finally, does the law, whatever its superficial appeal, violate some more general principle of political belief? This is not to say that all or even most of our subjects analyze so relentlessly most of the time, but these questions are tacitly being considered as the older adolescent considers the law proposed to him, while the younger one does not or cannot. Consider, as an example, the responses to a proposal that the island community draft a law prohibiting cigarette smoking. Our younger Ss were somewhat more likely to favor the idea; when asked, later on, what they would suggest if the law were widely violated, they tended to propose an Orwellian apparatus of spies, informers, secret police, and so on. Older Ss were more likely to question the feasibility of the proposal in the first place, pointing out that the law is not easily enforced, or that to enforce it would require costs far beyond the good achieved by it, that an unenforced law produces contempt for legal institutions, and that in any case the law violates the ideal of personal freedom.

THE CONCEPTION OF GOVERNMENT

Let us turn now to the conception of government. The trend toward decreased authoritarianism so visible in the child's formulation of law is also evident here. An exclusively restrictive view of government–that is, one which sees government only in its negative, constraining aspects–falls steadily from twenty-seven percent at age eleven to only one percent at age eighteen.

What is of greater moment is that the idea of government itself is an achievement only slowly won. The concept of government, or indeed of any collectivity, is too abstract for our younger subjects to manage. They recognize only dimly, if at all, the existence of a social order. Hence such terms as "society," "government," and "community" are essentially empty of meaning for them. What they can imagine are personal transactions; thus, education is not an abstract process, but is reduced to the interaction between teacher and student; law is what takes place between the police and criminal; and government is a mysterious territory occupied by mayors, presidents, and an omnipresent though obscure "them." In short, the abstract, ephemeral, intangible processes of the political domain are concretized and personalized by those adolescents below thirteen.

This cognitive limitation–the incapacity to imagine the social order, its structure, its functions–dominates, by its absence, the political discourse of the child younger than fifteen. It means that the youngster, in making political judgments, does not take into account the wider and more general social necessities. Let us offer several examples. In the area of health legislation, we asked about the purpose of a proposed law requiring vaccination and immunization. Younger Ss reply that it is to protect the health of the child; older Ss feel that its aim is to protect the health of the total community. In the area of education, we asked the purpose of a law requiring children to stay in school until they are sixteen. Younger adolescents answer in terms of the child's needs; it is to protect his future in life. Older adolescents may mention this, but they will also say that society needs an educated citizenry if it is to function adequately, or that it needs a supply of educated leaders for the future. In responding to a question on whether adults without children should pay school taxes, our older Ss point out that the society as a whole profits from public education. And we have already seen in our discussion of law that adolescents past fifteen are able to relate law to the larger purposes of society.

It will not have escaped your attention that cognitive maturation seems to be deeply involved in the developmental changes we have considered. This is quite obvious in regard to the conception of government, where a failure to achieve abstractness appears to underlie the failure to adopt a sociocentric stance on political discussions. But it is also involved in the decline of authoritarianism. The child's authoritarianism seems to be based upon cognitive simplicity, as well as upon limitations in social experience. The authoritarian doctrine is simpler conceptually and thus easier to manage cognitively. That there is marked cognitive shift in the level of abstraction with increasing age may be discerned from these results: a coding of level of abstraction—from concrete to low level to high level abstraction—reveals that in response to a question on the function of government, fifty-seven percent of eleven year olds are concrete, while none are highly abstract; at eighteen, none in the entire sample are concrete and seventy-one percent are abstract.

The importance of cognitive maturation is given added weight by the fact that, by and large, developmental changes are essentially similar in all three countries. For American, British, and German adolescents, then, we find a shift from concrete to abstract modes of discourse, and, in Piaget's terms, from concrete to formal operations in analyzing political problems; a decline in authoritarianism and a growth in democratic and humanistic views of social and political issues; a shift from a punitive to a rehabilitative emphasis in dealing with crime; an increased understanding of the needs of the total community as against the single individual; and, in general, a change from absolutistic to relativistic and pragmatic ways of formulating political issues. We have constructed indices for many of these variables, and we find almost uniformly, from analysis of variance estimates, that most of the variance is accounted for by age.

CROSS-NATIONAL RESULTS

Nevertheless, there are important national differences present, which the dominance of the age factor does not obscure. Because our findings here are both numerous and complex, we will be unable to document them fully. What we want to do is offer a discursive summary of the patterns of political thought unique to each of the national samples. Bear in mind that these samples cannot be taken as representative of the nations from which they are drawn; yet, we feel that the patterns discerned in these interviews reflect some common, though not necessarily universal, tendencies in the three countries.

GERMAN

Let us begin with the German sample. They are the easiest to understand, perhaps because German habits of political thought have already been the subject of so much analysis and commentary. Relative to the other countries, our German youngsters prefer having the government strong, and they see the citizen's duty as obeying the authority of the state. There is relatively less emphasis on the rights and privileges of the citizen. The preferred asymmetry of power between the rulers and ruled appears to rest upon a view of the citizen as weak, dependent, and inept; authority is idealized because it is competent and strong, and thus can protect the helpless and insecure citizen. The emphasis upon the confusion of the poeple is a constant refrain in the German interviews. Some excerpts may illustrate this: On the purpose of government, "People must all be guided somehow . . . they can't otherwise make sense out of what happens to them." On why laws are needed, "so that all the people can live in such a way that they don't have to think about what's going to happen to them very much." On why a law forbidding smoking is a good idea, "Otherwise people could have to decide for themselves if it's good or bad for their health or not." Related to this is a fear of diversity, for diversity breeds chaos and disunity. Our German subjects stress the need for a homogeneity of opinion. One S argues that laws must be uniform. "Everyone must have the same opinion." Another says that if people followed their consciences in regard to law, "a lot of different opinions would arise." The result would be anarchy, and anarchy seems to be seen not as people running around berserk and following their lusts, as an American imagines it, but rather people wandering about lost, confused, unguided. The solution to this is a strong, united state, centered upon a few wise leaders.

ENGLISH

Turning to the English, we find them to be the most surprising and the most difficult to understand of the three national groups. This is so perhaps because one can find traces of three political traditions in their interviews; the English are in part Hobbesian, in part nineteenth-century liberals, à la John Stuart Mill, in part children of the welfare state. They are Hobbesian in that they take a guarded view of human nature; men are greedy, selfish, willful; it is the war of all against all. The English sample comes through as intensely oral, obsessed about supplies, deprivation, self-indulgence, theft, and envy. They score highest of the three groups on an index measuring concern with impulse control. And because they see men as prepared to steal what is not rightfully theirs, they are prepared to see government take a strong hand in regulating public conduct. Thus, they are in some respects as authoritarian as the Germans are. But there is a vital difference in that the English do not idealize authority—far from it; they are suspicious and resentful of those who would rule them. Government is a necessary evil; hence, the English seek to limit the scope of government. They make much of the distinction between the private and the public. Government must not interfere with the private domain, especially the pursuit of pleasure; yet it must be strong enough to regulate the competition of private interests in the public domain. At the same time, the English are attuned to a welfare concept of government, and see it as the obligation of the state to distribute benefits equitably and assure minimal standards of subsistence. Government, then, emerges as a kind of stern headmaster, setting down rules which limit the invasion of one's terrain; at the same time, it is a kind of nanny who distributes supplies equally.

AMERICAN

Finally, we consider the Americans. They are, by a considerable margin, the least authoritarian of the national samples. We thought at first that this might be due to the fact that the American sample has a somewhat larger number of upper-middle-class subjects, but closer analysis suggests otherwise: Americans of working-class origin score lower on authoritariansim than upper-middle-class German or British subjects. The democratic emphasis in the American interviews stems from a benign view of both the citizen and the government. It is assumed that the citizen ought to be and in fact will be responsive to the needs of the total community, and will accommodate his interests to the general good; on its side, the government is seen as the executive of the general will. Thus, there is little felt distance between the citizen and collective authority. The American political philosophy, as it is revealed in these interviews, bears the stamp of John Locke's thought—an emphasis on consensus, on social harmony, on the rights of the governed. But this optimistic view of the political process does not altogether conceal certain tensions and dilemmas. One of these has to do with the restraint of individualism. Our American subjects value such individualistic ideals as autonomy, initiative, and achievement. They fear a strong central authority because it may inhibit the free exercise of these qualities. It is understood, as part of an implicit social contract, that the individual will not abuse these freedoms and will not infringe upon the rights of others, that he will exercise self-restraint. But there is no guarantee of this, and Americans seem preoccupied with finding some balance between allowing sufficient freedom for achievement and finding means of controlling rampant individualism. A second problem arises from the emphasis on consensus and social harmony. As many political commentators have noted, these can give way to a somewhat insipid politics of togetherness, one which stresses being a good fellow, not rocking the boat, going along with the majority.

NATIONAL PATTERNS

Since the intention of this paper is discursive, we have avoided to this point tabular presentations of the findings. However, some of the complex national patterns we have just discussed may be evoked more vividly by a presentation of specific national differences.

Table 1 reports some findings on the orientation to law. The subjects had been asked, apropos of a law which was commonly violated, whether it should be voted down or enforced more strictly. A code was devised which analyzed responses according to the underlying conceptions of the basis on which a law is felt to be legitimate. Thus, an *obedience* orientation is one which assumes that a law is given its legitimacy only when people are willing to obey it; the *pragmatic* orientation denies the legitimacy of a law when it cannot be enforced in practical terms; and the *popular will* category asserts that a law is legitimate when it reflects the decision of the populace. Table 1 shows that the obedience orientation is rarely found except among German youngsters, and more than half of the codable responses in that sample stress

TABLE 1

ORIENTATIONS TOWARDS THE LEGITIMACY OF LAW

	America %	England %	Germany %
1. Obedience orientation	02	05	27
2. Pragmatic orientation	33	29	20
3. Popular-will orientation	24	10	04
4. Not ascertained or other	42	56	49
TOTAL	101%[a]	100%	100%

n = 266

$X^2 = 46.93$; d.f. = 6; $p < .001$

a. Error due to rounding.

obedience as the criterion of legitimacy. The popular-will emphasis is most frequently found among the Americans. The pragmatic orientation is more evenly distributed among the three national groups, the Germans favoring it somewhat less than the others.

The degree to which the British youngsters were absorbed in issues of impulses and impulse-control is evident in Table 2. An impulse-control dimension was developed from a number of questions on law and government; responses to these questions were included in the dimension when they were felt to reflect a preoccupation with aggressiveness, self-indulgence, impulsiveness, greed, selfish pleasure, and the like. As the table makes plain, British youngsters were the most likely to score high on the dimension.

Table 3 reports national responses to an item which asked what would happen if there were no laws. Here again we note some characteristic national

TABLE 2

PERCENTAGE SCORING HIGH ON THE IMPULSE-CONTROL DIMENSION

	America	England	Germany
High	60%	84%	54%

n = 266

$X^2 = 19.38$; d.f. = 2; $p < .001$

TABLE 3

PROBLEMS FEARED IN A LAWLESS COMMUNITY

	America %	England %	Germany %
1. Impulse control or interpersonal conflict	37	63	42
2. Loss of guidance	19	21	28
3. Impulse control and loss of guidance	17	05	21
4. Community problems	15	09	04
5. Not ascertained or other	12	02	04
TOTAL	100%	100%	99%[a]

n = 266

$X^2 = 30.56$; d.f. = 8; $p < .001$

a. Error due to rounding.

tendencies. The British are the most likely to fear impulse problems and interpersonal conflict. The German youngsters most often stress the possible loss of guidance, a reflection, we take it, of their pervasive dependency. The Americans are the most likely to emphasize community problems, again a characteristic response, in that they consistently view specific problems in law and government in terms of their impact on the total community.

These national differences are intriguing, yet we should emphasize once again the importance of developmental similarities among the three national groups. For most of the concepts we have studied, the pattern of acquisition is essentially the same among adolescents in the three nations. There are some differences in tempo—for example, American subjects are precocious in attaining a sense of the community—but by the time they are eighteen, youngsters in all three countries are far more alike than different. They are alike in that they have acquired the fundamental concepts which equip them for reasoning about political issues; furthermore, they seem to share those assumptions about government and law common to the industrialized and democratic nations of the West. On the other hand, these cross-national uniformities by no means overcome certain national motifs—the German penchant for obedience, the British insistence on privacy, the American other-directedness—and who can deny that in their consequences, in their contributions to a nation's political temper, these motifs may prove to be more significant in the long run.

Chapter 8

Children and Compliance

A Comparative Analysis of Socialization Studies

SHEILAH R. KOEPPEN – *University of Minnesota*

Popular compliance with prescribed patterns of behavior is the fundamental constraint on social disruption.[1] Even the effectiveness of control by legal sanctions depends on the public's acceptance of their use by authorities. Inquiry into the sources of popular adherence to norms conducive to compliance with authorities has been an aspect of socialization research. This essay comments on political science research on socialization, and points out how it differs from the research reported by psychologist Joseph Adelson and his associates (1970) in this journal and in a previous study (1966). The socialization studies are compared in order to determine their utility for discerning the sources of compliant behavior.[2]

SOCIALIZATION: DEFINITION AND INTERPRETATIONS

Socialization is a process whereby the members of a society learn its norms and acquire its habits, values, and patterns of behavior. The theories of socialization are theories of behavioral development from early childhood to maturity and adulthood. (See Clausen, 1968.)[3] Three broad categories respectively entitled (1) psychoanalytic, (2) social-learning, and (3) cognitive-developmental, subsume socialization theories.

The following discussion points out the inducements for compliant behavior that are proposed by each type of socialization theory. Spokesmen for the socialization theories suggest how a child acquires the norms of moral behavior that are critical to ensuring that his actions contribute to, or at least do not threaten, the persistence of the social order. They all consider a child's awareness of his obligations toward others to be rooted in norms of moral behavior. They concur that for these norms to be effective in directing a child's judgment, he must internalize them. Internalized norms can be counted on to set continual restraints on a child's behavior. External controls are imposed by some agent other than the child himself and are, by themselves, insufficient restraints on behavior, varying as does the presence of the control agent and/or the child's awareness and response to the agent. Of course, it is difficult to determine to what extent adherence to moral behavior may result from both internalized values and an awareness of external sanctions against misbehavior (Maccoby, 1968: 258-262; Bandura and Walters, 1963: 206-207).[4] While acknowledging this problem, socialization theorists maintain that moral behavior rests on the comprehension of societal norms and the volition to comply with them.[5] The theorists agree also in citing conscience as the mechanism of internal control. Accordingly, a person's failure to honor his obligations to respect the rights of others is sanctioned by his conscience in the form of guilt feelings. The theorists differ with regard to the source of conscience and the relative importance of cognitive and environmental factors in the development of conscience. But there are points of similarity as well as differences among the theorists, and I shall delineate these as I discuss each theory.

PSYCHOANALYTIC LEARNING THEORY

A psychoanalytic interpretation of social learning, proposed by Harry Stack Sullivan (1953), and one proposed and developed by Erik Erikson (1963, 1968), describes a process whereby the child's acceptance of his parents' modes of conduct, which include norms of social behavior, is determined by how effective his parents are in providing him with the nurturance, instruction, and examples of how to act that he requires if he is to satisfy the particular drive or need appropriate to his (age) level of development.

According to psychoanalytic theory, conscience, manifest as guilt feelings, induces the child to comply with social norms. Erik Erikson (1968: 54-55, 71-74, 92-106) suggests that a child can feel guilt at any age because it results from his experiences rather than from a conscious understanding of taboos. In fact, he contends that a child can feel guilty over his misbehavior before he can understand why his behavior is inappropriate or wrong. A psychoanalytic theory of development attributes guilt to experiences and feelings. And Erik Erikson's (1969) psychoanalytic model treats cultural factors as determinants of the attainment of conscience.[6] He urges analysts to study child-rearing practices–which are culturally conditioned–because these are a critical source of children's experiences and how they learn to adhere to social norms.

SOCIAL-LEARNING THEORY

Social-learning theories have a more extensive bibliography than the other socialization theories.[7] The contemporary exposition of social learning, and the one followed here, draws on the work of Robert Sears (1957)[8] and Albert Bandura and R. H. Walters (1963). Social-learning theories and psychoanalytic theories provide parallel descriptions of how the child learns because both emphasize that learning is contingent on the affective relationship between the child and his parents. Social-learning theorists adopt and extend the analysts' stress on the effect proximal adults, notably the parents, have on a child. They propose that social learning occurs because a child acquires norms of behavior by imitating or identifying with "models," defined as persons whose activities he observes and who offer him rewards or inducements to reinforce his desire to act in a similar fashion. Robert Sears (1957: 154-157) suggests that an added or "secondary" reinforcement for learning comes from the child himself; the child is motivated to learn because he values identification with the model, and self-esteem is his reward for imitating or behaving like the model. Social-learning theorists allow that to some extent the child's ability to learn is associated with his level of maturity, and that his ability to learn affects how successfully he learns. For example, Robert Sears describes learning as an additive process whereby the child learns by imitating the behavior of persons with whom he identifies, and each successful identification is the basis for an identification at a higher and more complex level of development (Bandura, 1969: 255).[9]

The social-learning theorists share the analysts' emphasis on the role played by feelings in determining guilt. However, some social-learning theorists posit that guilt is learned in the same way as other responses, via identification with models. John Whitting (1961) suggests that guilt results from identification with the male role which is more punitive and unforgiving than is the female role. And social-learning theorists emphasize that the internalization of moral judgment is associated with the methods parents use to discipline their child. If external controls, such as physical punishment and verbal assault are used, the child is not likely to internalize moral norms. But when norms are communicated clearly to the child and punishment for transgression is withdrawal of love or the threat of withdrawal, he learns to value moral behavior (Sears, 1957; Aronfreed, 1961; Stephenson, 1966).

Social-learning theorists have reservations about whether all children learn to internalize moral norms. They recognize change and flexibility in behavior, and they point out that a child's behavior may be regulated by his fear of external sanctions and/or by his conscience, or may not be regulated at all. In the absence of models who act morally, or in the presence of stronger, more attractive models who are not acting morally, a child may not learn to adhere to moral norms. The realization of the possibility of another impediment to moral behavior is built into social-learning theory through its aforementioned proposal that if a child has experienced a punitive upbringing, he does not learn to value moral norms.

The social-learning theorists' attention to child-rearing practices is demonstrative of the importance they assign to culture (Whiting and Child, 1953). One cross-cultural survey based on social-learning theory reports an association between patterns of child-rearing and the incidence of theft in society.[10] And generally these theorists contend that cultural variation is maintained via the socialization process. They propose that as a child learns by imitating models, and as the models are "carriers" of cultural norms, a child learns to follow culturally acceptable patterns of behavior.

COGNITIVE-DEVELOPMENTAL THEORY

The cognitive theory of development, as introduced by Jean Piaget (1965, 1955, 1952)[11] and explicated and extended by Laurence Kohlberg (1964, 1969) posits that the ability to learn is critical; the child learns what he is able to learn, according to the level of development of the structure and organization of his thought processes (1969: 349-350). Kohlberg (1969: 352) explains that the core of the cognitive-developmental position is a doctrine of cognitive stages, each representing a level and a type of cognitive ability. A child's passage from one stage of cognitive maturity to the next is sequential and involves a transformation from simple to increasingly complex cognitive structures.

Cognitive-developmental theory shares the psychoanalytic view of development as a progression of stages, each of which rests on the previous stage, and both propose that what a child learns is associated with his level of maturity. The use of developmental stages by cognitive theorists differs from that by psychoanalysts with regard to the time encompassed by the stages. The stages posited by cognitive-development theory terminate in maturity, i.e., when cognitive structures attain their final form, whereas the stages of development examined by psychoanalytic theory cover the entire life cycle.[12]

Cognitive-learning theory does not overlook the role of the parents in the socialization process since it acknowledges the importance of communication between the child and an agent or model. Piaget also suggests that children learn a great deal from each other, in many instances more than they learn from their parents. However, according to the theory, whether the child absorbs the information communicated depends on how appropriate or how digestible the information is, given the child's level of development. The child's acquisition of social norms is associated with his ability to comprehend and conceptualize these norms himself. Hence the child cannot be expected to comply of his own volition with social norms until he learns them.

Piaget (1965) argues that the child cannot feel guilt until he has the intellectual ability to understand the cause and the nature of his guilt. According to Piaget, there are stages of moral development. In the first stage a child is able to judge the gravity of a deviant act according to the consequences of the act as determined by the extent of damages caused or the punishment incurred from authorities. In the second stage, which occurs after the age of seven, the child is capable of judging an act in terms of its intent and the punishment inflicted by his own conscience. These stages may overlap,[13] but there is a clear distinction in Piaget's scheme of moral development between moral conduct occasioned by the child being subject to external control, i.e., punishment by an adult, and moral conduct resulting from the child's belief in its desirability.

Laurence Kohlberg (1969: 398-412) distinguishes between moral judgment and moral behavior, recognizing that although a person comprehends social norms and is aware of his responsibilities toward others, he still may not adhere to norms. Kohlberg agrees that the internalization of moral judgment requires a change in the logical operations of thought processes. He develops the distinction between the objective and subjective bases of moral judgment into a complex, finely graduated schedule consisting of six stages. The final stage of the schedule marks the internalization of moral norms. At this point personal conduct is guided by the recognition and rational judgment as to the consequences of actions, and the desire to have a clear conscience. Kohlberg (1964: 407-409) reports that when children are found to progress at different rates in learning moral behavior, it is due to their having different abilities and being exposed to different values and beliefs. But he maintains that by adolescence all children can discern right from wrong; all children then have the capacity to exercise moral judgment.[14] In support of his contention, he has cited the findings of a cross-cultural study showing that regardless of country or cultural group, as children age, they come to judge acts in terms of motives (Zigler and Child, 1969).

Laurence Kohlberg (1964: 390-391, 398-399) recognizes that cultural variables influence child development. He claims that Piaget acknowledged cultural differences, especially differences in child-rearing practices, to be critical environmental factors that influence both the rate at which a child progresses through the stages of development, and the choice of norms by children at a similar stage of development. Cultural factors influence a basic developmental process in which cognitive maturity is a necessary but not always sufficient condition for the acquisition of moral judgment and maturity. Justin Aronfreed (1969: 303-306), in a review of cognitive theories of development, comments that cognitive capacity is not a sufficient source of compliance with social norms. Environmental conditions such as cultural norms, child-rearing practices, and particularly a minimal amount of parental nurturance also help to foster the internalization of norms of behavior.

TABLE 1

COMPARISON OF PSYCHOANALYTIC, SOCIAL-LEARNING, AND COGNITIVE-DEVELOPMENTAL THEORIES

		LEARNING THEORIES	
	Psychoanalytic	**Social-Learning**	**Cognitive-Developmental**
SOCIALIZATION: THE ACQUISITION OF MORAL BEHAVIOR			
1. How the child learns social norms:	From the affective relationship with parents who communicate the norms.	Children identify and imitate parents who adhere to norms.	From parents and peers and himself according to his ability to comprehend the norms.
2. How the child internalizes norms:	Guilt feelings.	Desire for parental approval and for his own self-esteem.	Ability to reproduce them through logical operations.
3. Effectiveness of internalization depends on:	The quality of his relationship with his parents.	The presence of attractive models and the choice of child-rearing practices.	The development of the ability to conceptualize and reason.
4. Influence of culture:	Critical: a determinant of the parent-child relationship.	Critical: a determinant of child-rearing practices.	Important in addition to cognitive development.

SUMMARY

The theories of socialization treat the internalization of moral norms as the basis of compliant behavior, but they differ in the relative importance given respectively to emotional, cognitive, and environmental factors. Each socialization theory acknowledges that cognitive maturity is a factor in learning. But only cognitive-developmental theory asserts that it is the fundamental condition for learning moral norms and exercising moral judgment. Each theory recognizes that culture, the overarching environmental factor, is a critical determinant of what children learn. But the view that cultural factors are an ancillary influence in relation to cognition is distinct to cognitive-developmental theory. Psychoanalytic and social-learning theories of development stress emotional experiences and the varieties of cultural experiences. The following table summarizes the learning theories' interpretations of the socialization process.

A description of how social norms are acquired and how they contribute to compliant behavior is derivative, in large part, from the socialization theory which is its reference. This point is brought out by distinguishing between the theoretical sources relied on by the psychologists and by the political scientists who study socialization.

SOCIALIZATION AND COMPLIANCE: POLITICAL AND PSYCHOLOGICAL STUDIES

The sources of compliant behavior will be delineated by examining data collected for the most part by survey research studies conducted by political scientists. In so doing the socialization theories applied by the political scientists will be contrasted with those applied by the psychologists with reference to their respective descriptions of how children develop ideas about the government. It would appear that their descriptions of this process are contradictory. For example, see Adelson and Beall's (1970) report in this journal on the decline of the authoritarian image of government from childhood to adolescence. They find that as children mature, they ascribe less punitiveness to government. Robert D. Hess and David Easton (1960), in one of the earlier political socialization studies, report that young children believe governmental authorities are kindly disposed to them, but that as they grow older, they grow wary of government.[15] Their findings have been replicated in other surveys on the political socialization of American children (Greenstein, 1965; Hess and Torney, 1967; Easton and Dennis, 1969; Jaros, 1967).[16]

Actually both the psychologists and political scientists provide a similar description of one aspect of socialization: the process whereby children learn about authority (Jaros, 1967: 372-376).[17] They report that as children acquire more information and the ability to comprehend it, children change their earlier views about government in favor of more complex and more realistic views (Hyman, 1959: 54).[18] Adelson and Beall (1970) say that children replace their belief that government is authoritarian first by a belief that government's laws are beneficial, and later by a belief that laws are useful devices for regulating society and assisting its members. The first change of view occurs when children are between eleven and thirteen years of age. The second occurs when they are between thirteen and fifteen. Hess and Easton (1962) find that the idealized image of authority held by young children is replaced progressively by a more realistic and critical view of authority. They find a change in attitudes among children from the fourth through the eighth grades, or among children from the age of ten to the age of fourteen.

The socialization studies concur also in finding that culture discriminates among children of a similar age. Adelson and his associates (1970) report finding cultural differences in adolescents' views of community and laws. Political socialization surveys explore differences in political attitudes that are attributable to cultural differences (Almond and Verba, 1963; Lambert and Klineberg, 1966; Hess, 1963).[19]

Notwithstanding the similarity of their descriptions of the process investigated, the political scientists and psychologists employ different indicators of law and authority as well as different theories of socialization. Adelson and his associates want to determine whether norms of moral behavior and compliance with laws have been internalized. He questions adolescents about what they would do in particular hypothetical situations. His inquiry is based largely (and implicitly) on a cognitive-developmental view of the learning process (Adelson and O'Neil, 1966: 296-297).[20] Political studies of socialization seek to determine the extent of children's attachment to political authorities as indicated by their evaluations of the President and the policeman. Children are asked to evaluate familial and governmental authority figures.[21] Social-learning theories and aspects of the psychoanalytic view of child development have guided political socialization research (Easton and Dennis, 1969: 14-15).[22]

Since the psychologists focus on the development of moral judgment and compliance with the laws and political scientists on perceptions about legal authorities, a comparison between their studies may be unfair. It is obvious that the questions raised, and answers suggested, by the psychologists are more pertinent to a determination of the source of popular compliance with laws. However political scientists claim, on behalf of their inquiries, to contribute to an understanding of compliance. For example, David Easton and Jack Dennis (1969: 54) report the results of a recent survey based on the indicators and proposals used in other political socialization studies, and propose: "Socialization represents an important mechanism that may help members of a system to internalize the need to comply or, as we say in legal systems, 'a need to obey legally constituted authority'."[23] Insofar as socialization studies in both disciplines are concerned about the source of compliant behavior, a comparison between them is in order. In the next section, through an analysis of the assumptions of the political science socialization studies, suggestions are made about how learning theory contributes to an understanding of compliant behavior.

POLITICAL SOCIALIZATION AND POPULAR COMPLIANCE

Why do political institutions persist and why do people comply with political procedures and prescriptions? These questions have encouraged political scientists to study the socialization process. There are several surveys of national and local populations that record the expectations that children have about how fairly political authorities use power, whether they believe the authorities use power for their own ends or for the public good, whether they believe it is important to obey the authorities (Greenstein, 1965; Hess and Torney, 1967; Easton and Dennis, 1969; Jaros, 1967). The findings from these surveys on American children's attitudes toward authorities are consistent, and show that by the age of seven, children are aware of the existence of political and legal authority as personified by the President and the policeman. Furthermore, children expect supportive, helpful, "benevolent" treatment from the laws and authorities, and they cannot conceive of themselves as disobeying them (Greenstein, 1960).[24]

The suggestions about the sources and implications of children's attachment to the President and policeman are illustrative of the political scientists' application of social-learning and psychoanalytic theories of child development. The most frequently cited suggestion about the source of children's affection for political authority figures is that young children, unable to differentiate between proximal and public figures, transfer both the high regard and the feelings of dependency they have for their father to other persons in authority (Hess and Easton, 1962: 262, 1960: 642-643; Easton and Hess, 1962: 161; Hess and Torney, 1967: 40, 99, 213-215; Greenstein, 1965: 46-47; Easton and Dennis, 1969: 137; Merelman, 1969: 758-759). A benevolent image of authority is said to result from this transference because, in general, American fathers are helpful rather than harsh and controlling, and because children defend themselves from feeling anxious about their helplessness and dependence by hoping for support from authorities (Hess and Easton, 1962; Hess and Torney, 1967: 47-48; Greenstein, 1965: 46).[25] One objection to this interpretation is that the experiences American children have with their fathers are not sufficiently similar to account for their common view of political leaders. There are many children whose fathers do not exercise authority benignly (Sigel, 1965: 36),[26] and the proportion of American children growing up in fatherless homes is increasing (Rainwater and Yancey, 1967: 55, 75; Moynihan, 1969: 8-9). Another objection to this interpretation is that it has not been confirmed by research. A survey of Detroit school children did not disclose an association among them between feeling dependent on authority and viewing the President as a benevolent leader (Jaros, 1967: 383). A survey of children in Appalachia did not find any connection between their affection for their fathers and their esteem for the President (Jaros et al., 1968: 572). And the most recent analysis of the national political socialization surveys of samples of white metropolitan-area public school children used by Hess and Torney does not find support for the proposed association between the affection children have for their fathers and the affection they have for the President.

A possible alternative explanation as to why American children, regardless of familial environment, have such similar and strikingly positive views of public authority is that, for the most part, children's sources of information—the family, churches, schools, and the media—portray the President, and (for the most part, until recently) the policeman as responsible men exercising power with the best intentions and to the utmost of their abilities (Easton and Dennis, 1969: 365-366). Parents who convey information about politics are predisposed to portray the President positively, regardless of their own beliefs (Greenstein, 1965: 45; Orren and Peterson, 1967: 398-402). Hence, a benevolent image of an official may be one that is taught to children rather than one adopted by them in order to cope with their fears and familial experiences.

The finding on children's attachment for the President and the policeman is interpreted, usually, as a source of support for the politcal order and for its rules. Analysts of the findings of political socialization surveys suggest that as children grow up and are able to differentiate between familial and governmental authorities, they retain a good deal of their earlier positive regard for political leaders and symbols (Hess and Easton, 1960: 643-644; Greenstein, 1965: 52-54; Hess and Torney, 1967: 58-59, 236-237; Easton and Dennis, 1969: 67-68, 116, 284-288; Dawson and Prewitt, 1969: 107-109). David Easton has expressed this interpretation often, and it is exemplified by his and Jack Dennis's (1969: 281) suggestion: "The favorable sentiments first extended to the personal figures he [the child] tends to shift toward those very organizations that he previously failed to notice."

This suggestion that the young child's regard for and deference towards leaders remains a part of his perceptions about politics as he grows up is an application of the "early learning" hypothesis. According to the hypothesis, the earlier in his life an attitude or value is learned, the greater endurance it is likely to have.[27] What is learned at an early stage of development is retained in the form and/or content of learning acquired at a later stage. Attitudes learned early in childhood persist into adulthood. Adoption of the emphasis on early learning prompts the inference that the youngsters' first view of authorities remains the basis for their later—adolescent and then adult—view of authorities. Although there have been criticisms about placing too great a stress on the impact of early learning on political behavior, the hypothesis has remained a source of inferences about children's retention of political attitudes. Fred I. Greenstein (1965: 71) explicitly invokes the hypothesis when he says, "Early learning takes place during a formative period and early learning affects later learning."

Easton and Hess (1961: 243-244) rest a claim for the relevance of the study of children's political attitudes on the importance of early learning.[28] And when Hess and Torney (1967: 31) report that around 95% of the second graders in their national survey agree, "America is the best country in the world," they comment: "Early attachment to the nation then is basic to political socialization and to subsequent learning and experience."

The political scientists' interpretation of the endurance of early learning requires them to explain how children cope with the information and sentiments about politics and government they acquire as they grow up. These explanations can be analyzed, and the utility of the inference on the retention of views assessed, if the political attitudes attributed to children are examined in terms of their components. Children's attitudes about government and authority have two major components: cognitions and affects. A third component, called value in some studies (Almond and Verba, 1963: 15-17), or evaluations in others (Easton and Dennis, 1969: 101),[29] represents orientations to political objects and is the manifestation, i.e., the active component of attitudes (Almond and Verba, 1963: 536). The formation and structure of attitudes is examined in terms of their affective and cognitive components. Cognitions are the knowledge pertinent to the attitude: the information about the subject of the attitudes and the intellect's organization of that information. Affects express the feelings, the emotive force of the attitude. In the political socialization studies, what children learn later is interpreted as information that alters the cognitions about authorities but has limited impact on their affects or feelings toward authorities. Greenstein (1965: 35, 53) expresses this interpretation as follows: "Political information increases substantially over the brief age span of the New Haven sample, but the structure of factual knowledge is erected on a foundation of feelings, assessments and opinions."

This description of social learning is based on either one or two of the following implicit assumptions about political beliefs. The first assumption is that a change in one component of an attitude may be independent of a change in the other component. A second assumption is that affect makes a particularly great—greater than cognition—contribution to the organization of the attitude.

The critical role given the affective component of children's attitudes seems to be a derivative of the social-learning theories used in the political studies.

Social-learning theory shares with psychoanalytic theory the view that affective needs are motivations for behavior whose direction and strength, formed at an early age, is a force for later action. In contrast, cognitive-developmental theory stresses the cognitive components of attitudes and the capacity for attitude change. The reasoning is that each stage of cognitive development represents a further unfolding and utilization of capacities which, when applied to external phenomena, enable children to develop new appraisals of the phenomena. The new attitudes are inherently richer due to their greater complexity, and they supplant the older, more primitive attitudes. Cognitive development necessitates affective development. The child's ability to feel an attachment for an object is associated with his ability to understand, to conceptualize that object. Each new level of cognitive capacity necessitates an adjustment of feelings, as Piaget (1962: 205) argues:

> Affective life, like intellectual life, is a continual adaptation, and the two are not only parallel but interdependent since feelings express the interest and the value given to actions of which intelligence provides the structure. Since affective life is adaptation, it also implies continual assimilation of present situations to earlier ones—assimilation which gives rise to affective schemas or relatively stable modes of feeling or reacting—and continual accommodation of these schemas to the present situation.[30]

I suggest that this interpretation of learning is appropriate to an understanding of the development of moral behavior and attitudes toward authority. Cognitive development is at least as critical to social learning and assessments of authority as is emotional experience. Studies of attitude change indicate an association between cognitions and affects. Their emphasis on early learning notwithstanding, political socialization studies record changes in levels and information and in feelings about political and legal authority associated with maturation. And the utility and meaning of the responses children give about political phenomena is limited when account is taken of the fact that before a certain age children do not understand the concepts in the questions they are asked.

Milton J. Rosenberg (1960) reports the results of experiments designed to determine the existence of an association between affect and cognition in the course of attitude change.[31] In these experiments manipulation of the affective component of the subjects' beliefs on a public issue important to them produced not only a change in their feelings toward the issue but also in their appraisal of information relevant to the issue. As Rosenberg manipulated the affective component of attitudes in order to observe a change in affects and cognitions, it might be argued that his results support, rather than challenge, the critical role assigned to affects by psychoanalytic and social-learning theories. But Rosenberg suggests that:

> The description of affective-cognitive congruence by alteration of either of the two components sets in motion processes of congruence restoration which will, under

> certain conditions, lead to attitude reorganization through complementary change in the previously unaltered component. [Rosenberg et al., 1960: 12]

Rosenberg's comment on affective-cognitive congruence is supported by earlier reports of experiments finding that changes in affects followed changes in cognitions (Carlson, 1956; Woodruff and DiVesta, 1948). All told, these studies support an argument for assigning equal strength to attitudinal components.

Political socialization studies report that adults have far less idealistic and affectionate images of authority and the laws than do children, and describe the loss of idealism about authority among children as they grow up. Yet, the studies suggest that older children, and by inference adults, do not feel so differently about authority. Their evidence does not support this interpretation.

No study investigating the development of attitudes among children as they mature has been completed, although Roberta Sigel (1969) has reported on a study of the same children over a two-year interval.[32] The only source of data available about how children's political ideas change as they grow up comes from the aforementioned surveys which question children in a progression of school grades at one time. The surveys report findings that the older the children are, the more they can and do learn about the government and laws (Greenstein, 1965; Hess and Torney, 1967; Easton and Dennis, 1969),[33] and they acquire different evaluations of the President and the policeman.

Older children have a more substantive view of the responsibilities and attributes of the President and the policeman (Hess and Torney, 1967: 45-49; Easton and Dennis, 1969: 176-177, 225, 236-238; Hess and Easton, 1960; Sigel, 1968: 221). For example, children's evaluations of President Kennedy were derived to a much greater degree from assessments of his policies than from an attachment to the symbolic value of the presidential role (Sigel, 1968: 225). Increasing the knowledge children have about the difference in skills between public authority figures and their fathers results in their making clearer distinction between how they feel toward officials and how they feel about their fathers. Older children have less affection for public officials than they do for their fathers (Hess and Easton, 1960; Greenstein, 1965: 70, 81-82; Hess and Torney, 1967: 39-40; Easton and Dennis, 1969: 274-277). In general, as children acquire information about what authorities do, their feelings about them change. Edward S. Greenberg (1969) reports that black children lose their affection for the President and the political system as they gain information that the treatment they can expect is far less benevolent than the treatment they anticipated earlier in their childhood and the treatment accorded to their white peers.

Once cognitive-affective interaction is acknowledged, evidence suggests that it is not valid to use children's expressions of affects toward symbols of authority such as the nation or the President in order to describe adult attitudes toward authority. Evaluations about politics and government that are made before cognitive maturity is attained are likely to change especially as there is information that children do not understand what national and political phenomena are or how to relate to such phenomena. Young children do not understand what a country is nor what their nationality is. Piaget and Anne-Marie Weil (1951)[34] questioned Swiss children of seven and eight. They report that their respondents could not correctly conceive of the spatial or power relationships among a city, state, and country. Not until the age of ten or eleven could the children distinguish town from country correctly. Gustav Jahoda's study (1963b: 58; 1963a: 143-153) of Scottish children suggests that even ten or eleven year olds may not comprehend such geographical or political entities, much less be able to relate to them. The Scottish children said they were both Scottish and British but could not conceive of Scotland as a part of Great Britain.

Cognitive development is associated closely with orientations toward authority. The results of one survey of grade school children in metropolitan areas throughout the United States reports that intelligence, as measured by standard IQ tests and age, as indicated by grade are associated with political efficacy while social class and participation in social group activities show little and no association (White, 1968: 716).[35] Roberta Sigel's (1965: 50) exploration of children's responses to Lee Harvey Oswald's assassination reports differences according to age illustrative of the cognitive-developmental description of moral learning. While children were, on the whole, more likely than adults to be glad Oswald was "punished" for assassinating President Kennedy, older children expressed less desire for vengeance which, Sigel suggests, may indicate greater awareness of the existence of more appropriate procedures for punishment.

SUMMARY AND CONCLUSIONS

Political socialization studies have focused on children's attachment to authority as a source of compliant behavior (Easton and Dennis, 1969: 54; Hess and Torney, 1967: 50-59). Evidence which casts doubt on this interpretation of compliance has been presented. Children change their opinions of authority as they grow up, and in doing so, they arrive at different estimates about the value of compliance. If this contention that attitudes toward authority change during maturation is acceptable, then an alternative interpretation of the findings that American children continue to have fairly positive attitudes toward their government is necessary. I suggest that this consistency is due largely to a lack of contradiction between what children are learning and what they learned earlier. While children do not seem to alter their appraisal of politics and government drastically, it is likely that as they grow older they have different reasons for expressing approval. People who have been exposed to congruent messages and who have not experienced critical change in their social and political institutions may have orientations to government that appear similar to those held in childhood.

But a general orientation to authority is no more adequate as a condition than it is as an explanation of compliance. And while emotional experiences and the imitation of "models" can be associated with behavior, these factors cannot tell us if a person is aware of the consequences of his behavior. If the socialization theorists' stress on the internalization of moral norms is accepted as the basis for compliance, then the cognitive-developmental theorists' insight and evidence on the acquisition of the ability to comprehend moral norms—to exercise moral judgment—are useful guides to expectations about standards of behavior. The cognitive-developmental interpretation has much to recommend it to a legal system based on premises about individual accountability. Cognitive-developmental theory proposes that by adolescence, an individual can be expected to discern right from wrong and to value the social utility of laws that punish misconduct. The interpretations and studies of development made by the social-learning theorists and the psychoanalysts offer insights as to why someone may not acquire an awareness of the value of law "on schedule," or why someone behaves contrary to moral standards. The information supplied by these socialization theories may be applicable in some phases of the legal process, for example, where rehabilitation is being considered. But a reliance on this information may create burdens for judges and attorneys who do not know what kind of evidence of child-rearing practices and early emotional experience to consider, and what kind of perspective to take with regard to weighing the impact of these experiences on the individual's ability to take responsibility for his behavior.

NOTES

1. John A. Clausen (1968) recognizes that this proposition is a major source of interest in the study of socialization. He reviews the development of research in this field.

2. An example is the question as to whether or not juveniles can be responsible for deciding to waive the privilege against self-incrimination. On this problem and court procedures, see Lefstein et al. (1969).

3. Goslin (1969) is an encyclopedia of the literature and critical evaluations of it.

4. Abraham S. Goldstein (1967) notes that the indicator of the ability to distinguish right from wrong in criminal cases is not only the defendant's conscience, but also his awareness of external sanctions. One dissenting view, offered by Dennis H. Wrong (1961) is that conformity is due to the desire people have to conform with the expectations of other people rather than with internalized norms.

5. Aronfreed (1969) posits cognitive and emotional maturity as critical to the development of conscience because maturity is the basis of the ability to internalize norms.

6. See Erikson's (1963: chs. 9, 10) interpretations of the motives and responses of

the subjects of his biographical studies. A statement on the psychoanalyst's concern with the interaction of the individual and his culture and its history is found in Erikson (1968: ch. 5).

7. For a summary, see Maccoby (1968: 240-242). Seminal studies in this area are Miller and Dollard (1941) and Whiting and Child (1953).

8. See especially Sears (1961) and Sears et al. (1957).

9. Henry W. Maier (1965: 196) attributes this view to Sears.

10. This study of 48 societies finds that deprivation of love in childhood is correlated with the incidence of theft in society (Bacon et al., 1963). See also McCord and McCord (1959) for an interpretation stating that crime is associated with the presence of a deviant model.

11. For an explication of Piaget's theory and investigations see Flavell (1963).

12. For more comments comparing cognitive with psychological and sociological interpretations of development, see Maccoby (1968: 290-292) and Baldwin (1969).

13. According to Flavell's interpretation (1963: 291-296) of Piaget, they may overlap. There are two phases within this stage. Until the age of eleven or twelve, the child demands that all misconduct receive equal punishment, while after, he becomes more attentive to what punishment is appropriate to the particular offense and offender.

14. Kohlberg (1964) says that such attributes as class and culture are not critical determinants of the ability to discern right from wrong but do influence expectations of treatment and of implications of behavior.

15. See also another analysis of this study, Easton and Hess (1962).

16. Greenstein (1965) questioned New Haven public school children and Jaros (1967) questioned Detroit public school children. The other studies are based on surveys of national samples of public school children. But the first review of political socialization hypotheses and research, based on a survey of the literature, was made by Hyman (1959).

17. Dean Jaros (1967) found that many children picture the President as both authoritarian and benevolent. He suggests that there is no inconsistency between these two images.

18. Herbert Hyman (1959) reports a survey showing that political knowledge increases between the lower and higher elementary school grades. The surveys of grade school children report a similar finding. See Greenstein (1965), Hess and Torney (1967), Easton and Dennis (1969), Jaros (1967), and Sigel (1968). Adelson and O'Neil (1966) report a growth in comprehension of what is a political community and what are the obligations of its citizens during the adolescent years.

19. Almond and Verba (1963) point out that persons having more than secondary education have similar orientations toward political authority regardless of country.

20. This interpretation of Piaget's theory is made by Henry Maier (1965: 140-141).

21. One recent paper reports on the application of another method of inquiry in political socialization research, a method that would allow the investigator to tap some of the richness of political ideas of children (Greenstein and Tarrow, 1969). Richard Merelman (1969) has suggested a means of applying some of the insights of cognitive developmental theory in political studies with regard to the conjunction between the development of moral behavior and of political ideologies.

22. In his review of political socialization research, Richard Dawson (Dawson and Prewitt, 1969) says that psychology, social anthropology, role theory, and small group studies have influenced political science research.

23. Hess and Torney (1967) discuss compliance with the law and images of the law as indicative of political socialization.

24. Greenstein (1960) introduced this term to characterize children's affective responses about the President and the policeman. See also Hess and Easton (1960), Hess and Torney (1967), and Easton and Dennis (1969). A study of children in Appalachia

found that despite disaffection from politics, they held a highly positive image of the President (Jaros et al., 1968).

25. Greenstein comments that children aggrandize adults.

26. The inquiry into the relationship between beliefs and personality traits of Americans is based on a premise that there are Americans who are raised by authoritarian fathers (Adorno, 1950). Fred L. Strodbeck (1958) reviews and assesses studies comparing the impact on children's behavior of authoritarian and democratic fathers. For an interpretation that authoritarian fathers have little impact on their sons' political beliefs, see Lane (1962: 272-279).

27. An example of an explicit statement of this hypothesis and an application of it, in this instance to a case of acculturation is Edward M. Bruner (1956). Benjamin S. Bloom (1964: 4-5) has collected, organized, and analyzed longitudinal studies on a variety of personal traits to determine the extent to which each is formed early in life and the extent to which each remains stable. He notes that interest in particular objects, learning particular subjects, and more superficial personality characteristics are less likely to be stable than are such traits as height, intelligence, and academic achievement. Alex Inkeles (1968: 92) suggests later social learning experiences can be critical for the acquisition of norms and skills, and he calls these experiences a "second wave" in the socialization process. Almond and Verba (1963) point out that school and job experiences and organizational membership and activity influence the acquisition of political values. Theodore Newcomb's study (1957) of Bennington students demonstrates that values acquired in college that conflict with parental values are likely to be retained after graduation. On the impact of grade school experiences see Langton (1969: Ch. 5).

28. They apply this interpretation in Easton and Hess (1962: 156) as do Easton and Dennis (1969: 162).

29. Jack Dennis (1968: 92-93) charts these components of attitude studies in socialization surveys.

30. See also Flavell (1963: 80-81) on Piaget.

31. See also Rosenberg et al. (1960: Chs. 1, 2). A summary and appraisal of Rosenberg's experiments and others on the components of attitudes is offered by Fishbein (1965).

32. Sigel (1969) points out that children's attitudes about politics are influenced by issues and events, and a change in these produces a change in their evaluations of the government.

33. The development of cognitive abilities is acknowledged as the source of this change.

34. Piaget has been criticized for having a cultural bias, and it may be pointed out that the nation is a less salient entity to Swiss children than to those in many other nations. Nonetheless, Piaget is concerned with children's abilities to comprehend concepts, and his observations here may be pertinent.

35. The findings may be qualified by the fact that a child's intellectual ability may be what is measured by the questions on efficacy. But this criticism may be made of many of the instruments used in the other socialization studies.

REFERENCES

ADELSON, J. and L. BEALL (1970) "Adolescent perspectives on law and government." Law and Society Rev. 4 (May).

ADELSON, J. and R. O'NEIL (1966) "Growth of political ideas in adolescence: the sense of community." J. of Personality and Social Psychology 4 (September): 295-306.

ADORNO, T., E. FRANKEL-BRUNSWIK, D. J. LEVINSON, and R. N. SANFORD (1950) The Authoritarian Personality. New York: Harper.

ALMOND, G. and S. VERBA (1963) The Civic Culture. Princeton: Princeton Univ. Press.

ARONFREED, J. (1969) "The concept of internalization," pp. 263-324 in D. A. Goslin (ed.) Handbook of Socialization Theory and Research. Chicago: Rand McNally.

--- (1961) "The nature, variety, and social patterning of moral responses to transgression." J. of Abnormal and Social Psychology 63 (September): 223-240.

BACON, M. K., I. L. CHILD, and H. BARRY III (1963) "A cross-cultural study of the correlates of crime." J. of Abnormal and Social Psychology 66 (April): 291-300.

BALDWIN, A. E. (1969) "A cognitive theory of socialization," pp. 339-345 in D. A. Goslin (ed.) Handbook of Socialization Theory and Research. Chicago: Rand McNally.

BANDURA, A. (1969) "Social learning theory of identificatory processes," pp. 213-262 in D. A. Goslin (ed.) Handbook of Socialization Theory and Research. Chicago: Rand McNally.

--- and R. W. WALTERS (1963) Social Learning and Personality Development. New York: Holt, Rinehart, & Winston.

BLOOM, B. S. (1964) Stability and Change in Human Characteristics. New York: John Wiley.

BRUNER, E. M. (1956) "Cultural transmission and cultural change." Southwestern J. of Anthropology 12 (Summer): 191-199.

CARLSON, E. R. (1956) "Attitude change through modification of attitude structure." J. of Abnormal and Social Psychology 52 (March): 256-261.

CLAUSEN, J. A. (1968) "Introduction: socialization, a concept and as a field of study," pp. 1-72 in J. A. Clausen (ed.) Socialization and Society. Boston: Little, Brown.

DAWSON, R. E. (1966) "Political socialization," pp. 4-11 in J. A. Robinson (ed.) Political Science Annual, Vol. I. Indianapolis: Bobbs-Merrill.

--- and K. PREWITT (1969) Political Socialization. Boston: Little, Brown.

DENNIS, J. (1968) "Major problems of political socialization research." Midwest J. of Pol. Sci. 12 (February): 85-114.

EASTON, D. and J. DENNIS (1969) Children in the Political System. New York: McGraw Hill.

EASTON, D. and R. HESS (1962) "The child's political world." Midwest J. of Pol. Sci. 6 (August): 229-246.

--- (1961) "Youth and the Political System," pp. 226-251 in S. M. Lipset and L. Lowenthal (eds.) Culture and Social Character: The Work of David Riesman Reviewed. New York: Free Press.

ERIKSON, E. (1969) Gandhi's Truth. New York: W. W. Norton.

--- (1968) Identity, Youth, and Crisis. New York: W. W. Norton.

--- (1963) Childhood and Society. New York: W. W. Norton.

--- (1958) Young Man Luther: A Study in Psychoanalysis and History. New York: W. W. Norton.

FISHBEIN, M. (1965) "A consideration of beliefs, attitudes, and their relationship," pp. 107-120 in I. Steiner and M. Fishbein (eds.) Current Studies in Social Psychology. New York: Holt, Rinehart, & Winston.

FLAVELL, J. H. (1963) The Developmental Psychology of Jean Piaget. Princeton: D. Van Nostrand.

GREENBERG, E. S. (1969) "Children and the political community: a comparison across racial lines." Canadian J. of Pol. Sci. 2 (December): 471-492.

GREENSTEIN, F. I. (1965) Children and Politics. New Haven: Yale Univ. Press.

--- (1960) "The benevolent leader: children's images of political authority." Amer. Pol. Sci. Rev. 54 (December): 934-943.

GREENSTEIN, F. I. and S. G. TARROW (1969) "An approach to the study of comparative political socialization: the use of a semi-projective technique." Delivered

at the American Political Science Association meeting, Washington, D.C., September.
GOLDSTEIN, A. S. (1967) The Insanity Defence. New Haven: Yale Univ. Press.
GOSLIN, D. A. (1969) Handbook of Socialization Theory and Research. Chicago: Rand McNally.
HESS, R. D. (1963) "The socialization of attitudes toward political authority: some cross-national comparisons." International Social Sci. J. 15, 4: 542-559.
--- and D. EASTON (1962) "The role of the elementary school in political socialization." School Rev. 70 (Autumn): 257-265.
--- (1960) "The child's changing image of the president." Public Opinion Q. 24 (Winter): 632-644.
HESS, R. D. and J. V. TORNEY (1967) The Development of Political Attitudes in Children. Chicago: Aldine.
HYMAN, H. (1959) Political Socialization. New York: Free Press.
INKELES, A. (1968) "Society, social structure and child socialization," pp. 73-129 in J. Clausen (ed.) Socialization and Society. Boston: Little, Brown.
JAHODA, G. (1963a) "Part II: national symbols and themes." British J. of Educational Psychology 33 (June): 143-153.
--- (1963b) "The development of children's ideas about country and nationality. Part I: the conceptual framework." British J. of Educational Psychology 33 (February): 47-60.
JAROS, D. (1967) "Children's orientation toward the president: some additional theoretical considerations and data." J. of Politics 29 (May): 368-387.
---, H. HIRSCH, and F. J. FLERON, Jr. (1968) "The malevolent leader: political socialization in an American subculture." Amer. Pol. Sci. Rev. 62 (June): 564-575.
KOHLBERG, L. (1969) "Stage and sequence: the cognitive-developmental approach to socialization," pp. 347-481 in D. A. Goslin (ed.) Handbook of Socialization Theory and Research. Chicago: Rand-McNally.
--- (1966) "A cognitive-developmental approach to socialization—morality and psychosexuality." Unpublished paper.
--- (1964) "Development of moral character and ideology," pp. 383-431 in M. L. Hoffman (ed.) Review of Child Development Research, Vol. I. New York: Russell Sage Foundation.
LAMBERT, W. E. and O. KLINEBERG (1966) Children's Views of Foreign Peoples, A Cross-National Study. New York: Appleton-Century Crofts.
LANE, R. (1962) Political Ideology. New York: Free Press.
LANGTON, K. (1969) Political Socialization. New York: Oxford Univ. Press.
LEFSTEIN, N., V. STAPLETON, and L. TEITELBAUM (1969) "In search of juvenile justice: Gault and its implementation." Law and Society Rev. 3 (May): 491-562.
MACCOBY, E. E. (1968) "The development of moral values and behavior in childhood," pp. 227-269 in J. Clausen (ed.) Socialization and Society. Boston: Little, Brown.
MAIER, H. W. (1965) Three Theories of Child Development. New York: Harper & Row.
McCORD, W. and J. McCORD (1959) Origins of Crime: A New Evaluation of the Cambridge Summerville Youth Study. New York: Columbia Univ. Press.
MERELMAN, R. (1969) "The development of political ideology: a framework for the analysis of political socialization." Amer. Pol. Sci. Rev. 63 (September): 750-767.
MILLER, N. E. and J. DOLLARD (1941) Social Learning and Imitation. New Haven: Yale Univ. Press.
MOYNIHAN, D. P. (1969) "Toward a national urban policy." Public Interest 17 (Fall): 3-20.
NEWCOMB, T. (1957) Personality and Social Change. New York: Holt, Rinehart, & Winston.
ORREN, K. and P. PETERSON (1967) "Presidential assassination: a case study in the dynamics of political socialization." J. of Politics 29 (May): 388-404.

PIAGET, J. (1965) THe Moral Judgment of the Child. New York: Free Press.

--- (1962) Play, Dreams, and Imitation in Childhood. New York: W. W. Norton.

--- (1955) The Child's Construction of Reality. London: Routledge.

--- (1952) The Origin of Intelligence in Children. New York: International Universities Press.

--- and A. WEIL (1951) "The development in children of the idea of the homeland and of relations with other countries." International Soc. Sci. Bull. 3 (Autumn): 561-578.

RAINWATER, L. and B. YANCY (1967) The Moynihan Report and its Critics. Cambridge: MIT Press.

ROSENBERG, M. J. (1960) "A structural theory of attitude dynamics." Pub. Opinion Q. 24 (Summer): 319-333.

---, C. I. HOVLAND, W. J. McGUIRE, R. P. ABELSON, and J. W. BREHM (1960) Attitude Organization and Change. New Haven: Yale Univ. Press.

SEARS, R. (1961) "The relation of early socialization experiences to aggression in middle childhood." J. of Abnormal and Social Psychology 63 (November): 466-492.

--- (1957) "Identification as a form of behavioral development," pp. 149-161 in D. Harris (ed.) The Concept of Development. Minneapolis: Univ. of Minnesota Press.

---, E. MACCOBY, and H. LEVIN (1957) Patterns of Child Rearing. Evanston: Row, Peterson.

SIGEL, R. (1969) "Two years after: change and stability in youth's political views." Presented at the Midwest Political Science Association, Ann Arbor, Michigan.

--- (1968) "Image of a president: some insights into the political views of school children." Amer. Pol. Sci. Rev. 62 (March): 216-226.

--- (1965) "An exploration into some aspects of political socialization: school children's reaction to the death of a president," pp. 30-61 in M. Wolfenstein and G. Kliman (eds.) Children and the Death of a President. Garden City: Doubleday.

STEPHENSON, G. M. (1966) The Development of Conscience. London: Routledge & Kegan Paul.

STRODBECK, F. L. (1958) "Family interaction, values, and achievement," pp. 135-191 in D. C. McClelland et al. (eds.) Talent and Society. Princeton: D. Van Nostrand.

SULLIVAN, H. S. (1953) The Interpersonal Theory of Psychiatry. New York: W. W. Norton.

WHITE, E. S. (1968) "Intelligence and sense of political efficacy in children." J. of Politics 30 (August): 710-731.

WHITING, J. (1961) "Socialization process and personality," pp. 335-339 in F. L. K. Hsu (ed.) Psychological Anthropology, Approaches to Culture and Personality. Homewood, Ill.: Dorsey.

--- and I. L. CHILD (1953) Child Training and Personality: A Cross-Cultural Study. New Haven: Yale Univ. Press.

WOODRUFF, A. D. and F. J. DiVESTA (1948) "The relationship between values, concepts, and attitudes." Educational and Psychology Measurement 8 (Winter): 645-660.

WRONG, D. H. (1961) "The oversocialized conception of man in modern society." Amer. Soc. Rev. 26 (April): 183-193.

ZIGLER, E. and I. L. CHILD (1969) "Socialization," pp. 450-589 in G. Lindzey and E. Aronson (eds.) The Handbook of Social Psychology, Vol. III. Reading, Mass.: Addison Wesley.

Chapter 9

Persuasion to Virtue

A Preliminary Statement

JUNE L. TAPP and FELICE J. LEVINE

American Bar Foundation and University of Chicago

With increasing incidences of deviance exemplified by campus disorders, community crime, civil disobedience, and interpersonal aggression, demands for law and order emanate from various segments of the general population. Concurrently, the search for effective means of assuring compliance to law becomes more fervent. Some policy-planners, legislators, policemen, judges, and educators seek new insights and greater understanding about obedience, but society's response is primarily expressed in terms of increased surveillance, detection, and punishment (which ironically may function to complicate compliance problems). In coping with disobedience, whether individual or collective, violent or nonviolent, little serious attention is paid to the origins of deviance and particularly to the antecedents of compliance. Yet it is from knowledge about the origins of obedience and the related ideas of normal populations about the legal process that the problems of deviance can best be understood and stratagems for social change most effectively realized.

AUTHORS' NOTE: *The analysis presented herein is derived in part from data gathered pursuant to a contract with the United States Department of Health, Education and Welfare, Office of Education, Project 2947 under Contract OE 5-10-219, entitled "Authority, Rules, and Aggression: A Cross-national Study of Socialization into Compliance Systems." The principal investigators in that study were Professor Robert D. Hess (project director), Professor Leigh Minturn (senior investigator), and the first author of the present paper (co-principal investigator). The results of that initial study have been submitted to*

In addressing the issues surrounding compliance to rules and laws, ultimately one must focus on what may be called legal socialization. To date, little is known about the "positive" or "negative" aspects of the legal socialization process on the attitudes and behaviors of the average citizen, i.e., how individuals learn both deviant and compliant modes. Socialization, rather than the threat of a particular legal sanction, is primarily responsible for compliance to social systems (Zimring and Hawkins, 1968). This process is perhaps society's central means of social control (Brim, 1963). Its primary objective is "to produce individuals who will not only conform to the socially prescribed rules [and roles] of conduct but will, as members of society, accept them as their own values" (Maccoby, 1968: 230).

Interest in how people learn to be rule-abiding is not an entirely new concern for the behavioral sciences. Developmental and social psychologists, as well as political scientists with interests in political socialization, have studied the growth of moral judgments and of ideas about law and government employing a range of techniques and in various settings (Piaget, 1932; Kohlberg, 1963; Almond and Verba, 1963; Bandura and Walters, 1963: Hess and Torney, 1967; Adelson, et al., 1969; Aronfreed, 1968; Easton and Dennis, 1969). Psychological theory and research in moral development provide an excellent perspective for initiating work on the development of legal values and law-abiding behavior. Both of the major psychological positions–the developmental, stage-theory viewpoint and the social-learning one–have had substantial influence on analyzing legal socialization. The moral development theorists emphasize the effect of maturational growth on all cognitive development, including moral development, while the social-learning theorists stress that the acquisition of moral behavior, like any other class of behavior, reflects the influence of training, modeling, and identification with socializing agents (Berkowitz, 1964).

From the perspective of internalizing legal values and behaviors, "both formulations turn out to be right to a degree" (Maccoby, 1968: 253). It is true that individuals at various maturational stages have different capacities for understanding, abstracting, and conceptualizing. Maturational processes are

---

U.S.O.E. in two volumes: Part I co-authored by Hess and Tapp with cross-national collaborators (March 1969), and Part II co-authored by Minturn and Tapp with cross-national collaborators (January 1970). Plans are in process to make this data available in other forms also.

The present authors are indebted to Professors Minturn and Hess, cross-national principal investigators for the project and senior investigators, for their initial collaborative efforts in the underlying research. We are also indebted to Roberta Tabor, research assistant, and Brenda Smith, secretary, for supportive services. Finally, we gratefully acknowledge the financial support of the American Bar Foundation which enabled completion of this work.

central in forming children's judgments of rules and laws as absolute or changeable, breakable or unbreakable. It is equally valid that modeling and reinforcement effects of parents and other socializing agents have a notably powerful effect on children's perceptions of and interaction with the legal system. The effectiveness of such characteristics of the authority as punitiveness and affection are differentially important for gaining legal compliance.

This paper looks at children's perceptions at various age levels in order to note, where applicable, maturational change as well as persistent, stable early learning apparently due to training and reinforcement experiences. Instead of studying compliance and deterrence in terms of criminality and the offender, the paper considers how ideas about rules, justice, authority, and punishment function in normal populations. Although socialization or resocialization continues throughout the life cycle, the present focus is on children because strong evidence indicates considerable persistence of values and modes of behavior learned early. In other words, societal reform may be needed to reach this group, but the young are also the ones most susceptible to change (Brim and Wheeler, 1966; Maccoby, 1968). Theoretically, an understanding of children's perceptions of authority, justice, and the role of law in society should illuminate (1) what is universal about compliance as distinct from cultural or situational, and (2) what conditions engender tendencies toward compliance. Practically, such findings should provide police, judges, parents, educators—the socializers of the legal system—with primal information in educating for responsibility, deciding about culpability, evolving mature (moral) ideas of law and fairness, and perfecting methods for effective compliance. The results might also reduce some of the pervasive tension between authority and citizenry across a wide spectrum of the population.

METHOD

SAMPLE

This analysis is stimulated in part by data collected for a six-country, seven-culture (Denmark, Greece, Italy, India, Japan, United States black and white) developmental study on children's perceptions of and behaviors toward authority, rules, and aggression in various "legal" compliance systems, e.g., home, school, government, community (Hess and Tapp, 1969: Minturn and Tapp, 1970). In the United States the two major racial groups, whites and blacks, were examined for assumed differential outlooks toward authority and the social order. The United States interview sample consisted of 124 preadolescents (middle school children) from three grade groups: 4, 6, and 8. The 61 white and 63 black United States subjects, with approximately 20 in each grade, were also equally divided between the sexes and socioeconomic status

(SES) groupings, representing high (professional and semiprofessional) and low (working) levels. The American children came from primarily inner-city and suburban communities within a large urban metropolis. The interview data was collected in late Spring 1965 during the early civil rights movement in areas where awareness of the problem was developing. The primary focus of this paper will be the responses of the United States sample groups. When the findings for the United States and other nations are similar, universal patterns will be noted.

INTERVIEW

The interview focused on 9 substantive areas: definition of rules and laws, nature of fair rules, breakability of rules (laws), consistency of rules (laws), function of rules (laws), power of enforcement and deterrence, inevitability of detection, worst deviations from rules and laws, and the justice of punishment. The interview was open-ended and contained 79 questions, of which 22 were analyzed using cross-national, empirically-derived categories. This paper will discuss 6 of the 22:

(1) What is a fair rule?
(2) What would happen if there were no rules?
(3) Is it ever right to break a rule?
(4) Who can make you follow a rule or law?
(5) Who is it worst to be punished by?
(6) Why is it worst to be punished by (that choice)?

These selected items provide an economical way of portraying children's conceptions of justice (fairness), legitimacy, enforcement, punishment, and the role of law.

The interviews were individually administered in school settings by experienced and trained personnel. Where possible, the interviewers were matched to the children by race, SES, and sex. The interview session was one to two hours long, depending on the culture and the child. All United States interviews were taped and transcribed verbatim; interviewers also took notes and recorded impressions. Since the questioning format was completely open-ended, children's responses may be assumed to reflect reliably their own associations and perceptions (or even myths).[1]

DATA ANALYSIS

The analysis of children's responses was based on percentages computed for total, age, sex and SES frequencies. Similarities and differences between blacks and whites were examined. Total black-white differences for each response category were analyzed using *t*-tests, and for sampling variation between ethnic groups using *chi*-square. Only total ethnic differences are indicated since there were no significant black-white differences in the age, sex or SES groupings. Also age, sex and SES sampling variations were measured within each United States culture by *t*-tests. No sex differences emerged. When significant age and SES differences occurred in one group, they are discussed comparatively.

Other national patterns paralleling those of United States whites and blacks are included. Percentages are compared for trends between cultures; the concentration is on cross-national or general patterns. For the cross-cultural perspective, rank order and trend analyses are deemed more important, relevant, and fruitful than the analysis of significant differences because such differences may only represent national differences in response set and are therefore not as telling as an analysis of general patterns across national samples.

An examination of the similarities and differences between subcultures and cultures suggests criteria for distinguishing between the idiosyncratic, the culture-bound, and the universal (Minturn and Lambert, 1964). What is considered uniquely American may turn out to be oddly human.

RESULTS AND DISCUSSION

Children's responses to "What would happen if there were no rules?" cogently expressed their ideas about the nature of man and the function of laws and rules in society. American children demonstrated a fearful, distrusting view of mankind; both blacks and whites most often thought violence and crime would erupt without rules. No significant differences appeared between the two cultural groups. Their reaction was typified by this boy's concern, "There would probably be all kinds of different murders and stuff like that. People would be going crazy. There would be all kinds of burglaries and stuff like that; stealing cars and stuff." Such ideas reflected internalization of American society's consuming sense that "violence lurks with us" (Toch, 1969). Children also thought anarchy, disorder, and chaos as well as personal desire would be rampant. Children from the other countries had a similarly somber view of the world. Although the United States children mentioned violence and crime more frequently than other national groups, the major predictions made by most children, despite national background, were that violence, anarchy, and personal gain would prevail in the absence of rules. The comment of this fourth grade American boy encapsulated the view of most children: "Well, it would be a lot of disorganizing in the world. You know, people would be going around killing each other. It wouldn't be

TABLE 1
WHAT WOULD HAPPEN IF THERE WERE NO RULES?[a]
(U.S. blacks and whites by grade and SES)

Categories		Blacks %	Blacks (n)	Whites %	Whites (n)
Personal desires, not principles	Grade 4	23	(5)	24	(5)
	Grade 6	33	(7)	10	(2)
	Grade 8	45	(9)	35	(7)
	Low SES	33	(11)	26	(8)
	High SES	33	(10)	20	(6)
	Total	33	(21)	23	(14)
Civil injury	Grade 4	9	(2)	24	(5)
	Grade 6	24	(5)	5	(1)
	Grade 8	15	(3)	10	(2)
	Low SES	21	(7)	13	(4)
	High SES	10	(3)	13	(4)
	Total	16	(10)	13	(8)
Violence and crime	Grade 4	50	(11)	67	(14)
	Grade 6	57	(12)	65	(13)
	Grade 8	65	(13)	50	(10)
	Low SES	58	(19)	64	(20)
	High SES	57	(17)	57	(17)
	Total	57	(36)	61	(37)
Anarchy, disorder, chaos	Grade 4	54	(12)	24	(5)
	Grade 6	19	(4)	55	(11)
	Grade 8	45	(9)	40	(8)
	Low SES	36	(12)	23[b]	(7)
	High SES	43	(13)	57	(17)
	Total	40	(25)	39	(24)
Wars	Grade 4	4	(1)	10	(2)
	Grade 6	14	(3)	5	(1)
	Grade 8	10	(2)	10	(2)
	Low SES	15	(5)	13	(4)
	High SES	3	(1)	3	(1)
	Total	10	(6)	8	(5)
Impossible to imagine world without laws	Grade 4	–	–	10	(2)
	Grade 6	5	(1)	–	–
	Grade 8	5	(1)	5	(1)
	Low SES	3	(1)	3	(1)
	High SES	3	(1)	7	(2)
	Total	3	(2)	5	(3)
Don't know, response not applicable, no response	Grade 4	4	(1)	–	–
	Grade 6	–	–	–	–
	Grade 8	–	–	–	–
	Low SES	3	(1)	–	–
	High SES	–	–	–	–
	Total	2	(1)	–	–

a. Categories "Property not maintained" and "No regulation of wealth or property" omitted because of few responses. Multiple coded; therefore, percentages total over 100.
b. Significant SES difference ($t = 2.73$, $p \leqslant .05$).

organized, there wouldn't be any school or anything like that." One girl succinctly noted, "Everyone would do what they wanted."

Since socialization seeks to produce individuals who will want to comply, agents of socialization may teach children that without rules and laws, chaos and conflict would reign. This is to say that children's apprehension about the violent and aggressive nature of man may ensue from the emphasis placed on obeying rules and the reinforcement effects of calls for law and order from authority models as much as from a basically pessimistic assessment of man. And stressing such concerns may be particularly prevalent within middle-class–and perhaps even white–homes. For whites significantly more high SES children anticipated anarchy, disorder, and chaos. No comparable class difference emerged for blacks.

While training may amplify certain attitudes, apparently children in many countries sustain a Hobbesian, not Lockean, perception of human nature. Few can imagine a world without rules and few dare suggest that good might survive without law (Adelson et al., 1969). Rules and laws provide the boundaries and limits. Accordingly, there is a pervasive recognition that they control and deter man's "instinctually" aggressive, egoistic motives.

Children evidently have internalized a strong prolegal inclination the compliance-inducing effects of which may be diluted if the rules that are wanted turn out to be in some way unfair. If so, it is important to know what kind of rule–the kind of legal system–children consider fair and what aspects of a rule result in its being regarded as unfair. Although there was variation within the United States and between the United States and other countries on "What is a fair rule?" the open-ended response answers addressed three dimensions of "fairness": equality (distribution), rationality (justifiable reason), and consensus (participation). Children presented a remarkably acute summary of the attributes believed inherent in a constitutional democracy. On equality, a white child observed "We should both get yelled at for talking, but it's not fair for one person to get yelled at"; a black specified "A rule that would apply to everyone fairly and it wouldn't put one person out and another person in." For rationality, a fourth grader summarized, "Something that's all right to do, not something that takes away your freedom." And their position on the consensual aspect was very simply described by "Everybody likes it" and "When somebody suggests a rule and everybody thinks it's right, then it's fair."

The United States blacks and whites diverged in one significant regard. In contrast to nineteen percent of the United States black children, forty-eight percent of the United States white children cited equality. Perhaps, as a minority culture, blacks are more concerned with compensatory justice than equal justice as an equitable principle for eventually realizing the distribution of equal rights and opportunities. However, unlike children from any other culture, *both* blacks and whites thought justifiable reason an important dimen-

TABLE 2

WHAT IS A FAIR RULE?[a]

(U.S. blacks and whites by grade and SES)

Categories		Blacks %	Blacks (n)	Whites %	Whites (n)
Equality	Grade 4	14	(3)	38	(8)
	Grade 6	24	(5)	45	(9)
	Grade 8	20	(4)	60	(12)
	Low SES	21	(7)	42	(13)
	High SES	17	(5)	53	(16)
	Total	19[b]	(12)	48	(29)
By authority	Grade 4	9	(2)	—	—
	Grade 6	—	—	15	(3)
	Grade 8	—	—	—	—
	Low SES	—	—	10	(3)
	High SES	7	(2)	—	—
	Total	3	(2)	5	(3)
Reasonable-rational	Grade 4	32	(7)	38	(8)
	Grade 6	43	(9)	40	(8)
	Grade 8	30	(6)	20	(4)
	Low SES	36	(12)	23	(7)
	High SES	33	(10)	43	(13)
	Total	35	(22)	33	(20)
Consensual-participatory	Grade 4	14	(3)	19	(4)
	Grade 6	38	(8)	35	(7)
	Grade 8	20	(4)	20	(4)
	Low SES	6[c]	(2)	19	(6)
	High SES	43	(13)	30	(9)
	Total	24	(15)	25	(15)
Institutional	Grade 4	4	(1)	10	(2)
	Grade 6	—	—	—	—
	Grade 8	5	(1)	—	—
	Low SES	6	(2)	6	(2)
	High SES	—	—	—	—
	Total	3	(2)	3	(2)
Absolute—all rules	Grade 4	4	(1)	—	—
	Grade 6	—	—	—	—
	Grade 8	10	(2)	—	—
	Low SES	9	(3)	—	—
	High SES	—	—	—	—
	Total	5	(3)	—	—
Don't know, response not applicable, no response	Grade 4	27	(6)	10	(2)
	Grade 6	10	(2)	—	—
	Grade 8	10	(2)	10	(2)
	Low SES	21	(7)	6	(2)
	High SES	10	(3)	7	(2)
	Total	16	(10)	7	(4)

a. Categories "One which favors the inherently disadvantaged" and "One which is not arbitrary" omitted because of few responses. Multiple coded, therefore, percentages total over 100.

b. Significant ethnic difference ($t = 3.44$, $p \leqslant .05$).

c. Significant SES difference ($t = 3.47$, $p \leqslant .05$).

sion of rule fairness. This decidedly American response may reflect a Deweyan ethos: Explain to children *why* something is done. Rules are rationalized, reasons articulated. This is consistent with Elder's (1963) research which found that, if parents explain rules, adolescents are more likely to use them as models. It may be an American "culture bound" trait to consider a rule fair if a "good" reason has been provided. Certainly this fourth grader's expression revealed early learning of the principle: "What makes it fair? Because it is a good thing and it is helping you from getting hurt."

Most surprising perhaps is the central role of consensus-participation in children's justice concepts in the United States and in other countries. That a fair system embrace participatory, mutual, and joint efforts has important implications for our legal authority system. Also the extremely low number of children in all cultures who saw fair rules as those made by a legitimate authority suggests, not that authorities are per se unfair, but that participation and power within the system are requisite characteristics of justice around the world. Perhaps if judges, law enforcement officials, and other community representatives are to be considered "fair" functionaries within a "just" system, they must bring children and adults together to confront problems of law-abiding behavior and develop programs for the control and prevention of delinquency. Such strategies emphasizing dialogue and cooperation, like the delinquency program in the San Francisco Bay area, may both reduce crime and resocialize a perception of "just" legal authority (Carter, 1968).

There was one significant SES difference on the consensus-participation response. Black, high social class children were more prone to define fairness in such democratic terms. The same difference, though not significant, was noted for United States whites. Presumably the high SES child has more exposure to democratic settings, greater opportunity for role-playing in participatory activities, and therefore favors this aspect of fairness (Maas, 1951; Tuma and Livson, 1960; Kohn, 1960; Kohlberg, 1963).

Children's views about rules were probed from an additional perspective; that is, "Is it ever right to break a rule?" United States children, like children in most other countries, thought rule-breaking might be right. A majority of both United States whites and blacks thought that breaking rules is permissible *if* the rule is less important than the reason for breaking it. Their position was concisely depicted in these answers: "Well, it depends on what's going on. If it's a matter of life and death or, you know, something pretty important, then it's all right. But it should be followed as much as possible," and "When you're hungry and you go in the store and steal something. When you need money [like for] someone kidnapped, someone in your family, and he stole it from the bank, paid the ransom and you try to pay the money back to the bank. Money and food could be replaced but the person in life couldn't." Substantial minorities of children in two other countries also felt rule violation could be legitimate when there is appropriate reason. Children even at

TABLE 3

IS IT EVER RIGHT TO BREAK A RULE?[a]

(U.S. blacks and whites by grade and SES)

Categories		Blacks %	Blacks (n)	Whites %	Whites (n)
Yes, unspecified	Grade 4	–	–	–	–
	Grade 6	5	(1)	5	(1)
	Grade 8	5	(1)	5	(1)
	Low SES	3	(1)	6	(2)
	High SES	3	(1)	–	–
	Total	3	(2)	3	(2)
No rule is breakable	Grade 4	46	(10)	33[b]	(7)
	Grade 6	5	(1)	5	(1)
	Grade 8	25	(5)	5	(1)
	Low SES	33	(11)	23[c]	(7)
	High SES	17	(5)	7	(2)
	Total	25	(16)	15	(9)
If it is unfair	Grade 4	4	(1)	10	(2)
	Grade 6	10	(2)	10	(2)
	Grade 8	10	(2)	25	(5)
	Low SES	15	(5)	13	(4)
	High SES	–	–	17	(5)
	Total	8	(5)	15	(9)
Less important than reason for breaking it	Grade 4	32	(7)	48	(10)
	Grade 6	76	(16)	80	(16)
	Grade 8	55	(11)	65	(13)
	Low SES	42[d]	(14)	55	(17)
	High SES	67	(20)	73	(22)
	Total	54	(34)	64	(39)
Don't know, response not applicable, no response	Grade 4	18	(4)	10	(2)
	Grade 6	5	(1)	–	–
	Grade 8	5	(1)	–	–
	Low SES	6	(2)	3	(1)
	High SES	13	(4)	3	(1)
	Total	10	(6)	3	(2)

a. Category "It is all right to break a rule but not a law" omitted because of few responses.

b. Significant grade difference ($t = 2.27$, $p \leqslant .05$).

c. Significant SES difference ($t = 1.75$, $p \leqslant .05$).

d. Significant SES difference ($t = 1.99$, $p \leqslant .05$).

these younger age levels recognized that the law is not infallible and absolute in its sovereignty, but that there are just and legitimate reasons for transgressions. Their judgments indicated that developmentally they have moved

TABLE 4

WHO CAN MAKE YOU OBEY?[a]

(U.S. blacks and whites by grade and SES)

Categories		Blacks %	Blacks (n)	Whites %	Whites (n)
Father	Grade 4	77	(17)	86	(18)
	Grade 6	67	(14)	70	(14)
	Grade 8	75	(15)	75	(15)
	Low SES	73	(24)	87	(27)
	High SES	73	(22)	67	(20)
	Total	73	(46)	77	(47)
Mother	Grade 4	96	(21)	86	(18)
	Grade 6	76	(16)	80	(16)
	Grade 8	80	(16)	70	(14)
	Low SES	85	(28)	90[b]	(28)
	High SES	83	(25)	67	(20)
	Total	84	(53)	79	(48)
Teacher	Grade 4	54	(12)	76	(16)
	Grade 6	52	(11)	80	(16)
	Grade 8	55	(11)	70	(14)
	Low SES	61	(20)	87[c]	(27)
	High SES	47	(14)	63	(19)
	Total	54[d]	(34)	75	(46)
Police	Grade 4	41	(9)	62	(13)
	Grade 6	67	(14)	70	(14)
	Grade 8	70	(14)	75	(15)
	Low SES	64	(21)	77	(24)
	High SES	53	(16)	60	(18)
	Total	59	(37)	69	(42)
Government officials	Grade 4	27	(6)	48[e]	(10)
	Grade 6	24	(5)	25	(5)
	Grade 8	15	(3)	10	(2)
	Low SES	21	(7)	32	(10)
	High SES	23	(7)	23	(7)
	Total	22	(14)	28	(17)
Relatives	Grade 4	18	(4)	10	(2)
	Grade 6	10	(2)	15	(3)
	Grade 8	10	(2)	20	(4)
	Low SES	15	(5)	23	(7)
	High SES	10	(3)	7	(2)
	Total	13	(8)	15	(9)
Self	Grade 4	4	(1)	–	–
	Grade 6	–	–	–	–
	Grade 8	5	(1)	5	(1)
	Low SES	3	(1)	–	–
	High SES	3	(1)	3	(1)
	Total	3	(2)	2	(1)
Others	Grade 4	27	(6)	48	(10)
	Grade 6	29	(6)	50	(10)
	Grade 8	30	(6)	45	(9)
	Low SES	30	(10)	36	(11)
	High SES	27	(8)	60	(18)
	Total	29[f]	(18)	48	(29)

a. Categories "Don't know," "Response not applicable," and "No response" omitted because of few responses. Multiple coded; therefore, percentages total over 100.

b. Significant SES difference ($t = 2.19$, $p \leqslant .05$).

c. Significant SES difference ($t = 2.17$, $p \leqslant .05$).

d. Significant ethnic difference ($t = 2.44$, $p \leqslant .05$).

e. Significant grade difference ($t = 2.67$, $p \leqslant .05$).

f. Significant ethnic difference ($t = 2.18$, $p \leqslant .05$).

beyond the stage of believing that rules and laws are fixed and unchangeable (Piaget, 1932; Kohlberg, 1963).

Significant and supportive developmental and SES trends in both United States groups were also illuminating. Younger American children were inclined to be more committed to the notion that no rule is breakable. This age difference was significant for whites and evident among blacks. The SES divergences coincided, perhaps predictably, with developmental differences. Low SES children were prone to believe no rule is breakable, while high SES preadolescents believed extenuating reasons justify rule-breaking. The former pattern was significant for whites; the latter, for blacks. Younger children as well as lower class children were likely to have internalized a more authoritarian conception of government, a rigid perspective on the absolute rightness of law, and an inflexibility about man's duty to obey (Kohlberg, 1963; Piaget, 1932; Maas, 1951; Dolger and Ginandes, 1946; Tuma and Livson, 1960). Paralleling Adelson and associates' (1969) findings on adolescents, older children were more willing to disavow or ignore an unworkable law while younger children felt obliged to obey authority or be subject to severe punishment.

Children's responses to the enforcement question: "Who can make you follow a rule?" suggested the efficacy of trust and affiliation over fear and distance. Blacks and whites differed only about the teacher; significantly more whites (75%) than blacks (54%) favored this figure. For whites, teacher perhaps represented a more nurturant individual with whom they identified more strongly.

Both black and white children in the United States, like children from all other cultures, indicated that authority figures with whom they share a closer relationship are most effective in inducing obedience. Children generally ranked mother first, father second, teacher third, and policeman fourth. Percentages for the more proximal parents were substantially higher than for the more distal policeman. In terms of societal role functions, it may be assumed that generally normal individuals experience a more affectionate and psychologically meaningful attachment to those who are in closer proximity.

Consistent with social-learning theory, strong affective attachment to authority is a more important feature than punishment power in enforcing rules and gaining compliance (Bandura and Walters, 1963; Aronfreed, 1968; Berkowitz, 1964). Affective attachment seems part of a general, pervasive loyalty to and identification with the authority figure, engendering feelings of support as well as resulting in modeling and obedience. Apparently, severe or hostile punishment, more typically meted out by less intimate figures, is not an effective technique for obtaining compliance. Close, personal affiliation may be the important element in the socialization process for encouraging the acceptance and internalization of social and legal norms. As Bandura and McDonald's (1963) experiment demonstrated, reward may not be enough;

TABLE 5

WHO IS IT WORST TO BE PUNISHED BY?[a]

(U.S. blacks and whites by grade and SES)

Categories		Blacks %	Blacks (n)	Whites %	Whites (n)
Father	Grade 4	32	(7)	14[b]	(3)
	Grade 6	19	(4)	60	(12)
	Grade 8	30	(6)	35	(7)
	Low SES	15[c]	(5)	29	(9)
	High SES	40	(12)	43	(13)
	Total	27	(17)	36	(22)
Mother	Grade 4	23	(5)	5	(1)
	Grade 6	14	(3)	25	(5)
	Grade 8	10	(2)	15	(3)
	Low SES	18	(6)	10	(3)
	High SES	13	(4)	20	(6)
	Total	16	(10)	15	(9)
Teacher	Grade 4	—	—	—	—
	Grade 6	—	—	5	(1)
	Grade 8	—	—	—	—
	Low SES	—	—	3	(1)
	High SES	—	—	—	—
	Total	—	—	2	(1)
Policeman	Grade 4	41	(9)	81[d]	(17)
	Grade 6	67	(14)	30	(6)
	Grade 8	60	(12)	60	(12)
	Low SES	64	(21)	64	(20)
	High SES	47	(14)	50	(15)
	Total	56	(35)	57	(35)

a. Categories "Don't know," "Response not applicable," and "No response" omitted because of few responses. Multiple coded; therefore, percentages total over 100.

b. Significant grade difference between fourth and sixth grades ($t = 3.06$, $p \leqslant .05$).

c. Significant SES difference ($t = 2.24$, $p \leqslant .05$).

d. Significant grade difference between fourth and sixth grades ($t = 3.30$, $p \leqslant .05$).

active participation in the learning process may also be necessary. Perhaps in the final analysis, it is the power of persuasion to virtue rather than coercion to virtue that induces compliance and institutionalizes deterrence.

The probable effects of physical and psychological distance on children's tendencies to comply suggest that the influence of formal, impersonal agencies is weak at best and can be altered only by dramatic or conspicuous events. If authority figures such as police, judges, and mayors are to have positive impact, it will be largely through strong and manifest displays of "good."

Conspicuously "bad" conduct by these figures, e.g., impoliteness, arbitrariness, brutality, is imposed on an already diluted and questionable position. If children are to exhibit "respect for law," parents–the key socializers–must also be persuaded that the law is respectable. Parents teach by example as well as by command; their styles and values are emulated (Berkowitz, 1964).

On the enforcement question, United States whites demonstrated significant developmental (age) differences for government. Younger children were more likely to think government was effective in obtaining compliance. The same pattern held for blacks. Also, for whites there were significant social-class differences in choosing both mother and teacher as effective enforcers. Low SES children more frequently chose these female figures. Although for blacks the social class frequencies were not significantly different, patterns for the figures were the same as those for the whites. Furthermore, pancultural SES patterns were indicated for mother, and strongly emerged in six out of seven cultures for teacher. These social class differences suggest the power of the matriarchy within the lower class milieu (Dolger and Ginandes, 1946; Maas, 1951; Tuma and Livson, 1960). Children from lower-class cultures have more direct influence exerted over them by female figures and perhaps also more positive reinforcement experiences (Berkowitz, 1964).

Children's ideas about "Who is it worst to be punished by?" further supported the notion that harsh punishment is *not* directly related to enforcement power. Consistent with the cross-cultural pattern, United States blacks and whites considered the policeman the worst punisher, substantially worse than any other figure. Since male authority figures are traditionally associated with punitive and severe disciplinary measures, it is not surprising that father was rated worse than mother or teacher. However, consistent with the enforcement power question, father–the proximal figure–was evaluated much more positively than policeman–the distal figure. The policeman was clearly the worst punisher, but on "Who can make you follow a rule?" was not the most effective enforcer. Overall, children seemed to define worst in punitive and severe terms. Although harsh authority figures may mete out the worst punishment, children are not motivated to obey.

For United States whites two significant age trends emerged. Unlike younger children, older children thought punishment by father was worst, but younger children were more inclined to feel that way about the policeman. Although there were no significant differences on these figures for blacks, a reverse age trend appeared on policeman. As for SES, two significant differences held for the blacks; parallel patterns held for whites. Unlike low-status children, high social-class children indicated father. But low social-class children more frequently believed that policeman was the worst punisher. Low-status children (and perhaps black children) may be reflecting the punitive, if not arbitrary, nature of their exchanges with police. High-status children may interpret worst in terms of the possibility of love withdrawal, a more preva-

TABLE 6

WHY IS IT WORST TO BE PUNISHED BY (PERSON LISTED AS FIRST CHOICE)?[a]

(U.S. blacks and whites by grade and SES)

Categories		Blacks %	Blacks (n)	Whites %	Whites (n)
Power	Grade 4	9	(2)	5	(1)
	Grade 6	–	–	10	(2)
	Grade 8	5	(1)	20	(4)
	Low SES	3	(1)	6	(2)
	High SES	7	(2)	17	(5)
	Total	5	(3)	12	(7)
Severity of punishment	Grade 4	82	(18)	57	(12)
	Grade 6	90	(19)	60	(12)
	Grade 8	85	(17)	50	(10)
	Low SES	82	(27)	64	(20)
	High SES	90	(27)	47	(14)
	Total	86[b]	(54)	56	(34)
Source of love and help	Grade 4	–	–	–	–
	Grade 6	–	–	5	(1)
	Grade 8	–	–	–	–
	Low SES	–	–	–	–
	High SES	–	–	3	(1)
	Total	–	–	2	(1)
Resultant bad reputation	Grade 4	–	–	5	(1)
	Grade 6	–	–	–	–
	Grade 8	10	(2)	5	(1)
	Low SES	3	(1)	3	(1)
	High SES	3	(1)	3	(1)
	Total	3	(2)	3	(2)

a. Categories "It is Person You Love Most," "It is Person You Should Respect," "It is a Relative," "It is Not a Relative," "Don't Know," "Response not Applicable," and "No Response" omitted because of few responses. Multiple coded; therefore, percentages total over 100.

b. Significant ethnic difference ($t = 3.69$, $p \leqslant .05$).

lent middle-class socialization technique (Bronfenbrenner, 1958; Sears et al., 1957).

Responses to "Why is it worst to be punished by (that choice)?" confirmed the foregoing analysis on the relationship between enforcement power and punishment power. The United States blacks and whites, reflecting the cross-cultural pattern that held for six of seven cultures, emphasized the severity of punishment. Although both groups most frequently indicated severity of punishment, significantly more blacks (86%) than whites (56%) gave this reason. This difference may reflect the greater exposure to, and resulting fear that black children have of punitive, harsh measures. The following are examples of children's ideas about police: "Because they can take you to the police office and you could be sentenced to live in jail for the rest of your life until you die"; "Because he can give harder punishments"; "Probably because they can do more to you, not more but worse things." The primacy of severe punishment is consistent with children's selection of policeman as worst punisher. While increasing the number or the severity of sanctions may in some cases deter deviance, there is little evidence that such procedures result in legal socialization *or* the resocialization of compliant modes. "Furthermore, a desirable outcome of the socialization process from the standpoint of the social group is that the individual will conform without constant surveillance from society's formal or informal policeman and, indeed, will be able to function as policeman and teacher of the norms to the next generation" (Maccoby, 1968: 241).

CONCLUSION

Black and white children in the United States with few exceptions were astonishingly alike in their views about human nature and the need for rules, the justice of rules, the legitimacy of rule-breaking, the power of enforcement, and the justice of punishment. Like children throughout the world, American children recognized the role of rules and laws in controlling crime and violence, as well as disorder and anarchy, and in establishing limits and boundaries for human behavior. They sought rules and laws to maintain order, but their motive for orderly compliance systems was not unconditional: with good reason, rules could legitimately be violated. Children required a fair system, one which was rational, emphasized equality, and stressed the importance of consensus and participation. Moreover, their perceptions of authorities were colored by their notions of justice (fairness). Figures to whom they felt attachment and trust were more likely to gain obedience than figures who were punitive, unilateral, or perhaps arbitrary. The latter were feared but certainly not revered or obeyed. Developmental processes affected children's conceptions of justice and of the role of law. Concomitantly, their perceptions of authority figures and the legal system itself were strongly influenced by social-learning experiences.

The impact of punitive figures may be diminished because of their enforcement techniques. Apparently trust, fairness, credibility, and affiliation as distinct from punitive power are important aspects for accepting the legitimacy of the authority system (Krause, 1968; Flacks, 1968; Gamson, 1968). Such characteristics influence the likelihood of obedience and may be even more crucial than power characteristics in obtaining compliance. Moreover, an authority system cannot assure tight surveillance over every individual (de Charms, 1968; Asch, 1952). Emphasizing the trust-affiliative characteristics of the authority figures, increasing the consensual or participatory nature of encounters with the authority system, and creating a sense of civic responsibility for maintaining order appear to be more powerful than the threat of sanction or the risk of legal penalty in internalizing compliance. Ultimately, the model of the persuasive socializer may achieve greater success than the coercive one.

NOTE

1. The coding categories were based on an analysis of 12 interviews from each culture and represented an integration of national codes. The reliabilities, both intra- and inter-country, were calculated for pairs of coders using percentage agreement on the whole interview and by response category, codable and noncodable. For the United States the range for the nine areas was 71% to 80% for whites, 75% to 82% for blacks. Cross-nationally, the overall reliability was 77% for the 42 translated interviews. More detailed methodological information is available in Parts I and II of the initial research reports.

REFERENCES

ADELSON, J., B. GREEN, and R. O'NEIL (1969) "The growth of the idea of law in adolescence." Developmental Psychology 1 (July): 327-332.

ALMOND, G. A. and S. VERBA (1963) The Civic Culture: Political Attitudes and Democracy in Five Nations. Princeton: Princeton Univ. Press.

ARONFREED, J. (1968) Conduct and Conscience: The Socialization of Internalized Control Over Behavior. New York: Academic Press.

ASCH, S. E. (1952) Social Psychology. Englewood Cliffs, N.J.: Prentice-Hall.

BANDURA, A. and F. J. McDONALD (1963) "The influence of social reinforcement and the behavior of models in shaping children's moral judgments." J. of Abnormal and Social Psychology 67 (September): 274-282.

BANDURA, A. and R. H. WALTERS (1963) Social Learning and Personality Development. New York: Holt, Rinehart & Winston.

BERKOWITZ, L. (1964) The Development of Motives and Values in the Child. New York: Basic Books.

BRIM, O. G., Jr. (1963) "Socialization through the life cycle." Russell Sage Foundation (mimeo).

--- and S. WHEELER (1966) Socialization After Childhood. New York: John Wiley.

BRONFENBRENNER, U. (1958) "Socialization and social class through time and space," pp. 400-425 in E. Maccoby, T. M. Newcomb, and E. L. Hartley (eds.) Readings in Social Psychology. New York: Holt, Rinehart & Winston.

CARTER, R. M. (1968) "Upper-class and middle-class delinquency." Medical Arts and Sciences: J. of Loma Linda Univ. School of Medicine 22, 1: 3-17.

DE CHARMS, R. (1968) Personal Causation. New York: Academic Press.

DOLGER, L. and J. GINANDES (1946) "Children's attitudes toward discipline as related to sociometric status." J. of Experimental Education 15 (December): 161-165.

EASTON, D. and J. DENNIS (1969) Children in the Political System. New York: McGraw-Hill.

ELDER, G. (1963) "Parental power legitimation and its effects on the adolescent." Sociometry 26 (March): 50-65.

FLACKS, R. (1968) "Social psychological perspectives on legitimacy." Prepared for the annual meeting of the American Psychology Association, San Francisco, September.

GAMSON, W. (1968) Power and Discontent. Homewood, Ill.: Dorsey.

HESS, R. D. and J. L. TAPP (1969) Authority, Rules and Aggression: A Cross-National Study of the Socialization of Children into Compliance Systems: Part I. Washington, D.C.: U.S. Department of Health, Education and Welfare.

HESS, R. D. and J. V. TORNEY (1967) The Development of Political Attitudes in Children. Chicago: Aldine.

KOHLBERG, L. (1963) "The development of children's orientation toward a moral order." Vita Humana 6 (Winter/Spring): 11-33.

KOHN, M. (1960) "Social class and the allocation of parental responsibilities." Sociometry 23 (December): 372-392.

KRAUSE, M. S. (1968) School Children's Attitudes Toward Public Authority Figures. Unpublished.

MAAS, H. S. (1951) "Some social class differences in the family and group relations of pre- and early adolescents." Child Development 22 (June): 145-152.

MACCOBY, E. E. (1968) "The development of moral values and behavior in childhood," pp. 227-269 in J. A. Clausen (ed.) Socialization and Society. Boston: Little, Brown.

MINTURN, L. and W. W. LAMBERT (1964) Mothers of Six Cultures. New York: John Wiley.

MINTURN, L. and J. L. TAPP (1970) Authority, Rules and Agression: A Cross-National Study of the Socialization of Children into Compliance Systems: Part II. Washington, D.C.: U.S. Department of Health, Education and Welfare.

PIAGET, J. (1932) The Moral Judgment of the Child. New York: Paul, Trench, Truber.

SEARS, R. R., E. E. MACCOBY, and H. LEVIN (1957) Patterns of Child Rearing. Evanston, Ill.: Row, Peterson.

TOCH, H. H. (1969) Violent Men. Chicago: Aldine.

TUMA, E. and N. LIVSON (1960) "Family socioeconomic status and adolescent attitudes to authority." Child Development 31 (June): 387-399.

ZIMRING, F. and G. HAWKINS (1968) "Deterrence and marginal groups." J. of Research in Crime and Delinquency 5 (July): 100-114.

Chapter 10

Power, Influence, and Behavioral Compliance

JAMES T. TEDESCHI, THOMAS V. BONOMA,

BARRY R. SCHLENKER,

State University of New York at Albany

SVENN LINDSKOLD – *Ohio University*

Social psychologists have traditionally been concerned with problems of social conflict, power, influence, and persuasion. Yet, when one looks for systematic theory and evidence regarding the determinants of behavioral compliance to rules, norms, or influence attempts, few prescriptions can be garnered by the practical man of affairs for developing policy in matters of law and order. In a day when shouts of black power, student protests, and antiwar demonstrations reverberate through the legitimate institutions of the country and when violence commissions report the degree of disorder existing in the urban centers of America, lack of social scientific evidence upon which to base policy is a disquieting comment upon the relevance of social scientific research.

For the past forty years, social psychologists have focused much of their interest upon the processes of attitude formation and change. The assumption motivating such research is that once we know how to measure attitudes, how to understand structural factors involved in belief systems, and how to produce attitude change, then the basis for predicting and controlling behavior will have been established. Unfortunately, after thousands of experiments have been performed and scores of theories have been developed, little evidence has been produced to prove that attitudes mediate behavior in any direct fashion. It is noteworthy that relatively few studies even attempt to establish the relationship between attitudes and behavior, but rather, studies are more concerned with the effects of behavior on attitudes (Festinger, 1964; Rokeach, 1968).

A plausible argument can be made that attitudes and behaviors actually follow different psychological laws and serve parallel but separate functions for the individual. For example, behavior may occur as a simple function of the cost-reward structure of the perceived environment, whereas the verbal expression of attitudes may serve the function of rationalizing the actions as "good" or at least necessary. Durkheim (1951) suggested that persons need to view their own actions as "good." A person who cannot find sufficient justification for his actions in his personal value system is likely to change his attitudes in a manner consonant with his behavior so that he can rationalize his conduct (Festinger, 1957). In addition to the function of rationalization for behavior, expressed attitudes can be used to legitimate a power position (authority) or as influence techniques to gain power over the behavior of other people. Also, it is clear that verbal behavior is seldom rewarded or punished to the same degree or in the same circumstances as are other behaviors. A person is brought to trial for a behavior he has allegedly shown, but a man who expresses remorse for his crime is likely to gain a more lenient sentence or to be paroled.

The above arguments provide reason to reject the basic assumption underlying most social-psychological research pertaining to the social influence processes—that a person's attitudes directly mediate his behaviors. Once this assumption is rejected, a number of different research strategies are suggested: (1) study how people use their attitudes for purposes of influence and power, (2) study how individuals use their attitudes to rationalize their behaviors, or (3) focus upon how influence attempts gain behavioral compliance and avoid the pitfalls associated with the labyrinth of attitude structures. The last strategy has been adopted by the present authors.

The deliberate attempt by one person to elicit behavioral compliance from another person has been viewed by political scientists, sociologists, and social psychologists as an attempt to use social power or exercise social influence. The concepts of power and influence are sometimes used interchangeably, but some theorists are wont to make fine distinctions between the two terms. The remainder of this paper will review some of the concepts of power and attempt to integrate them into a more comprehensive theory of influence within dyads. Evidence for the theory will be presented and some conclusions of interest to policy makers will be proffered.

THEORIES OF POWER AND INFLUENCE

In our everyday behavior to achieve certain goals and avoid certain unpleasantries, we are inevitably confronted with an obstacle. Whether the obstacle is in the form of the conflicting goals of another with whom we are interacting, or the norms and rules of the group to which we belong, we must decide to reach some mutual accommodation of interests, to exert pressure to achieve an all-or-nothing solution, or to just give up on that particular goal. As long as people desire similar or mutually exclusive goals, and as long as most societies inculcate similar values into their members, social conflict must be engendered. Social conflict may be simply defined as a struggle over values and claims to scarce status, power, and resources in which the aims of the opponents are to neutralize, injure, or eliminate their rivals (Coser, 1956).

In classical sociological thought, conflict was considered dysfunctional and detrimental to the social system. Parsons (1949) thought social conflict was a disease which should be treated by propaganda specialists as a doctor treats his patients. Lewin (1946) desired the social management of conflict to achieve harmony. However, Simmel (1950) recognized that groups require disharmony as well as harmony. Coser (1956) has pointed out some of the functional and beneficial effects of change which conflicts permit. Thus, the current view seems to place conflict in the role of a societal stimulant, which, if held within bounds, is essential to the development of progress.

However, whether one views conflict as functional or dysfunctional, beneficial or harmful, it nonetheless pervades all forms of social interaction, and its mitigation can only be temporarily achieved by the exercise of social influence which allows bargaining and the accommodation of interests, or alternatively, a settlement of the conflict in favor of the stronger adversary.

The resolution of conflicting interests has been a central problem in political science and in economics. Social scientists in these disciplines have developed a number of theories of power to help account for both the development and solution of conflicts. However, there has been little agreement as to a definition of power. Schur (1969: 85) defines power as the "ability to determine the behavior of others in accord with one's own wishes." MacIver (1964: 77) similarly considers power to be the "capacity to control, regulate, or direct the behavior of persons or things." Hans Morgenthau (1964) has offered the most general definition of power, which he defines as coextensive with any behavioral changes in one person which can at least partially be attributed to the actions of another person; the latter, as the controlling person or the causative agent, is considered the powerful individual. The breadth of these definitions is almost as broad as the area of social science and yields little precision in theory and no testable predictions either about the use of power or the compliance gained. Yet it can be seen from the above definitions that power and influence are in all social interactions. For example, Deutsch (1966) considers political science to be the study of how compliance is obtained. Similarly, Nieburg (1969) notes that politics is nothing more than the struggle for influence and authority within presently established formal authority structures. In this regard, Lord Acton considered the continental governments, formed after the French Revolution, to be based on the people's participation in power, not their security or freedom. Similarly, cries for black power are based not on a vague desire for the value of freedom, but on a share in the socioeconomic power base from which freedom will follow.

The range of a theory of power clearly exceeds the bounds of political science. For example, law was considered by Weber (1954) as orders which are externally guaranteed by a high probability of coercion, designed to bring about conformity and avenge violations and administered by a group possessing the legitimate right to do so. Thus, whether a subtle and frequently unadmitted power struggle occurs (the word "power" sometimes carries negative connotations in relations between friends) to decide whether the husband plays golf or the wife takes him to the opera, or the more overt struggle for power among nations is the focus of interest, much of social behavior seems ultimately to boil down to the question of how social influence is wielded.

As often happens in the field of science, concepts are continually redefined in an attempt to develop a coherent theory. In this tradition, Harsanyi (1962) suggests that compliance of one party to the wishes of the other constitutes the criterion for the successful exercise of power. In a condition of bilateral power, where each person has some influence over the behavior of the other, the amount of *P*'s power over *P* and *W*'s joint policy with respect to some controversial issue, "X," is defined as the probability (p) of *P*'s being able to get the joint policy X_p adopted when *P* favors this policy X_p and *W* favors a different policy X_w. For Harsanyi, a condition of a power relationship is that two or more individuals have conflicting preferences and a decision must be made as to whose preferences will prevail. Power is a relevant factor in social interactions only where social conflict exists. Harsanyi's analysis has the virtue of attempting to identify the conditions under which power is exercised. However, the possibility of compromise or the failure of a power attempt are not considered nor does the theory indicate the processes by which the conflicting parties resolve their differences.

Parsons (1963) analytically separates the concepts of power and influence. For him, power is a form of abstract currency and legitimacy and relies upon the psychological factor of trust. The influence processes are conceived as ways of getting results in interaction. In a manner of speaking, it may be said that Parsons' four systems of influence specify the processes by which conflicting parties resolve their differences and, consequently, serve to fill a gap in Harsanyi's theory of power. One form of influence, deterrence, relies on threats, coercion, and punishment for effectiveness. Promises of rewards or inducements constitute a second form of influence. Attempts to restructure the goals or attitudes of target individuals through the use of arguments or propaganda is a process labeled persuasion. Finally, Parsons suggests that the technique of activating commitments by appeals to norms may be effective in gaining compliance because the target individual reassesses what constitutes appropriate behavior for the situation.

Lasswell and Kaplan (1950) have developed a number of base values that they believe serve as basic resources for those who wield power and influence. These base values are respect, moral standing, affection, well-being, skill, wealth, enlightenment, and power (which can be used as a basis for accruing even more power). French and Raven (1959) have also delineated factors which serve as the bases of power. Reward power and coercive power derive from a source's ability to administer reinforcements and punishments and correspond with Parsons' distinction between inducements and deterrence and Lasswell and Kaplan's categories of wealth and power. French and Raven also suggest that a target individual often complies with a source's wishes because the former identifies with or is attracted to the latter—a form of attraction or referent power. Referent power can be viewed as equivalent to the categories of respect and affection in the Lasswell and Kaplan system and both inducements and activation of commitments in Parsons' system. Referent power is clearly related to Schopler and Bateson's (1965) proposal that the dependency needs of the target may be a basis of power for the source. Expert power is defined by French and Raven as a source's ability to persuade a target because of the former's superior knowledge or skill. It may be considered as equivalent to Parsons' persuasion process and the categories of skill and enlightenment in the typology of Lasswell and Kaplan. Persuasion systems appear also to be equivalent to Jones and Gerard's (1967) notion of information control. The fifth and last basis of power offered by French and Raven depends upon a target's belief that the source of influence deserves compliance because of the latter's role position (legitimate authority). Legitimate power is the only kind of power recognized by some theorists (Parsons, 1963; Gamson, 1968) and is consistent with the categories of moral standing and well-being among the bases of power suggested by Lasswell and Kaplan.

A number of social scientists define power as related to outcome control. March (1955) argues that the greater the power of *P*, the greater the ability of *P* to restrict *W*'s outcomes. Thus, if *P* cannot by his own actions lessen the range or value of outcomes for *W* in a situation, then *P* has no control over the future. Karlsson (1962), a sociologist, argues that the greater the range over which *P* can determine *W*'s rewards, the greater *P*'s power over *W*. At a more operational level of analysis, Thibaut and Kelley (1959) have offered an analysis of outcome control in dyadic interactions where the values in simple two-choice situations yield a matrix of payoffs to the two parties involved. When one player has absolute control over the other's outcomes, regardless of what the latter does, the former is said to possess fate control. Behavior control refers to a situation in which one or both parties in a dyadic interaction partially control the other's outcomes but do not possess fate control.

> Two suspects are taken into custody and separated. The District Attorney is certain that they are guilty of a specific crime, but he does not have adequate evidence to convict them at a trial. He points out to each prisoner that he has two alternatives: to confess to the crime the police are sure they have done, or not to confess. If they both do not confess, then the D.A. states he will book them on some very minor trumped-up charge such as petty larceny and illegal possession of a weapon, and they would both receive minor punishments; if they both confess they will be prosecuted, but he will recommend less than the most severe sentence, but if one confesses and the other does not, then the confessor will receive lenient treatment for turning state's evidence, whereas the latter will get "the book" slapped at him.

Thus, the PDG is a mixed-motive, non-zero-sum game in which both parties can win, both can lose, or one can win while the other loses. In the experimental situation, if both parties cooperate, both can win a certain number of points. If both parties compete, both lose a certain number of points. Finally, if one party competes while the other cooperates, the former will win points while the latter will lose points. A certain degree of conflict is thus built into the situation in that there is a temptation to exploit the other rather than cooperate and face the possibility of being exploited yourself. However, if both parties reason this way, both will continually lose. In the modified PDG, messages (e.g., threats and promises) can be intermittently exchanged by the parties. By using a simulated player as one of the parties, source characteristics, frequency of message use, and strategy selections can be systematically manipulated, and the effects of these independent variables on conflict and compliance can be delineated. All of the studies to be presented used the message-modified PDG as the research tool.

Figure 1 presents an overview of the concepts of the theory and indicates the relationships between them. Source characteristics are assumed to be measurable and constitute the independent variables of the theory. Source characteristics must be perceived or interpreted by the target and these second order variables are considered to be cognitive attributes of the target which correspond to the objective determination of the characteristics. Each of the second order variables are assumed to have specific functional relationships with the predictor variable, believability of the communication, which if the target cannot or chooses not to "leave the field" for some alternative social relationship, is directly related to behavioral compliance. The specific effects of each of the independent variables on compliance will now be discussed under their appropriate headings.

REWARD AND PUNISHMENT POWER

A source of influence who uses promises and threats to obtain compliance to his wishes from a target individual can be expected to be successful in proportion to the degree to which his deeds match his words. If a source

Many other issues have been raised concerning definitions of power and influence. For example, some reserve power for coercive influence attempts (Bachrach and Baratz, 1963), and others attempt to distinguish between power and force (Lasswell and Kaplan, 1950). However, the above review of concepts of power and influence and some of the factors contributing to compliance indicate that a wide range of phenomena are considered and that the language generally used by theorists (though often heuristic) does not meet the formal criteria expected for scientific theories. What is clearly needed at this point in the development of social science is a theory of power or influence which takes into consideration some of the analyses and definitions that have so far been offered, and which is clearly and precisely formulated so that testable theorems or predictions can be derived. Science is not just a process of intuitive analysis. It requires that concepts be imbedded in a system of functional relationships which can be empirically evaluated.

Theorists have delineated factors associated with the source of social influence, the types of influence attempts that might be made, the conditions under which influence takes place, and the target's characteristics rendering him influenceable, all of which are important for any theory of social influence. Thus, source characteristics, such as respect, moral standing, affection, wealth, skill, well-being, enlightenment, and power yield credits for future influence attempts. Different means of exercising influence correspond with inducements, deterrence, activation of commitments, and persuasion. The belief by the target-of-influence in the legitimacy of source's authority should be related to the degree of compliance or deference given to the source's influence attempts.

Tedeschi (1968) has developed a theory of social influence within dyads that attempts to capture most of the components of an influence system suggested by the above review of the concepts of power and influence. The theory predicts behavioral compliance by target individuals but also suggests factors relevant to source behaviors. The remainder of this paper will present Tedeschi's theory and will review evidence gathered to evaluate the theory.

A DYADIC THEORY OF INFLUENCE

The theory proposed by Tedeschi is deliberately simplified, first of all, to dyadic interaction and, second, to explicit contingent threats and promises sent from a specified source to a known target. The modes of influence thus correspond to Parsons' categories of deterrence and inducements, French and Raven's types of coercive and reward power, and Lasswell and Kaplan's bases of wealth and power. The theory is static in that it does not fully discuss opportunities for counterinfluence. The focus is upon behavioral compliance and largely ignores cognitive change (and thus the entire area of social persuasion). The source of influence is presumed to be motivated to maximize gains and has already chosen a target. Although specific characteristics of both source and target are defined operationally and linked to the ongoing influence process, the more complex cognitive factors that presumably help mediate the behaviors of both individuals are deliberately simplified. The result is a testable theory, the value of which will depend upon how well it predicts behavior. The theory is developed in a manner calculated to serve as a basis from which to develop a more complex theory once the simpler components are understood.

The basic components of a theory of influence are a source, a signal system, and a target. The present theory restricts the signal system to explicit contingent threats and promises. A threat takes the form "if-then" and asks for the performance of a behavior or the inhibition of a behavior and specifies the punishment for noncompliance. The punishment is an action, the withholding of an action, the production of a noxious stimulus, or the removal of a positive reinforcement, any of which may be perceived by the target as detrimental, costly, and punishing. Law, the nuclear deterrence system existing between the United States and the Soviet Union, and escalation are all examples of contingent threats. The classical theory of law reasons that if the punishment for noncompliance is large enough, man will stay within the bounds of cultural rules. The deterrence system tries to force decision makers into rational forms of behavior (i.e., aggression below certain specified limits) by the threat of annihilation. Escalation can be viewed as a contingent threat whose punishment is greater than the act which precipitated it (e.g., kill one of my soldiers and I will kill ten of yours). Contingent promises similarly take the form: "if you do X (or not X), then I will do Y," where Y is an action considered beneficial by the target. Bazelon (1965) has conceptualized the economic system largely in terms of contingent promises. For example, he reviews contracts as mutual contingent promises enforced by a court of law (threat system). Modern paper money can be considered a contract with unknown parties for the future delivery of pleasures which one can decide upon at a later date. A check is a promise from a bank that a bookkeeper will place a mark on his books in the appropriate place. The use of promises in political behavior to gain election support is known by every schoolboy. Advertising is also a promise made by a manufacturer that if their product is used, the purchaser will smell better, have more dates, and be happier than if he went without the product (the credibility of advertisements is another question). Contingent threats and promises thus seem to pervade our lives and are indeed essential for an individual who wants to maximize his outcome attainment when interacting with others who might have dissimilar goals.

The paradigm used for the study of compliance to contingent threats and promises is the message-modified version of the Prisoner's Dilemma game (PDG) developed by Horai and Tedeschi (1969). The important features of the unmodified form of this game are illustrated by Luce and Raiffa (1957: 95):

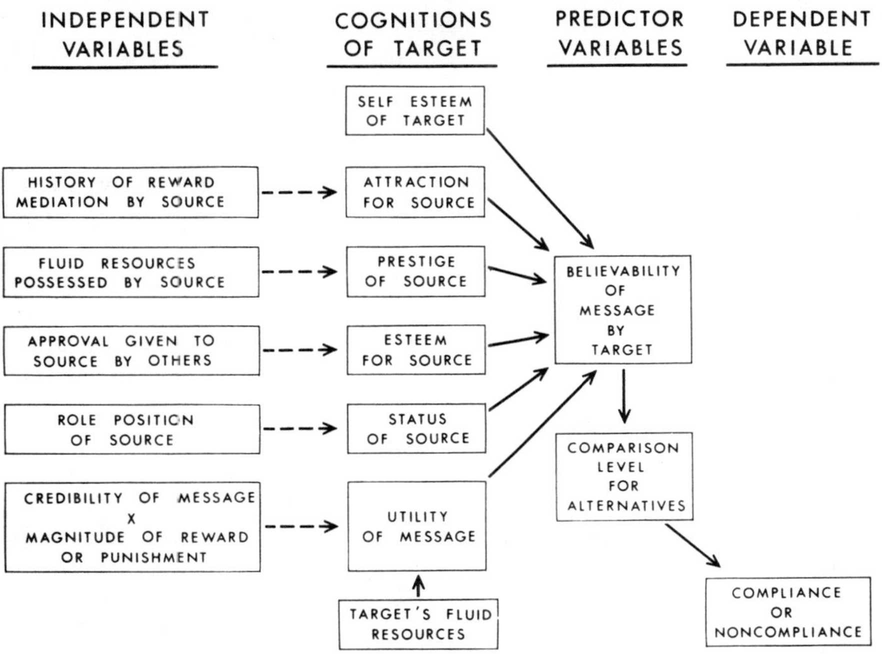

Figure 1.

offers rewards for compliance but does not follow through by giving the reward when the occasion arises, then the target should begin to doubt his word. Similarly, the believability of threats will be decreased if the target's defiance is not punished. As Nieburg (1969) has observed, the rational goal for the use of violence in carrying out a threat is the demonstration of the will and capability of action, thereby establishing high credibility for future threats. In addition, the degree of magnitude of rewards and punishments should be an important determinant of believability and subsequent compliance. MacIver (1964) notes that obedience to the law is a result of the costs for noncompliance, whether from the actual punishments or from guilt and loss of respect, and the like, being higher than costs of compliance. As has previously been noted, both the classical theory of law and the deterrence system rest on the premise that if the punishment is made severe enough compliance will result.

Source credibility can be operationally defined and measured as the proportion of times the source does what he says he will do. Thus, the proportion of times the source rewards compliance to promises is a measure of promise credibility, and the proportion of times the source punishes noncompliance to threats is a measure of threat credibility. It should be noted that these definitions explicitly assume that unsuccessful promises and successful threats have no objective credibility, although there is no presumption that such events either do or do not affect believability. It is quite possible that compliance to threats or noncompliance to promises will have cognitive effects on the target so that he rationalizes his responses by feeling that he definitely would have been punished had he not complied to the threat, or would definitely not have been rewarded if he had complied to the promise. Such rationalizations could produce increments in believability apart from objective credibility effects.

Since message credibility refers to the probability of an event, and magnitude of reward or punishment refer to the value of the event to the target, the concept of utility, as used by decision theorists and economists, seemed to be applicable to target's perceptions. The concept of utility has been used to express the subjective expected value of a future event perceived by a particular individual and is presumed to mediate the individual's choices (holding all else constant). The relationship between probability and value is usually believed to be multiplicative (Edwards et al., 1965). In a controlled laboratory experiment, both message credibility and value can be specified and measured. If the multiplicative relationship of credibility and value is assumed to be directly related to target's perception of message utility, and utility is assumed to be functionally related to believability, it can be predicted that compliance will be a direct function of message utility. Horai and Tedeschi (1969) were the first to test the relationship of message utility and compliance, and found that compliance to threats was a direct linear function of both credibility and punishment magnitude. The finding that as the negative utility of threats increases, compliance by target individuals also increases has been replicated a number of times (Lindskold et al., 1969; Faley and Tedeschi, 1969).

Tedeschi et al. (1968) found that when the punishment magnitude threatened for noncompliance was no greater than the costs to target for complying, the target resisted the threats, irrespective of message credibility. This result implies that the target is not indifferent when the punishment for noncompliance equals the costs of compliance but in fact derives some satisfaction from depriving the source of the gains to be gotten from the target's compliant behavior. Also, it could be inferred that when significant target values are at stake, threats are unlikely to be effective in gaining compliance.

It is quite clear that promises are not merely symmetrical to threats in that the former offers rewards and the latter offers punishments. Several studies (Lindskold and Tedeschi, 1969a; Lindskold et al., 1970; Schlenker, Bonoma, Tedeschi, et al., 1969) reveal that promise credibility, magnitude of reward, and positive message utility have no effects upon a target's compliance. Apparently, a promisor is perceived as generally benevolent, even when his promises are not fulfilled. In such a situation, the target is predisposed to be cooperative. Demos (1957) has suggested that promises create a moral obligation for the promisor, while threats carry no moral claim against the threatener. Our results suggest that promises connote normative obligations for the target as well as for the source. Apparently, a promisor is perceived as helpful and the normative rule is "help those who help you." Complementary to the effects of threats (when punishment for noncompliance is less than or equal to the costs of compliance), a target of promises ignores the small advantages to be gained by competitive noncompliant actions if he can gain almost as much by compliance. The important factor is that the promise itself, apart from source credibility or the magnitude of reward offered for compliance, carries strong normative connotations which are effective in mediating the target's compliance.

In the experiments so far reviewed, either threats or promises were sent by the source intermittently during the course of continuous dyadic interactions. Contrary to common sense, the use of threats does not exacerbate the ongoing conflict between individuals. However, the use of promises does ameliorate conflict. The strategist formulating policy must determine whether he prefers to use threats to gain compliance and accept a low level of cooperation by the target during other interactions in which threats are not used, or whether he prefers to use promises to gain a slightly lower level of compliance but more cooperative behavior by the target individual during interactions in which direct influence is not wielded.

ATTRACTION POWER

The degree of liking of the target for the source of influence may be considered a basis of power for the source. Festinger et al. (1950) demonstrated that the number of friendship choices in a group was positively correlated with conformity to group standards, a result that has been often replicated (Festinger et al., 1952; Gerard, 1953; Schachter, 1951; Lott and Lott, 1960; Thibaut and Strickland, 1956; Walker and Heyns, 1962). If attraction is a mediator of conformity to group norms, it may also be considered an important factor in mediating compliance to threats and promises.

Interpersonal attraction can be measured by various sociometric instruments. Experimental samples of existing friendships, strangers, or enemies can be obtained or attraction can be induced by manipulating attitude similarity in the laboratory (Byrne, 1969). In any case, the degree of the target's liking (or disliking) for source can be induced and measured.

The theory specifies that if a target likes the source, the target is more likely to believe promises of reward and to disbelieve threats of punishment. These predictions assume that the target will find it easy to believe that a friendly source will pay off for compliance to promises but will find it difficult to believe that a friendly source will use coercion. Alternatively, if the target dislikes the source, the target should be all too willing to expect punishment for noncompliance to threats and to disbelieve promises of reward. Thus, positive attraction for the source should lead to compliance to promises, while negative attraction should lead to compliance to threats.

Schlenker, Bonoma, Tedeschi, et al. (1969) have carried out two separate experiments to test the above hypothesis. The first study induced high or low attraction for source and exposed subjects to threats of either low or high credibility. Targets who disliked the source did comply as often to the low as to the high credibility threats, confirming that dislike does cause the target to overestimate message utility, increasing believability, estimated costs for noncompliance, and subsequent compliance. However, targets who liked the source were not prone to underestimate the credibility of the threats; such subjects were realistic in their appraisal of the situation and complied more often to the high than to the low credibility threats. Demos' comment that threats carry no moral obligation for either the source or target seems to be confirmed by the latter result. Dislike is a form of power when threats are used as the mode of influence, but positive attraction is not a basis of power in a coercive relationship. It may be concluded that when a source of threats does not have the resources or the intention of spending resources for punishing noncompliance, he can still be effective in exercising influence if he can gain the target's dislike. The exchange of attraction for power can occur in a coercive relationship. But if positive attraction is maintained, compliance can be gotten only with the resolute enforcement of threats.

In the second study, it was found that neither attraction nor message credibility significantly affected compliance to promises. Again, the operation of reciprocity norms (Gouldner, 1960) which apply to promises and which state that one should help those who help him caused compliance to occur about fifty percent of the time irrespective of credibility or attraction. It would appear that the mere statement of the promisor is enough to gain intermediate levels of compliance to promises even if the source is disliked. However, it was found that those subjects who were highly attracted to the "other" player cooperated more (over the course of the entire interaction) and were more trusting of the other than were subjects in the low attraction condition. Individuals who are highly attracted to one another generally seem to share the same attitudes (Byrne, 1969; Smith, 1957; Newcomb, 1961) and, thus, feel that they have similar goals which will not meet interference by cooperation. Thus, trust, which can be defined as the expectation that another will be helpful (Pruitt, 1965), can develop between highly attracted individuals and overall cooperation will increase without affecting compliance to specific promises. High attraction can be considered a base of power in an inducement relationship only when the interaction is taken as a whole and not when a specific promise of reward is dangled before the individual.

LEGITIMATE POWER

Authority derives from a role position rather than from the individual who holds the particular office or decision-making role (Freidrich, 1958). The authority is considered to be legitimized by a process of "reasoned elaboration"—the use of shared norms to demonstrate that the authority is worthy of deferential behavior. In a society of formal groups and organizations, hierarchies in role position as regards authority are often clearly established. The perception by a target individual that another person's role position deserves deference (compliance) is represented in the dyadic theory of influence as the perception of status. Within a group or institution it is assumed that status will be a direct function of role position. Furthermore, status is presumed to have a direct relationship to believability of and compliance to threats and promises.

Faley and Tedeschi (1969) have recently completed an experiment testing the relationship between status of source and compliance to threats by target individuals. They used ROTC cadets as the subject population. Cadets, who were themselves either low or high in authority or role position, were targets of threats from a simulated source, who was believed to be of either high or low status. The results confirmed the theoretical prediction; low status targets were more compliant (deferential) when the source was of high (rather than of low) status and high status targets were defiant of threats sent by a low status source. A somewhat surpising finding was that high status targets were as compliant to a high status source as were low status targets to the same source. The purely hierarchical notion of the effects of status is challenged by the latter result. Apparently, high status equals are likely to yield to each other's demands—presumably out of respect for rank or because similar deference is expected when the influence relationship is reversed, or because neither wants to be placed in the position of punishing the other. It is possible that, as long as they are equal in rank, the higher the authority positions of the two individuals, the more compliance they give to each other's verbal demands.

Intuitively, it seems reasonable that role position confers control over the allocation of decisions and resources. For this reason, there is a question whether status and message utility are really separate or orthogonal to one another in their effects on a target's level of believability and compliance. The Faley-Tedeschi study clearly shows that the effects of message utility and status are orthogonal to each other, but both contribute to the degree of compliance obtained by a source of threats.

At the moment, no evidence has been gathered concerning the relationship of status and compliance to promises.

DEPENDENCY POWER

A target may have certain needs that render him susceptible to influence. If an individual feels competent and feels that he deserves approval from others, presumably because of his own history of success in accomplishing objectives and solving problems, then he can be said to have high self-esteem. Such a confident individual could be expected to trust a source who promises rewards for compliance, while a low self-esteem person, who feels incompetent and disapproved of by others, could be expected to distrust the promisor. Thus, the theory predicts that a high self-esteem target is more likely to believe a promisor and more likely to comply to promises than is a low self-esteem target. On the other hand, a target who has low self-esteem is likely to believe that a threatener will punish him, and will comply more often with threats, particularly when the credibility of the threat is low and compliance is unwarranted.

Lindskold and Tedeschi (1969b) have only partially tested these predictions. Subjects were pretested on a measure of chronic self-esteem and divided into high and low groups. They were then sent either threats or promises by a simulated source who established one hundred percent credibility for each type of message. High self-esteem individuals were more compliant to promises than were low self-esteem targets, confirming the theory's prediction. However, high self-esteem targets were also more compliant to threats. It could be said that since the threats were one hundred percent credible, it was more realistic to comply with them and self-destructive to defy them, an interpretation not inconsistent with the theory. A second study is underway to find out whether targets of low self-esteem will comply more frequently than those of high self-esteem when threats have a low credibility. In any case, it is clear that the needs of the target are implicated in the degree of compliance he gives to influence attempts. The kind of influence attempt that will be successful in gaining compliance from a particular individual and the kind of source behavior which is likely to be most effective will depend upon the personality characteristics of the target. Lasswell and Kaplan's basis of power referred to as "well-being" may reside in the target, or the target and the wielder of power.

EXPERT POWER, RESPECT, AND ESTEEM

Although the discussion of legitimate power and the study by Faley and Tedeschi indicated that respect for another's authority (legitimacy) is an important factor in the social influence process, Lasswell and Kaplan apparently reserved the term, respect, for the person and not the office he holds. Homans (1961) has not been entirely consistent in his definition but has used the concept of esteem to refer to the perceived approval that another person has gained from those around him. An individual's esteem or respect would thus be orthogonal to his legitimacy and status. Esteem, a target cognition, should be a direct function of how much approval the other person (in this case, the source) is actually receiving from third parties. Homans suggests that a person will receive approval in direct proportion to the value and quantity of help he gives other people. Help is thus exchanged for the socially valuable reinforcer of approval. French and Raven's type of power referred to as "expert power" implies the value of, availability of, and ability to provide help or information. If help is directly related to approval, and approval produces the perception of esteem, then the concept of esteem considerably overlaps, and may even be coextensive with, the notion of expert power.

The present theory specifies that esteem for a promisor is directly related to believability and subsequent compliance by the target individual. A target who perceives another person as generally helpful will err on the side of believing the source's promises when such belief is unwarranted. On the other hand, low esteem for the source should lead the target to make the inference that the source is not generally helpful to others; the target should thus believe threats issued by a source perceived as low in esteem.

A pilot study conducted by Smith et al. (1969) attempted to establish high esteem by allowing the target subject to overhear another person give praise to a confederate for help rendered. Low esteem was established by allowing the subject to overhear another person admonish a confederate for having his father call the chairman of the psychology department in an attempt to affect a grade for a course. Unfortunately, this manipulation was unsuccessful in inducing the appropriate levels of esteem. Probably, the perception that the other was an active manipulator in either induction procedure led to the failure to produce the intended effects. Another attempt will be made to induce different levels of esteem by the manipulation of the perception of a passive or active source who either does or does not have anything to gain by giving help, or removing himself as an obstacle to the attainment of the other person's goals. At this time, no study of the esteem of another as it affects a subject's behavior or attitudes has ever been done in any context and certainly not in an influence situation.

PRESTIGE POWER

A threat from a court jester to his monarch is hardly taken seriously and may just cause robust laughter. The reason for this audience response is that the jester is not perceived as having the capacity to carry out the coercion which a king has. A threat is empty of coercive meaning for the target if the source is completely lacking in the resources required to levy the threatened punishment. Furthermore, even if the source is perceived as possessing the resources to punish noncompliance to his threats, he may still be perceived as unwilling to spend his resources for purposes of punishment, hence lacking the intentions to punish, and be defied by the target.

Analysis of the influence process reveals that when a threat is unsuccessful, the source is placed in the position of either punishing or not punishing the target but has not achieved the gains sought through the target's compliance. As Harsanyi (1962) has pointed out, opportunity costs are incurred by the source whenever he exercises his power. The source may be unwilling to spend the resources needed to punish the target unless there is concern about establishing a precedent (and credibility) for a future influence attempt. Similarly, when a target complies to promises, the source has already gained what he was after and will be tempted not to reward the target, unless concern for future interactions is present.

The target will be sensitive to the capabilities and intentions of the source (Pruitt, 1965; Singer, 1963). The source's available fluid resources will be perceived as his influence capability. The perception of intentions will depend upon how the source behaves in the interaction. Thus, even though a source sends threats, he may use them for the purpose of signaling in order to coordinate cooperative opportunities (Nardin, 1968). Additionally, the purely rational goal in the sending of a threat of violence is not provocation of actual violence but the coordination and accommodation of interests (Nieburg, 1969). Schlenker, Bonoma, Pivnick, et al. (1969) tested the hypothesis that a threat could be perceived as a signal to cooperate. Following the sending of a threat, they had the simulated source behave either totally accommodatively or totally exploitatively. Additionally, they had the simulated source send threats which were phrased in either a compellent or a deterrent form. Schelling (1966) has distinguished between compellent and deterrent threats by stating that the former is phrased in a form, "If you do *not* behave in a certain way, I will punish you," while the latter is phrased, "If you *do* behave in a certain way, I will punish you." The compellent threat thus specifies an action which the source must perform to escape punishment and thus can be perceived as more coercing, hostile, and manipulative than the deterrent threat, which only demands that the target not do a specified action to escape punishment. The results indicated that a subject faced with an accommodative source reciprocated that accommondation by being more compliant himself, while a subject faced with an exploitative source reciprocated exploitation with defiance. Also, subjects who received the more hostile compellent threats were more compliant than were those subjects who received the more static deterrent form of threat.

Singer (1963) has proposed that capability and intentions are multiplicatively related and, like utility, refer to the probability of the occurrence of an event based on the perception of source's intentions and the amount of costs or gains involved, based on the perceived capability of the source. Prestige, the target's perception, is considered to be a direct function of capability times intentions by the present theory. The higher the source's prestige, the more believable his influence attempts should be and the more compliance he should receive from target individuals.

Horai and Tedeschi (1970) manipulated the source's intentions while holding capability constant. They had a simulated source send threats to target subjects and behave either in a resolutely accommodative (i.e., the source was accommodative after sending a threat and always punished noncompliance), irresolutely accommodative (i.e., the source was accommodative after sending the threat but never punished noncompliance), or resolutely exploitative manner (i.e., the source was exploitative after sending the threat and always punished noncompliance). The results indicated that subjects who faced a resolutely accommodative source reciprocated the accommodative intentions by being both more compliant and more cooperative throughout the interaction, while subjects who faced a resolutely exploitative source reciprocated those exploitative intentions by being least compliant and least cooperative throughout the interaction. Sources who were perceived as irresolute in their accommodative intentions were intermediate on both compliance and cooperation. The results of Schlenker, Bonoma, Pivnick, et al. (1969) and Horai and Tedeschi (1970) indicate that when a source is clearly perceived as being accommodative in his intentions, and yet does not forfeit the capacity to punish noncompliance while striving for positive outcomes for both parties, more compliance ensues than when the source is perceived as being resolute in his intentions to exploit the subject. The Horai and Tedeschi (1970) study is consistent with Osgood's (1962) proposal for a series of unilateral conciliatory gestures which are clearly helpful to the opponent and which are aimed at the reduction of conflict in international affairs. The United States, a powerful nation with the acknowledged capacity to use its power in an enforcing manner, would thus appear to be able to initiate cooperative gestures and have them reciprocated by its targets. The results are also in direct opposition to theorists who desire to see a more aggressive policy on the part of the United States because they feel that a conciliatory response during conflicts will merely encourage aggression and exacerbate the conflicts.

The amount of resources possessed by a source can easily be manipulated while holding intentions constant. However, the study has yet to be done.

COUNTERINFLUENCE

So far, we have concentrated on the factors which cause the source of threats or promises to be more or less successful in gaining compliance from target individuals. The theory and evidence concerning these matters are potentially useful to those in a position to wield influence and power. However, what about the source himself? How can the relatively powerless affect the behavior of the powerful? Very few studies have been done in the entire field of social psychology concerning the behavior of persons in the position of power, the focus almost always centering on the targets of power.

Without the benefit of systematic theory but under the assumption that some of the same factors that affect the target also affect the behavior of the source, the authors have undertaken several exploratory studies of source behavior. Tedeschi, Horai, et al. (1970) investigated the plausible hypothesis that as opportunity costs to the source for using his punishment power increased, the less likely the source would be to punish noncompliance to threats. Surprisingly, they found that the frequency of sending threats decreased as opportunity costs increased, but no effect of opportunity costs on the use of punishment power was observed. The source of threats evidently considered his own costs before sending threats but once he committed himself by sending the threat, he was likely to punish noncompliance, whatever the costs for doing so.

Schlenker and Tedeschi (1970) induced high or low attraction in sources of threats, promises, or threats and promises for the targets of the influence attempts. Although no effects of attraction were found, the kind of power possessed by the source was important in determining his behavior. The source sent more threats and punished noncompliance more resolutely when he did not also have reward power and sent fewer promises and rewarded compliance less often when he did not also have coercive power. Thus, a powerful source is likely to be more benevolent and accommodating when he has both reward and punishment power than when he has either alone.

Tedeschi, Novinson, et al. (1970) compared the behavior of a source who was faced with a target who invariably retaliated when the source used his punishment power, with a source who incurred an opportunity cost (equivalent to the retaliation in terms of costs to the source) for using his power. Although the costs were the same in either condition, the source used his punishment power more often when the target was armed with retaliatory capability. These findings confirm those of Deutsch and Krauss (1962) and support the conclusion that conflict is more intense when both parties are armed than when only one is armed. Until recently the London police took this principle seriously.

It is a common belief that passive compliance to threats only encourages the source to send more threats since he is, in effect, being rewarded for his behavior. Halle (1967), in his history of the Cold War, noted that there is a deep-seated tendency in both men and nations to turn on one who appears stricken and helpless. Gamson's (1964) "cold warriors" feel that we must avoid conciliatory gestures following conflict intensification by the USSR so as not to encourage further exploitation. Tedeschi, Bonoma, et al. (1970)

faced a source with a simulated target who was either completely compliant or always defiant. Within each condition, the simulated target was either honest and open in announcing his intentions to comply or defy the source's threats or dishonest in concealing his intentions. Open defiance was successful in deterring the source from sending threats. Open compliance converted the source into a mutual cooperator; and although the source sent the most threats in this condition of the experiment, the threat was used by the source as a signal to coordinate mutual cooperation rather than for exploitative purposes. These results seem to deny the predictions of Halle and Gamson and further support Osgood's (1962) GRIT proposal, which calls for a clear statement of intentions before a conciliatory gesture to reduce conflict.

Obviously, there is a need to develop a theory of how a source of influence will use his power. Further experiments like those reported above may be necessary to develop a body of data suggestive of the relevant variables and functional relationships that will lead to such a theoretical development.

CONCLUSIONS AND IMPLICATIONS

A scientific theory of social influence within which is incorporated some of the more important and generally accepted definitions of power is only in its earlier stages of development. A systematic program of research is under way to evaluate, change, and expand the theory. The focus of the theory is on how behavioral compliance is gained from another person under conditions of social conflict and limited communications. This emphasis is a clear break with the tradition in social psychology which has been mainly concerned with attitude development and change.

It would probably be premature and also wrong to generalize from the theory and the laboratory results presented above to the serious problems of law and order in American society or to international conflict situations. However, a few such generalizations will be offered as a heuristic exercise and to point out the implications that could derive from the development of a mature and coherent theory of social influence.

Kaiser Wilhelm of Germany and Emperor Hirohito of Japan have both been quoted as pessimistic about the outcomes of the wars that each chose to enter. The Kaiser has been quoted as saying that at least Germany would make India bleed, while Hirohito succinctly expressed his position by noting that sometimes there is no alternative to leaping off a tower (Frank, 1967). If each of these leaders entered war with low expectancy of victory, why did they do so? Historians and strategic analysts, such as Tuchman (1962) and Kahn (1960), suggest each believed that he had no choice and that the alternative to war was perceived as worse than war itself. These historical events bear a striking resemblance to the results obtained in the laboratory when the punishment for noncompliance to threats is perceived by the target as being no worse than the costs of compliance. Given such a least-of-evils choice, when both alternatives are unsavory and relatively equivalent in terms of costs, the individual chooses to defy the source of threats rather than bear the ignominy of compliance and the detrimental costs associated with such surrender.

Analagous is the willingness of a few college students to defy the military draft system and accept incarceration implying that at least for these few, the legal punishment for their defiant actions is no worse in their hierarchy of values than serving in the armed forces. In corporate America, this principle is even more clearly illustrated. The penalties for price fixing and collusion are not severe. The profits to be gained by such activities are so vast that some large corporations have been tempted to violate the law many times (Nossiter, 1964). Only by increasing the penalty for price fixing to the point where it is "cheaper" to comply than to defy the law, while concomitantly establishing high probability of punishment or enforcement, can corporate recidivists be deterred.

An interesting finding in our research is that dislike is a form of power. Observation establishes that the young black militant is openly hostile to whites and challenges middle-class blacks, charging them with Uncle Tomming "the Man." The backlash in America is a reaction to this new form of black militancy. But, the finding that dislike is a form of power may indicate that the black militant is gaining some power and can be expected to be somewhat successful in threatening whites even though he does not have sufficient punishment power to enforce his threats. Thus, many jobs are opening to blacks from the fear that violence may occur if such action is not taken. However, the study by Tedeschi, Bonoma, et al. (1970) indicates that open and honest compliance to some black demands could be successful in converting even the most militant into cooperative partners in social change. The experience at many universities is that compliance to the demands of black students has not led just to more demands but rather has led black students to work closely with college administrators in developing new programs.

A process similar to that advocated by Charles Osgood (1962) for the mitigation of international tension could be employed as a matter of policy in domestic conflicts. Graduated reciprocation in tension reduction (GRIT) involves a series of announcements on the part of the instigating nation to the effect that some low-risk actions will be taken which are designed to benefit the other party. Such unilateral announcements are then followed by the performance of the stated behavior and require no specific reciprocation from the other party. GRIT is a strategy to build trust between nations, calculated to reduce tensions and elicit spontaneous reciprocation from the target nation. Our studies indicate that the proposal has a sound foundation, since both open announcement of accommodative intentions and the behavioral demonstration of good faith do result in mutual cooperation. Perhaps GRIT could be applied to ameliorate the distrust and conflict prevalent between blacks and whites in America.

The experimental findings that high self-esteem individuals are more compliant to both high credibility threats and promises than are low self-esteem individuals is a pessimistic one when applied to black-white problems, juvenile delinquents, criminals, or the deprived poor of America. For centuries the white man has taught the black man to believe that black is ugly and second-best, to accept a subservient blue-collar role in America, and to doubt that black men have the native ability to acquire the skills of a technological society. The consequences of such consistent inculcation is that most lower-class blacks have powerful identity problems and generally low self-esteem. Speedy social change toward integration may have been obviated by white Americans long ago by rendering blacks relatively uninfluenceable to the threats and promises of a white society. It would appear that a prerequisite for a true integration of American society presupposes that the average Negro believes that black is beautiful and that he is as competent and deserving of approval as the average white person. When black Americans have gained self-respect, they should be as compliant to the laws and norms of society as the average middle-class white American.

Young critics of "the system" are quite aware of the consequences of success in our society. Once an individual begins to work his way up the hierarchy of a structured organization, he receives rewards for the acceptance of responsibility, but he also necessarily becomes more conforming to the norms and goals of the organization. The fact is revealed indirectly by the experimental finding that high-status equals are very compliant to each other's social influence attempts. Giving an individual a stake in the institutions of the society is a way of gaining compliance and conformity to the norms of that society. This lesson has not been entirely lost on the social reformers of America. The disaffected, the poor, and the blacks must be given the skills by which they too can escape the confines of low status, as well as low self-esteem. This type of social therapy may be viewed as a hedge against disorder and possible large-scale violence.

Many other speculative generalizations could be made, but the purpose of demonstrating the potential importance of a general theory of social influence has been accomplished. The task now is to provide a firm scientific foundation that can be used with confidence by policy makers faced with the great issues of our time.

REFERENCES

BACHRACH, P. and M. S. BARATZ (1963) "Decisions and nondecisions: an analytical framework." Amer. Pol. Sci. Rev. 57 (September): 632-642.

BAZELON, D. T. (1965) The Paper Economy. New York: Vintage.

BYRNE, D. (1969) "Attitudes and attraction," pp. 35-89 in L. Berkowitz (ed.) Advances in Experimental Social Psychology, Vol. 4. New York: Academic Press.

COSER, L. (1956) The Functions of Social Conflict. New York: Free Press.

DEMOS, R. (1957) "Some reflections on threats and punishments." Rev. of Metaphysics 11 (December): 224-236.

DEUTSCH, K. W. (1966) The Nerves of Government. New York: Free Press.

DEUTSCH, M. and R. M. KRAUSS (1962) "Studies of interpersonal bargaining." J. of Conflict Resolution 6 (March): 52-76.

DURKHEIM, E. (1951) Suicide. Glencoe, Ill.: Free Press. [Original in French]

EDWARDS, W., H. LINDMAN, and L. D. Phillips (1965) "Emerging technologies for making decisions," in New Directions in Psychology, Vol. II New York: Holt.

FALEY, T. and J. T. TEDESCHI (1969) "Status and the reaction to threats." University of Miami (mimeo).

FESTINGER, L. (1964) Conflict, Decision and Dissonance. Stanford: Stanford Univ. Press.

--- (1957) A Theory of Cognitive Dissonance. Evanston, Ill.: Row, Peterson.

---, A. PEPITONE, and T. NEWCOMB (1952) "Some consequences of de-individuation in a group." J. of Abnormal and Social Psychology 47 (April): 382-389.

FESTINGER, L., S. SCHACHTER, and K. BACK (1950) Social Pressures in Informal Groups: a Study of Human Factors in Housing. New York: Harper & Row.

FRANK, J. D. (1967) Sanity and Survival. New York: Vintage.

FRENCH, J. R. P., Jr. and B. RAVEN (1959) "The bases of social power," pp. 118-149 in D. Cartwright (ed.) Studies in Social Power. Ann Arbor, Mich.: Institute for Social Research.

FREIDRICH, C. J. [ed.] (1958) Authority. Cambridge, Mass.: Harvard Univ. Press.

GAMSON, W. A. (1968) Power and Discontent. Homewood, Ill: Dorsey.

--- (1964) "Evaluating beliefs about international conflict," in R. Fisher (ed.) International Conflict and Behavioral Science. New York: Basic Books.

GERARD, H. B. (1953) "The anchorage of opinions in face-to-face groups." Human Relations 6 (May): 249-271.

GOULDNER, A. W. (1960) "The norm of reciprocity: a preliminary statement." Amer. Soc. Rev. 25 (April): 161-179.

HALLE, L. J. (1967) The Cold War as History. New York: Harper & Row.

HARSANYI, J. C. (1962) "Measurement of social power, opportunity costs, and the theory of two-person bargaining games." Behavioral Sci. 7 (January): 67-80.

HOMANS, G. C. (1961) Social Behavior: Its Elementary Forms. New York: Harcourt, Brace & World.

HORAI, J. and J. T. TEDESCHI (1970) "Attribution of intention and the norm of reciprocity." University of Miami (mimeo).

--- (1969) "The effects of credibility and magnitude of punishment on compliance to threats." J. of Personality and Social Psychology 12 (June): 164-169.

JONES, E. E. and H. B. GERARD (1967) Foundations of Social Psychology. New York: John Wiley.

KAHN, H. (1960) On Thermonuclear War. Princeton, N.J.: Princeton Univ. Press.

KARLSSON, G. (1962) "Some aspects of power in small groups," pp. 193-202 in J. H. Criswell, H. Solomon, and P. Suppes (eds.) Mathematical Methods in Small Group Processes. Stanford: Stanford Univ. Press.

LASSWELL, H. D. and A. KAPLAN (1950) Power and Society. New Haven: Yale Univ. Press.

LEWIN, K. (1946) "Action research and minority problems." J. of Social Issues 2 (November): 34-36.

LINDSKOLD, S. and J. T. TEDESCHI (1969a) "The effects of contingent promises on interpersonal conflict." University of Miami (mimeo).

--- (1969b) "Self-esteem and sex as factors affecting influencability." University of Miami (mimeo).

LINDSKOLD, S., T. BONOMA, and J. T. TEDESCHI (1969) "Impressions of and reactions to a threatening simulated opponent." University of Miami (mimeo).

LINDSKOLD, S., T. BONOMA, B. R. SCHLENKER, and J. T. TEDESCHI (1970) "Source accommodativeness, message utility, and compliance to contingent promises." University of Miami (mimeo).

LOTT, B. E. and A. J. LOTT (1960) "The formation of positive attitudes toward group members." J. of Abnormal and Social Psychology 61 (September): 297-300.

LUCE, R. D. and H. RAIFFA (1957) Games and Decisions: Introduction and Critical Survey. New York: John Wiley.

MacIVER, R. M. (1964) Power Transformed. New York: Macmillan.

MARCH, J. G. (1955) "An introduction to the theory and measurement of influence." Amer. Pol. Sci. Rev. 49 (June): 431-451.

MORGENTHAU, H. (1964) Politics Among Nations. New York: Alfred A. Knopf.

NARDIN, T. (1968) "Communication and the effect of threats in strategic interaction." Peace Research Society, Papers 9: 69-86.

NEWCOMB, T. (1961) The Acquaintance Process. New York: Holt.

NIEBURG, H. L. (1969) Political Violence. New York: St. Martin's.

NOSSITER, B. D. (1964) The Mythmakers. Cambridge: Houghton-Mifflin.

OSGOOD, C. E. (1962) An Alternative to War or Surrender. Urbana: Univ. of Illinois Press.

PARSONS, T. (1963) "On the concept of influence." Public Opinion Q. 27 (Spring): 37-62.

--- (1949) Essays in Sociological Theory Pure and Applied. New York: Free Press.

PRUITT, D. G. (1965) "Definition of the situation as a determinant of international action," pp. 393-432 in H. C. Kelman (ed.) International Behavior: A Social-psychological Analysis. New York: Holt, Rinehart & Winston.

ROKEACH, M. (1968) Beliefs, Attitudes, and Values, a Theory of Organization and Change. San Francisco: Jossey-Bass.

SCHACHTER, S. (1951) "Deviation, rejection & communication." J. of Abnormal and Social Psychology 46 (April): 190-207.

SCHELLING, T. (1966) Arms and Influence. New Haven: Yale Univ. Press.

SCHLENKER, B. R. and J. T. TEDESCHI (1970) "Interpersonal attraction and the use of threats and promises." U.S. International University (mimeo).

SCHLENKER, B. R., T. BONOMA, W. P. PIVNICK, and J. T. TEDESCHI (1969) "Compliance to threats as a function of the wording of the threat and the exploitativeness of the threatener." U.S. International University (mimeo).

SCHLENKER, B. R., T. BONOMA, J. T. TEDESCHI, S. LINDSKOLD, and J. HORAI (1969) "Interpersonal attraction and compliance to threats and promises." U.S. International University (mimeo).

SCHOPLER, J. and N. BATESON (1965) "The power of dependence." J. of Personality and Social Psychology 2 (August): 247-254.

SCHUR, E. M. (1969) Law and Society. New York: Random House.

SIMMEL, G. (1950) The Sociology of G. Simmel. Glencoe, Ill.: Free Press.

SINGER, J. D. (1963) "Inter-nation influence: a formal model." Amer. Pol. Sci. Rev. 57 (June): 420-430.

SMITH, A. J. (1957) "Similarity of values and its relation to acceptance and the projection of similarity." J. of Psychology 43 (April): 251-260.

SMITH, R. B., I. HABER, B. R. SCHLENKER, and J. T. TEDESCHI (1969) "Source esteem and targets compliance to threats." U.S. International University (mimeo).

TEDESCHI, J. T. (1968) "A theory of social influence within dyads." Presented at the Sixteenth International Congress of Applied Psychology, Amsterdam.

---, T. BONOMA, and S. LINDSKOLD (1970) "Threatener's reaction to prior announcement of behavioral compliance or defiance." Behavioral Sci. (forthcoming).

TEDESCHI, J. T., N. NOVINSON, and T. BONOMA (1970) "Fixed costs vs. retaliation as factors influencing the threatener." J. of Conflict Resolution (forthcoming).

TEDESCHI, J. T., J. HORAI, S. LINDSKOLD, and T. FALEY (1970) "The effects of opportunity costs and target compliance on the behavior of a threatening source." J. of Experimental Social Psychology (forthcoming).

TEDESCHI, J. T., J. HORAI, S. LINDSKOLD, and J. P. GAHAGAN (1968) "The effects of threat upon prevarification and conflict in the P.D.G." Proceedings of the Annual Meeting of the American Psychology Association.

THIBAUT, J.W. and H. H. KELLEY (1959) The Social Psychology of Groups. New York: John Wiley.

THIBAUT, J. W. and L. H. STRICKLAND (1956) "Psychological set and social conformity." J. of Personality 25 (December): 115-129.

TUCHMAN, B. (1962) The Guns of August. New York: Dell.

WALKER, E. L. and R. W. HEYNS (1962) An Anatomy for Conformity. Englewood Cliffs, N.J.: Prentice-Hall.

WEBER, M. (1954) Max Weber on Law in Economy and Society. Cambridge, Mass.: Harvard Univ. Press.

Chapter 11

Group Influences on the Helpfulness of Accident Victims

CHARLES KORTE – *Vassar College*

Action that occurs in a group or social context has always held a certain fascination for students of human behavior, partly because of our many notions about the powerful forces that groups exert on the individual. Impressions of group forces derive in part from Le Bon's (1895) early account of crowd behavior, which characterized the crowd's power over the individual as control that was essentially hypnotic, resulting in extremities of behavior, from brutal cruelty to altruism. More recent analyses of group influences have been concerned with the means by which groups elicit and maintain individual conformity to goals, values, and standards shared by the group. For example, Kelman's (1961) theoretical analysis of the processes of social influence has been a significant contribution to our understanding of the antecedents and consequences of conformity phenomena.

One of the most dramatic demonstrations of individual compliance to group standards has been contributed by Asch (1951). His research showed that a significant number of individuals, when confronted with a unanimous majority whose judgment on a simple perceptual task contradicted their own, would distort their own judgment so as not to appear in contradiction with the group.

AUTHOR'S NOTE: *This study was based on a dissertation submitted to the Department of Social Relations, Harvard University, in partial fulfillment of the requirements for the Ph.D. degree. The investigation was supported by the United States Public Health Service Pre-Doctoral Fellowship (1-F1-MH-40, 132-01) to the author. The author wishes to express his appreciation to Dr. Robert Rosenthal, who served as the dissertation advisor.*

Groups have also been found to exert considerable influence over their members in other diverse situations, e.g., in setting productivity standards among factory and office workers (Coch and French, 1948) and in shaping attitudes toward a tenants' organization in a housing project (Festinger et al., 1950).

This picture of individual compliance to the demands and expectations of the group seems to indicate that the group influence is largely detrimental, that it pressures the individual to act in a way contrary to his wishes and values. What has often been ignored is the possiblity that groups might function to bring about socially valued acts, or action that is actually more congruent with an individual's values than the behavior that would have occurred in the absence of the group. Milgram (1965) has carried out a study which demonstrated that the presence of a supportive group can facilitate an individual's resistance to authoritative commands which demand the cruel punishment of an innocent third party. It might seem intuitively true that acts of altruism would be facilitated by the presence of many people, who would provide a source of approval and potential assistance for the individual who chose to relieve the distress of some innocent victim. Yet the news media have revealed an alarming number of instances where large collections of bystanders have looked on helplessly while another person was robbed, beaten, crippled by a heart attack, or even murdered. Most infamous of these instances is the case of Kitty Genovese, who was murdered in the streets of Queens, while 38 of her neighbors watched from the safety of their apartments, without intervening or even calling the police. This case led Darley and Latané (1968a, 1968b) to hypothesize that the presence of a group might have an *inhibiting*, rather than *facilitating*, effect on the altruistic impulse of the single individual. When more people are present in an emergency situation, there are more people to whom the responsibility can be diffused, hence a decreased likelihood that any single individual will personally take the responsibility for helping the victim. Darley and Latané's laboratory simulation of the Kitty Genovese situation showed that when subjects overheard an epileptic attack by another subject, they were less likely to report his plight as the number of other potential helpers increased.

ABOUT THIS STUDY

The purpose of the present study was to take the assumption of an inhibitory group effect on bystander helpfulness and examine several possible mechanisms that might be responsible for the group inhibition. Darley and Latané based their "diffusion of responsibility" explanation on the decreased help-giving by individual subjects that occurred as group size increased. It is possible that other significant variations occur in addition to responsibility diffusion as group size varies, and the first aim of the present study was to make a direct test of the "diffusion of responsibility" explanation with group size held constant.

Responsibility diffusion was manipulated by varying the degree to which a target subject was the *only* bystander capable of initiating helpful intervention during an emergency. This suggests the hypothesis that an individual is more likely to offer assistance in an emergency when his fellow bystanders are incapacitated than when all bystanders are equally free to intervene. This first variable was labeled "focused versus diffuse responsibility."

In addition to diffusing the responsibility, it is possible that a group setting inhibits individual help-giving in another way. This second inhibitory mechanism is based on the premise that the crisis bystander experiences the need for a collective social reality and a confirmation of his own definition of the situation. What the social context may do is to confront the individual with fellow witnesses who fail to provide the feedback that allows the bystander to surmise that his situational assessment is shared by the other bystanders and thus is likely to be a correct reading of the situation. The lack of feedback from other bystanders, i.e., their silence and composed bearing, may occur as a result of the ambiguity and novelty of an emergency situation. Persons in such a situation are likely to hold in abeyance communication (verbalization, facial expression, and the like) of their initial perceptions and reactions until they have had some confirmation that their feelings and interpretations are shared by others in the situation rather than being some mistaken, idiosyncratic reaction which, expressed or acted upon, would prove embarrassing to the person and cause him to appear highly excitable, foolish, or the like. The inability of the individual to ascertain that there exists a mutual recognition among group members that the situation is in fact an emergency leaves him with an unstable definition of the situation that is insufficient as the grounds for action. If this explanation is correct, then we would predict that an individual faced with a distressed victim in a group context would be more likely to intervene when he receives feedback from the other bystanders which establishes the crisis as real than when there is only silence. A further hypothesis is that assistance is least likely to be offered when a "minimizing" feedback is received from the other bystanders, i.e., feedback that identifies the crisis as something less serious than what it appears to be. This leads to a second variable, "bystander communication," with the following predicted order of conditions from greatest likelihood of intervention to least: (1) communication of a crisis interpretation from the bystanders (true communication, TC, condition); (2) no communication received from the other bystanders (no communication, NC, condition); and (3) communication of a minimizing interpretation from the other bystanders (minimizing communication, MC, condition).

One direct approach to help-giving is to regard it as largely dependent on individual motivation and personality characteristics. Paradoxically, personality measures have proven to be poor predictors of helping behavior (see Darley and Latané, 1968a), the one exception being Rotter's measure of internal versus external locus of control. Midlarsky (1968) found that subjects low in fatalism, i.e., having a sense of internal rather than external control, were more likely to give aid to other subjects who needed help in completing some problem tasks in a laboratory setting. Yet for the most part, very few personality correlates of help-giving have been found. It may be that personality correlates are too small to be detected in relation to the much larger impact of situational determinants of help-giving or that any particular personality trait has associated with it tendencies toward both aiding the victim and suppressing the urge to help, the opposite effects thus canceling each other out. To pursue the question of the relationship between helping behavior and personality variables, three scales related to social dependency and other-orientation were included in the experimental design—Edwards' (1953) scales of deference and autonomy and Allport's (1928) ascendance-submissiveness scale. These scales were chosen because of their utility for the final hypothesis of the study—that the presence versus absence of group feedback or communication would be of greater significance for subjects high on social dependency and other-orientation. Thus we predict a significant interaction between bystander communication and the personality measures.

METHOD

Subjects

Sixty male subjects were recruited from the Harvard Summer School, ten subjects in each of the six conditions created by the 2 x 3 experimental matrix (two responsibility levels crossed with three communication levels). Subjects were paid two dollars for the sixty-minute sessions.

Procedure

Three subjects—a true subject, a confederate, and a phantom subject—were run in each session, which was described as an experiment in limited-contact group discussion. Upon arrival, subjects were placed separately in small adjacent rooms that were interconnected by intercom sets with attached headphones. The first half-hour was used for completing a background questionnaire and the personality measures. The subject was then instructed that the remainder of the experiment would be conducted via the intercom set. The three subjects were to discuss a particular topic, taking turns in a specified order. The true subject was assigned the middle position. After a certain point in the discussion, subjects were asked to complete a questionnaire that had been left with them by the experimenter, containing items which pertained to the quality of the discussion and the perception of the other participants, as well as a request for a short essay to be written as fast as possible.

As the experimenter delivered these instructions (over the intercom) he suffered what appeared to be a serious asthma attack; he had earlier made casual reference to an asthma condition when excusing a mild coughing seige. The experimenter's speech at first was only temporarily halted by a respiratory obstruction, but his condition quickly deteriorated, as choking sounds of greater severity were audible over the intercom. There was a final gasp, as the experimenter struggled to say "I-I-I . . . can't . . . seem to . . . breathe"; then there was silence. This sequence of events was accomplished by means of a tape recorder, which delivered the entire proceedings through the subject's intercom headphones. The tapes were designed with dead time at places where the subject himself was participating.

Experimental Conditions

Subjects run in the focused responsibility condition were led to believe that the other two subjects were strapped down during the session to allow for physiological recording. This was pointed out by the experimenter when the subject was placed in his room, referred to in the printed copy of the instructions each subject had at hand, and reiterated just before the experimenter began the instructions which terminated in the attack. This manipulation was simply excluded in the conditions of *diffused* responsiblity.

In the *no communication* condition, nothing was heard from the other subjects at any time once the asthma attack had begun. In the *true communication* condition, at the first sign of the asthma attack, the other two subjects were heard to say (in turn, rather excitedly) "Hey, are you all right? It sounds like you're choking!" and "He sounds in serious trouble–he seems to be–" And finally, in the *minimizing communication* condition, the subject heard the other two subjects give the following remarks (in turn, somewhat casually) at the first sign of the attack–"Should we start on the questionnaire now? . . . I mean you're all right, aren't you?" and "I guess he's O.K. Sounds all right, like–"

Dependent Measures

The criterion response was whether or not the subject emerged from his room and located the experimenter to see if he needed help. To do this it was necessary for the subject to leave his own room and find the experimenter by opening the door to the small room where he was located. The latency of this response was timed. At this point the subject was assured that the experimenter had recovered and was asked to return to his room. The subject was then carefully debriefed and given a final questionnaire. It was also possible to scale the suboptimal responses, which ranged from quick peeps out from the subject's room to extended but ultimately unsuccessful attempts to find the experimenter.

After four minutes had elapsed from the start of the attack, nonintervening subjects were interrupted in their rooms and informed of the true nature of the experiment. Any feelings of guilt or resentment were carefully discussed until the subject was in a satisfactory state of mind. A final questionnaire was then administered and the subject discharged.

RESULTS

Subjects gave clear indication that the crisis was an engaging and momentous experience. This was evident in their spontaneous comments at the moment of the experimenter's attack, recorded through the intercom set–"Where are you? We'll come and help you! Where are you?"; "Do you think we should see what–"; "I'll see what's wrong with him"; and "Hey, get that guy an inhalator, fast!" Only two subjects verbally expressed doubts about the genuineness of the accident as the crisis ensued; one of these subjects solicited advice from the other two subjects as to whether they thought it was real. A problem of interpretation was presented by twelve subjects who rated themselves in a postexperiment questionnaire administered subsequent to debriefing as completely skeptical of the genuineness of the experimenter's accident. These skeptics were evenly distributed across the experimental conditions. The clear possiblity that much of the skepticism was of a defensive nature, motivated by a failure to offer assistance and a subsequent need to justify one's performance, rather than genuine skepticism, precluded eliminating these subjects from the design and producing a possibly biased sample. Of the twelve self-described skeptics, eleven had failed to intervene in the crisis; only three of the twelve had gone so far as to emerge from their rooms. The situation of the subject who hears the cries of the experimenter and doubts that they are real is a genuine dilemma that is similar in many ways to the dilemma of the real-life bystander who is assailed by doubts that what he is seeing or hearing is not really a crisis, but rather something else, perhaps even a callous prank. But he must act in *spite* of his skepticism, as the experimental subject must, if there is any chance that the incident is in fact a real emergency. The dilemma of the skeptical subject was perhaps best portrayed by the introspection of one subject who remained in his room throughout the attack, and wrote the following remarks on the questionnaire that confronted him as the attack proceeded:

> I am wondering if this is a put-on job, and I am the only subject. Is this part of the experiment, not seeming to breathe–I'll bet it is–if not, the other two can take care of him; am I willing to risk someone's life just to prove I'm right? I guess so–No legal obligation, of course–should I just feel stupid or guilty for the rest of my life?

Confronted with the cries of the distressed experimenter struggling for breath, 73% of all subjects responded to the extent of emerging from their rooms. The latency time of this initial response ranged from 2 to 119 seconds, with a mean response of 40 seconds. Thus the first two minutes that elapsed after the onset of the attack appeared to be the crucial period for decision—everyone who was to emerge did so within this time period. The decision to leave his room did not guarantee that the person would undertake the task of locating the experimenter in his control room, hence intervening in the crisis. Of the 45 subjects who emerged, only 26, or 43% of all subjects, actually reached the experimenter in his room. The time that had elapsed before the experimenter was located varied from 28 to 115 seconds; the mean intervention time for intervening subjects was 74 seconds. All subjects who ultimately intervened had emerged from their rooms in the first 90 seconds after the onset of the attack. Efforts to utilize the intercom as a first response were quite common—25 of the 60 subjects, or 42%, tried communicating with the experimenter when the attack occurred, while 28% attempted communicating with the other subjects. Table 1 summarizes the behavior of subjects according to a five category continuum of action.

The diffusion of responsibility hypothesis was supported by the variation in intervention rates that occured between focused (FR) versus diffuse (DR) responsibility conditions (see Table 2). Fifty percent of all FR subjects intervened by locating the stricken experimenter in his room, while only 37% did so when the responsibility was diffuse. Variation in bystander communication likewise had an effect on the likelihood of intervention, but in a manner quite contrary to what was expected. The highest level of intervention, 55% of all subjects, occurred in the no communication (NC) condition, while the next highest was among minimizing communication (MC) subjects, 40%, and the lowest rate of intervention, 35%, occurred where the most was expected, among true communication (TC) subjects. Table 3 summarizes the analysis of variance of the arc-sin transformed percentage intervention rates (Snedecor, 1956). Both the responsibility and communication effects were found to be marginally significant ($p < .07$, $p < .08$, two-tailed, respectively). The Snedecor model,

TABLE 1

ACTION TAKEN BY SUBJECTS

		%	n
1.	Does not emerge from cubicle.	27	16
2.	Emerges from cubicle, returns without locating experimenter.	15	9
3.	Emerges twice from cubicle, both times returns without locating experimenter.	15	9
4.	Emerges twice from cubicle, locates experimenter on second occasion.	23	14
5.	Emerges from cubicle, locates experimenter.	20	12

TABLE 2

PERCENTAGE OF SUBJECTS LOCATING EXPERIMENTER

Communication	Responsibility Focused %	Responsibility Diffuse %	Total %
None	60	50	55
True	40	30	35
Minimizing	50	30	40
Total	50	37	43

NOTE: Cell percentages based on n=10.

TABLE 3

ANALYSIS OF VARIANCE OF PERCENTAGE INTERVENTION
(transformed into arc-sins)

Source	d.f.	M.S.	F	p(two-tailed)
Responsibility	1	92.82	16.20	$p < .07$
Communication	2	74.25	12.96	$p < .08$
Error	2	5.73		
Total	5			

suitable for single-cell entries, assumes no interaction between main effects, which can only be estimated from a three-way analysis, utilizing an additional independent variable (in this case the personality measures). This analysis showed the interaction between responsiblity and communication to be nonsignificant. Estimation of the significance of the differences between communication conditions (Snedecor, 1956) showed the NC-TC and NC-MC differences to be significant beyond the .05 level, while the TC-MC difference was not significant. We may conclude then that there was a marginally significant effect of responsibility on bystander intervention as predicted, and the unexpected finding of a significantly greater amount of help-giving in the absence of feedback than when feedback, of either a realistic or minimizing nature, was present.

An additional hypothesis of the study predicted an interaction between the communication variable and social dependency, on the basis that persons high in social dependency would be more influenced by the presence versus the absence of feedback. No significant interactions occurred between the communication variable and any of the three personality measures–Edward's Autonomy and Deference, and Allport's A-S. The data which showed feedback to inhibit rather

TABLE 4
MEAN SCORES ON THREE PERSONALITY SCALES: INTERVENERS VERSUS NONINTERVENERS

Scale	Interveners	Noninterveners
Autonomy	16.6	15.5
Deference	7.9	8.2
A-S	2.1	0.2

NOTE: All interveners-noninterveners differences are nonsignificant by t-test analysis.

than to facilitate intervention made the interaction hypothesis largely untenable, in that high social dependency was hypothesized to augment a presumed facilitative effect of feedback.

Interveners did not differ significantly from noninterveners on any of the personality measures (see Table 4). The pattern of differences was nevertheless consistent, with interveners more ascendant and autonomous, and less deferential than noninterveners. A cluster of individual test items which did discriminate significantly between interveners and noninterveners constitutes a central component of the autonomy scale:

(1) I like to avoid situations where I must do things in a conventional way ($p < .05$).

(2) I like to feel free to do what I want to do ($p < .02$).

(3) I like to do things that other people regard as unconventional ($p < .07$).

Thus, the only indication for personality correlates of help-giving in a laboratory crisis situation was a small cluster of items which tap a person's tendency to describe himself as unrestrained by conventionality. Other background information besides personality measures was collected from subjects–age, college level, birth order, number of siblings, size of home community, and college enrollment. The only one of these variables to show even marginally significant differentiation between interveners and noninterventers was age–interveners were slightly older than noninterveners (21.5 years versus 20.2 years, $t=1.8$, $d.f.=58$, $p < .08$).

DISCUSSION

It may be considered an encouraging sign that nearly three-quarters of all subjects were willing to break off from the proceedings by leaving their rooms in response to the experimenter's attack. Yet the fact that 57% of all subjects either remained in their rooms or returned to their rooms without locating the experimenter is significant, especially given the absence of any personal risk threatening interveners and the low incentive for subjects to maintain the experimental procedure by remaining in their rooms, with the experiment so apparently at an unfortunate end. Yet not all subjects saw the attack as terminating the session; in fact, 42% of all subjects reported that during the time of the attack they were reluctant to do anything that would "ruin the experiment." So it appears that subjects did not preclude the possiblity that the experimenter would be able to weather the present storm and bring the session to a successful conclusion. Was such faith built on a superlative respect for the perseverance of scientific investigators or wishful thinking that rationalized noninvolvement? It is quite possible that interpretations of the situation, such as the hardiness of the experimenter and the genuineness of the attack, are post hoc constructions used to justify whatever the subject has done or explanations forged in the heat of decision that allow the subject to act in accordance with a wishful reality. Latané (1967) has reported a study which demonstrated that a help-giving situation appears far more genuine to subjects when they do not have the responsibility for help-giving than when the responsibility for helping is solely theirs. The question of motivated distortions in the perception of situations remains an intriguing idea, not totally resolved by the present study but very much suggested by the nature of subjects' postexperiment reports.

The likelihood of help-giving was greater when subjects were in a situation of focused rather than diffuse responsiblity. This confirmation of the diffusion of responsiblity hypothesis was corroborated by data from the postexperiment questionnaire. Subjects were asked to rate the other two participants, P_1 and P_3, on the degree to which it appeared likely that (1) they had left, or (2) they were about to leave their rooms to check on the experimenter, using a scale from one (very unlikely) to five (very likely). In all instances, focused subjects had lower expectancies that the other two subjects had intervened or would intervene; in addition, they saw more dire consequences from their not helping the experimenter than did the diffuse subjects.

The effect of group feedback, the communication variable, was nearly the opposite of what had been expected. Greatest intervention occurred in the absence of any feedback, while a lesser degree of helpfulness was evident under conditions of minimizing feedback, and the least intervention occurred when subjects were exposed to feedback labeling the crisis as real. The obtained ordering of conditions can be handled by the alternative explanation that the communication variation acted more to define *responsibility*, i.e., variation in feedback created variations in the subject's expectation that someone else would respond to the experimenter's need for assistance. In TC and MC conditions, there was knowledge that the other subjects were aware of and concerned about the experimenter's plight and thus some reason existed to expect that they would intervene, especially since a public commitment of their awareness and concern had been made. This contrasts with NC subjects, who had no basis for believing that a response might be forthcoming from the other subjects. The difference in likelihood of intervention between TC and MC conditions, though very small and nonsignificant, is compatible with this new explanation for the feedback effect. While the two conditions exhibited similar awareness and public commitment on the part of the other participants, there was a greater show of concern in TC, and hence a greater reason for the subject to expect that the other participants would assume the responsibility for help-giving. Thus we are arguing that the feedback variable appears to operate through the mechanism of responsiblity diffusion: the feedback works primarily to determine a person's perception of the degree to which it is he that must offer assistance if the experimenter is to be helped at all.

This interpretation of the feedback effect was supported by data from the postexperiment questionnaire. In ratings of both P_1 and P_3, TC subjects were most likely to assume that the others had left or were about to leave their rooms, MC subjects were next most likely to make this assumption, while NC subjects were least likely to suppose that the other participants had intervened or would intervene. This pattern obtains for the sample as a whole, as well as within the nonintervening and intervening subsamples.

One pattern of data not entirely compatible with the diffusion of responsibility interpretation of the feedback variable is the occurrence of a feedback effect within the focused responsibility condition. Given the incapacitation of the other participants in this condition, it would not seem to make much sense that variation in the comments uttered by these subjects should affect the target subject's expectation that the other persons would provide the needed assistance for the experimenter. One possible explanation for the occurrence of a feedback effect here is that while focused subjects saw themselves as more able to help the experimenter, they did not see the other participants as totally *unable* to give assistance. This was clearly the case, as evidenced by the "likelihood of intervention ratings" of P_1 and P_3 by focused subjects, who generally attributed their incapacitated fellow bystanders with something less than the extreme "unlikely" ratings. Part of the experimental procedure, which admonished the subjects "not to remove any of the attachments yourself . . . wait until I am there to do it for you," implied the possibility that subjects could, if they had wanted to disengage themselves from the apparatus. The utterance of comments in TC and MC conditions may have created the basis for believing that such disengagement was a possibility.

Paradoxically, while effective as an inhibitor of help-giving, the communication received from other bystanders was perceived by the subjects as a factor making it *more* likely that they would leave their rooms to help the experimenter. Subjects also reported that the comments made them more certain both of what was happening and that the experimenter needed help (see Table 5).

TABLE 5

SUBJECTS' REPORTS ON THE EFFECTS OF FEEDBACK
(true and minimized combined)

Effect of comments on	Increase %	Decrease %	n
certainty of what was happening;	63	37	19
certainty that the experimenter needed help;	73	27	15
likelihood that I would help.	79	21	19

This contradiction between the real versus perceived effect of feedback points to the difficulty of postexperiment assessment of subjects' perception and motives. The contradiction in this case may be a matter of how the question is asked and how much the subject's defensiveness about his performance is engaged. Subjects' ratings of the likelihood of intervention by others showed quite consistently the increase in perceived likelihood that was associated with the presence of comments. Yet the logical extension of this, that comments make a person sure that others will help and hence have the effect of lessening the likelihood that he will intervene, was not admitted by subjects, who perhaps found this a distasteful admission to make.

A great deal of insight was afforded by creating some difficulties for the help-giver and making emergence from his room only a first step in the helping sequence. There were two thresholds that had to be crossed in the present situation. We can conceive of a certain amount of pressure that was necessary first to draw a subject out of his room, and then additional pressure necessary to set him on a determined search for the experimenter. Twenty-seven percent of the subjects were lost at the first threshold, while an additional 30% were lost at the second threshold. The fact that many experiments on altruism and help-giving utilize a single threshold may mean that we have underestimated the vulnerability of helping responses to situational and ecological barriers that often characterize real-life help-giving situations. Part of the dilemma of the emergency bystander is that frequently there are courses of action which when taken are found to be insufficient. The apartment dweller may find that his shouts are not enough to disrupt a sidewalk beating; he must then decide if he has done all that is possible or whether he must descend to the street and offer direct assistance. It is this second threshold which may often be the more crucial one in the help-giving process.

The centrality of the diffusion of responsiblity factor, demonstrated by the effect of the responsiblity variation as well as the utility of this explanation in accounting for the unexpected pattern of data relevant to the feedback hypothesis, might be disappointing to those who would hope that help-giving is a simple enactment of a person's altruistic impulse. It appears that the decision to offer assistance to some distressed person is not necessarily a first response to an emergency, but that emergencies may often produce Good Samaritans only by default. Persons will help out in a crisis, but most reliably when it seems apparent that the other available sources of help are not forthcoming.

REFERENCES

ALLPORT, G. (1928) "A test for ascendance-submission." J. of Abnormal and Social Psych. 23 (July-September): 118-136.

ASCH, S. E. (1951) "Effects of group pressure upon the modification and distortion of judgments," pp. 177-190 in H. Guetzkow (ed.) Groups, Leadership and Men. Pittsburgh: Carnegie Press.

COCH, L. and J. R. FRENCH (1948) "Overcoming resistance to change." Human Relations 1 (August): 512-532.

DARLEY, J. and B. LATANE (1968a) "Bystander intervention in emergencies: diffusion of responsibility." J. of Personality and Social Psych. 8 (April): 377-383.

--- (1968b) "When will people help in a crisis?" Psych. Today 2 (December): 54-57.

EDWARDS, A. (1953) Edwards' Personal Preference Schedule. New York: Psychology Corporation.

FESTINGER, L., S. SCHACHTER, and K. BACK (1950) Social Pressures in Informal Groups: A Study of a Housing Project. New York: Harper.

KELMAN, H. (1961) "Processes of opinion change." Pub. Opinion Q. 25 (Spring): 57-78.

LATANE, B. (1967) "The urge to help." Presented to meetings of the American Psychology Association, Washington, D.C.

LE BON, G. (1895) The Crowd. London: Unwin.

MIDLARSKY, E. (1968) "Some antecedents of aiding under stress." Presented to meetings of the American Psychology Association, San Francisco.

MILGRAM, S. (1965) "Liberating effects of group pressure." J. of Personality and Social Psych. 1 (February): 127-134.

SNEDECOR, G. (1956) Statistical Methods. Ames: Iowa Univ. Press.

Part Three

IMPACT ANALYSIS:

AGGREGATE AND CASE STUDIES

Chapter 12

Group Violence

Some Hypotheses and Empirical Uniformities

ANTHONY OBERSCHALL – *Yale University*

Definition of Terms and Review of Existing Approaches

Since group violence is but one of several means of conducting conflict, explanation for its occurrence must be embedded in a comprehensive theory of conflict. Yet violent conflict is so topical and important that an effort to reflect on it sociologically is well worth undertaking at this time even in the absence of a comprehensive theory of social conflict. Indeed, Max Weber (1947: 133) has written that "the treatment of conflict involving the use of physical violence as a separate type is justified by the special characteristics of the employment of this means and the corresponding peculiarities of the sociological consequences of its use." In this essay, I shall avoid definitional and typological exercises, and concentrate rather on specific, testable hypotheses and empirical uniformities of group violence that have been put forward and commented upon at various times. I shall also present some data and findings bearing on the hypotheses that, while not "testing" them in rigorous fashion, will do more than simply provide plausible illustrations that can always be found whenever a large body of historical and contemporary cases is carefully searched. The final aim of the paper is to link up these hypotheses and uniformities in more systematic fashion than is presently available although the paper does not spell out a systematic theory of group violence. At this stage of theory when a plausible case can be made for a large number of hypotheses, it is important to spell out the specific conditions under which specific hypotheses are thought to be applicable.

There are several aspects of my approach that bear some brief preliminary comments. First, I do not start with a typology of conflict (e.g., revolution rebellion, riot, coup d' état, guerrilla war, and so on) nor do I break up the topic by the social categories of the participants (peasant rebellions, race riots, labor wars). The reason is not that such typologies and distinctions are unimportant, but that a satisfactory theory of group violence ought to have some general applicability. Furthermore, when group violence breaks out, it is seldom clear until after some time has elapsed what type of conflict is actually taking place, and it may indeed change over time. There is also some theoretical gain in being able to explain differences of magnitude in group violence between urban and rural conflict and labor and race conflict with reference to variables common in all situations.

Second, I do not differentiate between legal and illegal use of physical violence as a basic category of analysis, even though Weber's (1958: 78) and others' definitions of the state rely so centrally on this distinction. The reason is that group violence is the result of interaction between two or more groups in a conflict process, one of which may be the state or its agents, and a theory ought to apply the same concepts and variables to all the parties locked in conflict. Moreover, the authorities often initiate violence under circumstances where its use is perceived as illegitimate and uncalled for, and this then becomes a further and often predominant issue in the conflict. The use of illegitimate violence by the authorities, whether provoked or not, is also a topic of interest in itself, and ought to be therefore explained as part of the theory.

Third, I avoid explanations based on psychological or social-psychological variables implying aggressive drives such as the "disposition to violence" of certain groups or a propensity to violence which is manifested in the national character. The reason is that many explanations based on these alleged dispositions or propensities are actually spurious insofar as they are no more than a statement of an empirical uniformity (e.g., low levels of group violence in recent British history) rephrased in tautological terms that really beg the question (e.g., peaceful British national character). Even if measures of aggressive tendencies independent of the occurrence of group violence are developed, the present approach seeks to exhaust the explanatory potential of sociological variables before these dispositional concepts are invoked. It is precisely the facile and exaggerated notions about innate aggression, irrational drives, the herd instinct and similar formulations, popular especially since the French Revolution in accounts of group violence and crowd behavior, that the present approach is meant to avoid and supplant. These remarks do not apply to other psychological and social-psychological concepts, variables, and processes. It is scarcely possible to come to terms with the question of group violence without discussing grievances, hopes, frustrated expectations, relative deprivations, ideologies, legitimacy, and a host of other attitudinal, motivational, and state of mind concepts.

For purposes of this paper, Coser's definition of social conflict (1967: 232) as "a struggle over values or claims to status, power and scarce resources, in which the aims of the conflicting parties are not only to gain the desired values but also to neutralize, injure, or eliminate other rivals" is adequate. The hypotheses on group violence developed below, however, are not meant to be applicable to all cases of conflict. Specifically, wars between states are excluded at one end and microconflict, such as gang wars, at the other. A borderline case would be protracted internal war or guerrilla war with outside intervention. In this situation, the hypotheses are applicable only to the initial stages of conflict. Since the distinction between legal and illegal use of force was rejected earlier, violence here simply means the employment of physical coercion for personal and group ends. By social turmoil, social disturbances, civil disorders, or some equivalent terms, I mean any episode of collective behavior, not necessarily violent, in which a group of people express grievances, voice demands, stage meetings, marches, demonstrations, or sit-ins, draft petitions, try to prevent or block the execution of unpopular actions, destroy property, assault other individuals or groups, and the like. The group itself I will refer to as protesters unless they are called by more specific designations such as strikers, demonstrators, squatters, or rioters. By agents of social control I mean the rank and file executors of the orders of the authorities or the government, namely police, troops, militia, national guard, yeomanry, constables, and the like, including their immediate commanders in the field situation.

Violence is a means used to pursue conflict, one of several means, and the same conflict can be simultaneously conducted using several means. Dimensions of conflict that readily come to mind are its duration, scale (measured by the number of participants in the confrontation and its geographic spread), intensity, and the magnitude of violence. Intensity, as Dahrendorf (1959: 211) points out, refers to the "energy expenditure and degree of involvement of conflicting parties. A particular conflict may be said to be of high intensity if the cost of victory and defeat is high for the parties concerned." Intensity stands for the importance attached to the issues under dispute by the parties to the conflict. Intensity is probably going to be a particularly difficult variable to measure. The magnitude of violence might be measured simply by the total number of casualties, fatalities, and injuries that result from it, although some researchers persuasively argue for the inclusion of property damage as well. The total magnitude of conflict will probably have to be constructed as an index with duration, scale, intensity, and magnitude of violence as its component parts. For a much more comprehensive discussion of the dimensions and measurement of conflict, the reader is referred to the interesting monograph of Tilly and Rule (1965). In any case, these are only meant to be suggestions for measurement, since a rigorous testing of hypotheses will almost always involve variations and improvisations in measurement techniques depending on the availability of data and the specific circumstances of the conflict process. In this paper I shall concentrate on the magnitude of violence as a key dimension of conflict and as the dependent variable of interest.

Conflict is an everyday, normal, ongoing, institutionalized process most of the time. Conflict theorists ask however: (1) under what conditions conflict will tend to increase and decrease; (2) under what conditions conflict will tend to be violent rather than nonviolent, and what accounts for the magnitude of violence; and (3) what consequences violence has for conflict regulation and institutionalization, its consequences (if you prefer, functions) for the conflict groups, the individuals in the conflict groups, and the social system. This paper will deal primarily with the second question.

The Likelihood of Violence

Although the same set of conditions that can account for an increase in conflict may well be able to account for an increase in the likelihood of violent conflict and the magnitude of violence, a number of theorists specify intervening variables between these two steps. Just about every theorist points out that increased social change or rapid social change produces dislocations, strain, grievances and an increase in the normal levels of conflict and the likelihood of violence. Some see a direct link between the magnitude of strain, social dislocation, grievances on the one hand and the magnitude of conflict and of violent conflict on the other. Others acknowledge this causal link but emphasize in addition the importance of intervening variables, in particular, social control variables such as the reaction of the authorities or the ruling strata to the grievances and demands of the protesters. One might further note that some stress the importance of long-range intervention and reforms by the ruling groups as a response to increased conflict while others focus more on the immediate tactical response of the agents of social control during the confrontation process, particularly if magnitude of violence is the variable of interest. Here are some representative views expressed by influential social theorists on these matters.

Smelser (1963: 48-49) holds that while "the more severe the strain, the more likely an episode of collective behavior," still "we should not search for specific causal laws such as 'economic deprivation gives rise to hostile outbursts,' " since social strain comes in a bewildering variety of concrete forms, and "any kind of strain may be a determinant of any kind of collective behavior." Elsewhere, he has emphasized that the translation into action of a specific combination of social strain and conduciveness depends "above all on the behavior of the agencies of social control" (1964: 122). Specifically, he argues that if disturbed groups are provided access to channels that influence social policy, their response will tend to be peaceful and orderly, whereas if access is blocked, the reponse will tend to be violent and even take on at times bizarre and utopian forms (1968: 143). Ted Gurr (1967: 5, 11-12) draws heavily on the frustration-aggression theory and hypothesizes that "the more severe the relative deprivation, the greater the magnitude and likelihood of violence." Yet he too recognizes in a subsequent hypothesis that "the likelihood and magnitude of civil violence varies inversely with available, institutional mechanisms that permit expressions of non-violent hostility." Writing on urban racial violence in the United States, Grimshaw (1960: 119) holds that

> there is no direct relationship between the level of tension and the eruption of social violence. While assaults in the accommodative structure doubtless lead to an increase in tensions, violence is constrained by the strength and mode of application of external agencies of control, in particular the police.

In the same spirit, Hodgkin (1957: 187) predicted that in Africa

> whether national movements in particular territories employ violent or non-violent, revolutionary or constitutional methods to gain their objects seems likely to depend primarily upon the attitudes of the colonial regimes, the flexibility of their policies, their willingness to make substantial political concessions, and generally upon tactical considerations.

Dahrendorf (1959: 213) also thinks that when oppressed groups are allowed the right to organize and voice their grievances, the chances of violent conflict are decreased. Coser (1967: 106-107) and Heberle (1951: 385-387) formulate hypotheses and generalizations along the same lines. Turner (1964: 126) emphasizes the importance of the general public as well as the authorities when he writes that "the public . . . observes, interprets, and labels the movement. The public definition affects the character of recruitment to the movement, the means which the movement is able to use, and thus the strategies which the movement evolves and the kind of opposition it encounters." While one can easily lengthen the list of supporting quotations, Killian (1964: 450) sums it up appropriately: "Whatever the influence of other variables, the influence of the opposition and of the public reaction to a movement cannot be overemphasized."

The great merit of all these views is that they do not look upon the values, goals, ideology, and especially the means of conflict used by a protest group as a fixed, constant quantity. Instead, the means used to pursue conflict are the result of a process of interaction between the conflict groups. In particular, the reception of the protest groups and the reaction of the authorities and agents of social control are singled out as very important. If the authorities are unresponsive, block channels of communication, do not provide the opportunity for peaceful protest, refuse to make concessions, and so on, the likelihood of violent conflict increases. While the magnitude of strain, type of strain, and the number of grievances account for the increase of conflict and threaten to overload and break down the existing institutions of conflict regulation, the magnitude and forms that conflict is likely to have are explained primarily with reference to the interaction between authorities and protesters. Still, the above viewpoints must be criticized for their lack of specificity since responsiveness or unresponsiveness, open or blocked channels of communication and influence, access or lack of access to decision makers are rather ill-defined, global conceptions that stand for complex social structures and processes. Moreover the above views assume that if the authorities are responsive and act in good faith, they are able to undertake effective reforms to relieve social strain and meet the grievances of the protest group. But what if reforms are ineffective or only partially effective? It is a commonplace that concessions and reforms can be "too little, too late." Furthermore, repression may under certain circumstances be an effective means of stopping a protest movement at its start with little violence. But how can one sociologically come to terms with the notion of an effective combination of the carrot and the stick for handling social disturbances and for defusing a potentially violent or revolutionary situation?

This issue has been discussed most recently by Huntington (1968: 362 ff.), who starts with de Tocqueville's observation on these matters, or what I would like to call de Tocqueville's paradox. In his discussion of the antecedent of the French Revolution, de Tocqueville (1955: 176-177) observes that

> it is not always when things are going from bad to worse that revolutions break out. On the contrary, it oftener happens that when a people which has put up with an oppressive rule over a long period without protest suddenly finds the government relaxing its pressure, it takes up arms against it. Thus the social order overthrown by a revolution is almost always better than the one immediately preceding it, and experience teaches us that, generally speaking, the most perilous moment for a bad government is one that seeks to mend its ways. Only consummate statecraft can enable a king to save his throne when after a long spell of oppressive rule he sets out to improve the lot of his subjects.

De Tocqueville's paradox has been noted in numerous instances in history and in the contemporary world, for instance in connection with increased social disturbances and urban racial violence in the United States concurrent with and following the most comprehensive social, economic, and political legislation and reforms to improve the condition of Negroes since the Reconstruction Era, and the East European anti-Soviet, anticommunist upheavals following shortly upon de-Stalinization and a period of relative "liberalization" in the Soviet orbit initiated after Stalin's death. Crane Brinton (1957: 40) long ago pointed out a more specific variant of de Tocqueville's paradox when he observed in his discussion of the antecedents of the English, American, French, and Russian revolutions that

> one of the most evident uniformities we can record is the effort made in each of our societies to reform the machinery of government. Nothing can be more erroneous than the picture of the old regime as an un-regenerate tyranny, sweeping to its end in a climax of despotic indifference to the clamor of its abused subjects.

Another student of revolution, Pettee (1938: 94) refers to the process of attempted reforms by an old regime as "erratic reformism":

> Erratic reformism is the only policy open to a ruling class divided in its attitudes, or strapped by unwieldy institutions . . . in Russia, the utmost repression and occasional barbarism was accompanied by spasmodic reforms in industry and agriculture and politics. The result of such reforms and reaction mixed might well be called the quickest way to make a revolution. The result is to cramp the privileged classes without relieving the exploited . . . . To the cramped, the reforms have an appearance of being forced concessions, and the reactionary measures an appearance of betrayal.

The paradox is, of course, less surprising if one recalls that the reform attempts tend to be half-hearted and ineffective because of institutional weakness and deliberate efforts by certain groups to undermine them. A period of liberalization after a long period of oppression allows the surfacing of long-dormant grievances and demands going far beyond those initially voiced to and anticipated by the authorities; it allows the mobilization of discontented groups and expectations of reforms that cannot be realistically instituted in a short time. The subsequent, half-hearted attempts to crack down upon the activities of the freshly mobilized groups creates a situation favorable to social disturbances on a wide scale.

Contemporary students of conflict are well aware of the consequences of erratic reformism. Eckstein (1964: 54) argues that a sudden relaxation of repression and the institution of a liberal policy after a regime has driven its opponents underground and inflamed their enmity creates a favorable context for violent confrontation. Smelser (1968: 114), in a similar vein, writes that "the type of response on the part of authorities that aggravates and intensifies an episode of collective protest is harshness and rigidity that alternates with evident weakness." On the other hand, "an agent of social control who is firm but patient, consistently prohibiting certain types of protest but consistently permitting and giving serious consideration to others . . . tends to contain the protest." It is immediately apparent from these quotations that the question of reform in the face of demands and social disturbances is an exceedingly complex topic, much neglected in contemporary theories of conflict, and not adequately captured by concepts such as open or blocked channels of communication, access or lack of access of disturbed groups to the authorities or ruling groups, or their responsiveness or unresponsiveness. Moreover to introduce qualifying terms such as "effective" and "ineffective" reform, access, or responsiveness into these hypotheses is to beg the question itself.

ECONOMIC FACTORS AND THE STRUCTURAL LOCATION OF GROUP CONFLICT

The relationship between social change, social strain and grievances, the authorities' response and the likelihood of social disturbances is further complicated by another and related set of issues also first raised by de Tocqueville (1955: 175-177) when he pointed out that the years preceding the outbreak of the French Revolution witnessed an increase, not a decrease, of economic prosperity.

> In 1780, there could no longer be any talk of France's being on the [economic] downgrade; on the contrary, it seemed that no limit could be set to her advance . . . . Twenty years earlier there had been no hope for the future; in 1780, no anxiety was felt about it . . . . It is a singular fact that this increasing prosperity, far from tranquilizing the population, everywhere promoted a spirit of unrest. The general public became more and more hostile to every ancient institution, more and more discontented . . . . Moreover, those parts of France in which the improvement in the standard of living was most pronounced were the centers of the revolutionary movement.

Even Marx, whose views are usually contrasted with those of de Tocqueville and who, in his theoretical works, tended to uphold the misery theory of political upheaval (deepening economic crises, falling profits, lower wages, increased exploitation and misery of the working class linked to increased revolutionary potential) took a much more flexible and varied approach in his brilliant case studies and commentaries on contemporary French and European political upheavals. Yet ever since Marx and de Tocqueville, there has been a continuous debate by historians and social scientists on just what are the precise links between economic changes and social conflict–in particular revolutionary outbreaks. There is no need to review this long controversy about the primacy or importance of economic as opposed to other factors. It is sufficient to recognize that economic changes broadly viewed are such a common, perennial, and central component of social change that a discussion of social change, social strain and social dislocations, grievances, and protest cannot proceed without thorough examination of economic processes. Short- and long-term economic trends, particular sequences of long- and short-term up- and downswings, migration patterns, rural-urban demographic shifts, the effects of the introduction of new technologies and novel modes of production and other structural economic changes, changes in the cost of living, of wages, of the cost of basic foods, and a host of other economic facts and processes have received close scrutiny by students of social conflict. Moreover, not only changes in absolute terms, but relative gains and losses have been discussed and the concepts of relative deprivation, rising expectations, or some other social-psychological concepts such as hope and cramp have been invoked to assess the reactions of various groups and social classes to absolute and relative economic gains and losses. The literature on these topics has grown immense. The conclusion that several diverse patterns of economic change must bear some direct and indirect links to social disturbances, and that these links are mediated by some intervening social-psychological processes is inescapable but not very helpful. I shall briefly review the major points in one of the most valuable papers on this topic by an economist and then list some of the most common patterns of economic change frequently linked to increased protest activity on the part of negatively privileged social strata and social classes.

In an article entitled "Rapid Economic Growth as a Destabilizing Force," Mancur Olson, Jr. (1963) points out that "economic growth . . . can significantly increase the number of [economic] losers," e.g., increase the absolute number of people whose standard of living has fallen, despite an increase in the average per capita income of the entire population. Moreover, in the early phases of economic growth, there is a tendency for increased inequality of incomes to come about as well. Rapid economic growth is frequently associated with changes in methods of production, new technologies, the type of labor and skills demanded and the geographic configuration of production. While some groups may therefore gain—and indeed gain a lot economically—other groups may lose in relative and even absolute terms if they are located in economically declining regions, in firms or industries caught with outdated technologies, and with outdated skills. Furthermore, levels of consumption may decline with economic growth when capital accumulation curbs spending through forced savings, taxation, or some other means. Olson also points out that economic growth as a long-term trend is often associated with short-term downswings, and for particular groups wages may rise slower than prices, increased unemployment may occur, and indeed short-run wage losses may occur as well. While Olson also stresses the potential for political unrest among groups that are economic gainers and the possiblity of rising expectations experienced by these groups, a central contribution of his analysis for sociologists is that nothing in economic theory contradicts the possibility of an increase in the number of economic losers during a period of economic growth, and that such growth might be associated with changes in the relative economic position of social strata and other population groups. A major conclusion of his paper is that detailed information on the impact of economic changes (both growth and decline) upon specific groups is needed for understanding the potential for social and political upheaval of different groups, strata, and classes in the population. Knowledge of aggregate national economic trends alone or comparative analyses of countries based on aggregate figures can lead to misleading inferences. Unfortunately, as Lawrence Stone (1965: 169 ff.) has pointed out, economic data sufficiently disaggregated and complete are difficult to come by even in the present, let alone locating data on state of mind variables such as relative deprivation, expectations, and aspirations for the past. As a result some researchers engage in the risky and often tautological business of inferring relative deprivation from the occurrence of social disturbances and then find their hypotheses on the relationship between these two variables confirmed. Here then follows a brief outline of the kinds of economic changes that commonly produce grievances and frequently result in social disturbances and protest among the lower social strata and classes.

Groups that are economically at the margins of subsistence will react at once to a short-term increase in food prices or a diminished food supply. Such shortages and price increases, often localized, occur frequently after a time of crop failures or of war. The protesters' response is typically the food riot, consisting of attacks upon grain hoarders or merchants and bakers who are holding back their grain stocks or selling them at a high price, forced food sales at the preshortage price, and the prevention of grain transfers out of a given locality after food supplies have been requisitioned elsewhere (Rudé, 1964). When such grievances and disturbances coincide with dissatisfaction among other social strata, the lower classes can be mobilized by them beyond the initial limited aims for the provision of cheap food. Writing about the French Revolution at a time when from twenty-five percent to ninety percent of the daily wages of urban working people were spent on bread (depending on their trade and skill level), Rudé (1959: 200) noted:

> Perhaps not surprisingly [an inquiry into the causes of social unrest among the *menu peuple*] reveals that the constant motive of popular insurrection during the Revolution, as in the 18th century as a whole, was the compelling need of the *menu peuple* for the provision of cheap and plentiful bread and other essentials, and the necessary administrative measures to insure it.

An effective response of the authorities in such a situation is to provide food supplies at the usual price, often by means of price control. The lack of support by the working people of Paris for Robespierre and the Jacobins at the time of their fall in 1794 was due in large part to the inability to assure a stable cost of living by means of wage and price controls (Rudé, 1959: ch. 9).

In the case of rural social strata, one should be careful to distinguish between peasants who are only marginally involved in commercial production for the market and farmers who are independent owner-cultivators producing commercial crops, often for export. Such farmers, especially single-crop farmers producing an export crop, are vulnerable to the fluctuations in the world market prices of their crops, and in particular to a drop in prices after a period of boom when they may have become excessively dependent for income on one particular crop. Examples of the processes of mobilization among farmers under such circumstances are the Populist movement in the American West in the 1880s and 1890s (Hicks, 1961: ch. 3), the disaffection and susceptibility to right-wing and Nazi appeals of farmers in North Germany in 1928 and later (Heberle, 1945), and the positive response of African farmers to nationalist movements in many colonies in the late 1950s and early 1960s after a drop in world market prices of cotton, coffee, cocoa, and other tropical crops following the World War II and early 1950s boom period.

Peasant disaffection on the other hand occurs most frequently over the issues of land shortage and an attempt by landlords to extract an increased economic surplus that frequently violates traditional norms of equity and distribution

(Moore, 1966: ch. 9). The occasion for peasant disturbances is provided by demographic pressure and the behavior of the landlords. Landlords may attempt to increase their income from rents and other extractions from the peasantry under pressure of conspicuous consumption and indebtedness in cities and the court. Gerschenkron (1964: 184) points to the attempt by the French nobility before the French Revolution to increase the peasant's financial burden and to revive some rights and claims on land that had not been exercised for a long time. Under such circumstances peasants are convinced that their grievances are legitimate. Peasant revolts resulting from these issues are extremely common. For China, for instance, Shu-ching Lee (1951: 512) reports that in a small border region between Kiangsi and Fukien, approximately the size of Iowa, an investigator found from local records 76 instances of peasant revolt, led mostly by tenants, over a period of some 180 years between 1448 and 1627. Another occasion for revolt occurs when a landlord class seeks to exploit its estates in a more rational and profitable fashion by consolidating land, evicting tenants, and seizing lands traditionally held in common ownership by the peasant community, as occurred at the time of the Mexican Revolution (McNeely, 1966). Furthermore, demographic pressures in rural areas often force peasants to become squatters or otherwise seize the uncultivated lands of neighboring landlords. Of course a part of the surplus population may migrate to the cities in search of industrial employment, but this alternative may not always be present or may become unattractive during periods of industrial depression and urban unemployment. For the peasant putting more land or unused land under cultivation using traditional techniques of production in order to increase or maintain his income is a more attractive and realistic alternative than to use more advanced agricultural technology on his existing holding, for which he may lack the skill and the capital. All of these forms of economic and demographic pressures operated on peasants in Russia before 1905 and led to widespread land seizures, illegal grazings, arson of manors, forest destruction, and other forms of peasant disturbances (Gerschenkron, 1964: 191).

Land reform is too broad a term to describe an effective response on the part of the authorities to meet peasant land hunger. Tilly (1964: 196) has shown in the case of the Vendée that the sale of church lands during the French Revolution became an occasion for increased disaffection among the peasantry when the prosperous farmers and bourgeois living in small towns managed to outbid the small tenants and farmers and grab most of the desirable land that rural people felt was rightfully theirs. Effective land reform means the transfer of available land (not only marginal land) to the peasants themselves. Land reform is likely to be successful if the landlords are foreign nationals: e.g. German barons in the Baltic area, Polish aristocracy in Lithuania, Hungarian nobility in Yugoslavia, and Turkish Bulgars in parts of Rumania, as was the case in the post-World War I period in Eastern Europe (Gerschenkron, 1966: 94). The nationalization of land and the impressment of tenants and small landholders into collective farms or state farms will also be highly unpopular solutions and will be resisted, although in these cases the state and its agents of social control may be strong enough to put down resistance, as happened in Soviet Russia. Nationalization of land is likely to be an acceptable solution in situations where the majority of rural working people had been a propertyless, wage earning, rural proletariat rather than an independent class of smallholders.

Among the urban working class three major groups have to be distinguished: unskilled recent rural migrants into cities in search of employment; working people in established and growing industries; and the "preindustrial" skilled workers and independent artisans and craftsmen who are losing their economic base because of competition from new methods of production. It is the last named group that has been particularly noted for its participation in social and political disturbances, at least in the Western European context (Rudé, 1959: ch. 13). Starting in the late eighteenth century, as a result of the industrial revolution, artisans and craftsmen have been a numerically declining stratum, threatened with being reduced to ordinary wage workers, economically insecure and caught in a spiral of downward social mobility, even while they were trying to maintain their economic grip and social status. Long-term economic growth did not benefit them, since it increased prosperity mainly in the new manufacturing and industrial sectors. Reform legislation regulating hours of work, conditions of work, safety, female and child labor seldom benefited them and more often than not represented a further immediate loss of income because of their reliance on family labor. Many of these groups sought a solution to their economic problems in the revival of preindustrial curbs on competition, price and wage controls, and other measures which were totally counter to the broader social and economic changes taking place and which were therefore not instituted. Because of a tradition of corporate association and collective action, these groups were susceptible to rapid mobilization to defend their interests.

On the other hand wage workers in new and growing industries did benefit directly from long-term economic growth and labor legislation but were hurt by unemployment and wage cuts during depressions. These wage earning groups, however, were subject to strain and grievances, most often manifested in strikes, over the reluctance of employers to restore wage levels when prosperity returned, over conditions and hours of work, over the right to form trade unions and engage in collective bargaining (which was itself a result of the workers' conviction that there was no other effective means of protecting their employment security, wage levels, and standard of life), and over the issue of job security when employers tried to hire unskilled workers, often recent migrants, to replace them. Especially explosive outbursts occurred when unskilled strike breakers, often drawn from an ethnic or racial minority, were introduced after workers had gone on strike against their employer, as was typical of United States industrial conflict. An increase in the standard of living of the working class, industrial legislation in the area of hours, child labor, hygiene, and safety, the recognition of the right to collective bargaining, and other reforms instituted during the nineteenth and twentieth centuries were the appropriate long-term responses that directed labor conflict into increasingly peaceful and institutionalized channels.

As for recent rural migrants with low skills, who are everywhere known to contribute a disproportionate share to all the social patholgies associated with the growing industrial city, a great deal depended on the opportunities they had for temporarily returning to their families in rural areas who provided them with an economic cushion in difficult times. At any rate, this group has not figured as prominently in large-scale collective disturbances, especially of a political sort, as the previous two groups, and has even at certain times been coopted by the ruling class to fight against other working class protesters as was the case with the Mobile Guard in Paris during the 1848 revolution (Rudé, 1959: 173), whereas at other times they have acted as strike breakers for employers. In effect, recent migrants are often so close to the margins of subsistence that they are very vulnerable to economic pressures, react positively to economic opportunities even when it means breaking the rank of working class solidarity, and are reluctant to take the economic risks that protest activity entails.

Noneconomic grievances, often coupled with the presence of economic grievances, also figure in lower-class social disturbances and are important in understanding the protest activities of economically privileged groups such as merchants and professionals and especially students and intellectuals. The last two groups often supply the ideological, organizational, and leadership resources that facilitate mobilization among the working class and peasants for protest activity.

The preceding paragraphs are not meant to be an exhaustive list of all types of strain and grievances, but only of the more common patterns of economic grievances that affect the lower classes who so frequently make up the bulk of participants in social movements and confrontations and who are likely to make up the majority of victims of group violence.

HYPOTHESES: STATEMENT AND DISCUSSION

Assuming that a situation of conflict or increased conflict exists as a result of economic and other changes—some of which were listed in the preceding section—what hypotheses and empirical generalizations can one make about the probability of violent conflict, and the magnitude of violence (measured roughly by the number of casualties)? Hypothesis 1 is that

> the protesters use violent means only after they have attempted other nonviolent means of seeking redress for their grievances.

Alternately (hypothesis la)

> the protest group waits for some time for reforms designed to reduce social strain to take effect, and only after these reforms have proved ineffective do they resort to violent means of protest.

Still another variation (hypothesis 1b) is that

> the authorities or ruling groups break a promise or agreement of reform, and thus provide little or no opportunity for nonviolent means of instituting desired changes before protest groups initiate violent actions.

For instance, Huntington (1962: 25) states that the Huk leaders in the Philippines first attempted to achieve their goals by peaceful means, but when the legislature refused to seat seven elected Huks, their leaders returned to the countryside to spark a revolt. Writing about the Zapata rising in Mexico in 1910-1911, McNeely (1966: 155-157) reports that Zapata's native village had a long record of contentions over its land rights, that the new governor paid little attention to the villagers' petitions despite the fact that their legal claims were upheld as valid, and that legal action by villagers in Mexico City also failed to produce results. Only after these institutional channels were exhausted did the uprising start. Concerning the Luddite outbreaks in England in 1811, Darvall (1934: 47-48, 64) explicitly states that the stockingers and weavers first tried to negotiate their grievances over wages, the rent of frames, the truck system, and other matters with the hosiers, but without any positive results. As for the June days in Paris during the 1848 revolution, the working people of Paris did not start erecting barricades until after Louis Blanc's Luxembourg Commission and the national workshops (the two major gains the Paris working people achieved after the overthrow of the July monarchy and one of the main sources of employment and livelihood for them at a time of economic depression) were dissolved and the workers given a choice of enlisting in the army, draining marshes, or remaining in Paris without work or pay (Rudé, 1964: 172). Examples can be multiplied, and in any case are only meant to be illustrative and suggestive.

A second set of hypotheses deals with some circumstances under which the casualties will be many in number rather than few in number. Hypothesis 2 is that

> in violent confrontations the authorities' actions produce the bulk, or at least more than half, of the casualties.

A subhypothesis (2a) is that

> violence is more often initiated by the authorities and their agents than by the protesters, as when peaceful demonstrations, marchers, petitioners, peaceful assemblies, and the like are broken up and attacked.

Of course, protesters often initiate actions which are illegal and coercive, but not destructive of life and property, such as squatting on land or cultivating land illegally, refusing to pay taxes, occupying factories and mines, or refusing to disperse, which represents a challenge to the authorities. I do not mean to imply that the authorities will randomly and lightly initiate violence as a rule. Another subhypothesis (2b) is that

> when the confrontation is not directly between the protesters and the authorities, but between two hostile population groups, such as employers and employees, or whites and blacks, the casualties tend to be higher when the authorities either openly side with one group against the other, or refrain from intervening in the situation and thereby legitimize the actions of the aggressor.

Moreover (hypothesis 2c)

> the magnitude of casualties will be greater if the agents of social control know that they will not be held accountable for the casualties they produce during repression.

This often happens when public opinion favors repression during a period of "Red" scare, of nationalism and jingoism, of religious enthusiasm, or of similar waves of fear and hostility during which the protesters have been identified as "Reds," "traitors," or "infidels" and "heretics," to cite some common examples. In other situations, social disturbances may occur in outlying areas, usually rural, with poor communications, so that little information about casualties and the details of the confrontation filters out other than through government-controlled sources. It may also happen in situations where the judiciary is subordinate to the executive branch and in any case is not much influenced by an unorganized public opinion. Another variant on this theme (hypothesis 2d) is that

> if the protesters belong to a negatively privileged or "pariah" social category, such as a religious minority or peasants, who have not enjoyed full citizenship rights and have traditionally been violently repressed, casualties will tend to be high,

again because public opinion supports repression, and because of low accountability for the use of force by the agents of social control. Finally, as Donald J. Black has pointed out to me, (hypothesis 2e)

> the probability of violence decreases to the extent that a third impartial party intervenes as buffer or mediator in the conflict.

This is in fact the rationale behind the U.N. peacekeeping force as it was put into operation in Cyprus and elsewhere.

We note, for instance, from the National Advisory Commission (1968: 68-69, 107, 115-116 fn. 20, 164) that in the 1967 urban riots in the United States, of the 83 persons who died in the 75 disorders studied, only about 10% were public officials, and that the overwhelming majority of the civilians killed were Negroes, most of these shot by the police or other agents of social control. In Detroit, rioters were responsible for three deaths at most, whereas the police and national guard accounted for between 27 and 30 deaths. In summarizing the detailed casualty figures resulting from popular disturbances between 1730 and 1848 in Western Europe, Rudé (1964: 255-256) concludes that "destruction of property, then, is a constant feature of the pre-industrial crowd; but not destruction of human lives . . . . From this balance sheet of violence and reprisal, it would appear, then, that it was authority rather than the crowd that was conspicuous for its violence to life and limb." During the Paris Commune of 1871, in contrast to the several hundred troops of the Versailles regiment killed and the 63 hostages shot by the Communards, at least 20,000 Communards were killed, shot as prisoners, or subsequently executed by the authorities, not counting the number of imprisonments and deportations to penal camps (Postgate, 1962: 286).

In going to standard historical sources one can produce similar figures for the discrepancy in magnitude of casualties produced by the authorities on the one hand and the insurgents, rebels, or protesters on the other in confrontations such as the June Days of Paris in 1848, the Russian Revolution of 1905-1906, the Mau Mau uprising, the Nyasaland disturbances of 1959, and so on. So far as the authorities initiating or escalating violence is concerned, history is filled with such examples. The precipitating event of the February 1848 revolution occurred when 50 to 100 demonstrators were killed or wounded by troops as they marched in support of the parliamentary opposition after the authorities had banned a large public banquet planned by the opposition in Paris (Rudé, 1964: 167). The precipitating event in the Russian revolution of 1905 occurred on Bloody Sunday when an immense procession of unarmed workers in their Sunday clothes, chanting church hymns and led by Father Gapon, sought to present a petition to the Czar and were attacked by the troops and the Cossacks, resulting in a massacre of about 1,000 petitioners. It should be pointed out that in conformity with hypothesis 1, Father Gapon had attempted before this event to seek redress of the workers' grievances through bureaucratic channels and had gotten nowhere.

In the Hungarian Revolution of 1956 (United Nations, 1957: 81-83) one of the precipitating events occurred when students, on the evening of October 22, demanded that the radio station broadcast their resolutions to the Hungarian people and were fired upon by security police inside the radio building after student representatives had already entered the radio building to negotiate with the officials of the radio. In a subsequent aggravating incident on October 25, a huge crowd of several thousand peaceful people, many of them women and children, were waiting for Prime Minister Nagy to appear when a number of flag-carrying demonstrators appeared in the square and the security police and possibly also Soviet troops opened up on everybody with machine guns, killing anywhere from 300 to 800 people.

Police partiality with an aggressor group during clashes between two population groups seems to result in inciting the aggressors to further violence, in prolonging the disturbances, and in the escalation of weapons used. These are all productive of a larger number of casualties than if the authorities had intervened impartially to separate the two sides. For example, Waskow (1967: ch. 10) has pointed out its importance in the 1919 race riots, and Lee and Humphrey (1943: ch. 4) for the Detroit riot of 1943. Furthermore, in communal or religious riots producing a very large number of casualties, the police or military actually join the aggressor group during the clashes, are directly responsible for many casualties, and often make weapons and ammunition available to one side, as happened in the Ibo massacres in Northern Nigeria in 1966 and the anticommunist massacres in Java in 1965. In these instances of communal riots the agents of social control did not play the part of the impartial buffer associated with lower casualties, as stated in hypothesis 2e. In some of the above confrontations, moreover, the protesters were drawn from negatively privileged groups (hypothesis 2d) and the agents of social control were operating in a tradition of low accountability for the casualties they produced (hypothesis 2c). The perfunctory manner in which inquests are often conducted—as they were in Los Angeles after the 1965 riot—to establish the cause and responsibility in the deaths resulting from police action is well described in Conot (1967: ch. 53).

Aside from these hypotheses which deal with the circumstance of confrontation, the social status of the protest group and the restraints operating on the agents of social control, other related hypotheses might be formulated, some, for instance, dealing with the relative social status separating the protesters and the agents of social control, the group membership overlap between them and past history of hostility and recriminations, and the capacity for repression of the authorities in the sense of their command over resources, their ability to organize an apparatus of social control, and the absolute size of this apparatus. Is violence more likely to erupt, and casualties likely to be higher, when Cossacks face peasants than if troops made up of peasant conscripts face them? Are they to be higher if black demonstrators or rioters are confronted by a white or a mixed white and black police force and other agents of social control in the United States? Are they likely to be higher if troops drawn from rural areas in France face the Paris working people than if troops are made up of urban recruits, and so on? The answers may well be in the affirmative in all these instances, but at this point I have simply not explored these matters in sufficient depth to formulate a set of clear and meaningful hypotheses. The evidence is, in any case, complicated. For instance, it is doubtful that there was less violence in the United States labor conflict when native employers, agents of social control, and armed guards were facing native, English-speaking workers than when they were facing immigrant workers of Southern and Eastern European origin.

Another set of hypotheses dealing with the magnitude of violence has to do with the ecological and technological aspects of the confrontation, although these matters have received little attention in the social science literature and are especially difficult to state unambiguously in terms of hypotheses. I would like to formulate (hypothesis 3) nonetheless that

> when two population groups are locked in conflict, and when a majority group attacks a numerical minority, casualties will be especially high if the minority group does not live in compact settlements but in small clusters dispersed among the hostile majority.

This ecological pattern existed in several instances of large-scale communal or tribal warfare productive of very high casualties, such as the Hindu-Moslem clashes on the Indian subcontinent at the time of partition, the clashes between Greek and Turkish Cypriots, the Ibo massacres in Northern Nigeria, the Tutsi–Hutu clashes in Ruanda-Urundi, the anticommunist massacres in Java, and rural violence in Colombia in the 1950s. On the other hand, compact settlement of a population group in a particular geographic area to the exclusion of other groups makes for the possibility of secession and civil war, as in Biafra and Buganda in 1966.

Access to weapons and the disparity of weapons technology also are important and independent factors in the production of casualties. According to hypothesis 4

> if only one side has access to modern weapons such as firearms, and the other side does not (it has only agricultural tools or spears and arrows) casualties tend to be higher than if there is no weapons disparity.

This occurs often in conjunction with a situation (compare with hypothesis 2b) as in Ruanda-Urundi and Northern Nigeria, where troops armed with modern weapons join one group against the other or make such weapons available to the side they favor. If there is no weapons disparity, access to lethal weapons becomes the crucial technological factor. Modern weapons used in a confrontation in and of themselves are not necessarily more productive of casualties than the use of premodern weapons and agricultural implements. If the groups in the confrontation have premodern weapons within reach in their own homes at a moment's notice and are skilled and accustomed in their use, casualties will tend to be high. Describing the communal riots in India in 1946-1948 that produced close to one million fatalities, Richardson (1960: 43) writes that "communal killing was mostly by sticks, small knives, small axes, swords, spears, with only a few shotguns, rifles, or automatics." Hypothesis 4a then is that

> in the absence of weapons disparity, possession of modern firearms by both sides is not in itself productive of higher casualties than possession of traditional weapons and agricultural implements.

Because access to traditional weapons by a large number of participants in the conflict is more probable in rural than in urban populations, hypothesis 4b is that

> violent clashes in rural areas between two hostile groups will be more productive of casualties than clashes in cities.

Furthermore, as Juan Linz has pointed out, visibility, both social and physical, is higher in rural areas. Group memberships of people in rural areas are well known by all, and potential victims will therefore not be able to disappear socially and physically in the anonymous settings of large cities, as is the case with urban violence. Of course, it often happens that the rural/urban distinction is correlated with ecological and other factors described in the set of hypotheses 2 and 3, all tending to favor higher casualties in the rural context, so that the test of hypothesis 4c might involve practical difficulties of locating enough cases for which the other factors can be controlled. There are other variables that are logical candidates for inclusion in hypotheses, especially the absolute and relative sizes of the conflict groups, or of the protesters and the agents of social control, but little thought has been so far given to "size" variables in the literature, and it may be premature to speculate about them at this point. Furthermore, the effects of size or relative size may well turn out to be less important than another set of structural variables to which I will now turn.

These structural variables concern the number and magnitude of grievances, the degree of mutually reinforcing, nonoverlapping social cleavages separating the conflict groups, the ideological level of the protesters' demands, the degree of organization of the conflict groups, and, finally, presence or absence of a recognition issue. In each case, we are asking what the relationship of these variables is to the likelihood of violence and its magnitude. For the first three variables, I shall hypothesize no systematic relationship. Hypothesis 5 then states that

> the number of grievances, the magnitude of strain, the magnitude of the frustrations experienced by the protesters, while making conflict more likely and increasing the intensity of that conflict, nevertheless bears no positive (or negative) relationship to the probability of violence and the magnitude of casualties.

In the same vein, if the conflict groups are separated by a number of nonoverlapping divisions–ethnic, religious, class, cultural-linguistic, and the like–rather than just one such division, conflict is more likely to involve more people, last longer, and have a higher intensity, but will not necessarily be more violent (compare with Dahrendorf, 1959: 213-215, for an extended discussion of this hypothesis). To state this idea as hypothesis 6:

> the number of reinforcing and nonoverlapping social cleavages separating the conflict groups bears no systematic relationship to the likelihood and magnitude of violence.

It may well be true empirically and historically that a number of other factors previously hypothesized as favoring violence is correlated with the last two named variables but I see no direct causal link. In other words, in technical parlance, the relationship is not "spurious," but an "intervening sequence."

The same lack of relationship is hypothesized here for the ideological level of the demands expressed by the protest group. Demands will have a higher ideological level insofar as they are not merely specific measures to relieve particular grievances, such as demands for higher wages, shorter work hours, lower food prices, or the dismissal of a corrupt or hated official. They will have a higher ideological level if they address themselves to major structural changes in the polity and the economy (such as the overthrow of the government) changes in the form of government (e.g., republic rather than monarchy), nationalization of industry and expropriation of private property (such as land reform backed up by radical philosophic and ideological appeals and justifications). Hypothesis 7 is, then, that

> the ideological level of the demands bears no systematic relationship to the likelihood and magnitude of violence.

Even if hypotheses 5-7 overstate the lack of relationship, the effects of these variables are dwarfed by the effects of the previously named variables and the next two (and last) variables to be considered–organization and recognition–whose importance for conflict theory Dahrendorf (1959: 223-227) has already pointed out. Hypothesis 8, briefly stated, is that

> the lower the level of organization of *both* conflict groups, the higher the likelihood and magnitude of violence.

By level of organization, I mean the degree to which there exists an effective, recognized, stable leadership structure exercising direction and control over the actions of the rank and file participants in the conflict, as opposed to the low level of organization of protest groups that more or less spontaneously collect as hostile crowds after precipitating incidents, and where at most temporary and local leaders may emerge. So far as the degree of organization of the agents of social control is concerned, it is higher to the extent that networks of communication, chain of command, and troop discipline are maintained. That is more likely to happen if the force is professional, has been trained, or is experienced in handling confrontations with protest crowds. A confrontation likely to be particularly violent is one in which an unorganized, spontaneously assembled hostile crowd faces a disorganized police force, troops, or another unorganized crowd. A corollary of this hypothesis is that (hypothesis 8a)

> if the protest group is split into rival camps and factions with competing leaders, the likelihood of violence is greater than if it is internally united.

By recognition I mean that the authorities, regardless of what position they may take on the substantive issues and demands, recognize the right to protest and are willing to listen to, sit down with, talk to, and negotiate in good faith with the leaders, deputies, representatives, or spokesmen of the protesters. Nonrecognition can be inferred from several indicators that signal to the protest group that recognition is not granted or is in the process of being withdrawn: refusal to receive, listen to, debate, discuss, or negotiate with the representatives of the protesters, arrest of their leaders, harrassment of their organizing efforts through arrest, blacklists, curbs on the right to free speech, and so on. Hypothesis 9 can now be stated:

> If recognition is granted, the likelihood and magnitude of violence tends to be lower than if recognition is not granted or is being withdrawn.

A subhypothesis (9a) is that

> even after violence has already broken out, it is likely to diminish when recognition is granted, but violence is likely to continue if it is not granted.

Some may object to this last hypothesis as self-evident or tautological, since recognition implies that the conflict is on its way to becoming institutionalized and regulated, if not resolved. Indeed, recognition is the major step in institutionalizing conflict. In a broader context than the social movements and episodes of collective behavior here discussed, recognition is analogous to the extension of political and civil rights to previously disenfranchised "new" groups or classes. Yet the above formulation stated in terms of recognition is more precise and measurable than if a hypothesis were worded in terms of the degree of institutionalization of conflict and the likelihood of violence. Furthermore, while recognition in some sense implies that the authorities have been responsive to the protest group and have opened previously blocked channels of communication and influence, similar hypotheses stated in terms of "greater responsiveness of the authorities" and "acceptance of the legitimacy of protest" are less precise than hypothesis 9. For regardless of the substantive issues and demands, lack of recognition may well and often does become the major issue of the conflict, so that even if the authorities promise or institute reforms and changes that will reduce the strain and are thus responsive, the conflict will still remain potentially high on likelihood of violence until the recognition issue is also resolved. Concessions extracted under popular pressures without recognition may perhaps be considered a very low or minimal form of recognition, and as such can lower the likelihood or level of existing violence, but it may not always do so. Furthermore, recognition, in itself, without immediate concessions on substantive issues, or even before reforms can take effect, will have a tendency to defuse a potentially violent confrontation or lower an already existing level of violence. It is nevertheless true, by virtue of hypothesis la, that if recognition does not eventually also bring concessions or reforms that will relieve strain on substantive matter, the likelihood of violent conflict is again increased.

Two exceptions are worth noting. There are situations in which the authorities might well grant recognition, but the protesters simply do not demand it because they lack literacy and education, because they lack a tradition of organization and leadership, or because curbs on freedom of assembly, association, and speech make even a rudimentary organization of the protest group unlikely. Hobsbawm's (1959: 108-125) description of the premodern city mob represents such a case of partly institutionalized conflict by means of direct action in which recognition was not yet an issue. According to the traditional conception of urban lower-class people, "if for one reason or another the usual livelihood of the people was jeopardized or broken down, it was the duty of the prince and his aristocracy to provide relief and to keep the cost-of-living down." The urban mob usually rioted against unemployment or a cheap cost of living, not for recognition. Immediate concessions on both these demands were therefore adequate and appropriate responses and would terminate the immediate conflict and stop violence. But as we move into the nineteenth century, the recognition issue assumes more and more importance relative to the substantive demands of the protest group.

The second exception is much more important in the contemporary world. In this situation, a highly organized and ideologically sophisticated group adopts the strategy of protracted violent conflict in order to overthrow the government, as in guerrilla insurgency, often with some foreign support or help. Since recognition is denied to the insurgents, we are led to predict violent conflict; nevertheless, since the insurgents are, or eventually become highly organized, according to hypothesis 8, conflict ought to be less violent than it usually turns out to be. Of course, many insurgencies actually start at a low ideological and organizational level, not much different from other protest movements, and only after recognition is withheld and reforms are ineffective or not instituted at all, do they become full blown, highly organized, ideological guerrilla movements. One might therefore formulate the following hypothesis 10:

> In a contemporary context, if the protest movement goes unrecognized and if it is not crushed by the agents of social control, the movement will tend to become highly organized and more ideological, and the likelihood of protracted, violent conflict will be high.

In other words, under modern conditions, the recognition issue is more basic for the explanation of violence than the level of organization of the conflict groups, although, given any single confrontation in an ongoing conflict, it is still hypothesized that the more organized both sides are, the lower the magnitude of violence and the number of casualties (hypothesis 8).

Support for Hypotheses 5 to 10

The following historical instances provide a few of many available illustrations, although it is difficult to isolate the operation of one variable at a time.

Compare, for instance, the February 1917 overthrow of the Czar with the Bolshevik coup in October 1917. In February, a week-long, unorganized, and spontaneous movement, which started as a protest for bread led by women and gradually developed into a general strike, produced 1, 315 casualties (Pettee, 1938: 102; Trotsky, 1959: 97-173) at a time when almost all revolutionary leaders were in Siberia or abroad, whereas in October, a highly organized and ideological party overthrew the Kerensky government with but a dozen fatalities (Trotsky, 1959: 336-436). This paired comparison would support both hypotheses 7 and 8.

Consider in addition the Detroit riot of 1967 and the casualties produced by the disorganized police and National Guard, in contrast with the disciplined and well-led paratroopers (National Advisory Commission on Civil Disorder, 1968: 99-102). The paratroopers who followed orders to unload their weapons and remain in evidence on sidewalks and in the street and expended only 201 rounds of ammunition, did not suffer any injuries from gunshot, and inflicted only one fatality. By contrast, the panicked police and National Guard disobeyed orders to unload their weapons, expended thousands of rounds of ammunition, sometimes at each other, were hiding behind walls and shooting out street lights in order not to be visible, and reacted to all conceivable rumors that kept flooding their communications system. Their actions accounted for between 27 and 30 fatalities:

Conot (1967: 218, 229, 234, 278, 325-326, 329, 339, 367) provides further evidence that in the Los Angeles riot of 1965 many fatalities were produced by police when they became disorganized, panicked, and acted on rumor, no matter how incredible those rumors now appear in retrospect. As a matter of fact, the more violent turn of the Negro movement in 1964 and later years can be explained by invoking hypothesis 8. As the Negro movement shifted from the more organized and better-led Southern Negroes to the previously unorganized Northern urban lower-class Negroes whom Martin Luther King and other civil rights leaders were unable to mobilize into their organizations, violence increased considerably. In the same vein, the relatively nonviolent summer of 1968 can also be explained partly in organizational terms. By 1968 in urban ghettoes, radical and militant blacks had managed to create at least a rudimentary organization network and following, and, in addition, many ghetto dwellers themselves had organized into block or neighborhood organizations for pressing their demands or for curbing youth and rioting. It is also possible that the agents of social control were more experienced and organized by the summer of 1968. Thus, unlike those who focus on magnitude of strain and frustration to explain the lower level of violence in 1968, I draw attention to the change in degree of organization of both conflict groups between 1968 and earlier years. There is no evidence that strain and frustration were lower in 1968 than in the previous four summers. Indeed, as formulated in hypothesis 5, these factors do not account for the magnitude of violence in any case.

So far as the recognition issue is concerned, Huntington (1962: 21) has noted that it is a crucial factor in protracted guerrilla wars:

> Insurrectionary war is almost always total. Neither side wants to recognize the legitimacy of the other, and negotiations, much less agreements, imply such recognition. Armistices and peace treaties are possible between governments, but rarely between governments and anti-governments.

Perhaps the most promising area to highlight the importance of recognition comes from comparative labor movements. Taft (1966: 127-134) has noted that a leading cause of violence in U.S. labor disputes was the refusal of management to recognize the union. "In cases where the union is recognized, strikes seldom lead to violent encounters. However, in unorganized strikes or in those which have arisen in an effort to gain recognition, the use of violence is more common." A comparison of the labor movements in the United States with those of Western Europe provides an appropriate illustration for several of the hypotheses under review. The U.S. labor movement was less ideological, less organized, yet more violent than European labor movements. Taft (1966: 127-134) writes that

> it may appear anomalous that the U.S., a country in which class feeling and class ideology are almost entirely absent, has experienced considerable amounts of violence in labor disputes .... With the exception of a small minority, American workers have not been attracted to the various branches of anarchism, communism, socialism, and syndicalism. Yet American history is dotted with clashes between strikers and strikebreakers and police authorities.

Another historian of labor movements, Val Lorwin (1957: 37-39), writes in this connection that

> American workers had to fight bloodier industrial battles than the French for the right of unions to exist and to function. Their political history knew nothing like the "June Days" or the Commune. But the rail strikes of 1877, the pitched battle of Homestead, the Ludlow massacre, were bloodier than Fourmies and Draveil and Villeneuve-Saint Georges .... France had nothing like the private armies, factory arsenals, and industrial espionage service exposed by the LaFollette Committee.... American employers came to recognize the unions only under the multiple pressures of public opinion, administration policy, a reversal of supreme court interpretations, and finally and essentially, worker self-organizations.

In fact, the history of the U.S. labor movement will provide an opportunity to test some of the hypotheses in somewhat more systematic fashion. Suffice it to remark here that it is not likely, as I have expressed in hypotheses 5 and 6, that American workers were under greater or more numerous forms of strain than French workers, or that there were a greater number of nonoverlapping divisions separating labor from management and the agents of social control in this country than abroad. To account for the greater violence in labor relations in this country it is the recognition issue and the level of organization of the conflict groups that are the most promising explanatory variables.

HYPOTHESES: SUMMARY

Hyp. 1 The protesters use violent means only after they have attempted other, nonviolent means of seeking redress for their grievances.

Hyp. 1a The protest group waits for some time for reforms designed to reduce social strain to take effect, and only after these reforms have proved ineffective do they resort to violent means of protest.

Hyp. 1b The authorities or ruling groups break a promise or agreement of reform, and thus provide little or no opportunity for nonviolent means of instituting desired changes before protest groups initiate violent actions.

Hyp. 2 In violent confrontations the authorities' actions produce the bulk, or at least more than half, of the casualties.

Hyp. 2a Violence is more often initiated by the authorities and their agents than by the protesters, as when peaceful demonstrations, marchers, petitioners, peaceful assemblies, and the like are broken up and attacked.

Hyp. 2b When the confrontation is not directly between the protesters and the authorities but between two hostile population groups such as employers and employees or whites and blacks, the casualties tend to be higher when the authorities either openly side with one group against the other, or refrain from intervening in the situation and thereby legitimize the actions of the aggressor.

Hyp. 2c The magnitude of casualties will be greater if the agents of social control know that they will not be made accountable for the casualties they produce during repression.

Hyp. 2d If the protesters belong to a negatively privileged or "pariah" social category, such as a religious minority or peasants, who have not enjoyed full citizenship rights and have traditionally been violently repressed, casualties will tend to be high.

Hyp. 2e The probability of violence decreases to the extent that a third impartial party intervenes as buffer or mediator in the conflict.

Hyp. 3 When two population groups are locked in conflict and when a majority group attacks a numerical minority, casualties will be especially high if the minority group does not live in compact settlements but in small clusters dispersed among the hostile majority.

Hyp. 4 If only one side has access to modern weapons such as firearms, and the other side does not (it has only agricultural tools or spears and arrows) casualties tend to be higher than if there is no weapons disparity.

Hyp. 4a In the absence of a weapons disparity, possession of modern firearms by both sides is not in itself productive of higher casualties than possession of traditional weapons and agricultural implements.

Hyp. 4b Violent clashes in rural areas between two hostile groups will be more productive of casualties than clashes in cities.

Hyp. 5 The number of grievances, the magnitude of strain, the magnitude of the frustrations experienced by the protesters, while making conflict more likely and increasing the intensity of the conflict, nevertheless bear no positive (or negative) relationship to the probability of violence and the magnitude of casualties.

Hyp. 6 The number of reinforcing and nonoverlapping social cleavages separating the conflict groups bears no systematic relationship to the likelihood and magnitude of violence.

Hyp. 7 The "ideological" level of the demands bears no systematic relationship to the likelihood and magnitude of violence.

Hyp. 8 The lower the level of organization of *both* conflict groups, the higher the likelihood and magnitude of violence.

Hyp. 9 If recognition is granted, the likelihood and magnitude of violence tends to be lower than if recognition is not granted or is being withdrawn.

Hyp. 9a Even after violence has already broken out, it is likely to diminish when recognition is granted, but violence is likely to continue if it is not granted.

Hyp. 10 In contemporary context, if the protest movement goes unrecognized and if it is not crushed by the agents of social control, the movement will tend to become highly organized and more ideological, and the likelihood of protracted, violent conflict will be high.

VIOLENCE IN U.S. STRIKES, 1870s to 1930s

For the purpose of testing some of the above hypotheses, a list of major strikes from the index of Commons (1918; 1935) and other sources for the period 1870 to 1930 in the coal, railroad, iron and steel, mining (other than coal), and cotton and silk (textiles, for short) industries was compiled. Details on each strike for a number of independent variables and violence were ascertained. Commons (1935) is especially thorough in providing information on violence, often listing fatalities, injuries and property damage in great detail and the circumstances under which these occurred. Because industries differ on so many of the independent variables and other characteristics that are relevant for industrial conflict, it was felt that major strikes in only these five industries would be analyzed so as to exercise some control over spurious variables. At the same time, there is considerable variation on the independent variables between the five industries, as will be discussed below. On an overall level of industrial conflict, we may note that Kerr and Siegel (1954: 211) rate coal as highest on "strike-proneness," textiles as medium-high, and transportation and iron and steel are rated as medium for the United States.

Measurement presents a real problem. The primary sources, which I did not check, are contemporary newspapers (including those of the unions), labor department reports of the various states, and the frequent state or congressional investigating commissions that were appointed after a period of acute labor violence. Commons (1918, 1935) and the other books I have relied upon are based on these primary sources. I have tried to rate strikes on three levels of intensity of violence—the lowest level, where no violence is mentioned; the next level, where reference is made to clashes, injuries, and property damage, but no fatalities; and, finally, the highest level, where one or more fatalities occurred. Since fatalities almost always occurred when clashes, injuries, and property damage also took place, the underlying variable is here treated as ordinal. It was unfortunately not possible to get sufficient information on the degree of organization of the strikers and the agents of social control, as well as on a number of other variables such as precise ethnic composition of the strikers and social control agents in order to check out degree of overlap of major social categories associated with patterns of group antagonism in the United States. However, since the causes of strikes are always reported, it was possible to check whether a "recognition" issue was present. This variable was also treated as ordinal. The issues at stake might simply be wages, hours, conditions of work, or the like, in which case there was no recognition issue. At the other end, the major issue, or the one explicitly stated demand of the workers before the strike, might be recognition of the union in the sense that they sought collective bargaining rights or the right to organize. In between, there are instances where the employer sought to weaken or "bust" a union, such as discharging union members, discriminating against them in employment, or otherwise harassing union organizing activities, but where recognition of the union was not explicitly demanded (aside from demands to reinstate discharged workers). I label this in-between category conveniently "union weakening." Since disputes over wages, hours, and conditions were usually present in all the strikes under review, recognition is treated here as an ordinal variable. For reasons stated earlier, I do not control for the number of strikers involved and duration of the strike, although in a more comprehensive investigation it might be desirable to do that at some point.

The findings on the association between presence of the recognition issue and degree of violence are summarized in Tables 1a through 1e separately by industry, and in Table 2 for the entire set of 54 strikes. In Table 2, it should be noted that gamma equals .52, which is fairly high considering the usual magnitudes of association found in sociological research, and therefore hypothesis 9 is supported, though this modest investigation is only a preliminary one. The major contrast is between the first two columns and the last one–wages and hours. There is not much difference on violence in strikes where recognition was an explicit issue, as opposed to being implicit in the attempts of employers to weaken an existing union or to prevent its establishment in the first place by harassing organizers, discharging union members, discriminatory employment practices directed at union members, and the like.

It is worth examining the patterns of violence separately by industry, for some impressionistic support for several other hypotheses can be provided in this manner. In railroads, there is a relatively low incidence of violence. Two exceptions should be noted. The railroad upheaval of 1877 produced over 100 fatalities, although at this early date recognition was not an issue, the strike wave being precipitated by a wage cut at a time of depression. The other major violent confrontation, the Pullman strike of 1894, with 25 fatalities, did involve as one of its causes union-busting activities by Pullman against the American Railway Union. The low incidence of violence in the railroad industry can be accounted for by the fact that after the Knights of Labor declined in the latter 1880s in the railroads, management adopted a policy of favorable treatment of the four major railway brotherhoods–the engineers, the firemen, the conductors, and the trainmen–with full recognition, a high wage scale, and acceptance of union seniority rules (hypothesis 9). Management also tended to accept outside mediation in railroad disputes by governmental bodies (hypothesis 2e), and the brotherhoods did win an eight-hour day in 1917 through national legislation after President Wilson, the Supreme Court, and Congress intervened. Many of the major strikes after the 1880s involved the shop crafts and switchmen, not the four favored brotherhoods (hypothesis 9).

In coal mining, strikes were especially numerous and major strikes tended to be violent throughout the period, the most productive of fatalities being the Colorado coal strike of 1913-1914, during which the Ludlow massacre occurred, and the 1922 strike during which the Herrin massacre took place. Most of the strikes took place in the coal fields of Pennsylvania and West Virginia, and the largest strikes involved hundreds of thousands of miners. The United Mine Workers was successful in getting recognition in the late 1910s in many of the Pennsylvania fields but had rather more difficulty in the decentralized bituminous coal industry and especially in the West Virginia fields. However, in the 1920s unionism was again weakened considerably. Apart from recognition, the relatively high incidence of violence can be accounted for by the frequent practice of employers in importing strikebreakers and armed guards, and in

TABLE 1A

OCCURRENCE OF VIOLENCE BY ISSUE: RAILROAD STRIKES

	Recognition Issue	Union Weakening	Wages, Hours, etc.	Total
Fatalities	1	1	1	3
Violence, no fatalities	0	1	0	1
No violence	0	1	5	6
Total	1	3	6	10

TABLE 1B

OCCURRENCE OF VIOLENCE BY ISSUE: COAL MINING STRIKES

	Recognition Issue	Union Weakening	Wages, Hours, etc.	Total
Fatalities	4	4	1	9
Violence, no fatalities	0	0	2	2
No violence	0	1	6	7
Total	4	5	9	18

TABLE 1C

OCCURRENCE OF VIOLENCE BY ISSUE: IRON AND STEEL STRIKES

	Recognition Issue	Union Weakening	Wages, Hours, etc.	Total
Fatalities	2	1	0	3
Violence, no fatalities	1	0	0	1
No violence	1	0	0	1
Total	4	1	0	5

TABLE 1D

OCCURRENCE OF VIOLENCE BY ISSUE: MINING (other than coal) STRIKES

	Recognition Issue	Union Weakening	Wages, Hours, etc.	Total
Fatalities	2	2	6	10
Violence, no fatalities	0	0	1	1
No violence	1	0	0	1
Total	3	2	7	12

TABLE 1E

OCCURRENCE OF VIOLENCE BY ISSUE: TEXTILES STRIKES

	Recognition Issue	Union Weakening	Wages, Hours, etc.	Total
Fatalities	3	0	2	5
Violence, no fatalities	1	1	1	3
No violence	0	0	1	1
Total	4	1	4	9

TABLE 2

OCCURRENCE OF VIOLENCE BY ISSUE: ALL INDUSTRIES STRIKES (in percentages)

	Recognition Issue	Union Weakening	Wages, Hours, etc.
Fatalities	75	67	38
Violence, no fatalities	12.5	16	15
No violence	12.5	16	46
Total	100	100	100
Total number	(16)	(12)	(26)
$\gamma = .52$			

evicting strikers from company housing and otherwise harassing the activities of the strikers (hypothesis 2a). Easy access to weapons was a factor in arming miners. Local authorities generally sided with the employers and operated in remote mountain districts, with low accountability, and against an ethnic, negatively privileged, immigrant work force (hypotheses 2b, 2c, and 2d).

In the iron and steel industry there are very few instances of strikes from which to generalize from, but recognition was a key issue in major strikes, as United States Steel set the pace in destroying the Amalgamated Association of Iron and Steel Workers after 1901. It was only in the latter 1930s that recognition was slowly achieved by means of a CIO-sponsored drive.

In mining other than coal, mainly in the Rocky Mountain states, the hypothesis linking recognition and violence is least supported, since almost all strikes tended to lead to violence regardless of the issues involved. The key factors here, present even more than in coal mining, were access to weapons and dynamite by the miners, the universal practice of employers in importing strikebreakers and armed guards, and the support of local authorities for strikebreaking activities (hypotheses 2b, 2c, and 2d). A frequent source of violence was the attack of armed miners upon trains of strikebreakers and the dynamiting of mines employing scabs, the attack of guards and deputies upon the tent colonies of strikers and their families, mass arrests of strikers, their imprisonment in bullpens, and their forced deportations (hypotheses 2 and 2a). In fact, Western labor conflict in the mining areas comes closest to continuous open warfare, yet lacks ideological issues (hypothesis 7).

In textiles, a relatively decentralized industry with a high frequency of strikes, unionism was hampered by the lack of skilled workers antedating machine production, the immigrant work force in New England after 1900, and the competition of Southern mills with New England. While violence and fatalities occurred frequently in major strikes despite a high proportion of female labor, overall casualties tended to be very low. Textiles is interesting, however, since it is one of the few industries were the I.W.W. and communist-dominated unions were trying to compete with the A.F. of L.-affiliated United Textile Workers in organizing the work force and frequently managed to lead the strikes. While not enough cases are available, it is interesting to note that so far as violence is concerned, it was equally likely to occur when the moderate U.T.W. was involved as when the more ideological I.W.W. and other unions were (hypothesis 7). For instance an appropriately matched comparison is provided during the 1929 drive to organize Southern textile workers. A strike in Gastonia, N.C., led by the communist-sponsored National Textile Workers' Union resulted in three fatalities, whereas in neighboring Marion, N.C., a strike over similar issues in a factory of roughly the same labor force composition and size led by the U.T.W. (A.F. of L.-affiliated) resulted in six fatalities. The Southern employers, authorities, and local population, of course, tended to perceive all unionization drives as Red-inspired and unpatriotic regardless of whether they in fact were, and the U.T.W. personnel as well as communist labor leaders were frequently assaulted and run out of town by vigilantes and mobs.

REFERENCES

BRINTON, C. (1957) The Anatomy of Revolution. New York: Vintage.

COMMONS, J. R. (1935) History of Labour in the United States, IV. New York: Macmillan.

--- et al. (1918) History of Labour in the United States, II. New York: Macmillan.

CONOT, R. (1967) Rivers of Blood, Years of Darkness. New York: Bantam.

COSER, L. (1967) Continuities in the Study of Social Conflict. New York: Free Press.

DAHRENDORF, R. (1959) Class and Class Conflict in Industrial Society. Palo Alto: Stanford Univ. Press.

DARVALL, F. (1934) Popular Disturbances and Public Order in Regency England. London: Oxford Univ. Press.

ECKSTEIN, H. (1964) Internal War. New York: Free Press.

GERSCHENKRON, A. (1966) Bread and Democracy in Germany. New York: Fertig.

--- (1964) "Reflections on economic aspects of revolutions," pp. 180-204 in H. Eckstein (ed.) Internal War. New York: Free Press.

GRIMSHAW, A. (1960) "Urban racial violence in the U.S." Amer. J. of Sociology 66 (September): 109-120.

GURR, T. R. (1967) The Conditions of Civil Violence. Princeton: Center of International Studies, Research Monograph 28.

HEBERLE, R. (1951) Social Movements. New York: Appleton-Century-Crofts.

--- (1945) From Democracy to Nazism. Baton Rouge: Louisiana State Univ. Press.

HICKS, J. D. (1961) The Populist Revolt. Lincoln: Nebraska Univ. Press.

HOBSBAWM, E. J. (1959) Primitive Rebels. New York: W. W. Norton.

HODGKIN, T. (1957) Nationalism in Colonial Africa. New York: New York Univ. Press.

HUNTINGTON, S. (1968) Political Order in Changing Societies. New Haven: Yale Univ. Press.

--- (1962) "Patterns of violence in world politics," pp. 17-50 in S. Huntington (ed.) Changing Patterns of Military Politics. Glencoe: Free Press.

KERR, C. and A. SIEGEL (1954) "The inter-industry propensity to strike," pp. 189-212 in A. Kornhauser, R. Dubin and A. Ross (eds.) Industrial Conflict. New York: McGraw-Hill.

KILLIAN, L. (1964) "Social movements," pp. 426-455 in R. Faris (ed.) Handbook of Modern Sociology. Chicago: Rand McNally.

LEE, A. M. and N. D. HUMPHREY (1943) Race Riot. New York: Dryden.

LEE, S. (1951) "Agrarianism and social upheaval in China." Amer. J. of Sociology 56 (May): 511-518.

LORWIN, V. (1957) "Reflections on the history of the French and American labor movements." J. of Economic History 17 (March): 25-44.

McNEELEY, J. (1966) "Origins of the Zapata revolt in Morelos." Hispanic-Amer. Historical Rev. 46 (May): 153-169.

MOORE, B. (1966) Social Origins of Dictatorship and Democracy. Boston: Beacon.

National Advisory Commission (1968) Report of the National Advisory Commission on Civil Disorders. New York: Bantam.

OLSON, M., Jr. (1963) "Rapid economic growth as a destabilizing force." J. of Economic History 23 (December): 529-552.

PETTEE, G. (1938) The Process of Revolution. New York: Harper.

POSTGATE, R. (1962) Revolution from 1789 to 1906. New York: Harper Torchbook.

RICHARDSON, L. (1960) Statistics of Deadly Quarrels. Chicago: Quadrangel.

RUDE, G. (1964) The Crowd in History. New York: John Wiley.

--- (1959) The Crowd in the French Revolution. New York: Oxford Univ. Press.

SMELSER, N. J. (1968) Essays in Sociological Explanation. Englewood Cliffs: Prentice Hall.

--- (1964) "Collective behavior and conflict." Sociological Q. 5 (Spring): 116-122.

--- (1963) Theory of Collective Behavior. New York: Free Press.

STONE, L. (1965) "Theories of revolution." World Politics 18 (January): 159-176.

TAFT, P. (1966) "Violence in American labor disputes." Annals of the Amer. Academy of Social and Pol. Sci. (March): 127-140.

TILLY, C. (1964) The Vendée. Cambridge, Mass.: Harvard Univ. Press.

--- and J. RULE (1965) Measuring Political Upheaval. Princeton: Center of International Studies, Research Monograph 19.

de TOCQUEVILLE, A. (1955) The Old Regime and the French Revolution. New York: Doubleday Anchor.

TROTSKY, L. (1959) The Russian Revolution. New York: Doubleday Anchor.

TURNER, R. (1964) "Collective behavior and conflict." Sociological Q. 5 (Spring): 122-132.

United Nations (1957) Report of the Special Committee on the Problem of Hungary. New York: General Assembly, Eleventh Session, Supp. No. 18 (A/3592).

WEBER, M. (1958) From Max Weber, Essays in Sociology. New York: Oxford Univ. Press.

--- (1947) The Theory of Social and Economic Organization. Glencoe: Free Press.

WASKOW, A. (1967) From Race Riot to Sit-in, 1919 and the 1960s. New York: Doubleday Anchor.

Chapter 13

Political Coerciveness and Turmoil

A Cross-National Inquiry

IVO K. FEIERABEND and BETTY NESVOLD

with ROSALIND L. FEIERABEND

San Diego State College

The central theme of this paper concerns the difficult question of whether the use of force, and, generally, the coercive character of a political regime stimulates or inhibits the occurrence of political strife and violence. More specifically, two questions are raised: First, what is the relationship between the degree of regime coerciveness and the amount of violence experienced within political systems? Second, in what way does the consistency or inconsistency with which force is applied affect internal political stability and turmoil?

Two contradictory views are commonly held regarding the use of force by political authorities. The deterrent view argues that the punishing arm of the law—the police or the army—discourages troublemakers, while permissive rule is an invitation to increased strife. The calling of the National Guard into

AUTHORS' NOTE: *We are grateful for the support of the National Science Foundation (Grant GS-1781), which made it possible to collect the cross-national data on permissiveness-coerciveness of political regimes as well as political violence and turmoil. In addition we should like to thank the following people for their help: Franz Jaggar, Harley Balzar, Howard Cohen, Mark Owens, and Fred Rosenbaum.*

strife-torn cities may be seen as guided by the notion of deterrence. On the other hand, it is also argued that the use of force creates more, rather than less, turmoil. Oppressive rule may well invite the wrath of the people, an untimely show of force may provoke anger, and coercion may radicalize previously peaceful opposition. As a consequence more, rather than less, violence will ensue. In this view, what is more likely to forestall political crisis and pacify a tense political situation is the permissiveness of the political regime.

The present inquiry into these questions is empirical in nature and extensive in scope. In a search for answers, 73 nations are scrutinized for more than 20 years of their recent history. In general, the patterns of coerciveness and the patterns of violence are ascertained for these countries and then compared. This broadly comparative, cross-national approach may reveal patterns that would go unnoticed in specific case studies. On the other hand, detail, depth, and even accuracy may be lost in the panoramic overview that would be more thoroughly preserved in the exploration of a single country or a single incident.

CROSS-NATIONAL DATA BANK OF REGIME PERMISSIVENESS-COERCIVENESS

The basic tools used in this analysis are cross-national collections of data on the permissiveness-coerciveness of regimes and on the occurrence of political instability and violence (Feierabend, Feierabend, and Boroviak, 1968; Feierabend and Feierabend, 1965).[1] Political permissiveness-coerciveness is a very complex notion. It invokes core concepts of political science such as force, power, control, and tyranny, as well as freedom, liberty, and democracy. However, the theoretical and observational definitions guiding the data collection are not so broad nor all-encompassing. Instead, the meaning of permissiveness-coerciveness of regimes is limited to fit the particular purposes of the study.

Coerciveness as a political category is understood in terms of the psychological concept of inhibition.[2] More precisely, it is the equivalent of punishment and negative reinforcement. Coerciveness is the set of restraints (inhibitions) instituted by the complex of office holders within the political system. It involves the use or threat of force or other severe sanctions. Political coerciveness can involve single restraining acts, such as arrests and imprisonments, or more complicated situations, such as martial law or press censorship. It can also involve coercive structures such as police, prisons and concentration camps. Furthermore, it should be pointed out that coerciveness entails aggressive, sometimes violent behaviors—that is, behaviors intentionally injurious to others.

All political systems by their very nature are coercive to some degree. And since permissiveness-coerciveness is a matter of degree, it is conceptualized as a continuous variable. Regimes with relatively low levels and narrowly defined spheres of application of force may be characterized as permissive, that is, at the low end of the coerciveness continuum. In summary definition, permissiveness-coerciveness of political regimes refers to the complex of inhibitory acts, situations, structures, and processes that entails the threat or use of force by the office holders within the political system.

This limiting definition excludes other restraints on political behavior that are not coercive, such as the legitimacy of the political system or restraints that stem from social, economic, or ecological systems. Yet this meaning remains sufficiently broad to include a variety of observable political behaviors, events, and institutions. To identify specific categories of restraints or freedoms is to probe into the position of individuals or groups within the system, as well as into the political roles and institutions that affect political coerciveness.[3] The following questions are all relevant to our inquiry: Are the civil rights of the individual citizen maximally respected, or are they sometimes or often violated? Are the freedoms of speech, press, religion, and assembly maximized within the political system? Is seditious speech punished? Is the individual afraid to speak freely? Are journalists prevented from criticizing governmental policies? Is there serious press censorship? Is there academic freedom? Is there freedom of arts and sciences in the country?

Questions concerning the status of groups within the political system are also important. Do minority groups enjoy freedoms? Is labor free to organize? How do other major associations–such as churches, business, landed interests, universities, social and cultural groups, and youth–fare within the system? Is political opposition tolerated? Are there competing parties in the political arena?

Finally, in order to estimate the degree of coerciveness within the political system, specific arrangements of political structures and institutions are relevant. How authoritarian is the executive? Does he arbitrarily perpetuate himself in office through the use or threat of force? Is the legislature endowed with rule-making powers, and is it representative? Does the country hold regularized, free elections, recognizing universal suffrage? Is the judiciary empowered to act independently from the executive? All of these questions refer to the specific variables which form the content of the cross-national data bank of regime permissiveness-coerciveness. In addition, the collection includes information on the role of the government in the economy, social reformism, the role of the military and the police, and arrangements of local autonomy.

It could be objected on several grounds that many of these questions are elusive, as are the civic freedoms or restraints which they explore. Freedom is a subjective perception; the philosopher may feel free even in jail, and a powerful king may feel himself a slave to his throne. Entire peoples accustomed to a long rule of tyranny may not feel oppressed. These claims may be true; the data collection, however, does not include subjective perceptions. The coerciveness variables rely on criteria that refer to objectively ascertainable behaviors or structures. For example, in the case of press censorship, we ask whether foreign correspondents are able to move freely within the country or whether they are expelled; whether newspapers are sometimes banned and editors jailed, and whether there are censors on the staffs of the news media. In the case of the relative freedom of labor unions, we may ask the following questions: Are strikes legal? Is there collective bargaining? Are labor unions organized by the management and the government, or are they independent? Or, in the case of political opposition, we want to ascertain whether extremist parties are outlawed, or, on the contrary, whether their activities are tolerated; whether there are members of opposition parties participating in the national legislature and, if so, how many.

COLLECTING THE DATA

The data collection phase was guided by these definitions, considerations, and questions. The task consisted of coding and rating relevant information from specific source materials, using a detailed set of criteria. For the most part, degree of permissiveness-coerciveness was rated on a six-point ordinal scale, with each scale point specifically defined for each separate behavior or measure. In general, point one refers to a very permissive set of conditions; point two, to permissive conditions; point three, to slight permissiveness; point four, to slightly coercive conditions; and points five and six, respectively, indicate coercive and extremely coercive situations, conditions, behaviors, or structures.

As mentioned earlier, independent national polities served as the units for which data were collected. Eighty-four nations were preselected which were independent, or close to independence, in 1945. Seventy-three of these serve as the units of analysis in this presentation. The decision not to code colonial territories meant that African nations were underrepresented in the data bank, although all other regional areas were included. All of the American and European and most of the Asian nations were independent or close to independence at that time. The data collection spans a 22-year period, 1945-1966, and each nation within the sample is rated at least once a year on each of the indicators of permissiveness-coerciveness. The data sources are concise chronicles of political situations and events. The three major sources are the yearbooks of the *Encyclopedia Britannica* and *Collier's Encyclopedia* and the *Political Handbook of the World* (Council of Foreign Relations, 1946-1966). For some measures, such as press censorship and trade union freedom, monograph sources were used that dealt specifically with these institutions. These sources were employed either to supplement the yearbook data or to serve as a check on source reliability.[4]

Some of the variables from the data bank are listed in Table 1, and the correlational matrix in this table affords a cursory look at the bank. The high intercorrelation among the coerciveness measures is striking. This supports the theoretical supposition that permissiveness-coerciveness is one underlying dimension of related characteristics in the political system. Nevertheless, the less than perfect relationships indicate that an overall score on permissiveness-coerciveness should combine several of these measures rather than rely on a single indicator. One can note, for example, that civil rights (general) correlates with freedom from internal press censorship at a rather high level (r = .72). This value shows that 52% of the variance in one variable is accounted for by its association with the other, but still leaves a significant amount of variance unexplained. On the other hand, civil rights (general) accounts for 86% of the variance in permissiveness of the executive. This latter variable, however, has a much lower association with most of the other measures on the matrix. One can also note the low association between variable 20 (absence of government participation in the economy) and all other measures in the matrix. This may indicate an aspect of the relative independence of the economic sphere from the political sphere.

STATEMENT OF HYPOTHESES

As mentioned previously, two hypotheses are explored in the cross-national empirical analyses. The first postulates a curvilinear relationship between coerciveness of regime and political violence.

> Hypothesis 1: Low levels of political coerciveness (that is, political permissiveness) and high levels of coerciveness are associated with internal stability while mid-levels of coerciveness are associated with political violence.

The second hypothesis postulates inconsistency in the use of force as the predictor of political violence. More specifically, the hypothesis may be formulated as follows:

> Hypothesis 2: The greater (lesser) the fluctuation in level of political coerciveness, the higher (lower) the level of political violence.

It is assumed that these two variables—the level of coerciveness and the consistency with which it is applied—are largely unrelated. Furthermore, if they are combined, they will in combination predict political violence more efficiently.

The logic underlying the relationships postulated in the two hypotheses is not self-evident. It may be explicated within the framework of the frustration-aggression theory in social psychology. This is a complicated and elaborate doctrine; however, in its most basic insight it specifies aggression (as well as certain other behaviors) to be the result of frustration. Frustration itself is defined as interference with attainment of goals, aspirations, and expectations.[5]

This motivational concept of frustration is often thought more appropriate to individual than to social circumstances. The notion of *systemic frustration*,

TABLE 1

RELATIONSHIPS AMONG LEVELS OF COERCIVENESS

	1	2	3	4	5	6	7	8	9	10	11	12	13	14	15	16	17	18	19	20	21
1. Freedom of speech	–																				
2. Freedom of religion	.63	–																			
3. Academic freedom	.94	.61	–																		
4. Freedom of arts and sciences	.88	.83	.86	–																	
5. Freedom of assembly	.92	.58	.90	.76	–																
6. Civil rights (general)	.96	.62	.94	.82	.95	–															
7. Freedom of minority groups	.78	.68	.75	.65	.80	.80	–														
8. Freedom from internal press censorship	.78	.59	.81	.82	.72	.76	.62	–													
9. Freedom from external press censorship	.78	.60	.82	.79	.75	.78	.67	.94	–												
10. Freedom from radio censorship	.75	.43	.75	.67	.71	.75	.60	.83	.78	–											
11. Freedom of labor	.81	.46	.83	.73	.81	.84	.72	.69	.72	.65	–										
12. Freedom of landed interests	.67	.76	.56	.88	.53	.62	.65	.67	.63	.53	.44	–									
13. Freedom of business	.67	.71	.65	.92	.74	.81	.75	.75	.78	.71	.74	.85	–								
14. Freedom of churches	.64	.79	.57	.80	.60	.65	.65	.53	.53	.46	.49	.80	.80	–							
15. Freedom of universities	.88	.58	.94	.81	.86	.89	.73	.75	.77	.72	.84	.77	.76	.56	–						
16. Freedom of associational groups (general)	.90	.61	.91	.83	.88	.93	.76	.75	.77	.69	.88	.67	.87	.68	.92	–					
17. Opposition in the lower house	.70	.50	.73	.79	.65	.67	.49	.75	.72	.79	.66	.49	.66	.50	.67	.69	–				
18. Permissiveness of the executive	.90	.53	.90	.75	.89	.92	.75	.74	.76	.76	.81	.56	.76	.59	.87	.88	.64	–			
19. Party opposition	.86	.57	.89	.81	.81	.83	.59	.83	.81	.83	.76	.63	.76	.60	.84	.83	.82	.83	–		
20. Absence of government participation in the economy	.21	.43	.20	.64	.12	.16	.13	.11	.15	.02	.09	.68	.44	.59	.15	.28	.18	.08	.08	–	
21. Suffrage	.72	.40	.74	.57	.73	.72	.68	.64	.69	.63	.69	.37	.63	.41	.77	.69	.64	.70	.74	.05	–

however, makes it available to the analysis of behavior within social systems. Systemic frustration is defined in reference to three criteria:

(1) as frustration interfering with the attainment and maintenance of social goals, aspirations, and values;
(2) as frustration simultaneously experienced by members of social aggregates and hence also complex social systems; and
(3) as frustration that is the result of processes within social systems.

Systemic frustration and social strain are thus frustrations experienced collectively within societies (Feierabend, Feierabend, and Nesvold, 1969).[6]

Three general propositions further qualify the notion of systemic frustrations:

Proposition 1: Systemic frustration at any given time is a function of the discrepancy between present social aspirations and expectations, on the one hand, and social achievements on the other.

Proposition 2: Present estimates or expectations of future frustrations (or satisfactions) are also responsible for level of present frustration (or satisfaction).

Proposition 3: Uncertainties in social expectations in themselves increase the sense of systemic frustration.

The first proposition focuses on the discrepancy between aspirations, expectations, and attainments within the present situation. Further refinements of this proposition relate level of frustration to the number of unfulfilled aspirations, their level of valuation, their frequency of occurrence within various population strata, their expected level of attainment, and the degree of certainty with which these expectations are held. Similar criteria apply to the notion of social attainment. It should also be pointed out that it is perceived, rather than actual, social attainment that is important. Aspirations in our definition include the goals that people wish to attain as well as the desired values already in their possession. Expectations, on the other hand, include only the portion of aspirations which we expect to achieve and maintain. Strictly speaking, expectations refer always to the future. Yet expectations are disappointed (or fulfilled) in the context of the present. This is the measure of systemic frustration as formulated in the first proposition.

An expectation of future frustration or satisfaction may also intensify or counteract present predicaments. The second proposition recognizes this possiblity and hence uses the term "expectation" in a somewhat different sense. It does not refer to expectations regarding the present situation but rather to present expectations of future occurrences. The third proposition singles out uncertainty as a separate source of systemic frustration and social strain. Uncertainty is a special quality of expectation. Ambiguity as to whether the future will bring disaster or salvation should be considered a distressful experience, adding to the present sense of frustration.

In more usual usage of the frustration-aggression hypothesis to explain political violence, systemic frustrations have been sought in the economic circumstances of a society. Inequality of land distribution, level of development, income, health, and other socioeconomic circumstances all have been explored in relation to level of political unrest.[7] It is the tenet of this paper, however, that political coerciveness can also be regarded as a special instance of systemic frustration. In fact, it fits the stated definition as a set of restraints that regulates the attainment of social goals, aspirations, and expectations. Most of the 21 variables listed in Table 1 could be classified as social values or aspirations, or else as instrumentalities for achieving these values. The coerciveness level of the regime thus equals the degree to which the attainment of these goals is blocked or frustrated.

However, the function of coerciveness is more complex than this. Coerciveness is not only a frustration interfering with the attainment of social goals and hence an instigating condition for political violence; it also has quite an opposite function. In the frustration-aggression theory, as well as in common sense, punishment is an inhibitory force that prevents the overt expression of the aggressive impulse. In this role, coerciveness may act as the controlling, inhibiting factor, muting or preventing outbursts of political violence and turmoil (Gurr, 1970: esp. ch. 8). These two functions of coerciveness must be kept separate, and it is to the first function—coerciveness as frustration—that we are directing our attention at this time. Thinking of coercion as frustration and not as inhibition, it follows that high levels of coerciveness should result in high levels of systemic frustration and hence should instigate high levels of internal political turmoil. This inference may be further refined in reference to expectations and achievements as formulated in the first two propositions. According to proposition 1, the higher the expectations of permissiveness (coerciveness) and the higher (lower) the actual level of coerciveness, the greater (less) the systemic frustration. According to proposition 2, the higher the expectation of future permissiveness (coerciveness), the lower (higher) the sense of systemic frustration experienced in the present. In other words, if coerciveness is in fact expected, then less systemic frustration will ensue when it actually occurs. If it comes unexpectedly, a sense of outrage may stimulate political violence.

This recognition could be further extended by speculating that a justifiable use of force is the one kind of force that is both accepted and expected. Such legitimate use of force or coerciveness stemming, for example, from a legitimate government, should be considered the least serious creator of frustration. In fact, neglecting to use legitimate force may be frustrating if indeed coerciveness was fully expected by the members of the political system and was viewed as an appropriate technique to maintain valued social goals.

It must be pointed out that our data do not tap the dimension of expectation but only the actual level of coerciveness. However, expectancy could be inferred from the data, even if imperfectly. It may be assumed that any sudden changes in the level of coerciveness may be evidence of a sudden change in expectation regarding coerciveness. Political regimes employing consistent levels of coerciveness, either high or low, reinforce social expectations of similar levels to follow, Hence previously permissive regimes which suddenly turn coercive will sharply disappoint social expectations of permissiveness. Furthermore, it may be that this fluctuation in level and deterioration of political liberties may be felt as illegitimate and tyrannical by the citizens.

The hypothesis that fluctuation in coerciveness levels breeds violence finds an additional justification in the third proposition elaborating the notion of systemic frustration. Undue and repeated flux in any social, political, and economic performance or environmental condition is postulated as an important source of systemic frustration and social anomie. It is likely to create feelings of ambiguity and uncertainty of present as well as future expectations. Not knowing what to expect, the members of social systems must feel that they live in a haphazard, perplexing, and insecure environment.[8] The wider and the more salient the social domain that experiences this flux, the more threatening its nature, and the greater the resultant social strain. Permissiveness-coerciveness of regime might so qualify, especially in the context of the modern, highly politicized world of the twentieth century. Fluctuation between the extremes of political permissiveness and coerciveness must be considered an important source of frustration and social strain.

Turning to the second function of political coerciveness, it can in addition be conceptualized as inhibiting the overt expression of aggressive behavior. This is by far the more usual perception of the role of force and punishment. Hence, coerciveness may be said to be cast in a dual role. It created a condition of systemic frustration instigating the impulse to violence, but at the same time it has the capacity to curb the actual manifestation of violence. This may lead to yet another reason that fluctuating levels of coerciveness instigate violent responses. If punishment, or an expectation of the use of force, is suddenly removed, the deterrent power of coerciveness is gone and the accumulated impulse to aggression may find its release. Highly coercive regimes that suddenly are weakened, for whatever reason, in their coercive prowess should expect to experience violent, perhaps even revolutionary behavior.

The dual role of punishment explains the first hypothesis, which postulates a curvilinear relationship between coerciveness and political violence. Permissive regimes must be presumed to give little impulse to political aggressiveness; minimally punishing, they give minimal offense. Extremely coercive regimes, although they must be presumed to frustrate maximally, are nonetheless also maximally able to inhibit the expression of violence. Regimes at the median levels of coerciveness must bear the brunt of internal turmoil. Although instigating violence by being coercive, they are not sufficiently coercive to inhibit it.

While a curvilinear relationship is postulated between level of coerciveness and violence, a linear relationship is indicated between violence and degree of inconsistency, or fluctuation in level of coerciveness. Fluctuation may be said to create systemic frustration for the three reasons discussed above: (a) Inconsistency in coerciveness may be an indirect indicator of an unexpected and perhaps even illegitimate use of force. The sharp increase in coerciveness that disappoints an expectation of permissiveness and stimulates violence is depicted in Figure 1. It is the discrepancy between the social expectations of permissiveness and the sudden introduction of coercion that causes frustration. (b) A sudden decline in coerciveness may also breed violence. In the first place, it can create an exaggerated expectation of permissiveness which is bound to be disappointed (see Figure 2). Secondly, it means the removal of the inhibitory mechanism, but not necessarily the removal of the instigation to violence that still may linger as the heritage of the previously coercive regime. (c) Significant and repeated fluctuations in the level of coerciveness, as demonstrated in Figure 3, add yet another dimension. Uncertainty of expectations regarding the coerciveness of the regime must be presumed to create social strain and hence, under certain circumstances, a readiness to recruit the populace for turmoil and violent activity. In addition, fluctuation of permissiveness-coerciveness could be presumed to bear witness to an arbitrary use of force and hence also suggests a lack of legitimacy of the regime.

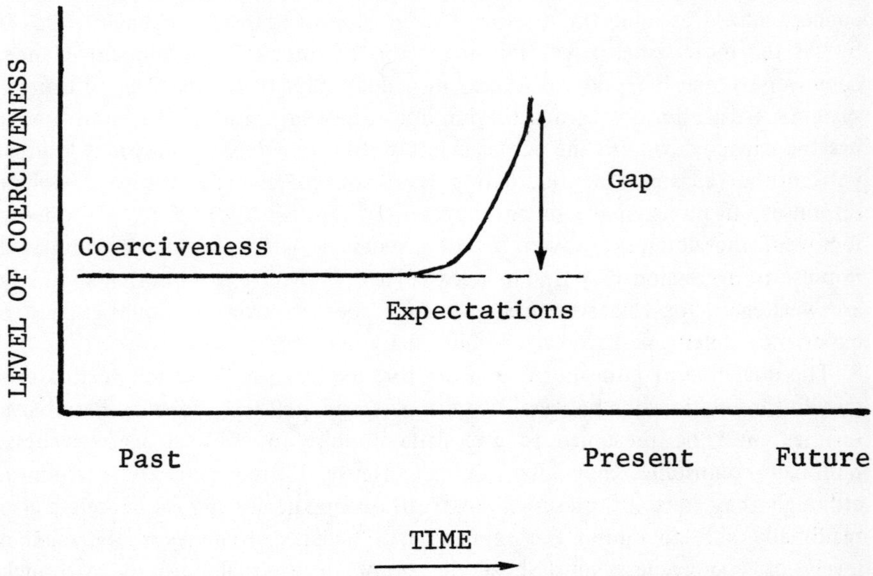

Figure 1.

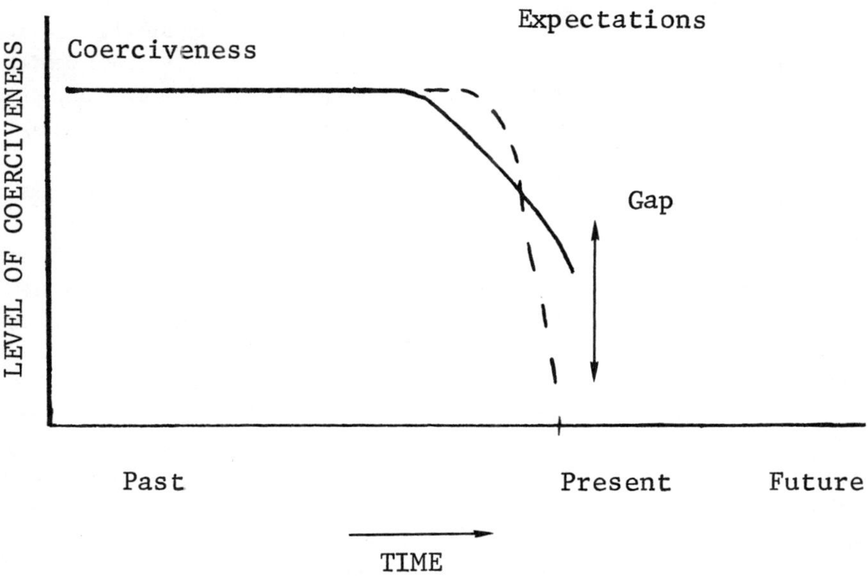

Figure 2.

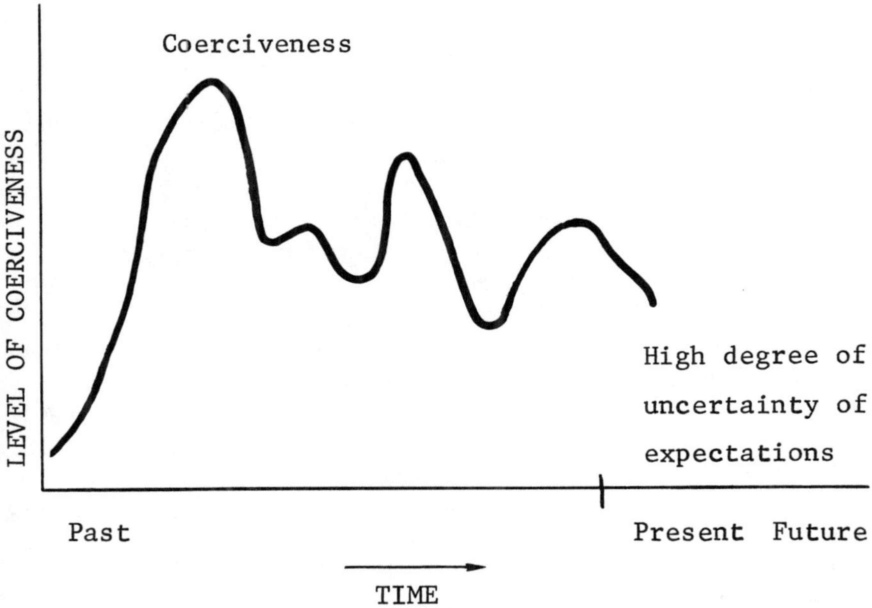

Figure 3.

Contemplating the relative merits of the first and second hypotheses, it is possible to consider inconsistency as the overriding stimulus leading to discontent. Inconsistency in coerciveness, as depicted in Figure 1, may be experienced in usually permissive regimes, while highly coercive regimes experience the type of fluctuation illustrated in Figure 2. If this is the case, very permissive and very coercive regimes, although predicted to be stable in terms of hypothesis 1, still might experience an outburst of political violence.

FINDINGS

From the set of 21 coerciveness variables reported in Table 1, 5 were selected as representing different facets of the permissiveness-coerciveness syndrome: (1) suffrage, (2) internal press censorship, (3) party opposition, (4) general civil rights, and (5) permissiveness of the executive. These 5 were among those with the most complete yearly scores for each of the 73 nations in our study. A mean score on all 5 measures for each of the 22 years was calculated to serve as a summary value denoting the level of coerciveness of each nation. These scores are listed in Table 2. A value of 1.00 reflects consistently permissive behavior for each of the years 1945-1966, for each of the five measures. On the other hand, a score of 6.00 reflects consistently coercive conditions during that time. No nation was scored at this extreme level of coerciveness, but Albania and East Germany come close to this limit. The Communist nations occupy the top six positions at the coercive end of the scale, and the highly permissive nations are all Western European-type polities. This is not a surprising finding, and it lends initial face validity to the scoring endeavor.

Table 3 reports the profiles of consistency or inconsistency in coerciveness-permissiveness for the 73 nations. These scores represent a mean number of fluctuations for each country for the 22-year period calculated from the same 5 coerciveness variables. It was constructed by recording the absolute difference in scale value each time a nation underwent a change in level of permissiveness-coerciveness. The greater the number of changes in policy within a nation, the larger the number of difference scores. These difference scores were summed for each of the 5 measures separately, for the 22-year period. The 5 scores were then averaged to create an index of fluctuation for each nation.

It may be seen in this table that there is a considerable range of values, from zero, indicating no changes in regime coerciveness, to fourteen, indicating frequent reversals of policy. The countries lowest in fluctuations are the highly permissive regimes, a finding which will be explored further below. The countries exhibiting the most fluctuations are principally Latin American states, and the Communist nations are scattered throughout the table. Some, such as Albania and East Germany, show very little evidence of regime change. Others, such as Czechoslovakia and especially Poland, indicate considerable change in policy over time.

TABLE 2

LEVEL OF COERCION MAP, 1945-1966
(n = 73)

Country	Score	Country	Score	Country	Score
Iceland	1.00	Ceylon	2.26	Sudan	4.07
Luxembourg	1.00	India	2.34	Republic of South Africa	4.10
New Zealand	1.00	Panama	2.52	Tunisia	4.18
Norway	1.00	Brazil	2.72	Egypt	4.24
Sweden	1.00	El Salvador	2.86	USSR	4.38
Finland	1.02	Cyprus	2.92	Indonesia	4.44
Ireland	1.02	Liberia	2.92	Syria	4.50
United States	1.02	Bolivia	2.94	Dominican Republic	4.52
Netherlands	1.04	Libya	3.00	Nicaragua	4.54
Belgium	1.08	Laos	3.10	Cuba	4.60
Canada	1.08	Ecuador	3.12	Paraguay	4.62
United Kingdom	1.14	Turkey	3.12	Cambodia	4.66
Italy	1.20	Lebanon	3.26	Afghanistan	4.68
Costa Rica	1.22	Ethiopia	3.34	Iraq	4.74
Uruguay	1.28	Morocco	3.34	Portugal	4.96
Israel	1.36	Honduras	3.42	Haiti	4.98
Australia	1.40	Colombia	3.46	Saudi Arabia	4.98
France	1.40	Venezuela	3.46	Spain	5.00
Austria	1.44	Peru	3.48	Czechoslovakia	5.26
Japan	1.44	Argentina	3.72	Romania	5.28
Philippines	1.48	Jordan	3.82	Hungary	5.30
Switzerland	1.54	Pakistan	3.84	Bulgaria	5.36
Mexico	1.60	Poland	3.88	East Germany	5.76
West Germany	1.66	Thailand	3.98	Albania	5.98
Chile	2.08				

A question which arises in connection with these fluctuations in coerciveness is whether they can be viewed as independent of the absolute level of permissiveness-coerciveness exhibited by the regime. A mean score close to one or close to six on level of coerciveness in Table 2 means, mathematically, that the amount of fluctuation in coerciveness *must* be very low. Freedom to fluctuate is thus primarily associated with intermediate levels of permissiveness-coerciveness. Since there are a large number of nations close to a mean value of one on level of coerciveness, it was expected that they would also be close to the zero value on fluctuation of coerciveness, and this is the case. On the other hand, there are very few nations which approach a mean value of six on level of coerciveness. Thus the logical possibility remains that the coercive nations, with the exception of East Germany and Albania, could experience considerable fluctuation. It was postualted that a modest loosening of extreme controls and immediate reinstatement of them would be as unsettling as frequent and perhaps

TABLE 3

FLUCTUATION OF COERCION MAP, 1945-1966
(n = 73)

Country	Score	Country	Score	Country	Score
Iceland	0	United Kingdom	1.40	Egypt	5.20
Luxembourg	0	Cyprus	1.80	Haiti	5.80
New Zealand	0	Ethiopia	2.00	Poland	5.80
Norway	0	Japan	2.00	Chile	6.00
Sweden	0	Morocco	2.00	Dominican Republic	6.50
Finland	0.20	Bulgaria	2.20	Panama	6.50
Italy	0.20	France	2.20	Cuba	7.20
Philippines	0.20	Spain	2.20	Brazil	7.60
Ireland	0.25	Liberia	2.25	Jordan	7.60
Albania	0.40	Libya	2.25	Colombia	7.80
Netherlands	0.40	Costa Rica	2.60	Lebanon	8.20
Switzerland	0.40	Mexico	2.80	Paraguay	8.20
United States	0.40	Republic of South Africa	2.80	Syria	8.20
Belgium	0.60	Tunisia	3.00	Sudan	8.25
Canada	0.60	Romania	3.20	Thailand	8.60
Israel	0.80	Iraq	3.60	Argentina	9.20
Saudi Arabia	0.80	West Germany	3.60	Indonesia	9.80
Australia	1.00	Nicaragua	3.80	Laos	10.20
Cambodia	1.00	Hungary	4.00	Turkey	10.20
USSR	1.00	India	4.60	Honduras	10.40
Uruguay	1.00	Pakistan	4.60	Peru	10.40
Austria	1.20	Czechoslovakia	4.80	Ecuador	11.00
Portugal	1.20	Ceylon	4.90	El Salvador	11.20
Afghanistan	1.40	Bolivia	5.20	Venezuela	14.20
East Germany	1.40				

larger changes at the more moderate levels of coercion. The patterning between level of coerciveness and fluctuation in coerciveness is shown on the scatterplot in Figure 4. The two most coercive nations are low in fluctuation, as are all of the most permissive nations. Beyond this, however, there is wide variation in the relationship between these two variables.

To measure the dimension of political instability, acts were recorded that denoted aggressive behaviors within polities. Specific instances of overt aggression were selected as evidence of political instability. Events such as civil war, riots, mass executions, and guerrilla warfare are good examples of the more extreme hostilities. Less violent events, such as general strikes, attempted assassinations, and demonstrations were also selected. The data were collected from the yearbooks (1945-1966) of the *Encyclopedia Britannica* and *Deadline Data on World Affairs* (1945-1966), and although these chronicles are cursory, they were deemed sufficiently detailed and and accurate to provide the required material.[9]

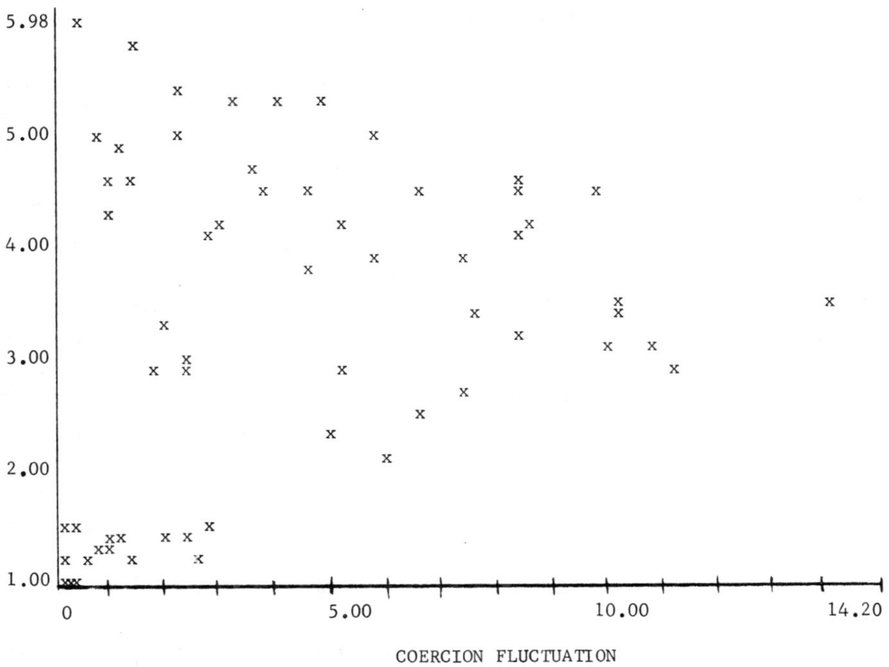

Figure 4.

All instances of political aggression in each of the 73 countries were recorded for the period 1948-1965. Twenty-eight different items were selected as being representative of all the specific disturbances that occurred in these countries.[10] Examining these 28 types of events, it seemed obvious that they implied different degrees of severity or intensity of social disturbance. For example, the intensity of aggression in a civil war may certainly be judged greater than that of a general strike. For this reason, it seemed feasible to arrange these items on a continuum ranging from those denoting the least aggression or disturbance to those denoting the most aggression.

Specifically, these 28 items were arranged on 7-point scale. The continuum ranged from extreme stability, point 0, to extreme instability, point 6. Point 0 indicates an absence of disturbance within the political process, which proceeds in a completely peaceful and institutionally prescribed manner. Point 1 on the scale indicates a mild strain in the political system. Although policies are still carried out in a prescribed manner, an aura of mild crisis is noticeable. Point 2 on the scale indicates the presence of some disturbance, and incipient aggressive tendencies can be noted. Point 3 identifies overt social aggression which is, however, not so widespread that the political leadership cannot be expected to cope with the disturbance effectively. The initial indicator of instability is point 4. Disturbances have become more widespread than at point 3; overthrow of the government is a distinct possibility and may even have been attempted. Point 5 on the scale identifies even more intense and widespread disturbance. If a coup d' état has taken place, it has been accompanied by riots and violence. If a plot to overthrow the government has been uncovered, serious and widespread repercussions such as mass arrests and violent activities follow. Point 6 indicates a situation of the utmost instability and aggression. Civil war, mass executions, and revolution that involve a large segment of the society fall within this last category.

On the basis of the scale values, stability profiles for the 73 countries were computed. The entire time period was divided into 3 6-year periods, and each nation's score was calculated for each subperiod separately. A grouped scoring method was used which weighted both the intensity and the frequency of occurrence of instability events. The grouped scores for each of the 3 subperiods were then summed to yield a nation's instability profile. The instability index calculated in this manner appears in Table 4.[11]

We see in this table that Indonesia was the most unstable country in the world during these eighteen years, experiencing a civil war during each of the three six-year subperiods. Latin American and Middle Eastern countries also show high levels of political unrest. At the opposite end of the continuum, among the highly stable countries, we find primarily modern industrialized democracies, as well as some very traditional states such as Saudi Arabia and Afghanistan. The Communist bloc of countries are fairly spread throughout the table. Albania shows the highest level of political stability and East Germany the highest level of unrest in this bloc of nations. The United States is close to the center of the distribution, as is the USSR. Of all the modern western-style democracies, France is the most unstable.

In the theoretical discussion, it was postulated that political turmoil would be curvilinearly related to the level of coercion within a society, and linearly related to the degree of fluctuation of coerciveness. In testing these hypotheses, the measures were intercorrelated, using first a product-moment coefficient in which linearity is assumed, and second an *eta* which makes no assumptions of linearity. The results are in Table 5.

If we examine first the product-moment correlation between fluctuation of coercion and political instability, we find evidence of a relatively strong linear relationship (r = .67). Thus 44% of the variance in instability is accounted for in its relationship to fluctuations in coerciveness. Furthermore, this level of relationship stays essentially the same when the eta calculation (.66) is performed. Turning to the level rather than the fluctuation of coercion, we find a more complex association with instability. A sizeable amount of variance in instability (33%) is accounted for by making assumptions of linearity in the relationship with level of coercion (r = .58). Furthermore, the joint relationship

TABLE 4
POLITICAL INSTABILITY MAP, 1948-1965
(n = 73)

Country	Score	Country	Score	Country	Score
Luxembourg	03012	Chile	10156	Portugal	13190
Netherlands	04021	Belgium	10162	Morocco	13194
New Zealand	05015	Albania	11067	Brazil	13209
Saudi Arabia	05018	Bulgaria	11071	Republic of South Africa	13422
Ireland	05031	Japan	11123	France	13435
Sweden	06020	Ceylon	11152	El Salvador	14079
Australia	06026	Dominican Republic	11195	Panama	14101
Finland	06056	Spain	11284	Honduras	14105
West Germany	06087	United States	11318	Tunisia	14126
Iceland	07026	Nicaragua	12096	Laos	14129
Austria	07057	Ecuador	12117	East Germany	14138
United Kingdom	07112	USSR	12165	Paraguay	14141
Norway	08034	Sudan	12189	Egypt	14152
Switzerland	08042	Pakistan	12231	Lebanon	14212
Canada	08084	India	12360	Peru	15196
Afghanistan	09029	Cambodia	13071	Haiti	15205
Costa Rica	09058	Czechoslovakia	13100	Syria	15329
Romania	09060	Philippines	13105	Venezuela	15429
Libya	09069	Hungary	13113	Colombia	16244
Italy	09192	Cyprus	13123	Iraq	16274
Ethiopia	10034	Jordan	13145	Cuba	16283
Liberia	10036	Thailand	13152	Bolivia	16318
Israel	10064	Poland	13179	Argentina	16445
Uruguay	10100	Turkey	13189	Indonesia	18416
Mexico	10111				

between fluctuation and level of coercion accounts for 58% of the variance in political instability, an unusually strong association for this type of complex cross-national study (R = .76). Nevertheless, the eta coefficient between instability and level of coercion (.69) exceeds the linear value, a finding that brings modest support to our postulate suggesting a curvilinear patterning between these two variables.

A final association described in this table concerns the two measures of permissiveness-coerciveness: level and fluctuation. Here we find evidence of a strong curvilinear relationship (.78) as against a weak linear one (.36). These statistics describe the patterning shown in Figure 4, in which very high levels of coerciveness and very low levels of coerciveness (permissiveness) show the least amount of inconsistency of policy. The highest levels of fluctuation occur in states which are at mid-levels of coerciveness.

To clarify the relationships between political instability and the two measures of coercion, scatterplots were drawn. Figure 5 plots the relationship between

TABLE 5

RELATIONSHIPS AMONG MEASURES OF COERCIVENESS AND POLITICAL INSTABILITY

Product-Moment Correlation Coefficients[a]	1	2	3	Eta Coefficients	1	2	3
1. Fluctuation of coercion	–			1. Fluctuation of coercion	–		
2. Level of coercion	.36	–		2. Level of coercion	.78	–	
3. Political instability	.67	.58	–	3. Political instability	.66	.69	–

a. Multiple Correlation Coefficient $R_{3.12} = .76$

fluctuation of coercion and instability, and Figure 6, level of coercion and instability. It is possible to see the linear patterning in Figure 5, in which increasing fluctuation is accompanied by increasing political instability. In Figure 6, however, the most unstable countries are at mid-levels of coerciveness. No countries at the highest levels of coerciveness fall into the highest scale position on instability. On the other hand, only one highly coercive country falls at the most stable end of the political violence scale. In these plots we can see that the strong tendency for permissive nations to be peaceful has an overriding effect on the correlational analyses. If these permissive nations are removed from the plot, linearity is still noticed between inconsistency in coercion and political instability, but a modest tendency toward curvilinearity appears in the relationship between level of coercion and political unrest.

Two further analyses were performed to combine the postulated curvilinear association of level of coercion and the linear association of fluctuation with political instability. The first analysis is an expanded contingency table in which countries are first dichotomized into stable and unstable groups (see Table 6). They are then further subdivided into two degrees of fluctuation of coercion (high and low) and three levels of coercion (permissive, coercive, and moderate). By ordering the three levels of coercion so that a moderate level indicates greatest political instability, we find a striking linear pattern in the table. Permissive nations with a low level of fluctuation of coercion (high consistency) are overwhelmingly stable, while countries at mid-coercive levels with high levels of fluctuation (inconsistency) are predominantly unstable. It is especially among highly coercive countries that the notion of consistency adds a particular refinement. Coercive countries with high fluctuations of policy are predominantly unstable (10: 3), while highly coercive countries which are consistent in these controls are predominantly stable (6: 4). We also find that those very few moderately coercive countries which are consistently moderate in their policies tend to be politically stable (3: 2).

In the final analysis of these interrelationships, a mean instability score was calculated for the three levels of coercion and the two degrees of fluctuation, in combination. These values are reported in Table 7, where the only really deviant score is found in the upper right-hand cell. However, with only two cases in this

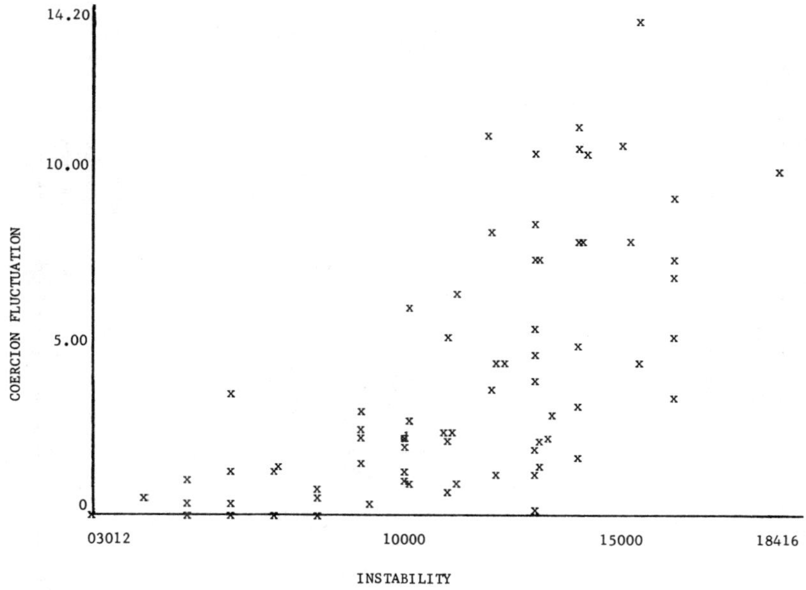

Figure 5.

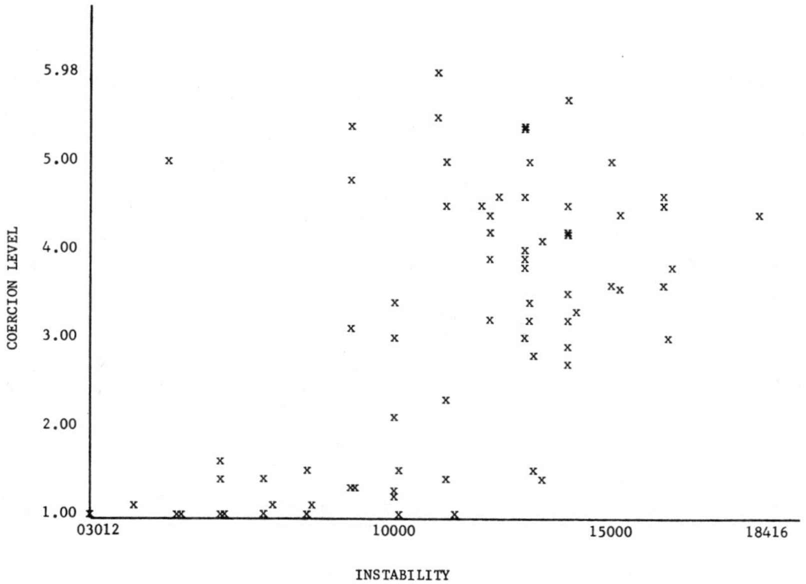

Figure 6.

TABLE 6

RELATIONSHIP BETWEEN LEVEL AND FLUCTUATION OF COERCION AND POLITICAL INSTABILITY

	Low Fluctuation of Coercion			High Fluctuation of Coercion			Totals
	Permissive	Coercive	Moderate	Permissive	Coercive	Moderate	
Stable	Australia Austria Belgium Canada Costa Rica Finland Iceland Ireland Israel Italy Japan Luxembourg Netherlands New Zealand Norway Sweden Switzerland United Kingdom United States Uruguay (20)	Afghanistan Albania Bulgaria Saudi Arabia Spain USSR (6)	Ethiopia Liberia Libya (3)	Mexico West Germany (2)	Dominican Republic Nicaragua Romania (3)	Ceylon Chile Eduador (3)	37
Unstable	France (2) Philippines	Cambodia (4) East Germany Iraq Portugal	Cyprus (2) Morocco	(0) Egypt Indonesia	Cuba (10) Czechoslovakia Egypt Haiti Hungary Indonesia Paraguay Sudan Syria Rep. of South Africa	Argentina (17) Bolivia Brazil Colombia El Salvador India Jordan Laos Lebanon Pakistan Panama Peru Poland Thailand Tunisia Turkey Venezuela	35
Totals:	22	10	5	(2)	13	21	72

cell, it is difficult to draw any statistical conclusions. What is illustrated is that high fluctuation completely overwhelms the original curvilinear pattern between level of coercion and political instability. The high fluctuation countries, with the exception of the two that are at a permissive level, are significantly more unstable than the low fluctuation nations.

CONCLUSIONS

In summary of our findings, let us repeat that some support was found for the first hypothesis and considerable support for the second. A significant relationship between coerciveness level and political instability is present. However, the finding is ambiguous, since it is difficult to decide whether a linear or a curvilinear relationship obtains. Leaning on the theoretical formulations, one could reflect that the deterrent power of punishment that is predicted for the highest levels of coerciveness is considerably modified by its violence-instigating mechanism.

On the other hand, the analysis seems to indicate a striking linear relationship between inconsistency in coerciveness and violence. When combined, the two variables provide a powerful predictor of political instability. A multiple correlation of .76, accounting for 58% of the variance, is a sizeable relationship for this kind of cross-national correlational research. While this association is not perfect, and much of the variance in instability remains unexplained, it is surprising that two political variables chosen from an enormously complicated social field should exhibit this degree of association. It must be stressed that no intuitively persuasive preconditions of violence stemming from the economic, social, and international domains entered into the present analysis. The present findings could be used as an argument for the importance of political determinants of internal peace and violence.

We may interpret the relationship between level of coerciveness and violence in light of previous cross-national studies conducted by Bwy (1968), the Feierabends (1966b), Gurr (1969), and Walton (1965). For the Feierabends, as well as for Walton and the present endeavor, permissiveness-coerciveness is operationalized as a structural dimension of political regimes. In the studies by Bwy and Gurr, coerciveness is estimated in terms of the size of the army or the internal security forces. Bwy assesses defense expenditures and Gurr, manpower resources supplemented by two indices of the past loyalty of coercive forces. All these studies undoubtedly have the same theoretical variable in mind: the permissiveness-coerciveness of the political regime. All four studies find empirical support for a curvilinear relationship between the use of force and the level of overt violence within society. The Feierabends and Walton, for example, obtain a linear product moment correlation (r = 41) but a significantly improved eta of .72 between these two variables. Bwy, in a study of twenty Latin American republics, finds a striking curvilinear relationship between coercion and

TABLE 7

MEAN INSTABILITY AND COERCIVENESS

		Fluctuation of Coercion	
		Low	**High**
Level of Coercion	Low	$\bar{M}$ Instability = 08048 (n = 22)	$\bar{M}$ Instability = 08099 (n = 2)
	Moderate	$\bar{M}$ Instability = 11091 (n = 5)	$\bar{M}$ Instability = 13707 (n = 20)
	High	$\bar{M}$ Instability = 11115 (n = 9)	$\bar{M}$ Instability = 13873 (n = 15)

his category of anomic violence. However, either a linear relationship or no relationship is indicated for his category of organized violence, depending on the time lags which are employed in the analysis. Gurr also determines a nonlinear relationship between the size of coercive forces and the total magnitude of civil strife within society. He obtains a linear relationship, however, when the size of coercive forces is weighted by their loyalty to the regime. This weight of evidence from previous studies helps to interpret the present findings. It persuades us to accept the curvilinear relationship between level of coerciveness and political violence.

The second finding, concerning the relationship between inconsistency and violence, is striking and perhaps more intriguing. It would seem that the impact of an inconsistent use of force overrides the results of degree or level of force. This perhaps is not surprising if it is true that some fluctuation can occur even at the highest level of tyranny. It may well be that force as a social technique is sufficiently persuasive only if it is constantly and consistently employed. With fluctuation, the deterrent power is impaired, perhaps because inconsistency creates a credibility gap. Relaxing oppressive rule may create an expectancy of permissiveness and hence diminish the fear of reprisal.

Since this finding of a relationship between inconsistency of coerciveness and violence appears to be the first such result in the cross-national literature, it should await replication before being accepted with confidence. With the exception of the study of violence in colonial Africa by Robert LeVine (1959), no cross-national comparisons using inconsistency of policy have been attempted. In the psychological and sociological literature, however, there is more evidence of a relationship between inconsistent application of discipline and consequent aggression.[12]

Finally, let us speculate on the implications of our study both for officeholders in the political system and for protestors, conspirators, or insurgents. In permissive regimes, the protestors, conspirators, or insurgents will have the least chance of creating turmoil if the incumbents persist in their permissive policies. However, it may also be, although our study passes no direct judgment on this point, that the legitimate use of force to "fit the crime" should be scrupulously used in the interests of internal peace. With such a policy, the incumbents may have the best chance of preserving internal peace and tranquility. The alternative of resorting to force in the face of provocation would seem only to add fuel to future unrest, unless high levels of coerciveness are involved. However, here our data offer a somewhat ambiguous answer. It is not certain whether the energetic use of force will have a pacifying effect. Undoubtedly, if high coerciveness is applied, it should be applied consistently. Probably the officeholders of a previously permissive system might find it difficult to persuade the populace that they are turning the system irrevocably to high coercion. This may be difficult unless the regime itself changes substantially. It may be successful in a country like Czechoslovakia which has previously known a coercive regime and where the imposition of new coercion is backed, or perhaps itself is coerced by the presence of foreign troops or the threat of foreign occupation. Even then it may take awhile before protest activity and turmoil subside.

Regimes with mid-levels of coerciveness must be judged as the most conducive to violent insurgent activity, while at the same time they should cause maximum anxiety for the officeholders. In view of our findings, such a statement comes close to being an ironclad rule if a high flux in coerciveness is combined with a mid-level of intensity. Without such flux, however, this implication is less certain.

Highly coercive regimes, when they lose hold for whatever reason, are likely to be subject to great turmoil. This was illustrated in the Hungarian revolution of the fifties, in the Poznan uprising in Poland, and most recently in the Czechoslovak spring revolt of 1968. Another example is the Dominican Republic after the demise of the Trujillo family.

All of these speculative reflections must be seen against the larger background of other forces stimulating, inhibiting, or facilitating violent behavior. The two main hypotheses explored in this analysis do not represent the complete dynamics governing the relationship between coerciveness and political violence, nor can coerciveness be considered the only inhibitor of political violence. Other factors, such as the legitimacy of the political system, also serve as a restraint. Furthermore, coerciveness is only one among many possible sources of systemic frustration. Thus this research does not represent the development of a comprehensive theory of the use of force and violence. Rather, it has explored a significant subset of theoretical and empirical variables.

NOTES

1. The Instability Data Bank is deposited with the Inter-University Consortium for Political Research, Ann Arbor, Michigan. Plans are made for deposition of the Coerciveness Data Bank.

2. See, for example, the discussion of inhibition and punishment in Buss (1961).

3. For a discussion of social and political freedoms and their restraints, see Bay (1958) and Oppenheim (1961).

4. For a discussion of the validity and reliability of the data see Feierabend, Feierabend, and Boroviak (1968). It is sufficient to indicate here that several raters were employed, at different times, coding the same variables, sometimes for the same countries, and often from different sources. These ratings were compared, and the degree of agreement between raters and source materials was judged satisfactory. For example, correlation coefficients comparing the ratings from the source materials listed in the text for 73 countries on 14 variables ranged from a satisfactory level (r = .77) to a very high one (r = .97).

Comparing the ratings of 2 coders on 6 countries rated in common, of 8,428 data points there was 1 scale point difference on 1,166 data points, 2 points' difference on 146 data points, and 3 or more scale points' difference on 20 data points.

Some additional confidence in the data bank is also gained because of the independent efforts of other researchers to assess coerciveness cross-nationally. For example, press censorship profiles correlated (r = .88) with those reported in Nixon (1965). The coercive profiles calculated in Walton (1965) had a high correlation coefficient (r = .84) with our measure of press censorship. A major property of Cutright's (1963) measure is the notion of political opposition and competition. This variable was also correlated with our measure of press censorship (r = .75).

5. For the classic theoretical statement of the frustration-aggression hypothesis see Dollard et al. (1939). Also there are several more recent general restatements, among which we may name Berkowitz (1962) and Buss (1961).

6. For a comprehensive statement of theory of political violence that relies in part on the frustration-aggresion hypothesis, see Gurr (1970).

7. Several studies in the cross-national literature are available, among which are Gurr (1969), Feierabend, Feierabend, and Nesvold (1969), Gurr (1968), Bwy (1968), Feierabend and Feierabend (1966a) and Russett (1964).

8. Under certain circumstances, it should be assumed that the highest level of coerciveness, that is, a reign of terror, also creates great uncertainty and insecurity. This is not because of the high level of coerciveness, but because terror implies an arbitrary use of force. If severe punishments are meted out regardless of crimes committed, if innocent as well as guilty people are punished, the resultant situation of fear and uncertainty must give rise to high social strain.

9. This data bank is described in Feierabend and Feierabend (1965). In an initial test of source reliability, assassinations (including attempted assassinations) were coded from the *New York Times Index* for the same period of time as from *Deadline Data on World Affairs*. The scores of each country on this event were correlated from the two news sources, and this proved to be a satisfactory level (r = .80). We are now coding political instability events from daily issues of the *New York Times* (1955-1970) and will make further reliability checks. We have also compared our political instability profiles with Gurr's scores of total magnitude of civil violence. The level of agreement between the two sets of scores for the same nations and the same time period (1961-1965) ranges from .66 to .69, depending upon which scoring method for political instability we use.

10. These events are: elections, dissolution of the legislature, resignations of politically significant persons, dismissal of politically significant persons, fall of cabinet, significant change of laws, plebiscite, appointment of politically significant persons, organization of new government, reshuffle of government, severe trouble within a nongovernmental organization, organization of opposition party, governmental action against specific groups, strikes, demonstrations, boycotts, arrests, suicide of significant political persons, martial law, executions, assassinations, terrorism, sabotage, guerrilla warfare, civil war, coup d' état, revolt, and exile.

11. Intercoder reliability on these scale values was very high (r = .93). For additional discussion of the measurement of political violence, see Feierabend and Feierabend (1966a), and Nesvold (1969).

12. See, for example, Sears, Maccoby, and Levin (1957) and Whiting and Child (1953).

REFERENCES

BAY, C. (1958) The Structure of Freedom. Palo Alto: Stanford Univ. Press.

BERKOWITZ, L. (1962) Aggression: A Social Psychological Analysis. New York: McGraw-Hill.

BUSS, A. (1961) The Psychology of Aggression. New York: John Wiley.

BWY, D. (1968) "Political instability in Latin America: the cross-cultural test of a causal model." Latin American Research Rev. 3 (Spring): 17-66.

Collier's Encyclopedia (1945-1966) Yearbook. New York: Crowell-Colliers.

Council of Foreign Relations (1946-1966) Political Handbook of the World. New York: Harper & Row.

CUTRIGHT, P. (1963) "National political development: measurement and analysis." Amer. Soc. Rev. 28 (April): 253-264.

DOLLARD, J., N. MILLER, L. DOOB, O. MOWRER, and R. SEARS (1939) Frustration and Aggression. New Haven: Yale Univ. Press.

Encyclopedia Britannica (1945-1966) Yearbook. Chicago: William Benton.

FEIERABEND, I. and R. FEIERABEND (1966a) "Aggressive behaviors within polities, 1948-1962: a cross-national study." J. of Conflict Resolution 10 (September): 249-271.

--- (1966b)"The relationship of systemic frustration, political coercion, international tension, and political instability." Presented at the annual meeting of the American Psychological Association, New York.

--- (1965) Cross-National Data Bank of Political Instability Events. (Code Index) San Diego: Public Affairs Research Institute.

FEIERABEND, I., R. FEIERABEND, and D. BOROVIAK (1968) "Cross-national data bank of regime permissiveness-coerciveness." Unpublished.

FEIERABEND, I., R. FEIERABEND, and B. NESVOLD (1969) "Social change and political violence: cross-national patterns," pp. 606-667 in H. Graham and T. Gurr (eds.) Violence in America, Report to the National Commission on the Causes and Prevention of Violence. Washington, D.C.: Government Printing Office.

GILLESPIE, J. and B. NESVOLD [eds.] (1970) Macro-Quantitative Analysis: Conflict, Development, and Democratization. Vol. 1. Sage Readers in Cross-National Research. Beverly Hills: Sage Publications.

GRAHAM, H. and T. GURR (1969) Violence in America, Report to the National Commission on the Causes and Prevention of Violence. Washington, D.C.: Government Printing Office.

GURR, T. (1970) Why Men Rebel. Princeton: Princeton Univ. Press.

--- (1969) "A comparative study of civil strife," pp. 544-605 in H. Graham and T. Gurr (eds.) Violence in America, Report to the National Commission on the Causes and Prevention of Violence. Washington, D.C.: Government Printing Office.

--- (1968) "Causal model of civil strife: a comparative analysis using new indices." Amer. Pol. Sci. Rev. 62 (December): 1104-1124.

LeVINE, R. (1959) "Anti-European violence in Africa: a comparative analysis." J. of Conflict Resolution 3 (December): 420-429.

NESVOLD, B. (1969) "A scalogram analysis of political violence." Comparative Pol. Studies 2 (July): 172-194.

NIXON, R. (1965) "Freedom in the world's press: a fresh appraisal with new data." Journalism Q. 42 (Winter): 3-14.

OPPENHEIM, F. (1961) Dimensions of Freedom. New York: St. Martin's.

RUSSETT, B. (1964) "Inequality and instability: the relation of land tenure to politics." World Politics 16 (April): 442-454.

SEARS, R., E. MACCOBY, and H. LEVIN (1957) Patterns of Child Rearing. Evanston: Row, Peterson.

WALTON, J. (1965) "Correlates of coerciveness and permissiveness of national political systems: a cross-national study." Unpublished. San Diego State College.

WHITING, J. and I. CHILD (1953) Child Training and Personality. New Haven: Yale Univ. Press.

Chapter 14

Comparative Analysis of Patterns of Compliance with Supreme Court Decisions

"Miranda" and the Police in Four Communities

NEAL MILNER – *Grinnell College*

Political scientists until recently have ignored the study of the process involved in complying with Supreme Court decisions. As Richard M. Johnson (1967: 4) has stated, to neglect such studies "is to neglect an indispensable segment of the total judicial process." Despite the increasing awareness of the importance of this aspect to the judicial process, there are still almost no studies which attempt a comparative analysis of patterns of compliance with or resistance to Supreme Court decisions.

Many of the compliance studies have been concerned with response to Supreme Court decisions involving religious activities in schools (Johnson, 1967; Patric, 1957; Birkby, 1966; Sorauf, 1959; Muir, 1968). This concentration on a single policy area would be more worthwhile if these studies could be easily compared with one another. Unfortunately, they provide neither the conceptualizations nor the methods which would facilitate such comparisons. The foci of the studies vary greatly. For example, some of them attempt to give a detailed account of the reaction to Court decisions in one small geographic area (Johnson, 1967; Muir, 1968). Others are less systematic in discussing patterns of compliance, but discuss the impact of Court decisions on a much more general scale (Sorauf, 1959; Patric, 1957). Not only is it difficult to generalize from these studies, but also one finds very little agreement over the meaning of such concepts as "impact" or "compliance."

The present study compares four Wisconsin police departments (see Table 1) in their process of complying with the Supreme Court's Miranda v. Arizona (1966) decision. Primarily, it relates this process to the degree of professionalization

TABLE 1

POPULATION AND SIZE OF POLICE DEPARTMENTS—FOUR WISCONSIN CITIES (population from 1960 Census unless otherwise indicated)

	City			
	Green Bay	Kenosha	Racine	Madison
Population	76,888[a]	62,899	89,144	160,000[b]
Size of department	120	120	158	202

a. Includes 1963 annexation of about 14,000.

b. Special census, 1964.

found within each department. In the majority opinion of the Miranda case, Chief Justice Warren established certain procedures that the police must follow before and during the interrogation of a suspect. Prior to interrogation, the police must advise a suspect of his right to remain silent. The suspect must also be told at this stage that anything he says may be held against him. The police officer must further inform the suspect that, even if the suspect decides to talk, he may discontinue talking at any time. The suspect must also be told that he has a right to have an attorney present during the interrogation, and that, if he is indigent, a lawyer will be provided at government expense. Confessions or other self-incriminating statements made during the interrogation are inadmissible in court unless the suspect was informed of these rights and, prior to making these statements, intelligently waived such rights.

Compliance and deviance are both regularized and routine patterns of behavior on the part of all classes in organized society. One cannot divide society into two groups—individual compliants (or conformists) and deviants. Because of the regularity with which both compliance and deviance occur, and because both manifest a complex combination of behavior and attitudes, one must study the *conditions and distribution* of compliance (Krislov, 1963: 5). Only certain aspects of these conditions and distribution of compliance will be considered in this study.

Aspects of Compliance

This study investigates the *degree* of compliance with a Supreme Court decision. Degree of compliance depends upon perceptions and attitudes held by those who evaluate whether a decision-making body is complying with the Court decision. For example, a civil rights organization might have far more stringent criteria for evaluating school board compliance than does the school board itself. Both the school board members and members of the civil rights group might agree on what the school board's behavior was, but might violently disagree about whether such behavior should be considered compliance. In the present study the goals that the Supreme Court justices posited in the Miranda majority opinion will be used as the criteria. Other important actors in the communications process may have different standards and goals, and other sources may be more important and more frequently used than is the opinion of the Court. Nonetheless, the opinion sets the initial standards and can be used as an indicator of the goals which the majority of the justices desired to communicate about police interrogation.[1] One cannot assume, however, that these goals and standards are automatically communicated from the Court to the decision makers who are expected to implement the Court's decision. Thus the communications process must also be studied.

There are several reasons why I compare police organizations according to the degree of their professionalization. Police response to legal change is often discussed in terms of police professionalization. In fact, FBI officials, prosecuting attorneys, and other influential members of professional organizations discussed the Miranda decision in these terms (Milner, 1968: 180-200). In their discussion of police reform, advocates of such reform often use criteria of professionalization which are similar to criteria usually used to measure the extent of professionalization in other occupational organizations (compare President's Commission on Law Enforcement [1967: 43-61, 120-143] with Carr-Saunders [1966: 3-9]). Furthermore, it is possible to obtain indicators of professionalization which can be used to compare organizations.

A profession is defined as an ideal type which serves as the model for an occupational group. Professionalization is thus considered to be the *process* involved in developing toward this ideal type (Vollmer and Mills, 1966: vii-viii). Organizations can be compared according to the stages they have reached in this process (Hall, 1968). Writers concerned with the concept of professionalization generally agree that, to some degree, specialization and expertise are criteria for professionalization (Greenwood, 1966).[2] The extent of professionalization can thus be established by criteria which measure the degree of expertise and specialization, and by criteria which indicate the nature of incentives that exist to sanction the development of expertise and specialization.

Using these criteria, I ranked the departments according to an index of professionalization. The following items were used as indicators of the degree of professionalization in each of the four departments:

(1) patrolman's monthly salary;
(2) detective's monthly salary;
(3) the percentage of full-time civilian employees in the department;
(4) the percentage of criminal investigators in the department;
(5) the percentage of officers with at least a high school diploma;
(6) the percentage of officers with at least some college;
(7) weeks of required police recruit training;
(8) annual in-service training hours per officer.

In order to rank the departments and compare them according to their degree of professionalization, I computed the sum total of each of these eight variables and then established the fraction of this total that each department composed. For example, the Green Bay department required 10 weeks of recruit training, Kenosha required 8 and Racine and Madison required 12 and 14, respectively. The sum of the required hours equals 44. Thus, for that item Green Bay received a score of .23, that is, 10/44, while Kenosha's score was .18, Racine's .27, and Madison's was .31. For all of these items, a higher score was equated with a greater degree of professionalization. Both Green Bay's and Kenosha's mean score was .22. Racine's was .26 and the Madison department's mean score was .30. The Green Bay and Kenosha departments are the least professionalized, followed in order by Racine and Madison (see Appendix).

The data for this study were gathered between June 1966, and April 1967. Data came from literature published by local police departments (especially their annual reports), from questionnaires submitted to all police officers in the four cities, and from nonstructured interviews with informants in these cities.[3] Additional information about behavior during interrogation was obtained in each community through direct observation of the interrogation process and through field work with detectives.

FINDINGS

SOURCES OF POLICY INFORMATION

The process of disseminating law enforcement information from state to local authorities involved neither a hierarchical nor a centralized communications structure. Consequently, the four Wisconsin police departments had a great deal of discretion in choosing from which sources, if any, they would obtain information about the Miranda decision. The state attorney general made a special effort to disseminate such information, but he had no formal powers to require departments to accept his information, much less his viewpoint (Milner, 1968: 220-268). Advocates of increased police professionalization contend that professionalized police departments are more interested in receiving information about changes in law enforcement policy (President's Commission on Law Enforcement, 1967: 32-35). On the surface, the data support this contention. The officers in Green Bay, one of the least professionalized departments, received information from an average of 4.95 sources, while the averages for all the other departments were higher; Kenosha (5.20), Racine (5.24), and Madison (5.82).

Conferences which were organized at the behest of their respective departments and in-service training sessions were the sources of information most frequently mentioned by the officers in each department. Table 2 further compares the departments' communication processes. Table 2 shows that the degree to which officers remembered being exposed to conferences or training sessions varied almost directly with the degree of professionalization of the departments. Ninety-two percent of the Madison officers remembered learning about the Miranda decision at such sessions, while only 69% of the Racine officers, 67% of the Kenosha officers, and 61% of the Green Bay officers learned about Miranda from these sources.

While not varying directly with professionalization, the other variables in Table 2 nevertheless help elucidate the differences between Madison and the other cities. The two least professionalized departments fall between Madison and Racine in their likelihood to consider training sessions as the best source of information. Of all four departments, the officers in the Madison department were *most* likely to rate the training sessions that were organized by their departments as the best source of information about the Miranda decision, and they were *least* likely to rate local officials (judges, prosecutors, and other local attorneys) as the best source. Officers in Racine, the second most professionalized department, reacted in completely the opposite manner. That is, of the officers in the four departments, those in Racine were *least* likely to perceive the training session as the best source but *most* likely to choose local officials as the best source of information. These conclusions might surprise certain advocates of police professionalization who frequently suggest that the most professionalized police departments are most amenable to information from sources other than those from the law enforcement occupation (President's Commission on Law Enforcement, 1967: 32-35). Local judges and lawyers could conceivably have participated in the Madison in-service training program, and thus the officers might not have listed local officials as a separate source of information,

TABLE 2

OFFICERS' SOURCES OF INFORMATION IN THE *MIRANDA* COMMUNICATIONS PROCESS (by department)

Source	Department: Green Bay (n=70)	Kenosha (n=64)	Racine (n=58)	Madison (n=78)
Percentage Responding:				
Learned about decision at conference training session.	61	67	69	92
Conferences, training sessions rated *best* source of *Miranda* information.	37	34	24	45
Local officials rated the *best* source of *Miranda* information.	7	13	17	4

but in fact this was not the case. Neither the local judiciary, the local prosecutor, nor local lawyers were asked to participate in these programs. Moreover, all departments used other law enforcement personnel, namely the FBI, in their training sessions, although, as we shall see, the degree of the use of this organization varied.

Other studies of professionalization help to shed light on the reasons for this reversal of the pattern expected by advocates of police professionalization. As an occupation becomes more specialized, and as it begins to develop a systematic body of abstract principles governing the behavior of the occupation, its members begin to feel that they have a monopoly of expertise about the nature and proceeding of that occupation (Greenwood, 1966). One should then expect that, as a police department undergoes professionalization, its members would have more confidence in their ability to determine the proper rules of occupational behavior. This confidence was particularly apparent among the high-ranking policy-making officers in the Madison department. In the words of the most knowledgeable of these officers:

> FBI agents are the best teachers of the police .... Attorneys don't know how to talk to the police. This includes the district attorney. He is not a law enforcement official; he's an attorney, and his perspective differs .... He [the district attorney] contributed very little [to the process of disseminating information about Miranda]. In fact, I invited his staff to sit in on the FBI lectures.

This official not only refused to recognize the expertise of a local official who was in constant contact with the police, but in fact specifically listed a member of the law enforcement profession, albeit from a different agency, as the best source of police information. Although all departments used the FBI as a source of information, this sentiment about the value of the FBI was most clearly expressed in Madison. In Racine, the second most professionalized department, the district attorney was a more important source of information than his counterparts were to any of the other departments.[4]

In all four communities, information furnished by the FBI was based on lectures prepared by that bureau's expert on police education. This information was presented in a more thorough manner in Madison than it was in any of the other cities. Although these lectures stressed that police must be aware of the ramifications of Miranda, the information was generally presented in a manner which suggested that the FBI was especially concerned with allying the anxieties of law enforcement officers. Although cautioning against resistance to Miranda, these lectures definitely emphasized ways of maintaining pre-Miranda procedures.[5]

The Madison department was thus most exposed to this source of information which quite explicitly tried to minimize the degree to which Miranda changed the status quo. The most professionalized department, then, made greatest use of information offered by an organization that attempted to express views that were congruent with the values and attitudes of the law enforcement profession.

THE DEGREE AND PATTERN OF COMPLIANCE

The goals of the Miranda v. Arizona (1966) majority can be summarized as follows:

(1) to discourage whenever possible the use of confessions, *all* of which are obtained under circumstances which *inherently* lead to coercion of the suspect (444-445, 467-476);

(2) to make certain that all suspects are informed of their right to remain silent and their right to have an attorney present to protect this right, even if the suspect could not afford to hire his own lawyer (480-481);

(3) to improve the quality of police officers so that the officers would be able to perform their jobs effectively while still operating under the norms of due process (447, 452, 460); and

(4) to allay police anxieties by specifically stating that, despite these new constraints created by the Court, interrogation can still at times continue to be a legitimate and effective weapon (477-478).

Both the Court and the FBI sought to ease the anxieties of the police, but the FBI more greatly emphasized that the police could continue to use interrogation techniques of the type which in fact the majority of the Court in Miranda seemed to disapprove (compare Dalbey, 1967 with Miranda). Both the Court in Miranda and the FBI agreed that under certain circumstances police questioning was still possible without being preceded by a Miranda warning. The difference was one of emphasis; clearly the Miranda majority was more anxious to discourage the use of confessions.

Police perceptions of the meaning of the decision were obtained from responses to the following question: "Recently the Supreme Court decided the case *Miranda v. Arizona*. This case resulted in a rule about interrogation procedures. Describe this rule as best as you can by putting an 'x' next to *all* of the following statements which you think apply to the rule." On all but two items there was little difference between the departments' ability to identify the stipulations of the rule. Table 3 presents a comparison of these two items. The pattern of these perceptions, as shown in Table 3, did not vary directly with the degree of professionalization. The Green Bay department's relatively great response (forty percent) to the first item can be partially attributed to a Wisconsin Supreme Court case which explicitly sanctioned such behavior on the part of that department (State v. Miller, 1967). Still, the officers in Madison were most likely to perceive correctly stipulations consistent with the Court's

TABLE 3

OFFICERS' "CORRECT" PERCEPTIONS OF STIPULATIONS OF THE *MIRANDA* RULE (by department)[6]

	Department			
Stipulation	Green Bay (n=70)	Kenosha (n=64)	Racine (n=58)	Madison (n=78)
Percentage Giving "Correct" Response:				
Can still ask person to come voluntarily to the police station.	40	38	35	63
May still talk to person without advising him of his rights.	21	34	33	54

goals of allaying police anxieties because these stipulations (Table 3) *limit the constraints* placed on police departments by the procedures stated in the Miranda opinion. Admittedly these findings are ambiguous, but it is interesting to note that the perceptions of the officers in the most professionalized departments were most congruent with both the Court's and the FBI's goals stressing limitations of Miranda's scope.

The degree of approval of the decision also varied directly with the degree of professionalization. Eleven percent of the Green Bay officers, 11% of the Kenosha officers, 17% of the Racine officers, and 36% of the Madison officers approved of the decision. Advocates of police professionalization would probably expect such findings. They contend that the more professionalized police departments are, the more amenable are these organizations to accepting the views of those advocating police reform. In order further to investigate the relationship between professionalization, attitudes toward the decision, and perceptions of its impact, we must investigate the ideology of these organizations, that is, the degree of their "professionalism" (Vollmer and Mills, 1966: vii-viii).[7]

The degree of the departments' professionalization should be related to the nature of the departments' professional ideology in regard to the *Miranda* decision. The nature of this ideology was investigated on the basis of the officers' responses to the following question: "If you so desire, please make any other comments about the *Miranda* rule. Why, for example, do you think the Supreme Court decided the *Miranda* case the way it did?" Sixty percent of the respondents answered this question, and all departments were represented in virtually the same proportion as they were in the larger number of respondents. The more professionalized the department was, the more likely were its members to discuss this question in terms of what police professionalization advocates would probably call an ideology of professionalism. That is, the officers in the two most professionalized departments more frequently either approved of Miranda on the grounds that the decision's stipulations would help improve the police profession *or* discussed the decision in a manner similar to the discussions by advocates of police professionalization.[8] Of the respondents to this question, 14% of the Green Bay officers, 23% of the Kenosha officers, 28% of the Racine police, and 33% of their Madison counterparts responded in terms of professionalism. This relationship between professionalization, attitudes, and perceptions cannot simply be explained in terms of amenability to non-law enforcement sources of information because earlier evidence indicated that Madison did not consider most outside, non-law enforcement sources of information to be very important in the Miranda information process. Factors other than professionalization must be considered.

The Green Bay organization was one of the least professionalized, yet it was also the department least likely to encounter the situations where interrogations were necessary. This community had by far the lowest crime rate of the four communities, and interrogation occurred quite infrequently. This lack of need to use the Miranda stipulation seems to be an important reason why only 24% of the Green Bay officers thought their jobs changed greatly because of Miranda. The Kenosha, Racine, and Madison departments all operated in a milieu in which interrogation situations frequently arose. Sixty-three percent of the Kenosha department, 45% of the Racine department, and only 32% of the Madison department thought their jobs had been greatly changed by the Miranda decision. Of these three departments, the extent of perceived job change varied *inversely* with the degree of professionalization. Thus Kenosha, a relatively unprofessionalized department which operated in an environment where interrogations were often deemed necessary, was most likely to see a great change as a result of Miranda.[9] The more professionalized departments facing roughly the same situation were less affected.

Each officer was also asked to list the two greatest effects Miranda had on his own job. Changes in methods of obtaining evidence and changes in the education process were the most frequently mentioned in all four organizations. Table 4 compares the departments according to the frequency of these responses.

The responses to the two items in Table 4 follow the same pattern as the responses concerning the extent of job change. Officers in the departments toward the extremes of the professionalization ranking—Madison and Green Bay—least frequently mentioned changes in the methods of obtaining evidence or in education programs. Certainly the fact that the Green Bay department received fewer sources of information about Miranda and had a relatively less-pervasive intradepartmental training system is significant in explaining these responses. In addition, the nature of the Green Bay department's tasks did not require that Miranda be made more salient. The need for change was less visible both because of the communications process and because the lack of need for crime investigation lessened the perceived need for change. For the same reasons, Kenosha police were more likely to perceive great change. The Kenosha officers

TABLE 4

OFFICERS' PERCEPTIONS OF EFFECTS *MIRANDA* HAD ON THEIR OWN JOBS (by department)

	Department			
Effects	Green Bay (n=70)	Kenosha (n=64)	Racine (n=58)	Madison (n=78)
Percentage Responding:				
New methods of obtaining evidence now must be used	47	70	64	49
Education and training has increased.	41	72	53	50

were far more likely than their Green Bay counterparts to see such specific changes resulting from Miranda.

Perhaps among the other departments, where interrogations were more frequent and visible, the more professional organizations, prior to Miranda, had adjusted their education and interrogation procedures in anticipation of such a decision. Madison officers, however, were similar to Green Bay and Kenosha in their failure to anticipate the Miranda decision. Twelve percent of the Green Bay officers, 14% of Kenosha, 22% of Racine, and only 13% of the Madison police anticipated that decision. This finding is particularly surprising because of the relationship between approval and anticipation. In the complete sample, 32% of the officers who anticipated the decision approved of Miranda, while only 16% of those not anticipating the decision approved. As stated previously, Madison had the greatest percentage of approving officers, but, *despite* the differences both in the communications process and degree of approval, the Madison department was no more likely to anticipate the decision than were the two least professionalized departments.

The Racine communications process might be an important factor in explaining the greater degree of anticipation in the Racine department. Of the four departments, Racine officers were least likely to consider conferences and training sessions as the best source of Miranda information and most likely to look toward local groups for such information. This also seemed to be the case prior to Miranda. These non-law enforcement groups might have emphasized anticipation of future decisions more than the in-service training programs featuring FBI officials. There were, of course, important differences between Madison and the two least professionalized departments in regard to their in-service training programs, and these differences also existed prior to Miranda. The FBI training, which did not emphasize anticipation, was exceptionally important in Madison and may have decreased anticipation of future court decisions even though after Miranda the Madison department was more likely to approve of that decision. This explanation is tenuous, and it may well be that the differences in professionalization were not related to this difference in anticipation.

There is another possible explanation for the lack of perceived change in more professionalized departments. Perhaps, contrary to the assumptions of police reformers, more professionalized departments like Madison were simply less willing to change their procedures. Officers in the two most professionalized departments with high interrogation visibility were least likely to perceive change in interrogation methods. Admittedly, the more approving attitudes of the more professionalized departments and the greater congruence between their perceptions of some of the Court's goals and the actual goals suggest that such departments are more likely to react to the Miranda decision in ways which disseminators of information about the Court's decision would call compliance. There was no apparent difference, however, between the degree of a department's professionalization and the interrogation behavior of its detectives. The Miranda stipulations were quite regularly given in all departments, but this procedure was to a great extent *pro forma*. The detectives informed the person of his rights but then required this person to make an *immediate* decision about whether he wished to waive these rights. Usually waiver was obtained, and the suspect was then immediately questioned. Psychological ploys, which, according to Chief Justice Warren's majority opinion in Miranda, made confessions inherently coercive, continued to be used. Thus the officers' behavior may be considered congruent with the Court's goal of stressing the advisement of right, but interrogation behavior was not congruent with the Court's goal of encouraging alternatives to confessions as sources of evidence. In fact, in all departments the general procedure was to attempt at least initially to obtain incriminating statements. Also contrary to the Court's goals was the fact that lawyers played almost no active part in actually supervising the interrogation process. As previously mentioned, most suspects waived their rights to an attorney. If an attorney was called into the case, he usually told his client to say nothing.[10] Consequently there occurred either interrogations using pre-Miranda techniques or no interrogations at all.[11]

The evidence suggests that despite a more sympathetic attitude toward the decision, professionalized departments did not change interrogating behavior any more than did less-professionalized departments. Changes were minimal perhaps because upper-level police administrators were unable to supervise such isolated and often decentralized police activity (Wilson, 1968: 57-83). Furthermore, officers in more professionalized departments who might be more concerned with bringing formal action against a suspect and thus pressure for a confession would consequently be greater in these departments (compare Wilson, 1968). Two limitations in the methods of gathering the interrogation behavior data must be noted. First, no attempt was made to observe the interrogation behavior differences between officers who approved of Miranda and those who did not, and no such comparison was made between officers who viewed Miranda in a manner more characteristic of professionalism and those who did not. Second, the time obstacles faced by a single observer who investigated interrogation behavior over a relatively short period of time (from 45-60 hours in each community) perhaps limit the reliability of my conclusions. These findings, however, were consistent with those of other recent studies of post-Miranda interrogation behavior (Reiss, 1968; Yale Law J. [Note], 1967).[12]

CONCLUSION

The concept of professionalization was helpful in explaining the differences between the sources of Miranda information which were visible in the four departments. The more professionalized departments received information from more sources and the most professionalized department was most likely to isolate itself from non-law enforcement sources. This isolation seemed consistent with characteristics attributed to relatively highly professionalized organizations. Among the four departments, however, the degree of isolation did not vary directly with the degree of professionalization.

To a lesser extent, the data showed a relationship between the professionalization of a police department and the perceptions and attitudes its members had about the Miranda decision. Attitudes toward the decision and the likelihood of perceiving it in terms of professionalism varied rather directly with professionalization, but the likelihood of anticipating Miranda did not. In Green Bay, one of the least professionalized departments, great change was not perceived, probably because the low crime rate made interrogation relatively infrequent. In the other departments, where the interrogation process was more visible, the degree of perceived change varied inversely with the degree of professionalization.

Despite these organizational and task differences, interrogation behavior was similar in all departments. Both our limited knowledge of interrogation behavior and our limited knowledge of the methods of compliance, however, prevent us from completely accepting as yet such a sweeping conclusion. Thus, along with refining independent variables for comparative analysis, we must also refine one important dependent variable; the degrees of behavioral compliance with Court decisions. We know that it is inaccurate to distinguish simply between deviance and compliance becuase there are degrees of each, yet we still know little about what these degrees are.[13] Because only four departments in one state were studied, the reliability of the conclusions are limited. I did not choose to study these four cities because of the difference in departmental professionalization. I investigated professionalization only after I chose the cities. Thus, it may be that these four departments, when compared to a larger sample, are relatively homogeneous in their professionalization, and the present study may underestimate the differences between professionalized departments.[14] But a good portion of the data used as the basis of the index of professionalization is relatively easy to obtain, especially from public organizations. We have, then, the clear opportunity for further exploration of the hypotheses with which some work has been done in this study. A comparison of a large number of organizations should allow some firmer statements than were possible here with regard to the relationship between professionalism in police departments, and a tendency to comply with Supreme Court requirements.

NOTES

1. Judicial opinions may not be accurate reflections of a judge's motives, goals, or policy preferences, but, regardless of the accuracy of the opinions' reflections, others must use them to determine what the legal rules are supposed to be. Martin Shapiro (1968: 36, 38-39) calls this communications function "the most vital function of an appellate [court] opinion [because these opinions] provide the constraining directions to the public and private decision-makers."

2. For a critical view of the use of such criteria alone, see Skolnick (1966: 235-239).

3. Questionnaires were distributed to each department, and in the two departments where each officer had his own mailbox (Madison and Green Bay), a questionnaire was placed in each mailbox. Otherwise, superior officers distributed them at roll calls. The questionnaires were sent back in postpaid envelopes. The response rate was as follows:

Green Bay	58%
Kenosha	54%
Racine	37%
Madison	39%
Total	45%

There is, of course, no sure way to check for sampling error in such a sample. Generally, detectives were overrepresented especially in the larger departments (see Milner, 1968: 524-528).

4. The anticipated relationship between professionalization and the perceived importance of local officials held for Racine, Kenosha, and Green Bay. Thus, it is perhaps somewhere between the stages of professionalization in Madison and Racine that the great emphasis on specialized knowledge and on the occupation's monopoly of expertise occurs.

5. Inspector Dwight Dalbey is the FBI specialist spoken of here (see Dalbey, 1967.)

6. The following are the stipulations presented to the officers: "Recently the U.S. Supreme Court decided the case Miranda v. Arizona. This case resulted in a rule about police interrogation procedures. Describe this rule as best you can by putting an 'x' next to *all* of the following statements which you think apply to the rule. (1) A person in custody must be advised of his right to remain silent. (2) A person in custody must have an attorney whether he wants one or not. (3) Confessions may no longer be used as evidence. (4) A person in custody must be advised that anything he says may be held against him in court. (5) A policeman may no longer talk to a person about a crime without first informing the person of his right to remain silent. (6) Wiretapping will no longer be tolerated. (7) Any person in custody has the right to an attorney if he wants one. (8) A person in custody who cannot afford to hire his own attorney has the right to have one appointed at county

expense. (9) Voluntary confessions are no longer legal sources of information. (10) A police officer can still ask a person to come voluntarily to the police station without first advising him of his constitutional rights." Items 1, 4, 7, 8, and 10 are considered to be stipulations consistent with the Miranda rule. Thus an officer responded correctly to each of items 1, 4, 7, 8, and 10 if he marked these items and responded correctly to each of items 2, 3, 5, 6, and 9 if he did not.

7. For a discussion of the importance of ideology in the professionalization process, see Skolnick (1966: 238-239) and Wilson (1966: 184-193).

8. The following criteria were used as a measure of professionalism. An officer was considered to view Miranda in terms of professionalism if: (1) the reasons that he gave for the Court's decision were generally consistent with those given by those advocates of police professionalization whose views of the Court's Miranda goals are consistent with the Court's view; or (2) he approved of the Miranda decision on the grounds that it would improve the police profession. Choosing item 1 does not necessarily mean that the officer approved of the decision.

9. The particularly great emphasis on change in Kenosha can partially be explained by the fact that a suspect in an especially brutal murder, which was quite important in the community and in the department could not be interrogated by the police because his attorney would not allow it. The detectives insisted that this suspect was the killer, and attributed to the Miranda rule their inability to question him.

10. Interrogation behavior could conceivably have been influenced by the presence of an outside observer. Such observer bias in this study is limited for two reasons. First, the data showed that despite the presence of an observer, detectives did not always behave in a manner which seemed consistent with the goals of Miranda. Second, to check on such influence, I listened to some interrogations unbeknownst to the investigators.

11. For a criticism of the Court's refusal to consider the differences between its goals and the goals of organizations involved in the local criminal process, see Blumberg (1968: 169-184).

12. All such studies could be improved if more sophisticated methods of observing behavior in nonexperimental settings were available. See Deutscher (1966). A similar point is made from a different perspective in Froman (1968: 43-44).

13. Muir (1968) offers some insight about this in his discussion of how the subjects of his study avoided dissonance created by certain school prayer decisions.

14. For a study comparing two police departments which vary greatly in professionalization, see Wilson (1968). He finds distinct differences in the ways these departments handle juveniles. Also, departments may be more similar in the way they carry out such law enforcement as opposed to order maintenance behavior. Compare Wilson (1968).

APPENDIX: Testing and Construction of Index of Professionalization

I used an analysis of variance to test the null hypothesis that all the data used to construct the index were drawn from the same sample. The formula is as follows:

$$F = \frac{m\Sigma(\bar{x}i - \bar{\bar{x}})^2 / n-1}{\Sigma(x_{ij} - \bar{x}_j)^2 / n(m-1)}$$

where

x_{ij} = individual deviation for i^{th} row, j^{th} column

$\bar{x}_j$ = column mean of column j

$\bar{\bar{x}}$ = mean of all observations
m = number of rows
n = number of columns

F = 6.13473, which means that the null hypothesis is rejected; the statistic is significant at the .01 level. The table below presents the data which were used to construct the index of professionalization discussed in the text. It also presents an alternative method of constructing the index. The rank order of each department on each variable is presented, with the absolute number for each variable presented in parentheses. Because this alternative index does not take into consideration the extent of departmental differences in any single variable, I chose not to use it, and employed instead the index explained in the text. Note, however, that according to the alternative index Kenosha is more professionalized than Green Bay.

ALTERNATIVE COMPARATIVE PROFESSIONALIZATION INDEX: FOUR CITIES

	Green Bay		Kenosha		Racine		Madison	
Item:	Rank	Amount	Rank	Amount	Rank	Amount	Rank	Amount
Patrolman's Monthly Salary[a]	4	($530)	3	($586)	1	($588)	2	($575)
Detective's Monthly Salary[a]	4	($610)	3	($648)	1	($655)	2	($651)
% Full-time Civilian Employees[b]	3.5	(9.6%)	2	(10.7%)	3.5	(9.6%)	1	(23.8%)
% Investigators in Department[c]	3.5	(13.5%)	2	(15.4%)	3.5	(13.6%)	1	(18.3%)
% Officers with at least High School Diploma	3	(89.0%)	1	(94.3%)	4	(83.0%)	2	(89.7%)
% Officers with some college	3	(26.5%)	4	(17.1%)	2	(34.5%)	1	(37.2%)
Weeks of Required Recruit Training	3	(10 wks.)	4	(8 wks.)	2	(12 wks.)	1	(14 wks.)
Annual In-Service Training Hours per Officer	4	(55 hrs.)	3	(61 hrs.)	1	(100 hrs.)	2	(90 hrs.)
Total Rank Score	28		22		18		12	
Average Rank	3.50		2.75		2.25		1.50	

a. Average based on annual salary ranges.
b. Includes stenographers, janitors, police cadets, radio operators, dog pound, and meter officials.
c. Includes detectives, juvenile investigators, and special non-traffic investigators.

CASES

MIRANDA v. ARIZONA (1966) 384 U.S. 436.
STATE v. MILLER (1967) 35 Wis. 2d 454; 151 N.W. 2d 157.

REFERENCES

BIRKBY, R. H. (1966) "The Supreme Court and the Bible Belt: Tennessee reaction to the *Schempp* decision." Midwest J. of Pol. Sci. 10 (August): 304-319.

BLUMBERG, A. (1967) Criminal Justice. Chicago: Quadrangle.

CARR-SAUNDERS, A. M. (1966) "Professionalization in historical perspective," pp. 3-9 in H. M. Vollmer and D. E. Mills (eds.) Professionalization. Englewood Cliffs: Prentice-Hall.

DALBEY, D. (1967) Police Interrogation and the Miranda Rule. Washington: FBI National Academy.

DEUTSCHER, I. (1966) "Words and deeds: social science and social policy." Social Problems 13 (Winter): 235-254.

FROMAN, L. A. (1968) "The categorization of policy content," pp. 41-54 in A. Ranney (ed.) Political Science and Public Policy. Chicago: Markham.

GREENWOOD, E. (1966) "The elements of professionalization," pp. 10-19 in H. M. Vollmer and D. G. Mills (eds.) Professionalization. Englewood Cliffs: Prentice-Hall.

HALL, R. H. (1968) "Professionalization and bureaucratization." Amer. Soc. Rev. 33 (February): 92-104.

JOHNSON, R. M. (1967) The Dynamics of Compliance. Evanston: Northwestern Univ. Press.

KRISLOV, S. (1963) "The perimeters of power: patterns of compliance and opposition to Supreme Court decisions." Presented to the American Political Science Association, New York.

MILNER, N. A. (1968) "The impact of the *Miranda* decision on four Wisconsin communities." Ph.D. dissertation. University of Wisconsin.

MUIR, W. (1968) Prayer in the Public Schools. Chicago: Univ. of Chicago Press.

PATRIC, G. (1957) "The impact of a court decision: the aftermath of the McCollum case." J. of Public Law 6 (Fall): 455-463.

President's Commission on Law Enforcement and the Administration of Justice Task Force (1967) Report: The Police. Washington: Government Printing Office.

REISS, A. J., Jr. [ed.] (1968) President's Commission on Law Enforcement and the Administration of Justice, Studies in Crime and Law Enforcement in Major Metropolitan Areas. Washington: Government Printing Office.

SHAPIRO, M. (1968) The Supreme Court and Administrative Agencies. New York: Free Press.

SKOLNICK, J. (1966) Justice without Trial. New York: John Wiley.

SORAUF, F. J. (1959) "*Zorach v. Clausen*: the impact of a Supreme Court decision." Amer. Pol. Sci. Rev. 53 (September): 777-791.

VOLLMER, H. M. and D. G. MILLS (1966) Professionalization. Englewood Cliffs: Prentice-Hall.

WILSON, J. (1968) Varieties of Police Behavior. Cambridge: Harvard Univ. Press.

--- (1966) "The police and the delinquent in two cities," pp. 184-193 in D. Bordua (ed.) The Police: Six Sociological Essays. New York: John Wiley.

Yale Law J. [Note] (1967) "Interrogations in New Haven: the impact of Miranda." 6 (July): 1519-1648.

Chapter 15

Severity of Formal Sanctions as a Deterrent to Deviant Behavior

RICHARD G. SALEM – *Ohio State University*

WILLIAM J. BOWERS – *Northeastern University*

The imposition of penalities for violation of criminal laws has been traditionally justified for such reasons as social justice and retribution. Today, perhaps the main justification for imposing severe penalties on those who violate the law is that such punishments serve as a specific deterrent to future violations by the offender and as a general deterrent to violations by others who might be tempted to follow his lead.

The extent of this deterrent force and the way in which it operates are, however, largely a matter of conjecture. One explanation relies on a rationalistic conception of human behavior. The individual is seen primarily as one who optimizes resources in the pursuit of his goals. The more costly a particular form of behavior becomes for him, the less likely he is to engage in it (Homans, 1961). Imposing severe sanctions for deviant behavior, it is anticipated, will make the potential offender realize that "crime does not pay." In Bentham's words, "The value of the punishment must not be less in any case than what is sufficient to outweigh that of the profit of the offense" (Pincoffs, 1966: 78).[1]

Yet, this perspective leaves out a significant dimension–the importance of sanctions for normative stability. Durkheim formulated this argument clearly by stressing that the deterrent effect of formal sanctions occurs, not so much by means of the direct impact they may have on potential offenders, but more through their indirect effect in strengthening and buttressing social norms. Thus he asserts (1964: 108) that punishment:

> does not serve, or else serves quite secondarily, in correcting the culpable or in intimidating possible followers. From this point of view, its efficacy is justly doubtful, and, in any case, mediocre. Its true function is to maintain social cohesion intact, while maintaining all its vitality in the common conscience.

Hence formal punishment acts to affirm the rule which has been transgressed and to restore the unanimity of the collective sentiment. For Durkheim, then, the effect of formal sanctions in deterring deviant behavior occurs only secondarily by way of the individual's "calculus of utilities." The sanctions' primary effect is through their capacity to strengthen the normative climate of the community—to reinforce and mobilize informal social disapproval (Coser, 1967; Toby, 1964).

Durkheim's contention that the imposition of sanctions validates the conformist's behavior and reclarifies the norm for the general community is reflected in Cohen's (1966: 4-5) observation that "the most destructive impact of deviance on organization is probably through its impact on trust, on confidence that others will, by and large, play by the rules." Here again deviance must be pointed up and defined as inappropriate in order to assure the community that the "old rules" are still in effect. We see, then, that formal reaction to deviance can be conceived of as acting directly as a deterrent, or as acting indirectly in the reaffirmation of rules.

While it is generally assumed, as in both the above arguments, that formal sanctions have some kind of deterrent effect on deviant behavior, there is little systematic evidence on the nature or extent of such an effect. We know from small-group studies that an individual's attitudes and especially his behavior can be modified by the prospect of informal social sanctions (positive as well as negative). However formal sanctions as part of the legal structure of the society or community are another matter. They are more remote and often irrelevant to the large bulk of the population. Seldom do they figure in the activity of most people.

Moreover, available research—largely studies of capital punishment—seriously questions the deterrent effect of formal sanctions. Thus Sellin (1966), in examining the effect of the death penalty on homicide rates, presents data which show, for example, that during 1917-1918, when the death penalty was abolished in Arizona, the number of people convicted of murder was no different from previous and subsequent periods when the death penalty was in effect.[2] Schuessler (1969), in comparing contiguous abolition and death penalty states over a period of approximately thirty years, demonstrates the similarity of homicide rates. In fact the rates for abolition states are sometimes lower than those for death penalty states, and certainty of execution does not lower the homicide rates among the 41 death penalty states. He concludes that "statistical findings and case studies converge to disprove the claim that the death penalty has any special deterrent value" (Schuessler, 1969: 388).

This research, however, is limited to a rare crime of passion and perhaps the most severe punishment of all. But what about less serious crimes and less extreme punishments? Gibbs (1968) has recently tried to assess the effects of durations of imprisonment, rather than the death penalty, on homicide rates. He concludes (1968: 525) that

> even though the relation between severity and the criminal homicide rate is obviously not a close one by any standard, the evidence of an additive effect [with certainty of sanctions] cautions against entirely rejecting the possibility in some way operates as a deterrent.

A reexamination of his data, however, shows that Gibbs' claim that there is an independent relationship between severity of sanctions and homicide rate appears unfounded (see Bowers 1970).

In a more comprehensive attempt to isolate the separate effects of severity and certainty of formal sanctions, Tittle (1969: 417) examines rates of homicide, robbery, burglary, larceny, assault, auto theft, and sex offenses. He concludes that the

> examination of the relationship between severity and offense rate at constant levels of certainty reveals that severity of punishment has little consistent independent or additive effect.

Tittle's findings on the deterrent effects of certainty of penal sanctions have been challenged, but there is no indication that his findings on severity of sanctions—that it "has little consistent independent or additive effect"—must be qualified (see Chiricos and Waldo, 1970).

Chambliss (1969) cites evidence that certain less serious forms of deviance are definitely responsive to formal sanctions. In particular he cites parking meter violations and shoplifting (by nonprofessional thieves) as examples of behaviors which are reduced by increasing the severity of formal sanctions. The research he cites, however, unlike that of Gibbs and Tittle, makes no effort to separate the effects of severity and certainty of sanctions. On the basis of this limited evidence, then, it would seem that deviant behavior is relatively unresponsive to direct formal sanctions, and that when such effects do occur, they are highly contingent upon the type of behavior considered, the conditions under which it occurs, and the nature of the individuals involved (Ball, 1955: 348-351).

Perhaps the main reason for the limited amount of research on the deterrent effects of formal sanctions lies in the methodological difficulties of isolating such effects. In particular it is difficult to find a sample of societies, communities, or institutions sufficiently alike in other respects that differences in their rates of deviant behavior can be attributed to differences in formal sanctions and not to other factors.

For the purposes of this work, college communities will be examined to determine whether: (1) formal sanctions have a *direct* deterrent effect on deviant behavior, and (2) they have an *indirect* deterrent effect through their ability to stimulate and reinforce informal social norms. To evaluate the influence of these formal and informal mechanisms we will be using data on: (1) the rates of specific forms of deviant behavior; (2) the extent to which these actions are disapproved; and (3) the usual legal or institutional sanctions imposed for these forms of misbehavior in a number of different social contexts. These data have been obtained by Bowers (1964) in a nationwide study of academic dishonesty among college students.

The Data

Information on formal sanctions: During the school year 1961-1962 a survey was made of deans and student body presidents from all regionally accredited, four-year, degree-granting colleges and universities, asking for information on the usual reactions of their institution to various forms of student misconduct. Deans and student body presidents from 838 colleges and universities responded.

Information on deviant behavior and normative climate: During the 1962-1963 academic year 100 of these institutions were selected for more intensive study. At each of these schools, questionnaires were sent to a sample of 75 to 100 students who were drawn randomly from institutional directories or records of the registrars. Sixty percent of the sample returned completed questionnaires; 91 schools were represented by at least 40 students. One school had to be dropped because of difficulties in reaching the students, leaving a total sample of 5,422 students from 99 colleges and universities. (For further details of the sampling procedure see Bowers, 1964: app. c.)

The students in this survey were asked to indicate their attitudes toward and involvement in various forms of campus behavior. Five of the actions about which students report their attitudes and behavior in the 1962 survey correspond quite closely to offenses for which deans and student body presidents indicated the usual formal sanctions at their institutions a year earlier. Thus the merging of data from these two surveys permits us to examine the interrelationships among formal sanctions, normative climate and rate of violation for each of the five forms of behavior at 99 colleges and universities. (See Bowers and Salem, 1970, for a discussion, based on the same data, of variations in rates of misconduct and institutional sanctioning policies by type of institution.)

Formal Sanctions and Deviant Behavior

In this section we shall examine the extent to which formal sanctions for a given offense affect its prevalence; the next section will investigate how this effect occurs—whether, as Bentham would argue, by making the action more costly to engage in or, as Durkheim holds, by strengthening the force of informal normative constraints.

If formal sanctions have a deterrent effect on behavior, we must find that the rates of the various offenses decline as the penalties for them become increasingly severe. Table 1 shows the relationship between formal sanctions and rates of involvement in five different forms of deviant behavior. For purposes of comparison, the column to the right shows the percentage difference per interval as a rough index of the effect of formal sanctions on behavior.[3]

Generally speaking, this table shows that deviance decreases as the sanctions become stronger. There is, however, substantial variation in the *extent* of the

TABLE 1

MEAN PERCENTAGE ENGAGING IN FIVE DEVIANT ACTIONS BY FORMAL SANCTION[a]

	Sanctions Imposed for Drinking and Library Offenses						
Offense	Dismissal %	(n)	Suspension %	(n)	Restriction of Privileges %	(n)	Percentage Difference per Interval
Violating alcohol-use rules	19	(15)	35	(35)	39	(35)	-7.6
Getting drunk[b]	25	(17)	35	(44)	41	(30)	-7.4
Stealing library books	15	(13)	13	(39)	21	(31)	-5.0
Marking up library books	–	(0)	28	(7)	24	(70)	+4.0
	Sanctions Imposed for Cheating[c]						
	Suspend or Expel		Fail Course		Fail Specific Piece of Work or Less		Percentage Difference per Interval
Cheating index[d]	38	(19)	52	(43)	56	(30)	-7.9

a. The mean percentage in each cell is computed by averaging the rates for all schools in that cell. The numbers in parentheses represent schools rather than students. The number of respondents for any cell will be approximately 55 times the number of schools in that cell. The danger here is not that the number of respondents will be too small to yield reliable percentages, but rather that the number of schools from which they come will be too few to adequately represent institutions with a particular sanctioning policy. Where the dean and student body president disagreed about the sanction usually imposed at their school, the report of the dean was used. When both responded, the dean and student body president usually agreed.

b. Penalty imposed, according to dean's reports, is for "being drunk and disorderly"; offense reported by students is simply "getting drunk."

c. Items referring to cheating on a midterm exam, a final exam, and plagiarism on a term paper were combined to produce a cheating sanctions index which is used to represent this form of behavior.

d. Students are classified as cheaters by this index if they have "used crib notes during an exam," "copied from another student during an exam," "plagiarized on a term paper," or "turned in work done entirely or in part by another student." (See Bowers, 1964: ch. 3 for further details.)

deterrent effects of formal sanctions by type of offense. A relatively strong effect is to be found among the offenses involving the use of alcohol. These two items show a seven- to eight-point percentage difference per interval. A weaker effect occurs among the items referring to property offenses in the library. In the case of marking up library books there is actually a slight reversal; misconduct is a little more prevalent where the punishments are more severe. (It should be noted, however, that formal sanctions for this offense are not very severe at most schools. The effect we do find is dependent upon a small minority of only seven schools which may depart in other relevant ways from the rest.) Finally, cheating is affected to about the same degree as the alcohol-related offenses (although, of course, the sanctioning categories differ).

There is also variation in the *pattern* of effects of formal sanctions by type of misconduct. Hence for the two drinking violations the most pronounced deterrent effect occurs only when the maximum formal sanction–dismissal from school–is usually imposed. For stealing books from the library, however, dismissal and suspension show approximately the same ability to deter the deviance. Similarly, in the case of cheating, the difference in rates of misconduct comes largely between dismissal and suspension on the one hand and the lesser sanctions on the other.

Clearly, then, the effects of formal sanctions are uniform neither in extent nor pattern. They are, however, evident at least to some degree in four of the five cases at hand, suggesting that formal sanctions have a modest deterrent effect on the incidence of deviant behavior. Next, the normative climate will be examined as a mechanism through which formal sanctions may have their effect.

The Role of the Normative Context

In a recent study using these data, Bowers (1968) has shown a strong negative relationship between the climate of disapproval of a given action at a college and the incidence of that action. The study indicates that the climate of disapproval has a deterrent effect on behavior in two distinct ways: through "the effect of the individual's own sense of disapproval, and the effect of the normative feelings of others in his social context" (Bowers, 1968: 383). The measure of the normative context we are using for this analysis thus combines both of these effects.

Following Durkheim, we would expect to find a relationship between formal sanctions and the strength of normative sentiments toward a particular form of behavior. Table 2 shows this relationship for the five offenses under consideration. As in Table 1, strong effects are found for drinking-related behavior. In fact, formal sanctions show an even stronger relationship with disapproval (Table 2) than with behavior (Table 1). For library offenses, the relationship between formal sanctions and disapproval is again relatively weak. In the case of marking up library books, there is no relationship whatsoever. (Consequently the slight negative effect of formal sanctions in Table 1 cannot be attributed to differences in normative climate. This suggests that severe formal sanctions for this action provoke a slightly greater incidence of it.)

Perhaps the greatest surprise in Table 2 occurs with the cheating offenses. Whereas Table 1 showed a modest deterrent effect of formal sanctions, Table 2 shows essentially no association between formal sanctions and disapproval. Apparently students' attitudes are relatively insensitive to the formal sanctions imposed for cheating, although their behavior is not. Obviously the normative climate, at least as represented by students' reported feelings of disapproval, does not account for the apparent deterrent effect of formal sanctions in the case of cheating behavior.

With the exception of cheating, the *pattern* of effects in Table 2 is also very similar to that in Table 1. For the two alcohol-related offenses, the largest effects come between dismissal and all other sanctions; and for stealing library books, the effect appears primarily between dismissal and suspension on the one hand and lesser penalties on the other.

Thus we find that both the extent and the pattern of variations in disapproval (Table 2) are quite comparable to their variation in behavior (Table 1) for most

TABLE 2

MEAN PERCENTAGE STRONGLY DISAPPROVING[a] OF FIVE DEVIANT ACTIONS BY FORMAL SANCTION

	Sanctions Imposed for Drinking and Library Offenses						
	Dismissal		Suspension		Restriction of Privileges		Percentage Difference
Offense	%	(n)	%	(n)	%	(n)	per Interval
Violating alcohol-use rules	62	(15)	41	(35)	35	(35)	+10.5
Getting drunk	62	(17)	48	(44)	39	(30)	+10.8
Stealing library books	64	(13)	67	(39)	58	(31)	+ 5.5
Marking up library books	–	(0)	56	(7)	56	(70)	0.0
	Sanctions Imposed for Cheating						
	Suspend or Expel		Fail Course		Fail Specific Piece of Work or Less		Percentage Difference per Interval
Cheating index	38	(19)	35	(43)	39	(30)	- 1.3

a. Single items were used to measure personal disapproval for the drinking and library offenses. In the case of cheating, students were classified on the basis of their strong agreement with four items: under no circumstances is cheating justified; students are morally obligated not to cheat; the individual's personal integrity and self-respect should be the basis for the decision not to cheat; and cheating directly contradicts the goals of education. (See Bowers, 1964: ch. 5, for further details.)

of these actions. And, since there is a strong negative association between the normative climate and the incidence of deviant behavior (Bowers, 1968), the deterrent effects of formal sanctions in Table 1 may occur largely through their association with the normative climate.

Formal Sanctions, the Normative Context, and Deviant Behavior

Table 3 shows the relationship between formal sanctions and misconduct, controlling for the normative context. Beginning with the drinking-related items, we find that the control for normative context removes virtually all of the effect of formal sanctions on behavior. For both getting drunk and violating alcohol-use rules, the per interval effects within the five disapproval contexts are very small; overall or average effect is less than one percent per interval in both cases.[4]

For stealing books from the library, the results are similar. The relationship between formal sanctions and behavior is reduced except in the lowest disapproval context. And only a few schools are responsible for the deterrent effect in this category. (In fact, it would take a modest increase in the rate of library theft at only one of these schools to virtually eliminate the deterrent effect.) For marking up library books, the positive effect shown in Table 1 reappears—again based on a very small minority of the colleges under investigation.

In the case of cheating, the results are quite unlike those for the other four offenses. Although the overall deterrent effect of formal sanctions is reduced slightly from -7.9 to -6.7% per interval, this remaining effect is considerably greater than that shown for any of the other violations. Apparently academic dishonesty, unlike the other behaviors, is directly responsive to the imposition of formal sanctions. Perhaps this is because cheating is the most instrumental and rationally motivated form of deviance under consideration. Chambliss (1969: 368-372) argues that instrumental deviance is significantly more susceptible to the impact of sanctions than deviance of a more expressive nature, e.g., violations involving the use of alcohol.

Yet the effect of formal sanctions on cheating behavior varies by college context. There is generally an increase in their deterrent effect as the context of disapproval becomes stronger. Apparently the weight of severe sanctions is more clearly brought home to potential offenders where informal disapproval is more intense. We know from previous research (Bowers, 1964: ch. 10) that disapproval levels are generally higher at schools that employ the academic honor system. It could be that in these more disapproving contexts the honor system, which often requires students to report their peers for cheating, makes more salient the formal sanctions which may remain relatively remote under other systems of control.

TABLE 3

MEAN PERCENTAGE ENGAGING IN FIVE DEVIANT ACTIONS BY FORMAL SANCTIONS AND NORMATIVE CLIMATE OF COLLEGE

Type of Deviant Action	Percentage on Campus Strongly Disapproving	Sanctions Imposed for Drinking and Library Offenses: Dismissal %	(n)	Suspension %	(n)	Lesser Penalty %	(n)	Percentage Difference per Interval
Violating alcohol-use rules	1-20	–	(0)	56	(7)	57	(12)	- 1.0
	21-40	45	(2)	43	(9)	42	(9)	+ 1.2
	41-60	24	(6)	29	(13)	28	(11)	- 1.1
	61-80	9	(4)	15	(5)	8	(1)	- 3.4
	81-100	6	(3)	5	(1)	2	(2)	+ 1.8
				Average Percentage Difference				- 0.5
Getting drunk	1-20	–	(0)	65	(7)	64	(7)	+ 1.0
	21-40	61	(2)	49	(7)	47	(8)	+ 4.0
	41-60	32	(6)	30	(18)	33	(11)	- 1.2
	61-80	14	(7)	17	(10)	19	(2)	- 2.8
	81-100	5	(2)	7	(2)	7	(2)	- 1.0
				Average Percentage Difference				- 0.1
Stealing library books	21-40	23	(1)	–	(0)	40	(3)	- 8.5
	41-60	18	(5)	22	(11)	27	(14)	- 4.7
	61-80	12	(6)	10	(23)	12	(14)	- 0.8
	81-100	11	(1)	7	(5)	–	(0)	+ 4.0
				Average Percentage Difference				- 3.1
Marking up library books	21-40	–	(0)	43	(1)	48	(5)	- 5.0
	41-60	–	(0)	29	(3)	26	(41)	+ 3.0
	61-80	–	(0)	21	(3)	16	(24)	+ 5.0
				Average Percentage Difference				+ 3.1
		Sanctions Imposed for Cheating: Suspend or Expel		Fail Course		Fail Specific Piece of Work or Less		Percentage Difference per Interval
Cheating index	1-20	–	(0)	71	(3)	62	(3)	+ 9.0
	21-40	46	(13)	56	(26)	59	(17)	- 6.0
	41-60	25	(5)	40	(13)	50	(8)	-11.9
	61-80	11	(1)	49	(1)	39	(2)	- 6.0
				Average Percentage Difference				- 6.7

The Academic Honor System and Peer Disapproval

Information is available on whether the schools in our sample operate under the honor system, thus permitting us to determine if the effectiveness of formal sanctions for cheating is somehow enhanced by this system of social control. Table 4 shows the relationship between formal sanctions and cheating, controlling for normative context and whether or not the college has an honor system.

Several things are evident from the table. First, as we noted above, the level of personal disapproval of cheating is generally higher at the honor system schools. Second, the honor system schools more regularly administer severe sanctions for academic dishonesty. Third, rates of cheating are generally lower at the honor system schools even when their counterparts without honor systems are comparable in normative climate and severity of sanctions.

More important for the purposes of this analysis is the fact that the direct deterrent effect of formal sanctions seems to be concentrated at the honor system schools. The average per interval effect of formal sanctions at the honor system schools is higher than the value for all schools (shown in Table 3), while at the schools without honor systems this effect is considerably reduced. Apparently the honor system does make formal sanctions more relevant to the potential offender. Clearly, personal disapproval does not absorb the effects of formal sanctions as it does for other forms of misconduct.

Peer attitudes of disapproval may be of greater importance than personal sentiments in the honor system context. Under most honor systems the individual is responsible not only for his own behavior but also for the conduct of his peers. Thus the peer group is a prominent source of informal social sanctions under this system.

TABLE 4

MEAN PERCENTAGE CHEATING BY FORMAL SANCTIONS, NORMATIVE CLIMATE, AND CONTROL SYSTEM OF COLLEGE

		Honor System						
	Percentage Strongly Disapproving	Suspend or Expel %	(n)	Fail Course %	(n)	Fail Specific Piece of Work or Less %	(n)	Percentage Difference per Interval
Cheating index	21-40	34	(5)	28	(3)	47	(5)	- 6.6
	41-60	24	(4)	33	(7)	52	(1)	-11.0
	61-80	11	(1)	–	(0)	39	(2)	-14.0
			Average Percentage Difference					- 9.0
		No Honor System						
Cheating index	1-20	–	(0)	71	(3)	62	(3)	+ 9.0
	21-40	53	(8)	60	(23)	65	(12)	- 5.8
	41-60	27	(1)	49	(6)	49	(7)	- 2.8
	61-80	–	(0)	49	(1)	–	(0)	–
			Average Percentage Difference					- 3.6

Fortunately the data include the respondent's perceptions of the disapproval of his peers. Table 5 allows us to compare levels of personal and peer disapproval at schools with and without honor systems.

Both types of disapproval are, of course, stronger at the honor system schools. Their relative strength is reversed, however, in the two contexts. At the large majority of institutions, those without honor systems, strong personal disapproval is more often reported than is strong peer disapproval. At the honor system schools, on the other hand, more students perceive strong disapproval among their peers then say they personally feel a strong sense of disapproval of cheating.

In effect, at the honor system schools the perceived climate of peer disapproval is quite strong relative to the level of personal disapproval that prevails. Personal attitudes seem to have become *social reality* under the honor system so that students are aware of and sensitive to the disapproval of their peers. It seems quite plausible, then, that this heightened sense of peer disapproval is what conveys the deterrent forces of formal sanctions under the honor system.

Table 6 shows the relationship between formal sanctions and cheating, controlling for the climate of peer disapproval and the system of control at the college. As in Table 4, the direct deterrent effects of formal sanctions continue to be clearly evident at honor system schools, contrary to our expectation that peer disapproval might account for this effect. On the other hand, peer disapproval produces a reduction in the deterrent effects of formal sanctions. The average per interval effects for both honor system and others are slightly lower in Table 6 than they were in Table 4.

Thus peer disapproval is generally more effective than personal disapproval in accounting for the relationship between formal sanctions and cheating behavior,[5] yet neither peer disapproval nor personal disapproval accounts for the deterrent effects of formal sanctions against cheating at the honor system

TABLE 5

LEVEL OF PERSONAL AND PEER DISAPPROVAL BY CONTROL SYSTEM OF THE COLLEGE

	Honor System	Other System
Mean percentage expressing strong personal disapproval	43%	33%
Mean percentage perceiving strong peer disapproval[a]	51%	28%
Number of schools	(28)	(64)

a. The measure of perceived peer disapproval is constructed from two items which ask the respondent how strongly "a close friend" and "the students you go around with" would disapprove if they learned that you had cheated. (See Bowers, 1964: ch. 8 for further details.)

TABLE 6

MEAN PERCENTAGE CHEATING BY FORMAL SANCTIONS, PEER DISAPPROVAL, AND CONTROL SYSTEM OF COLLEGE

		Honor System						
	Percentage Strongly Disapproving	Suspend or Expel %	(n)	Fail Course %	(n)	Fail Specific Piece of Work or Less %	(n)	Percentage Difference per Interval
Cheating index	1-20	48	(1)	–	(0)	–	(0)	–
	21-40	34	(2)	36	(2)	44	(2)	- 5.0
	41-60	29	(3)	33	(5)	47	(5)	-10.3
	61-80	19	(4)	25	(3)	40	(1)	- 7.8
				Average Percentage Difference				- 8.3
		No Honor System						
Cheating index	1-20	63	(3)	66	(13)	71	(7)	- 4.4
	21-40	57	(3)	58	(15)	57	(11)	+ 0.6
	41-60	31	(3)	40	(3)	44	(3)	- 6.5
	61-80	–	(0)	46	(2)	47	(1)	- 1.0
				Average Percentage Difference				- 2.5

schools as well as they do at schools without the honor system, or as well as personal disapproval does for drinking and library offenses at all schools.

Our assumption that peer disapproval would account for the deterrent effects of formal sanctions at honor system schools was clearly mistaken. If we examine our argument and the data more closely we may find out why. We argued that under the honor system, the student's peers become an important source of disapproval—that formal sanctions may activate peer disapproval which, in turn, discourages cheating. (To be sure, the slight reduction in deterrent effects in Table 6, as compared to Table 4, may very well reflect this fact.) Yet under the honor system, responsibility for the behavior of one's peers usually involves more than simply expressing disapproval informally to an offender. Most systems have a "reporting clause" that requires a student who has witnessed a cheating incident to report the offender to appropriate authorities, or to ask the offender to report himself and then to report him if he fails to do so. The honor system is thus designed to increase the likelihood that formal sanctions will be brought to bear. The student's peers are directly responsible for activating the formal sanctioning machinery. As a result, formal sanctions, which are often imposed by a student court, are far less remote from the would-be offender. And indeed we might expect them to be more salient to him as the proportion of his peers who are strongly committed to the system increases.

Table 6, in fact, supports this interpretation. Not only does it show a generally greater deterrent effect of formal sanctions at honor system schools for a given level of peer disapproval, but it also shows an interaction effect between peer disapproval and formal sanctions at these schools. Thus the stronger the climate of peer disapproval, the greater the reduction in cheating behavior resulting from a given increase in formal sanctions.[6] Although this pattern is based on a limited number of schools, it holds without exception. It strongly suggests that the reason for the direct deterrent effects of formal sanctions at honor system schools lies in the ability of these systems to bring formal sanctions into play, or at least to make students think they will come into play.[7]

Preselection versus Conversion Effects of Formal Sanctions

There is little support in our data for the rationalistic view that potential offenders are directly inhibited by the prospect of severe formal sanctions, as Bentham and the general utilitarian viewpoint would contend. Except for a minority of schools which seem to have a unique capacity for making formal sanctions relevant through the academic honor system, no direct deterrent effects vis-à-vis drinking, library, and cheating offenses remain after we control for the normative climate of the school. This is not to say that formal sanctions have no effect on behavior, but simply that by and large the effects they do have seem to occur largely through informal normative processes.

What, then, is the connection between formal sanctioning policy and the normative processes of the school? Perhaps the most straightforward assumption is that formal sanctions influence the attitudes of students *after* they reach the campus. It is quite possible, however, that the sanctioning policy of an institution affects the *kinds of students it attracts*. Thus since the use of alcohol is central to much of campus social life, and since potential students are attracted to colleges at least in part on the basis of the schools' social reputations, it is quite plausible that a punitive sanctioning policy in this area will attract students who diapprove and repel those who do not. Rules of conduct and sanctions imposed for library offenses, on the other hand, would seem to be less relevant as criteria in deciding what college to attend. And indeed, Table 2 showed that there is a stronger relationship between severity of sanctions and feelings of disapproval for the drinking-related items than for the library offenses. Do these relationships come about as a result of a selection process in which students gravitate toward schools where the sanctioning policies are compatible with their own predispositions? Or are they a result of a conversion process in which a change in attitude occurs after the students have made the decision to attend a particular school?

The answer is contained in Table 7. It shows how students with a particular level of drinking or cheating behavior in high school[8] are distributed among colleges with varying sanctioning policies.

There is no evidence to speak of in Table 7 that students who are predisposed toward drinking or cheating choose to attend schools with more lenient policies in these areas. Sanctioning policy of the college attended is virtually unrelated to the previous behavior of students. The relationship between formal sanctioning policies and personal feelings of disapproval with regard to drinking offenses therefore appears to be a function of normative changes which take place after students reach college, not of a selection process that occurs either before or during college.[9]

Yet the case of cheating casts doubt on the power of formal sanctions to produce a change in normative sentiments. The fact that formal sanctions in this area show no association either with students' predispositions before coming to college (Table 7) or with their attitudes in college (Table 2) seriously questions the possiblity of any pervasive or consistent connection between formal sanctions and the normative climate that emerges. The suggestion is that some broader, more fundamental aspect of the insitution determines the normative climate, and perhaps in some cases the formal sanctions as well. Indeed, the institution's sponsorship or type of control, or the particular forms of disciplinary administration in effect may strongly influence the normative climate. Obviously further research will be required to establish the links between formal sanctions and the normative climate, which seem to exist with respect to some offenses and not others.

Discussion and Conclusion

In view of our findings that the severity of formal sanctions has no direct deterrent effect on deviant behavior except under the special conditions of an academic honor system, it is time to seriously consider why this should be the case. There is little doubt that man is in part a rational animal who seeks to minimize his losses or potential losses in terms of power, prestige, popularity, and self-esteem (compare with Homans, 1961). How is it that sanctions which are essentially designed to deprive him of these things seem not to affect his behavior?

Certainly the foremost answer, one we have suggested above, is that formal sanctions are extremely remote to most people. There is evidence that most people, notably those who have had little contact with the law, are not aware of the prescribed legal sanctions for various criminal offenses (California State Legislature, 1968: 12 ff.). Formal sanctions for drinking, library, and cheating offenses are probably remote from most students at most colleges. Only a tiny fraction of those who violate in these areas ever come to the attention of authorities (Bowers, 1964: ch. 1). Even if students are aware of the appropriate sanctions in these areas, knowing many others who have violated without consequences will certainly contribute to the impressions that there is little risk of formal sanctions.

Studies which purport to demonstrate the deterrent effects of formal sanctions generally focus on offenses of relatively high certainty and low severity

TABLE 7

FORMAL SANCTIONS OF COLLEGE ATTENDED BY HIGH SCHOOL DRINKING[a] AND CHEATING BEHAVIOR

Formal Sanctions For:		Level of Behavior in High School: % Non-drinker	% Moderate Drinker	% Heavy Drinker
Violating alcohol-use rules	dismissal	19	19	16
	suspension	42	49	42
	restriction of privileges	39	32	42
	total	100	100	100
	number of students	(2284)	(320)	(1901)
Getting drunk	dismissal	18	17	16
	suspension	50	49	50
	restriction of privileges	32	34	34
	total	100	100	100
	number of students	(2425)	(346)	(2128)
		% Noncheater		% Cheater
Cheating index	suspend or expel	24		21
	fail course	45		49
	fail specific piece of work or less	31		30
	total	100		100
	number of students	(2263)		(2554)

a. Here the drinking of beer and/or liquor is considered. A moderate drinker has used one or the other at least once, while a heavy drinker has used both at least once in high school.

of formal sanctions, such as parking violations (Chambliss, 1966), speeding violations (Ross and Campbell, 1968), and violations of the income tax laws (Schwartz and Orleans, 1967; Schwartz, 1969). In these cases, detection is routine, and the sanction is a monetary one. The potential offender can assess the risk of detection from his own past experiences and the experience of others; he can evaluate the sanction in terms of financial loss. People will talk in calculative terms about the chances of getting caught and whether they can afford it.

There is no specific evidence in these studies, however, that *severity* of sanctions plays an important part. No attempt is made to examine the effects of severity *independently* of certainty. Moreover, those studies which do attempt to separate the effects of severity and certainty (Tittle, 1969; Gibbs, 1968), whatever their methodological shortcomings, indicate that certainty rather than severity of legal sanctions is the primary deterrent factor. In fact, in Tittle's data, severity showed no consistent relationship to offense rates even under conditions of relatively high certainty. This latter point calls the simple, rationalistic formulation still further into question since, according to this logic, increasing certainty should add to the weight given severity of sanctions in the decision to act.

Perhaps there are "negative feedback processes" at work which tend to offset the expected deterrent effect of formal sanctions. Schwartz (1969) has recently provided evidence that the threat of formal sanctions generates what he calls "resistant side effects." While most people increased their compliance with income tax laws under threat of sanctions, a minority responded with substantially increased claims for deductions, as if they had been provoked to "beat the system."

More generally, severe formal sanctions or punitive threats may produce a certain degree of alienation, hostility, and rebelliousness, particularly when they do not reflect informal sentiments.[10] Under these circumstances, violation can become a symbolic act, one predicated on a commitment to social justice or personal pride. When those who feel these reactions also share other social attributes, especially common group membership, noncompliance may even become a subcultural response. Thus the willingness to risk severe sanctions will be a sign of commitment to the subgroup and will elicit the respect of the other members–noncompliance, then, will be socially motivated and reinforced, at least within the subgroup. Thus, for example, Erikson (1966: esp. 114-126) writes of the Quakers of Puritan Massachusetts argues that, with increasing severity of punishment for their offenses, increasing numbers of violators appeared as if to invite legal sanctions.

There may be another closely related source of resistance to severe formal sanctions–the insulating effect of peers. We know from previous research on cheating (Bowers, 1964: 141) that students are much more willing to express their disapproval informally to an offender than to report a fellow student to the authorities for that offense. Moreover there is evidence that when the offender is a close friend, students will actually take steps to protect him from the authorities (see also Stouffer, 1949; Stouffer and Toby, 1951; Turner, 1959). This protective tendency among particularistic or primary group relations may grow even stronger as formal sanctions become more severe. While the motivation in this case may be the loyalty of personal friendship rather than the injustice of alien sanctions, the effect is the same–to neutralize or counteract severe formal sanctions.

In effect, the academic honor system is designed to remove or to offset these sources of resistance by making peers themselves the agents of formal control. Formal sanctions are imposed not by an outsider to insure conformity with his norms, but by insiders to enforce norms to which the members of the group subscribe. Under these conditions, formal sanctions may actually take on the meaning and functions that informal social sanctions possess in most groups.

Perhaps honor systems have been less effective in controlling excessive drinking, disorderly social conduct, and other more expressive forms of misconduct because such behavior is more closely tied in with the collegiate subculture. It will be difficult to extract a commitment within the peer group to report those who break the rules when the behavior is a group enterprise supported by subcultural values.

Chambliss (1969) has argued that instrumental actions which the offender adopts as a specific means to an end (e.g., cheating) are more subject to control through formal sanctions than are expressive actions in which an offender engages as part of a broader style of life to which he is committed (e.g., drinking violations). The data in Table 3 do tend to confirm this proposition; formal sanctions against cheating continue to show a deterrent effect after we control for the normative climate, whereas this effect totally vanishes in the case of drinking-related offenses. More specifically, the data suggest that the deterrent effects remain in the case of cheating because, and to the extent that, peers become the agents of formal control. Thus the deterrent effect is concentrated at honor system schools, particularly where a large proportion of peers are perceived to strongly disapprove of cheating. Presumably objective and subjective certainty of formal sanctions are the greatest under these circumstances.

In conclusion, then, we find little evidence of a direct deterrent effect of severe formal sanctions. More substantial is their role in anchoring and buttressing the normative climate. For most of the offenses under investigation, the level of formal sanctions appears to influence students' attitudes and thus to affect the normative climate that develops at a college. This "conversion effect" is not, however, uniform in pattern or extent. For drinking-related offenses it is strong and clear; for cheating offenses it is altogether absent.

Since we find only modest and irregular deterrent effects, either direct or indirect, it might be appropriate at this point to consider briefly some effects of severe sanctions apart from deterrence. The fact that the commonly assumed direct deterrent effects are largely a myth should focus our attention on those for whom the myth may serve some function. One possibility is that severe sanctions have important implications for those who impose them. As long as everyone believes in their deterrent effects, severe sanctions represent a powerful tool for authorities in meeting their responsiblities, and a sign to the broader community that they are taking those responsibilities seriously. Thus, when authorities are having difficulty catching offenders, they can impose more severe sanctions "to insure that violations will be curbed." Or when the rate of violations is increasing and pressure is mounting for more effective control, authorities can "crack down" with more severe sanctions. In both these cases, the imposition of severe sanctions is a visible sign of action in response to failure in the system of social control.[11]

Research on the deterrent effects of formal sanctions is still at a relatively primitive stage. Different methods are being employed, including ecological analysis, natural and controlled experimentation, and survey research. Yet most of the studies to date have not uncovered processes through which formal sanctions may be having effects. In fact, the balance of evidence thus far collected weighs against a deterrent effect directly attributable to the severity of formal sanctions. Only under exceptional conditions do they directly deter deviant behavior. The evidence concerning the deterrent effects of certainty of formal sanctions is only slightly more convincing. Needless to say, further work in separating and evaluating the relative effects of severity and certainty of formal sanctions is required. In view of the largely negative findings in the area of deterrence, at least in the research to this point, it would also seem advisable in future research to examine other possible functions of formal sanctions. These might include their role in stimulating and reinforcing the normative climate of the community—what we have here described as indirect deterrent effects—and their role as resources and signs of performance for those who impose them.

NOTES

1. Of course Bentham is only one of a group of legal philosophers and criminologists who developed theories of deviant behavior and social control upon the assumption that individuals who engage in deviant acts rationally respond to the administration of formal penalties. In summarizing the contribution of classical theory, Vold (1958: 23) indicates: "Puzzling questions about the reasons for or 'causes' of behavior, the uncertainties of motive and intent, the unequal consequences of an arbitrary rule, these were all deliberately ignored for the sake of administrative uniformity."

2. This assumes that the potential murderers of Arizona were aware of the changed situation in 1917-1918. Although the prospect of death as the punishment for their crimes did not seem to faze them, it could be argued that this two-year interlude was not long enough to produce a weakening in the normative climate and hence was not an adequate test of the indirect effects of formal sanctions.

3. The percentage difference per interval is a weighted average computed as follows:

$$\frac{(a-b)na \cdot nb + (b-c)nb \cdot nc}{na \cdot nb + nb \cdot nc} = \frac{(a-b)na + (b-c)nc}{na + nc}$$

where a, b, and c are the rates of a given form of deviant behavior under the most severe, the intermediate, and the most lenient sanctioning categories respectively, and where na, nb, and nc are the number of schools contributing to a, b, and c respectively. Where nb=o, we let $b = \frac{a+c}{2}$.

4. In addition to percentage difference per interval for each context of disapproval, the table also shows the average percentage difference for the several normative contexts of a given offense, as a rough index of the overall deterrent effect of formal sanctions after the effects of the normative context have been removed. The average percentage difference is computed as follows:

$$\frac{\Sigma_i [(a_i - b_i)na_i + (b_i - c_i)nc_i]}{\Sigma_i(na_i + nc_i)}$$

where the i's represent control categories 1,2,3, . . . , n, on the independent variable. (For preliminary considerations, see note 3.)

5. It is, of course, quite possible that peer disapproval would have accounted for the deterrent effects of formal sanctions against drinking and library offenses; however measures of perceived peer disapproval were not available for these other forms of behavior.

6. This pattern is not reflected in the index of percentage difference per interval because the differences are weighted by the number of schools on which they are based. If we were to disregard the number of schools in our per interval measure, the differences would read: 5.0, 9.0, and 10.5 respectively for the 21-40, 41-60, and 61-80 disapproval contexts, showing that deterrent effects increase with increasing peer disapproval.

7. Further research reveals that students at honor system schools believe that fewer students cheat and that more of them get caught than do their counterparts at schools without such systems. Moreover, students under the honor system are more likely to know of existing incidents that have come to the attention of authorities, but less likely to know the students involved on a personal basis than are students under other systems. In effect, students' knowledge and perceptions seem to reflect a sense of more effective control under the honor system.

8. Ideally we would have wanted high school attitudes measured *prior* to college. We know, however, that there is a relatively close association between behavior and attitudes in these areas. (There is a strong negative relationship between attitudes and behavior in college and between high school behavior and college attitudes.) Therefore this recall information on high school behavior should serve as a rough index of predisposition in these areas.

9. Had we found a relationship between sanctioning policy and high school behavior, it would not have been possible to determine whether (or to what degree) selective recruitment as against selective attrition was at work without information on dropouts. Since the two variables are unrelated, however, the data in Table 7 discount both processes.

10. This reaction may also occur when severe formal sanctions are imposed selectively in an effort to control the behavior of some subgroup in the population or when they are used to curb some other associated form of behavior.

11. If severity of sanctions imposed were largely a response to variations in the rate of misconduct, there would actually be a *positive* association between these two variables. The fact that we find no relationship suggests the possiblity of two countervailing effects: a deterrent effect of formal sanctions on misconduct; and a crackdown effect in which variations in misconduct produce corresponding variations in formal sanctions. In effect, the two could be linked in a negative feedback circuit which is in turn influenced by the normative climate of the college or the expectations of institutional authorities. (For a model of this kind of functional process, see Stinchcombe, 1968: 87 ff., esp. Figure 3.7.)

REFERENCES

BALL, J. C. (1970) "Crime, punishment, and deterrence: a reexamination." Unpublished.

--- (1955) "The deterrence concept in criminology and law." J. of Criminal Law, Criminology and Police Sci. 46 (September/October): 347-354.

BOWERS, W. J. (1968) "Normative constraints on deviant behavior in the college context." Sociometry 31 (Winter): 370-385.

--- (1964) Student Dishonesty and Its Control in College. New York: Bureau of Applied Social Research, Columbia University.

--- and R. G. SALEM (1970) "Student disciplinary administration." pp. 7/36-7/63 in A. S. Knowles (ed.) Handbook of College and University Administration. New York: McGraw Hill.

California State Legislature (1968) Deterrent Effects of Criminal Sanctions. Progress report of the Assembly Committee on Criminal Procedure.

CHAMBLISS, W. J. (1969) Crime and the Legal Process. New York: McGraw-Hill.

--- (1966) "The deterrent influence of punishment." Crime and Delinquency 12 (January): 70-75.

CHIRICOS, T. G. and G. P. WALDO (1970) "Punishment and crime: empirical evidence?" Presented at the meetings of the American Sociological Association, Washington, D.C.

COHEN, A. K. (1966) Deviance and Control. New York: Prentice-Hall.

COSER, L. A. (1967) Continuities in the Study of Social Conflict. New York: Free Press.

--- (1962) "Some functions of normative flexibility." Amer. J. of Sociology 68 (September): 172-182.

DURKHEIM, E. (1964) The Division of Labor in Society. New York: Free Press.

ERIKSON, K. T. (1966) The Wayward Puritans. New York: John Wiley.

GIBBS, J. P. (1968) "Crime, punishment, and deterrence." Southwestern Social Sci. Q. 48 (March): 515-530.

HOMANS, G. C. (1961) Social Behavior: Its Elementary Forms. New York: Harcourt, Brace & World.

PINCOFFS, E. L. (1966) The Rationale of Legal Punishment. New York: Humanities Press.

ROSS, H. L. and D. T. CAMPBELL (1968) "The Connecticut speed crackdown," pp. 30-35 in H. Lawrence Ross (ed.) Perspectives on the Social Order. New York: McGraw-Hill.

SCHUESSLER, K. F. (1969) "The deterrent influence of the death penalty," pp. 378-388 in W. J. Chambliss (ed.) Crime and the Legal Process. New York: McGraw-Hill.

SCHWARTZ, R. D. (1969) "Sanctions and compliance." Presented at the American Sociological Association meetings, San Francisco.

--- and S. ORLEANS (1967) "On legal sanctions." Univ. of Chicago Law Rev. 34 (Winter): 274-300.

SELLIN, T. (1966) "Effect of repeal and reintroduction of the death penalty on homocide rates," pp. 339-351 in H. A. Bedau (ed.) The Death Penalty in America. Chicago: Aldine.

STINCHCOMBE, A. L. (1968) Constructing Social Theories. New York: Harcourt, Brace & World.

STOUFFER, S. A. (1949) "An analysis of conflicting social norms." Amer. Soc. Rev. 14 (December): 707-717.

--- and J. TOBY (1951) "Role conflict and personality," pp. 481-496 in T. Parsons and E. A. Shils (eds.) Toward a General Theory of Action. Cambridge: Harvard Univ. Press.

TITTLE, C. R. (1969) "Crime rates and legal sanctions." Social Problems 16 (Spring): 409-423.

TOBY, J. (1964) "Is punishment necessary?" J. of Criminal Law, Criminology and Police Sci. 55, 3: 332-337.

TURNER, R. H. (1959) "An experiment in the modification of role conception." Year Book of the Amer. Phil. Society: 329-333.

VOLD, G. B. (1958) Theoretical Criminology. New York: Oxford Univ. Press.

Chapter 16

The Perimeters of Power

The Concept of Compliance as an Approach to the Study of the Legal and Political Processes

SAMUEL KRISLOV – *University of Minnesota*

Increased and more explicit attention by students of the legal order to the processes of compliance and the securing of compliance seems in order. "The spectrum of means available for the enforcement of legal norms," writes Herbert Packer (1962: 586), "is rapidly becoming a central preoccupation of students of the legal order. It has not so far progressed much beyond the recognition that the problems are important, intricate and almost entirely unexplored."[1] As Robert MacIver has trenchantly observed, under various names social scientists have for long been principally preoccupied with the problem of social control.[2] Yet the explicit recognition of compliance as a basic problem is only a scattered and a recent phenomenon.

The emphasis upon compliance is basically a reversal of the elitist, leader-centered power approach. The preoccupation with elites and the powerful, at least in part, results from the convenience and the attractiveness of research among the higher social echelons of society as opposed to mundane research throughout society. A possible corollary to the findings that middle-class pollsters prefer to deal with middle- and upper-class respondents is that

---

AUTHOR'S NOTE: *This paper was originally presented to the American Political Science Association in 1963. Although never published, it has frequently been cited. It seemed appropriate to preserve it in the form in which it was revised immediately after the 1963 meetings, revisions which were essentially copyediting. I am indebted to conversations with Edwin Fogelman, University of Minnesota, and Abraham Goldstein, Yale Law School, for help in clarifying my own position.*

social scientists too have preferred to associate with the rich and the powerful, and to center their work upon the problems of the attractive elite. Social scientists too can suffer from the F. Scott Fitzgerald syndrome.

Compliance is, of course, the correlative of power. Yet it is not simply a matter of changing focus. To emphasize the totality of the process "stands the problem on its feet" and restores the mutuality of social interaction. The emphasis upon power, on the contrary, dichotomizes where there is no dichotomy and suggests unidirectional and invariant types of relations. The conundrum-like discussions of power and authority, and power and influence, are products of this segmentation as opposed to a recognition of the continuum of power relationships.

Looking at the real world, few indeed–although there are those few–would acknowledge as correct a portrait of concentrated, instant omnipotence. On the contrary, to most observers, the striking phenomenon of modern civilization, if not of all civilizations, is the relative weakness of the individual in the face of his physical and social environment. One might in consequence reverse the more usual approach with a good deal of profit–"politics is the study of the uninfluential and the powerless." Everywhere we find degrees of helplessness. Presidents feel they are constrained by Congress, and Congressmen that their powers are being usurped from all directions. So, too, powerful social groups complain constantly of deprivation, of being hemmed in, of loss of independence and the sense of creativity. Businessmen bemoan the loss of their authority to labor, and labor its decline in the face of automation. Emphasis upon the process of compliance and the conditions of compliance, then, accords well with our intuitive perceptions of the political world as most of us really see it.

Such a change of focus would be consonant with conceptual developments in social science. I think it is an objective (and not merely idiosyncratic or pollyannaish) evaluation, that there has been a progressive improvement in basic terminology and conceptual clarity of the field. Specifically, there has been a refinement and evolution of terms from notions of sovereignty to power to decision-making and, perhaps now, to compliance. All of these terms seem to aim at the same general problem of social control, but they focus with increasing sharpness upon the real phenomena at issue.

This development is perfectly in accordance with the trends in the physical sciences. A study of the development of the most analogous concept in the physical sciences–force–suggests that it had a very similar evolution. Max Jammer's *Concepts of Force* (1963; a book which would be most appropriate for courses in methodology) indicates that terminological clarification within a science is a vital and integral part of the development of empirical findings as well. Physical force was, in its first usage, loosely identified by ancient and medieval thinkers, as coterminous with power, virtue, and other similar terms. Gradually a more direct and more refined meaning developed. Finally, the stage of mathematization was reached, and the concept was incorporated into relational equations. In its last stages, force became merely regarded as the relations suggested by the equations, and the concept itself effectively disappeared.

This is not the history of an "incorrect" or useless concept. On the contrary, this is the most successful of all possible developments a concept may have. The gradual increase in precision and its final reduction and absorption into equations lacking any mystical anthropomorphic or extrasensory overtones is the final triumph of scientific method. Indeed, the refinement of concepts, in terms of their applicability to real phenomena, is the history of scientific development.

The narrowing down of the mystical questions of "sovereignty," the avoidance of the highly similar—indeed, at one time synonymous—debates over the essence and "virtu" of man in the social sphere, the preoccupation, in short, with the relative influence rather than the categorization of power, is simply an analogous development in the social sciences. We have, in the general emphasis upon decision-making in various spheres, centered upon the problem of how the imprimatur of legality is acquired, while thrusting under the rug with words like "authoritative" the problem of how much attention is paid to the results. A decision by Hitler in 1943 had rather more consequence than one made in the bunker in 1945.

> I can call spirits from the vasty deep; Why so can I, or so can any man, but will they come when you do call for them? [Henry IV, Part I, Act II]

It is perhaps relevant that the most authoritative elitist power analyst—Harold Lasswell—has himself in recent years been attracted to a compliance framework—addressing himself to the problem in a full-scale work—*In Defense of Public Order* (Arens and Lasswell, 1962).[3]

II

The inexorable relationship of compliance to law is too obvious to have escaped attention. The literature has generally, however, concerned itself with the problem of criminality and recidivism. The notion implicit in such a concern is one of deviance. Research has been primarily in terms of typifying individual behavior and categorizing individuals as good citizens or deviants. Even here great problems have arisen with regard to statistical techniques and data available for measuring criminality and deviance.[4] Subjectivity in the definitions of crime, differential reporting according to class, and cycles in vigorous enforcement all figure among these problems. With this dualistic approach, our data often tell us more about social structures than they do about social behavior.

The principal intellectual virtue of Sutherland's (1961) concept of white-collar criminality is not that it satisfied populistic social voyeurism (which has unfortunately been its chief attraction), but that it restores criminality and deviance to a place of expected and, indeed, normal behavior in organized society. Compliance and deviance, rebellion and conformity, can be seen as regularized and routine behavior among all classes of citizens. This is perhaps clearest in the fine studies of OPA violations, done in the wake of Sutherland's efforts, by Clinard (1952) and Hartung (1953). In a similar vein, the Kinsey studies suggest precisely the same conclusion–that "antisocial" behavior is an inevitable product of an ongoing social system. Thus, the recognition that compliance is a psychosocial phenomenon, distributed more or less normally throughout the population, leads in turn to a more explicit problem–not one of identifying two types of breeds, but of determining the conditions and distribution of compliance and opposition.

Studies like those of Professor Macaulay (1963) of the Wisconsin Law School deal with the extent of reliance upon legal contract and legal enforcement as the basis of business relationships. Stouffer (1955) and Cohen (1958) have investigated the relationship between perceived values and legally enforced behavior. The operating function of the Bar as an instrument of legal enforcement and recruitment of cases is also relevant. In short, the adoption of this view of a normal distribution of obedient and disobedient behavior opens up a broader vista of possible research problems and can lead to more creative and relevant studies in the field of law and human behavior.[5]

While courtroom drama remains the preoccupation of the novelist and the journalist, the increasingly interesting question to the social scientist should be that of placing the courtroom scenario within the broader area of the interaction between the individual and society. The relationship between the discrete and relatively small number of court trials and the gigantic machinery of social behavior and social regularity is not only a more sophisticated problem but, on closer view, a more dramatic and challenging one.

Within the field of inquiry of public policy, too, the importance of compliance has not been neglected. John P. Frank has discussed the general problem in his *The Marble Palace* (1958: 20-41) as one of "the practicalities of power."[6] He suggests that the Supreme Court is most effective in securing compliance when the issue attracts public interest, when the position of the Court is clearly enunciated, and publicity attends the policy set by the decision. Resistance from other governmental officials is also a key variable. Unfortunately Frank's discussion, while interesting and novel, is somewhat ad hoc and impressionistic like much of his relatively popularized book.

While Frank's discussion remains one of the few efforts to deal with the overall problem, similar studies have been made in specific areas of law. The effect of court decisions as to prayers in the public schools has been studied by two political scientists, partly in response to the suggestions made in Jack

Peltason's (1955) pioneering *The Federal Courts in the Political Process.* Gordon Patric (1957) and Frank Sorauf (1959) were early venturers into the field to inquire into the behavior patterns of superintendents and school teachers resulting from the McCollum and the Zorach decisions.

The issue of the subsequent discounting of a court decision, the problem of the practical effect of a legal verdict, comes particularly to the fore in connection with the segregation decision. The greatest effect of the decision in Brown v. Board of Education, for example, was to educate students as to the limits and operations of the court system generally. (I am sure this was not a motive of the judges in enunciating the decision, but we may nonetheless be grateful to them.) While the problems of the thirties served to focus the attention of the public lawyer on policy and the rights and wrongs of particular decisions, the fifties and sixties seemed to call upon us to investigate the manner in which limits on power imposed by courts must operate.

Implementation is, after all, a key question, even from the standpoint of social policy and the realities of so-called commonsense politics. Thus, the study of the implementation of decisions and compliance with them is not appropriate only for the development of an academic understanding of the legal process, but also for steps in unravelling of the mysteries of social control and social regularity. Even for those who still regard the social scientist's role as preeminently one of contemplative journalism and moralizing, it would seem to be a most appropriate focus. But the need for immediate societal solutions should not preclude the possibility of greater development of the understanding of the social process.

In a peculiar sense, too, current emphasis on international relations and the growth of our interests abroad contribute to this new concern. As the international situation has contributed to the social problem so may its study contribute to our analytic understanding. Schelling's brillant *The Strategy of Conflict* repeatedly follows simplified models from the legal order, and he explicitly suggests his task would be simpler if legal scholars had a greater concern for theory: "Deterrence has been an important concept in criminal law for a long time. One might have supposed the existence of a well cultivated theory, already available for international applications" (1960: 10).[7]

The reverse now looms as true–the attempt to develop a theory of international deterrence is now applicable to public law. Schelling's essential notions, such as tacit bargaining, are right to the point. Indeed, the current Negro strivings can be put into the context of revolutionary–radically revised bargaining situations–that have occurred in history. Similarly, the current emphasis on social change reflects a preoccupation with purposive manipulation of institutions, while discussions of political socialization represent the recognition that formal sanctions are merely one means of inducing loyalty. We are all compliance specialists now.

The slice of research undertaken by the public law men in the early days of political science was dictated by interests similar to those of the practicing lawyer–case analysis and doctrine. Creatively, they added the dimension of the political origin of law and won the fight for political interpretation. Corwin, Cushman, Haines, and Grant dominate the *Selected Essays on Constitutional Law* chosen by a committee of the Association of American Law Schools (1938). During the 1920s and 1930s, the immediate issue and the problems of policy created by the Court were an irresistible focus for scholarly concern. The successful treatment of constitutional law by legiopolitical specialists proved itself again and again.

The 1937 Court fight and the newfound agreement on a more modest judicial role provided an opportunity for reexamination of method. The response was meager; the efflorescence of judicial biography was valuable, but hardly earth-shaking.

The advent of the Legal Realist converted old iconoclasm into tired cliche, and even the Thermidorean effects of the fifties and sixties have not totally eroded their essential insights. The advanced law professors are hardly, if at all, behind the sociologist in assimilating behavioral literature and are probably still ahead of the political scientist.

The postwar trend toward creativity in political science came with Pritchett's use of bloc analysis. This was succeeded by Schubert's much more sophisticated methods of analysis of judicial votes; he not only consolidated Pritchett's effort, but actually revived it as Pritchett progressively withdrew from active use of the technique. Paralleling this was Peltason's development of a broader political framework by emphasizing a Bentleyite perspective. Peltason's concept of the judicial process was certainly a broad enough platform for any political scientist to stand on. But the recent effect of his appeal has been the production of intrinsically noncumulative case studies, as the lack of explicitness of Bentleyite analysis makes itself felt. The conceptual tool he developed was blunted in general use (see Krislov, 1963).

But the broad perspective is, after all, what is most attractive about *Federal Courts in the Political Process* and *Fifty-Eight Lonely Men* (Peltason, 1955, 1961), and it is this approach to the broad agenda of the political behavior of judges, not in isolation but as it interacts with the political behavior generally that unites the best of the public law of the past with its possibilities for the future.

III

There are currently many loose generalizations about the degrees of compliance with Supreme Court decisions and legislative policies. Prohibition was a failure; segregation has had rough going. Baker v. Carr (1962) has witnessed extraordinary positive response. These, however, are at best loose impressions; they imply a basis for comparative degrees of compliance which is not only undefined but actually nonexistent.

Specifically, if we probe beyond the bald assertions, we can find at least a plausible case for prohibition as a successful program (see Wickersham Commission, 1931; Encyclopedia Britannica, 1960). If we include the elimination of educational programs of real or potential segregation in Kansas and the southwestern states, the school desegregation record is quite comparable with their record for voting progress and higher education, and more successful than the early interstate commerce segregation efforts.

Unfortunately, as the preceding discussion suggests, assessment of compliance is not a matter of "objective reality"; but rather it is defined by what is acceptable at a given time. This is a two-fold problem. The zone of compliance varies according to social perception, and the degree of compliance is normally difficult to ascertain with any level of confidence.

Since the zone of acceptance is a consequence of either tacit or direct bargaining, it is thus by no means an independent variable. If token compliance were to prevail in every part of the South, the original intent of Brown v. Board of Education would not be fulfilled (though a number of decisions have suggested that the Court would indeed settle for this).[8]

Similarly, figures on prosecution and conviction cannot be the sole basis for evaluation of compliance, for they depend upon complex calculations of feasibility and desirability of enforcement which vary according to the nature of the case. A high rate of convictions may be associated with high compliance, and a low rate with no enforcement at all. If it is true that there is a Nebraska law that pi shall equal 3.0, or a Kansas law that trains going in opposite directions shall both stop until the other has passed, the compliance rate is no more indicated by the record of prosecutions than King Canute's effectiveness was by the response to his order.

Further, the degree of compliance is dictated also by the intensity of the enforcers' demand. It is sufficient for compliance with daylight saving time that railroads should put the black clockhand ahead while introducing a red hour-hand and printing their schedules in the old time. But it is not permissible to evade the primary decision by holding a pre-primary primary.

But if we bear these complexities in mind, we may establish degrees of compliance with *enunciated* doctrines and deal simply with the effectiveness of the announced policy—leaving aside for separate treatment the problem of the enunciator's intent. Prosecutions may thus be an index of effectiveness, though great care must be exercised. With this caution in mind, we may then be able to suggest an acceptable zone of degrees of compliance.

Richardson (1948) has argued that when the death rate in war goes above a certain line, fighting always ceases and society finds further slaughter, particularly of young males, intolerable.[9] In the same way, socially crucial measures may have limits beyond which nonconformity is intolerable. Further, it is likely that, within a broad range, compliance is largely self-generating, while, below a minimum level of acceptance, enforcement would become impossible.

Whether we might expect a specific base line rather than a zone of compliance is another question. I think it is clear that a given social measure would have differing crucialities in different political systems, and that compliance requisites consequently will be different as well. Enforcement of laws forbidding murder would probably be intensified rather than relaxed if incidence doubled; but, as the history of dueling shows, would not necessarily be enforced under all circumstances. A slight increase in the incidence of homosexuality, on the other hand, might make it acceptable in society regardless of its previous frequency. Possibly it would be viewed with more tolerance in a society that felt it had reached a state of overpopulation. Thus the violation rate for the prohibition statute might have been considerably lower than those for many other laws and still be at a violation point intolerable to the social system, while Michigan's deer hunting law, according to estimate, is less than 50% successful without producing excessive agitation for change.

(1) The Targets of Policy: Geographic Distribution

A good deal of ingenuity has gone into the comparative study of data on voting patterns, and not a little of what we know in political science depends upon electoral sociology. Similarly, Zeisel et al. (1959: 220-240) have shown that some locales are consistently more "litigation-prone" than others, and have even suggested an ecological law to account for the phenomenon. Similarly, Durkheim's *Suicide* (1951) can be viewed as a study in factors of compliance.

It is possible similarly to delimit geographical areas of resistance to social programs. It is feasible to take, for example, a simple rank order of percentage of Negroes in integrated public schools and a similar rank order in higher education in various states. The apparent anomalies of Louisiana and Virginia reflect their complex social problems, their dynamics of leadership, and their "might-have-beens."[10] Indeed, the generalization that "black belt" counties are more likely to defy court orders in race matters is already well known.

Of course, we continuously do something like this in evaluating the success or failure of social policies. But the notion that the process by which we do this is of major concern to political science is not common. By studying, comparing, and working out patterns of resistance and acquiescence to particular policies, we may learn to detect clusters of issues. That is to say, patterns of resistance and acquiescence seem to go together as attitudes and personality attributes do. It should be possible in many instances to develop scales of social attitudes for regions and states. The resultant clusters of compliance could in any event be compared with the clusters of judicial attitudes and values. With the growing literature available on the nature of judicial values, the possibilities of comparison with general population perceptions become exciting.[11]

Cohen et al. (1958) have produced a study showing that community values differed sharply from the state of the law in the field of parental authority and liability. For some reason, lawyers have not seized upon the study as evidence of the essential independence of law from ephemeral opinion, or as suggesting the complexity of the relationship of legal doctrine to changing functional needs, but have naively attacked it as a threat to the structure of the law of personal liability. In so doing, it is quite likely that they have merely taken the authors' intention at face value and have thereby lost many opportunities for interpretive insight. We may find that the crucial variables are not the positive or negative content of the sentiment, but the systematic direction of the preferences or the ordering of the preferences of the judges and the citizens.

The study of patterning of resistance and acquiescence also might take into account the problem of the "spillover of defiance" from one type of issue to another, the dynamics of defiance. South Carolina, with its history of resistance to desegregation of schools, "intends to ignore court ruling" on prayer (New York Times, 1963), the state superintendent of schools announcing a program of "massive resistance" to the Schempp decision. Similarly, however, Wallace threatened to pray in the schoolhouse door. Various types of patterns can be similarly developed. The characteristic that distinguishes the apportionment most sharply from the segregation decision is not the speed but the direction of compliance. Baker v. Carr has been obeyed soonest in the areas of greatest abuse—Georgia, for example—effecting major changes in the social pattern. The reverse has been notoriously true of the school decision. In one instance, the improvement came from the center out, while in the other it has been moving in from the periphery. Determining which issues fall into one category or another is a task for the researcher.

(2) The Targets of Policy: Individuals

The effects of a policy upon decision processes at other levels is presumably closely related to the relative power relations of those who effect and those who would be affected by a new policy. Perhaps the most nearly established "fact" in the literature on this matter is that prescriptions are relatively ineffectual in reversing the actions of officials who have previously based a policy upon their own predilections and political evaluations. It is presumably for these reasons that the patent office and the school boards in the prayer cases have persisted in their course of conduct (Frank, 1958; Sorauf, 1959). Sutherland's "differential association" may explain these instances of demonstrated and continued noncompliance, though it seems inadequate for the instances in which compliance did in fact occur.

The more general question of whether institutionally based individuals are more or less likely to comply with legitimated policy decisions seems to be open. It is closely related to such central problems as the role of bureaucracy and the realities of mass society. While leaders may be more likely to comply with higher-level decision makers because of their own coordinative experience, as

Stouffer suggests, they can also afford to resist more effectively. More precise statements of the controlling conditions should be possible. Some light might be shed by the various studies undertaken in the name of "group dynamics" if imaginatively projected to broader and less artificial social settings.

Among areas relatively accessible for study is compliance within the executive branch, such as the presidential order on Negro employment in federal agencies and differential compliance with the order. Similarly, such interbranch matters as court convictions for congressional contempt citations provide many possibilities for study. This latter suggests, in fact, two sets of interrelationships–between Congress and the Department of Justice, and the subsequent conviction rate. It is perhaps not too surprising that only about one-third of the contempt citations ultimately result in convictions. The factors involved present some interesting possibilities for interpretation.

(3) The Sources of Policy and the Effects on Compliance

If we regard power as distributed continuously, all agencies and all participants are capable of exercising it. Corwin displayed a form of this insight in his discussion of judicial review when he pointed out that the summons server or the postal clerk might exercise the power of declaring a law unconstitutional.

Does it, in fact, make any difference what the source of the policy is or at what level it is enunciated? Common sense suggests and organizational studies seem to bear out, that the higher the level at which policies are enunciated, the stronger their legitimating overtones will be, in most instances.[12] But this is by no means established, and it is not always clear which is the higher legitimating authority.

In American government, this is even overtly a problem. The House of Representatives from time to time wages war on its "lower house" label. But it is usually assumed that congressional approval or even presidential endorsement of the Court's decision on segregation would lead to greater compliance, though there is no solid evidence for such an assumption. It is true, polls have shown, that an Act once passed by Congress gains in social approval. But no comparable inquiries have been made into the legitimating effects on Court decisions of congressional approval or presidential proclamation.

Further, there are other authorities as well. There is considerable evidence to suggest that violence and defiance in different states have varied in accordance with gubernatorial or legislative approval of defiance, but none to prove whether this was cause or effect.

The wide variety of means whereby policies are promulgated in the American system provides us with a laboratory for examining the relative effectiveness of different types of authority in our political structure. Thus, compliance with programs such as minimum-wage legislation could be reviewed for determining executive versus legislative effectiveness. The difficulty is that the subsequent actions of various bodies are usually correctives of the previous measure and not, strictly speaking, comparable. Congress not only enacted minimum-wage legislation but improved upon the executive orders.

There are more usual patterns—e.g., action taken by Congress subsequently rather than immediately—in our political spectrum which would make comparison difficult. Nonetheless, studies which might show one institution's superiority in effectiveness over another's would be highly interesting, and there is sufficient variation to make comparisons possible.

If such a study should reveal a pattern of differential support for decisions of different authorities among different parts of the population, it would be of major significance for the current speculations on interest support for specific branches of the government. Whether distasteful decisions are in fact made less so when enunciated by an authority which normally supports one's values could certainly be tested, and the results used as a collateral test of currently assumed theories about interest groups. Similarly, whether certain types of issues are more successfully handled by one institution than another could be explored. Determination of whether people respond to different types of legitimation is probably as possible as finding out whether they orient themselves by issue, by group affiliation, or by candidate.

(4) The Content of the Policy Statement

Thomas Emerson once estimated that in the OPA "from 50 to 75 percent of our enforcement success depends upon the regulation itself" (Clinard, 1952: 206). While on the surface this is a statement whose remarkable precision is beyond the limits of knowledge (Cardozo, 1947: 22), Emerson's generalization seems reasonably defensible, since unworkable and unenforceable regulations can obviously be promulgated with no change of compliance.

John P. Frank (1958: esp. 23) concludes that a policy is most likely to be accepted if it has a clearly enunciated domain and secures widespread attention. This is, in part, semantic sleight-of-hand, since a policy obviously cannot be complied with, except perhaps by accident, if the subject of the order does not know that compliance is expected or what direction it should take. Further, as indicated above, defiance also is a product of knowledge and precision, and the individuals who can (by skill) and should (by position) know what is expected are often the most recalcitrant.

Yet the notion is apparently not all a parlor trick. Murray Edelman (1958) has shown quite persuasively that prescriptions only vaguely implicit, at least in one realm, have had no effect on administrative action. Relatively precise statements do have some role as they are regarded by an administrator as a major variable to be assessed, particularly in view of the possibility of court reversal of agency action.

By the same token, it would appear that ambiguity is ineffectual not only because it makes it hard to tell what is wanted, but also because it is often an index of the intensity of the determination to carry a policy through. Where the object of the prescription believes the ambiguity will not be translated into action, he is unlikely to feel compulsion. Thus, the avoidance of the New York question in the McCollum case (1948) produced an opportunity for evasion, and the total murkiness of the Zorach "distinction"—really an overruling—suggested very weak Court resolutions indeed.[13]

But where there is in fact no determination, and many alternatives are apparently available, the foolish and unnecessarily rigid position invites disaster. Successful statesmen, of course, are notably expert in avoiding positions from which there is no available retreat. Judges, aware of the almost boundless time afforded by the judicial process, have generally assumed that there is a basic advantage in things left unsaid. But there are, in fact, advantages both ways. In the McCollum aftermath, school superintendents found it easy to justify any existing pattern of religious education as falling within the context of the decision, precisely because the Court chose to reserve for itself an almost infinite variety of alternative courses of future action. On the other hand, President Kennedy successfully followed a course of "irrevocable commitment" in several key instances—Cuba and Alabama, to cite two somewhat disparate cases. At the same time, he was unsuccessful with more ambiguous pronouncements in Mississippi and the steel case and was finally forced into a "no retreat" stand. There are clearly strong advantages to such commitments on certain occasions, and the possible gains and losses with different strategies under various conditions are being systematically and brilliantly studied on the international level. The transference of the method to the domain of domestic compliance is inevitable.

(5) The Sanctions Utilized

The range of available sanctions has long been a subject of discussion; they extend from the most legalistic to the totally informal. Macaulay's study (1963) shows that in a highly competitive low-margin business—the paper box industry—legally enforceable contracts are the exception rather than the rule; this illustrates, if we need further illustration, that the use of force is not the best index of effectiveness. Force, deprivation, threat, shame, and the like can be elaborated endlessly by human ingenuity for a desired end.

The study of the relevance and appropriateness of different sanctions to meet different situations has been avoided, perhaps because it comes so close to the essential purpose of the law itself. In a sense, the legal order regards itself as a testing ground for the efficacy of sanctions, an empirical method for arriving at appropriate conclusions. Thus, as Dean Landis (1958: 907) has suggested, remedies regarded as legitimate in one area have never been utilized in what appears to be a similar situation, simply and precisely because the law enforcement officials have set it up that way. To investigate the problem is, or appears to be, to duplicate the decision maker's function. The "informer's share" is used in some tax matters, but not in private fraud cases. The utility in each instance has been "evaluated" only by the most generous use of the term. But the taint of reformist literature seems to inhibit more precise inquiry.

An important exception is Clinard's *Black Market* (1952) which sets forth the methods used by the OPA and attempts to evaluate alternatives that had been available in various instances. In the end, though, he is the prisoner of data collected mainly by the agency for its own purposes, and the backward look gives little evidence of the relative effectiveness of the sanctions.

Today the outstanding possibilities for development of notions seem to lie in a domain outside domestic politics. Schelling's inventive and provocative discussions of deterrence seem equally applicable to the question of the strategy of punishment.

In essence, bargaining takes place between groups of society on intent to comply with prospective legislation. At some levels of action, the bargaining is explicit and overt where a group threatening defiance is powerful enough and respectable enough to openly enunciate its own existence and the limits to which it will accept adverse decisions. Once a group falls below a level of respectability and power, its bargaining becomes more involuted and is done largely through the medium of interpretation of its demands by its regulators or supervisors. Thus the Narcotics Bureau, for all practical purposes, evaluates definitively the likelihood of compliance for any narcotics policies. Further, to a large extent, it controls subsequent accounting of the degree of compliance with or evasion of the policy. The analogy to international relations, however, does not break down here. For to a considerable extent, the same processes are operative in the relationship of foreign affairs. A country's diplomats and international experts maintain this interpretive role in their formulation and execution of policy. The more estranged and remote a foreign country is, the more its reactions and demands are filtered, through the views of the recipient nation's policy members.

The whole field of game-theory-like discussions of response and anticipation suggests matters most relevant for the behavioral student of the legal order. When, indeed, do deterrents deter? And when do they anger and provoke? When does an increase of punishment result in a loss of effect and a weakening of authority? A total answer to this problem would result, of course, in a utopian formula for the ideal set of criminal laws. But it would seem that an understanding of the general principles and overall effect of sanctions on compliance is possible.

IV

The politicization of public law has, as V. O. Key once suggested, been a dominant trend since World War II. That is to say, we have come more and more to share the general approach and techniques of behavioral science.

The desirability of this is, of course, hardly self-evident, particularly for those who reject even what has already been done. I should, therefore, like to make two points explicit. First, that compliance is in fact a vital component of political relations, and second, that public law is an appropriate—in my view, the most appropriate—area in which to study it.

According to the naive behaviorist, the essence of politics is individual action. But the process of interrelationships of individuals constitutes the core and the fascination of politics. Not even the simple result from the interaction of individuals could or should exhaust the concerns of the political scientist. Even if we accept the triad "who, what, and how" as the basis of politics, we would have to assert that not the least of these is the "how." Lasswell himself seems to embrace this in his statement that politics is concerned with "the shaping and sharing of power" (Lasswell and Kaplan, 1950: xiv).

And the "how" cannot include only the interrelationships until the moment of prescription, for that itself is in fact not a moment but a succession of almost infinite events. As we have suggested, even if the actions of the postal clerk and the corner cop were assembled under the rubric of decision-making, the vital response of the client-citizen would be ignored. It is, after all, large-scale compliance that differentiates prescription from edicts of lunatics, brigands from governments, and revolutionary cabals from political societies. Social science is one-sided if it regards power as simply a matter of decision-making or prescribing. The translation of prescription into action is an absolute prerequisite to the understanding of politics.

Why, however, should the field of public law be concerned with compliance? Essentially, I suggest it as appropriate because public law is not concerned with most of the preprescription linkages of political life and is oriented primarily toward the postprescription phase. It should add compliance to its concerns in order to maintain its roots in political reality.

This is not intended as an exercise in mere symmetry—a tidy distribution whereby students of legislatures study parties and pressure groups, and students of judicial processes deal with enforcement. It is based upon a recognition that compliance is the focal problem in the study of law, that the potentially resistant citizen is the inherent constituency of the courts. As the student of the legislative process wants to know how public characteristics comport with voting behavior, so the student of the courts should concern himself with the interaction of decision and compliance.

And there is a special and further reason—the appeal to the sense of intellectual and professional craftsmanship—which should be at least as important for the scholar as Llewellyn suggests it should be for judges. The dangers that lie in estrangement from truly political categories and interrelationships are self-evident, and include the possibility that the study of public law will degenerate into a kind of subnational area study, wtih a language, history, and self-concern all its own. And the danger of studying public law as a political phenomenon which has no base in any precisely defined political relationships, is that it may lead to the kind of vague and grandiose generalizations that so often characterize loose historical writing. Portentous remarks about "political forces" may mean nothing more than a feeling that people should have reacted in some particular way, and generalizations about "social forces" can be so vague and unfocused that they amount to nothing more than normative judgments. On the other hand, the danger of a preoccupation with judges and their voting patterns can too easily lead to biographical or psychological reductionism. But combining the study of political interrelationships, of which compliance is an important component, with investigations into legal and judicial activity will add scope to the study of public law and justify our claims to be social scientists.

NOTES

1. A leading example of a compliance approach, though bearing some of the characteristics of a tour de force is Etzioni (1962).

2. The concept of "social control" in fashion during the twenties and thirties (see the "Index of the First 25 Years" of the *American Sociological Review*) seems to be making a comeback (see the discussions by Parsons in William Evan [1962] and Peter Berger [1963]). The assumption that the study of social control is equivalent to the development of technocratic social engineering differentiates the approach in Beutel (1957).

3. "By 'compliance' I mean the securing of general public behavior, in a direction and to a degree acceptable to the enunciators of policy, as a consequence of articulated or otherwise manifested wishes of official policy makers. Sanctions, education, and enforcement are all then instrumental means in the achievement of such compliance" (Arens and Lasswell, 1962).

4. The work of Thorstein Sellin has been most useful in clarifying problems of criminal statistics. It should be noted, however, that there are problems in using most of the statistics we employ without question. Thus, as Eldersveld has shown, election returns are not as immutable as they appear; indeed, recounts and postelection analysis constantly reveal new and unsuspected problems. For example, in some states it is the practice not to tally the ballots of late-reporting precincts whose vote cannot affect the final election returns.

5. The need for such a "normal distribution" view of compliance is dramatically epitomized in Joseph Borkin (1962: especially 11)–"Nor is there a discernible type of corrupt judge." The dynamics of the bar are discussed in Carlin (1962). The recruitment of cases has been explored by the Columbia University Project for Effective Justice and has appeared in various forms in the *Columbia Law Review* under the authorship of Rosenberg, Franklin, and others.

The difference is sharply drawn in Suchman, Dean, and Williams (1958: 26-30). Their discussion of power centers on well-known distinctions, attempts to improve on terminology, and concludes that the power framework is largely irrelevant; only "traditional legitimation" seems promising in effecting change of attitudes. More, I venture to say, would have been adduced in a compliance framework.

6. See Arthur Miller (1965) and Robert Dixon (1951, 1949).

7. See also Schelling (1960: e.g., 37, 43). See also Schwartz and Orleans (1967), continuing the work of Schwartz and J. H. Skolnick (1963).

8. The Court seems to have upped the requirement, however. See Watson v. Memphis (1963).

9. Richardson suggests modification in the notion of the rate dependent upon selective death of "hostiles" at the front and the gregariousness of the home populace affecting the velocity of discouragement as a result of the attrition.

10. Derived from data supplied by Jim Leeson of the Southern Education Reporting Service, April 22, 1963 and the *Southern School News* annual summaries.

11. See various leading articles by Schubert (notably 1962, 1963).

12. Peter Blau and Richard Scott (1962: 153-157) indicate that detachment is functionally related to effectiveness of leadership in organization.

13. The Legal Realists have suggested that "rules of law" have little or no compulsion. Yet administrative theorists assume codification can be extremely effective, particularly together with a high degree of internalization of values and significant institutional checks (see, in this regard, Herbert Kaufman, 1960). This anomaly can be explained partly in terms of continuous response to interpretation on the lower level. That is, the higher authorities in administrative organizations respond by enunciating further policy statements designed to "correct misinterpretations" and enforce compliance. The expectancy of such responses, of course, builds into persistence. Frank is quite good in indicating the frustration of a "higher authority" in the face of persistent error, where the Supreme Court is unlikely to expend the energy involved in continued exercise of discretion, and therefore freeing the lower agency–i.e., the patent office. At the same time, Osborne (1963: 149-204) shows that such reaction is not by any means automatic. He depicts the possibility of persistence in the segregation matters where the Court demand is sufficiently intense to cause them to systematically pursue their policy in the face of any opposition.

In this view, the reason for Court rule in effectiveness vis-a-vis administrative rules lies principally in the more circumscribed nature of Court opportunities for correction of lower policy maker misinterpretation. At the outer limit in fact, opportunities are completely controlled by the outside forces–that is to say, the Court cannot be sure of the possibility of acting to follow up this enunciated policy and make unmistakable the fact of compliance or lack of compliance. The temporal facts of changes in personnel and, indeed, of resolve, are known to the proposed object of the policy and, together with this problem of continued communication, emerge as a conscious discount of the need for compliance.

CASES

BAKER v. CARR 369 U.S. 186 (1962).
BROWN v. BOARD OF EDUCATION 347 U.S. 483 (1954).
McCOLLUM v. BOARD OF EDUCATION 333 U.S. 203 (1948).
WATSON v. MEMPHIS 373 U.S. 526 (1963).
ZORACH v. CLAUSEN 343 U.S. 306 (1952).

REFERENCES

ARENS, R. and H. LASSWELL (1961) In Defense of Public Order: The Emerging Field of Sanction Law. New York: Columbia Univ. Press.

Association of American Law Schools (1938) Selected Essays on Constitutional Law. Chicago: Foundation Press.

BERGER, P. (1963) Invitation to Sociology. Garden City, N.Y.: Doubleday.

BEUTEL, F. K. (1957) Some Potentialities of Experimental Jurisprudence as a New Branch of Social Science. Lincoln: Univ. of Nebraska Press.

BLAU, P. and W. R. SCOTT (1962) Formal Organizations. San Francisco: Chandler.

BORKIN, J. (1962) The Corrupt Judge. New York: C. N. Potter.

CARDOZO, B. N. (1947) "Paradoxes of legal science," pp. 251-337 in M. Hall (ed.) Selected Writings of Benjamin Nathan Cardozo. New York: Fallon.

CARLIN, J. (1962) Lawyers on Their Own. New Brunswick, N.J.: Rutgers Univ. Press.

CLINARD, M. B. (1952) The Black Market. New York: Holt, Rinehart.

COHEN, J. et al. (1958) Parental Authority. New Brunswick, N.J.: Rutgers Univ. Press.

DIXON, R. G., Jr. (1951) "Public power and critical labor disputes." J. of Politics 13 (November): 511-535.

--- (1949) "Tripartitism in the national war labor board." Industrial and Labor Relations Rev. 2 (April): 372-390.

DURKHEIM, E. (1951) Suicide: A Study in Sociology. (J. A. Spaulding and G. Simpson, translators). New York: Free Press.

EDELMAN, M. (1958) "Interest representation and policy choice in labor law administration." Labor Law J. 9 (March): 218-226.

Encyclopedia Britannica (1960) "Prohibition." Volume 18: 566-570.

ETZIONI, A. (1962) Complex Organizations: A Sociological Reader. New York: Holt, Rinehart & Winston.

FRANK, J. P. (1958) Marble Palace: The Supreme Court in American Life. New York: Alfred A. Knopf.

HARTUNG, F. E. (1953) "Common and discrete group values." J. of Social Psychology 38 (August): 3-22.

JAMMER, M. (1963) Concepts of Force. New York: Harper.

KAUFMAN, H. (1960) The Forest Ranger. Baltimore: Johns Hopkins Univ. Press.

KRISLOV, S. (1963) "What is interest? The answers of Bentley, MacIver and Pound." Western Pol. Q. 16 (December): 830-843.

LANDIS, J. (1958) "The study of legislation in law schools," p. 907 in H. M. Hart and A. M. Sacks (eds.) The Legal Process: Basic Problems in the Making and Application of Law. Cambridge: Harvard University. (tentative edition.)

LASSWELL, H. and A. KAPLAN (1950) Power and Society. New Haven: Yale Univ. Press.

MACAULAY, S. (1963) "Non-contractual relations in business: a preliminary study." Amer. Soc. Rev. 28 (February): 55-67.

MILLER, A. S. (1965) "On the need for 'impact analysis' of Supreme Court decisions." Georgetown Law J. 53 (Winter): 365-401.

New York Times (1963) June 21: 100.

OSBORNE, G. R. (1963) "The NAACP in Alabama," pp. 149-203 in C. H. Pritchett and A. F. Westin (eds.) The Third Branch of Government: Eight Cases in Constitutional Politics. New York: Harcourt, Brace & World.

PACKER, H. L. (1962) "Review of Arens and Lasswell, *In Defense of Public Order.*" Univ. of Chicago Law Rev. 29 (Spring): 586-593.

PARSONS, T. (1962) "The law and social control," pp. 56-72 in W. Evan (ed.) Law and Sociology. New York: Free Press.

PATRIC, G. (1957) "The impact of a court decision: aftermath of the McCollum case." J. of Public Law 6 (Fall): 455-464.

PELTASON, J. W. (1961) Fifty-Eight Lonely Men: Federal Judges and School Desegregation. New York: Harcourt, Brace & World.

--- (1955) The Federal Courts in the Political Process. New York: Doubleday.

RICHARDSON, L. F. (1948) "War moods." Psychometrica 13 (September): 147-174; (December): 197-232.

SCHELLING, T. C. (1960) The Strategy of Conflict. Cambridge, Mass.: Harvard Univ. Press.

SCHUBERT, G. (1963) "Judicial attitudes and voting behavior: the 1961 term of the United States Supreme Court." Law and Contemporary Problems 28 (Winter): 100-142.

--- (1962) "The 1960 term of the Court: a psychological analysis." Amer. Pol. Sci. Rev. 56 (March): 90-107.

SCHWARTZ, R. and S. ORLEANS (1967) "On legal sanctions." Univ. of Chicago Law Rev. 34 (Winter): 274-300.

--- and J. H. SKOLNICK (1963) "Televised communication and income tax compliance," pp. 155-165 in M. Arons and M. Mays (eds.) Television and Human Behavior. New York: Appleton-Century-Crofts.

SORAUF, F. J. (1959) "*Zorach* v. *Clauson:* the impact of a Supreme Court decision." Amer. Pol. Sci. Rev. 53 (September): 777-791. (Reprinted in 1963 in C. H. Pritchett and A. Westin [eds.] The Third Branch of Government: Eight Cases in Constitutional Politics. New York: Harcourt, Brace & World.)

STOUFFER, S. (1955) Communism, Conformity and Civil Liberties. New York: Doubleday.

SUCHMAN, E., J. P. DEAN, and R. WILLIAMS, Jr. (1958) Desegregation: Some Propositions and Research Suggestions. New York: Anti-Defamation League of B'nai B'rith.

SUTHERLAND, E. H. (1961) White Collar Crime. New York: Holt.

Wickersham Commission (1931) Official Records of the National Commission on Law Observation.

ZEISEL, H., H. KALVEN, Jr., and B. BUCHHOLZ (1959) Delay in the Courts. Boston: Little, Brown.

Bibliography

The entries which follow in this bibliography are intended to provide some feel for the wide range of social science material relevant to a concern with compliance. That such a wealth of information and perspectives is available is a conclusion to which the editors quickly came in addressing the topic of compliance. We have consciously attempted to reflect that conclusion here, as well as in our introduction to this volume and in the wide-ranging selection of articles. We have a second, related assumption, too, noted in the introduction. It appears to us that the lack of any comprehensive and carefully outlined theory of compliance is in part due to the fact that scholarly efforts have been largely noncumulative: the phenomena of obedience and revolt have been treated as parallel, never-intersecting lines by different professions.

With these considerations in mind, we rejected the idea of presenting a bibliography which categorized entries according to the discipline from which they came and to which they were addressed. For some articles, that would have been somewhat difficult; for others, unfair and unduly restricting, in that they have rich implications for scholars in related fields. And this last consideration applied to all of the entries, with special force, perhaps, for a work which has hopes of beginning to bridge disciplinary gaps. In most cases, the field will be fairly apparent. But where it fruitfully is not – where, for example, a scholar from one field finds the bibliography useful in discovering some related work from another field – our decision will be justified.

In place of an indication of the discipline to which the work "belongs," then, and also in order to provide an economical annotation system, we have coded the entries to indicate some relevant aspects of the work. (In moving to such a system we were frankly influenced by Blau and Scott's [1962] coded bibliographical annotations, which we felt did a good job of indicating the nature of the works listed there.) The code itself is presented in detail below.

Four aspects of each study are indicated: *type of study,* meaning by that primarily methodology; *focus* of the study, indicating under that section whether, e.g., attention is directed toward the characteristics of nations or of individuals; *mechanism for gaining compliance,* where a key concern for this topic is laid out; and *conceived as contributing toward,* where we mean to distinguish whether the work has primary implications for empirical theory, policy, or normative theory, or is straight-forwardly a piece concerned with substantive knowledge or description.

Type of Study

LA	Laboratory experiments on animals, usually concerned with learning theory
LI	Laboratory experiments using individuals as subjects
LG	Laboratory experiments concerned with groups, group behaviors, and pressures
CL	Clinical observation technique in a controlled or largely controlled environment
QSR	Questionnaires and survey research
I	In-depth interview
QCS	Quantified case study or quasi-experiment
FE	Field experiment or other experimenter-induced change in a nonlaboratory situation
PO	Participant observation or other field observation
ADA	Focus on aggregate data and associations over time, not on specific decision or circumstance
E	Empirical study employing other methodology
CS	Case study focusing on nonquantitative phenomena
H	Historical study not classifiable as a case study
N	Philosophical and normative studies
T	Theoretical and methodological analyses
D	Discussions, surveys of the literature
R	Readers, texts, collections not classifiable into a single category

Focus

1	Individual
2	Groups
3	System perspective, social structure
4	Subsystem comparison
5	Cross-national and system comparative
6	Concept analysis, usually philosophical
7	Multiple foci

Mechanism for Gaining Compliance

*	Indicates that the article deals directly with the concept of compliance
m	Maturation, human development
ms	Socialization
l	Avoidance learning, reinforcement, identification
s	Sanctions, rewards, deterrents in general (informal structure)
grs	General rules structure: mainly philosophical considerations
sp	Specialized law structures
b	Bargaining
f	Feedback effects on system, change in system demands for compliance
e	Environmental variables as causal agents
o	Other, not discussed specifically

Conceived as Contributing Toward

I	Empirical theory
II	Policy and reform
III	Substantive knowledge and description
IV	Development of normative theory

It will be quickly seen that these are not all the things we could have said about each entry. The code is not exhaustive in that sense and is probably not perfectly exhaustive within each category either. We have tried to cast our net broadly in order to be able to say something meaningful about each entry; the reader will have to judge for himself how well we have succeeded with regard to exhaustiveness and mutual exclusiveness, as well as sheer utility. Of these, the last-mentioned seems paramount: we are not as concerned with the elegance of the scheme as we are that it be useful.

The code uses upper-case letters to indicate type of study, numbers for the focus, lower-case letters for mechanism for gaining compliance, and Roman numerals to indicate toward what the study appears to contribute. The categories are separated by slashes: an example would be Koeppen's article in this volume, coded as *T,D/1/ms/I. The interpretation would be that the article is a contribution to empirical theory (I), focusing on individual (1) socialization (ms), and is primarily a theoretical analysis (T) which includes a survey of literature (D). The asterisk indicates that Koeppen's article overtly addresses the problem of compliance. In order to include as much information as possible, more than one entry per category is used without hesitation where appropriate. Entries are ordered, the first representing the primary thrust or importance of the work, with subsequent entries in a category representing sub-topics, purposes, or uses. Koeppen's article thus is coded T,D for the category "Type of Study." The major points she makes are theoretical, but a good discussion of relevant literature is an important part of the exercise.

More than one coder has gone over a number of the entries, and though a formal measure of intercoder agreement was not taken, such agreement is gratifyingly high. Partly this is due to an attempt to be inclusive, to include more than one code per category where appropriate. But we also take it to mean that we are tapping a meaningful set of characteristics. Again, the criterion on which we would prefer to be judged is whether something useful and meaningful has been said, not whether some number of entries might have been coded somewhat differently. There were a few clearly appropriate items which proved to be unavailable for our inspection. They are included here without a coded annotation in the hope that they will enhance the utility of this listing. We are indebted to Ann Walcott and Joseph Price for special help in preparing the coded entries.

Keith O. Boyum, Jerry N. Clark,
Samuel Krislov, and Roger C. Shaefer

ADELSON, J., B. GREEN and R. O'NEIL (1969) "The growth of the idea of law in adolescence." Developmental Psychology 1 (July): 327-332. I/1/m/I

ADELSON, J. and R. O'NEIL (1966) "Growth of political ideas in adolescence: the sense of community." J. of Personality and Social Psychology 4 (September): 295-306. QSR/1/ms/III

ADORNO, T. et al. (1950) The Authoritarian Personality. New York: Harper. QSR,I/1/ms/III

ALLEN, F. A. (1964) The Borderland of Criminal Justice. Chicago: Univ. of Chicago Press. N/6/s,grs/IV,II

ALLPORT, G. W. (1954) The Nature of Prejudice. Reading, Mass.: Addison-Wesley. R/1-5/o/I

ALMOND, G. and S. VERBA (1963) The Civic Culture. Princeton: Princeton Univ. Press. QSR/5/ms,o/III

ANDENAES, J. (1952) "General prevention: illusion or reality?" J. of Criminal Law, Criminology and Police Sci. 43 (July-August): 176-198. N/3/s/II

ARENS, R. and H. LASSWELL (1961) In Defense of Public Order: The Emerging Field of Sanction Law. New York: Columbia Univ. Press. ADA,T/1,3,4/s,sp,f/II,IV,III

ARONFREED, J. (1969) "The concept of internalization," pp. 263-324 in D. A. Goslin (ed.) Handbook of Socialization Theory and Research. Chicago: Rand McNally. T/1/ms/IV,III

--- (1968) Conduct and Conscience: The Socialization of Internalized Control Over Behavior. New York: Academic Press. T/1,4/s/I

--- (1961) "The nature, variety, and social patterning of moral responses to transgression." J. of Abnormal and Social Psychology. 63 (September): 223-240. CL/3/ms/III

ARROW, K. (1951) Social Choice and Individual Values. New York: John Wiley. T/1/o/I

ASCH, S. E. (1960) "Effects of group pressure upon the modification and distortion of judgments," pp. 189-200 in D. Cartwright and A. Zander (eds.) Group Dynamics. Evanston, Ill.: Row, Peterson. LG/1/s/I

AUSTIN, J. (1832) The Province of Jurisprudence Determined. London: J. Murray. *N/1,3/s,grs/IV

AZRIN, N. H. and W. C. HOLTZ (1965) "Punishment," pp. 380-447 in W. K. Honig (ed.) Operant Behavior: Areas of Research and Application. New York: Appleton. D,T/4/o/I

BACON, M. K., I. L. CHILD, and H. BARRY III (1963) "A cross-cultural study of the correlates of crime." J. of Abnormal and Social Psychology 66 (April): 291-300. ADA/5/ms/III

BALDWIN, A. E. (1969) "A cognitive theory of socialization," pp. 339-345 in D. A. Goslin (ed.) Handbook of Socialization Theory and Research. Chicago: Rand McNally. T/1/ms/III,I

BALL, H. V. (1960) "Social structure and rent control violations." Amer. J. of Sociology 65 (May): 598-604. QSR/3/sp/III

BALL, J. C. (1955) "The deterrence concept in criminology and law." J. of Criminal Law, Criminology and Police Sci. 46 (September-October): 347-354. T,D/3/ms/I,III

BANDURA, A. (1969) "Social learning theory of identificatory processes." pp. 213-262 in D. A. Goslin (ed.) Handbook of Socialization Theory and Research. Chicago: Rand McNally. T, LI/1/ms/III,I

––– and F. J. McDONALD (1963) "The influence of social reinforcement and the behavior of models in shaping children's moral judgments." J. of Abnormal and Social Psychology 67 (September): 274-282. LI/1/l,m/I

––– and R. H. WALTERS (1963a) "Aggression," pp. 364-415 in National Society for the Study of Education Yearbook, Part I. Chicago: Distributed by Univ. of Chicago Press. D/1/o/I

––– (1963b) Social Learning and Personality Development. New York: Holt, Rinehart & Winston. T,D/1/l,ms,m/I

BARKUN, M. (1968) Law without Sanctions. New Haven: Yale Univ. Press. T/3,5/e,sp/III,IV

BARNARD, C. I. (1938) The Functions of the Executive. Cambridge: Harvard Univ. Press. CS/2/s/III,I

BARRETT, E. L., Jr. (1962) "Police practices and the law – from arrest to release or charge." California Law Rev. 50 (March): 11-55. ADA/4,2/sp,b,f/II,III

BARTH, T. (1968) "Perception and acceptance of Supreme Court decisions at the state and local level." J. of Public Law 17 (June): 308-350. QSR/1/o/I

BAUER, R. A. [ed.] (1966) Social Indicators. Cambridge: MIT Press. T/3/o/I,II

––– (1966) "Detection and anticipation of impact: the nature of the task," pp. 1-67 in R. A. Bauer (ed.) Social Indicators. Cambridge: MIT Press. T/3/f/I

BAUMRIND, D. (1964) "Some thoughts on ethics of research: after reading Milgram's behavioral study of obedience." Amer. Psychologist 19: 421-423. T,N/1/oI

BAY, C. (1958) The Structure of Freedom. Palo Alto: Stanford Univ. Press. N/6,1/grs/IV

BEANEY, W. and E. N. BEISER (1964) "Prayer and politics: the impact of *Engel* and *Schempp* on the political process." J. of Public Law 13, 2: 475-503. CS/2/o/III

BECKER, H. S. (1963) Outsiders: Study in the Sociology of Deviance. New York: Free Press.

BECKER, T. L. [ed.] (1969) The Impact of Supreme Court Decisions: Empirical Studies. New York: Oxford Univ. Press. R/3,4/sp,b/I

BEISER, E. N. (1968) "A comparative analysis of state and federal judicial behavior: the reapportionment cases." Amer. Pol. Sci. Rev. 62 (September): 788-795. E/1/l/III

BENNETT, J. W. and M. M. TUMIN (1948) Social Life. New York: Alfred A. Knopf. R/1,2,3/o/III

BERGER, M. (1952) Equality by Statute. New York: Columbia Univ. Press. H/3/sp/III

BERKOWITZ, L. (1964) The Development of Motives and Values in the Child. New York: Basic Books.

——— (1962) Aggression: A Social Psychological Analysis. New York: McGraw-Hill. T,D/1,2/l/I

BEUTEL, F. K. (1957) Some Potentialities of Experimental Jurisprudence as a New Branch of Social Science. Lincoln: Univ. of Nebraska Press. T,LG,D/2,3,6/sp,f/I,III

BICKEL, A. M. (1970) The Supreme Court and the Idea of Progress. New York: Harper & Row. N/6/o/II,IV

BIRKBY, R. (1966) "The Supreme Court and the Bible Belt: Tennessee reaction to the *Schempp* decision." Midwest J. of Pol. Sci. 10 (August): 304-319. QSR/4/e/I,III

BLAU, P. (1964) Exchange and Power in Social Life. New York: John Wiley. T,D/1,2,3/s,l/I

——— and W. R. SCOTT (1962) Formal Organizations. San Francisco: Chandler. T,D/3,2/s/I

BLAUSTEIN, A. P. and C. C. FERGUSON (1957) Desegregation and the Law. New Brunswick, N. J.: Rutgers Univ. Press. CS/2/o/III

BLUMBERG, A. S. (1967) Criminal Justice. Chicago: Quadrangle Books. CS/1,2/b/II,III

BLUMROSEN, A. W. (1965) "Antidiscrimination laws in action in New Jersey: a law-sociology study." Rutgers Law Rev. 19 (Winter): 189-287. QSR,T/3,2,1/sp,f,ms,e/II,III

BOLES, D. F. (1965) The Bible, Religion and the Public Schools. Ames: Iowa State Univ. Press. H,E/4/sp,grs/III,II

BORDUA, D. (1966) The Police: Six Sociological Essays. New York: John Wiley. R/3,4/sp,s,l,ms,e/I,III

BOWERS, W. J. (1968) "Normative constraints on deviant behavior in the college context." Sociometry 31 (Winter): 370-385. QSR/1,2/s,l/I

——— (1964) Student Dishonesty and its Control in College. Bureau of Applied Social Research, Columbia University, New York. QSR/1,2/s,o/I,III,II

BREHM, J. W. and A. R. COHEN (1962) Explorations in Cognitive Dissonance. New York: John Wiley. T,LI/1/1/I

BRIM, O. G., Jr. (1963) "Socialization through the life cycle." Russell Sage Foundation. (mimeo) T/1/ms/IV

——— (1957) "The Parent child relation as a social system: I. Parent and child roles." Child Development 28 (September): 343-364. ADA/1/m,ms/I

——— and S. WHEELER (1966) Socialization After Childhood. New York: John Wiley. T/1,2/ms,m/I

BRINTON, C. (1957) The Anatomy of Revolution. New York: Vintage. E,H/5/e,o/I

BRONFENBRENNER, U. (1963) "Developmental theory in transition," pp. 517-542 in National Society for the Study of Education Yearbook, Part I. Chicago: Distributed by the Univ. of Chicago Press. D,T/1/o/I

--- (1958) "Socialization and social class through time and space," pp. 400-425 in E. Maccoby, T. M. Newcomb, and E. L. Hartley (eds.) Readings in Social Psychology. New York: Holt, Rinehart & Winston. ADA,QSR/2,3/ms/I

BROOM, L. and P. SELZNICK (1968) Sociology. New York: Harper and Row. R

BUCHANAN, J. and G. TULLOCK (1962) The Calculus of Consent. Ann Arbor: Univ. of Michigan Press. T/1,2,3/s,b/I

BUSS, A. (1961) The Psychology of Aggression. New York: John Wiley.

BWY, D. (1968) "Political instability in Latin America: the cross-cultural test of a causal model." Latin American Research Rev. 3 (Spring): 17-66.

BYRNE, D. (1969) "Attitudes and attraction," pp. 35-89 in L. Berkowitz (ed.) Advances in Experimental Social Psychology, Volume 4. New York: Academic Press. ADA,T/1,3/o/I

CAHN, E. (1966) "Law in the consumer perspective," in L. Cahn (ed.) Confronting Injustice: The Edmond Cahn Reader. Boston: Little, Brown. N,ADA/3,2/sp,f/IV

California State Legislature (1968) Deterrent Effects of Criminal Sanctions. Progress report of the Assembly Committee on Criminal Procedure. ADA/1/grs,f/II

CAMPBELL, D. T. and H. L. ROSS (1968) "The Connecticut crackdown on speeding: Time-series data in quasi-experimental analysis." Law and Society Rev. 3 (August): 33-53. QCS/3/sp/II,III

--- and J. C. STANLEY (1963) "Experimental and quasi-experimental designs for research on teaching," pp. 171-246 in N. L. Gage (ed.) Handbook of Research on Teaching. Chicago: Rand McNally. T/3/e/I

CARLSON, E. R. (1956) "Attitude change through modification of attitude structure." J. of Abnormal and Social Psychology 52 (March): 256-261. LI/1/l/III

CARMEN, I. (1966) Movies, Censorship and the Law. Ann Arbor: Univ. of Michigan Press. I/2,4/sp/III

CARTWRIGHT, D. [ed.] (1959) Studies in Social Power. Ann Arbor: Univ. of Michigan Press. R,T/1,2/s/I

CHAMBLISS, W. J. [ed.] (1969) Crime and the Legal Process. New York: McGraw-Hill. R/3/grs/III

--- (1967) "Types of deviance and the effectiveness of legal sanctions." Wisconsin Law Rev. 1967 (Summer): 703-719. T/3/s/I

——— (1966) "The deterrent influence of punishment." Crime and Delinquency 12 (January): 70-75. I/1,3/s,f/I

CLARK, A. L. and J. GIBBS (1965) "Social control: a reformulation." Social Problems 12 (Spring): 398-414. T/3/grs/I

CLAUSEN, J. A. [ed.] (1968) Socialization and Society. Boston: Little, Brown. R/1-5/ms/III,I

——— (1968) "A historical and comparative view of socialization theory and research," pp. 18-72 in J. A. Clausen (ed.) Socialization and Society. Boston: Little, Brown. D/1-3/ms/III,I

——— and J. R. WILLIAMS (1963) "Sociological correlates of child behavior, Part I." pp. 62-107 in National Society for the Study of Education, Child Psychology. Chicago: Univ. of Chicago Press.

CLINARD, M. B. (1964) Anomie and Deviant Behavior: A Discussion and Critique. New York: Free Press. R,D/3/o/I

——— (1963) Sociology and Deviant Behavior. New York: Holt, Rinehart & Winston. R/1,2,3/o/III

——— (1952) The Black Market. New York: Rinehart. E/4/sp/III,II

COCH, L. and J. R. FRENCH (1948) "Overcoming resistance to change." Human Relations 1 (August): 512-532. FE/2/f/I

COHEN, A. K. (1966) Deviance and Control. Englewood Cliffs, N. J.: Prentice-Hall. D/1,2,3

COHEN, J. et al. (1958) Parental Authority. New Brunswick, N. J.: Rutgers Univ. Press. QSR/1,3/sp,f/I

COHEN, L. J. (1962) "A critical note on *The Concept of Law* by H. L. A. Hart." Mind 71 (July): 395-412. N,T/6/grs,sp/IV

COLEMAN, J. S. (1966a) "Foundations for a theory of collective decision." Amer. J. of Sociology 71 (May): 615-627.

——— (1966b) "Individual interests and collective action." Papers in Non-market Decision-making, I. Charlottesville: University of Virginia Center of Political Economy.

COSER, L. (1967) Continuities in the Study of Social Conflict. New York: Free Press. T,R/3/o/I

——— (1956) The Functions of Social Conflict. New York: Free Press. T/2/s/I

COUNTRYMAN, V. (1964) "Bankruptcy boom." Harvard Law Rev. 77 (June): 1452-1461. ADA/3/o/II

CRAIN, R. L. et al. (1968) The Politics of School Desegregation: Comparative Case Studies of Community Structure and Policy-Making. Chicago: Aldine. CS/4/f/III

CRESSEY, D. R. (1964) Delinquency, Crime and Differential Association. The Hague: Nijhoff. R

——— (1953) Other People's Money: A Study in the Social Psychology of Embezzlement. New York: Free Press. 1,CS,T/1,3/l,s/I,III

——— and D. A. WARD (1969) Delinquency, Crime and Social Process. New York: Harper & Row. R/3/o/III

CULP, M. S. (1929) "A survey of proposals to limit or destroy the power of judicial review by the Supreme Court of the United States." Indiana Law J. 4 (March, April): 386-398, 474-490. H,D/4/sp,f/III,II

DARLEY, J. M. and B. LATANE (1968a) "Bystander intervention in emergencies: diffusion of responsibility." J. of Personality and Social Psychology 8 (April): 377-383. LI,LG/1,2/o/I

——— (1968b) "When will people help in a crisis?" Psychology Today 2 (December): 54-57. T,LG/1,2/s,l/I

DARVALL, F. (1934) Popular Disturbances and Public Order in Regency England. London: Oxford Univ. Press. H/3/o/III

DAVIS, F. J., H. H. FOSTER, Jr., C. R. JEFFERY, and E. DAVIS (1962) Society and the Law. New York: Free Press. R/3/sp/III

DAWSON, R. E. (1966) "Political socialization," pp. 4–11 in J. A. Robinson (ed.) Political Science Annual, Volume I. Indianapolis: Bobbs-Merrill. T,D/1,3/ms/III

——— and K. PREWITT (1969) Political Socialization. Boston: Little, Brown. R/1-5/ms/III

DEMOS, R. (1957) "Some reflections on threats and punishments." Rev. of Metaphysics 11 (December): 224-236. N,E/1,6/s/IV,I

DENNIS, J. (1968) "Major problems of political socialization research." Midwest J. of Pol. Sci. 12 (February): 85–114. T/5/ms/I

DENTON, J. H. (1967) "The effectiveness of state anti-discrimination laws in the United States." Race 9 (July): 85–92. CS/3/sp/II

DEUTSCH, M. and R. M. KRAUSS (1962) "Studies of interpersonal bargaining." J. of Conflict Resolution 6 (March): 52-76. LG/2/s,b/I

DEVLIN, P. (1965) The Enforcement of Morals. London: Oxford Univ. Press.

DIENES, C. T. (1970) "Judges, legislators and social change." Amer. Behavioral Scientist 13 (March-April): 511-521. T/4,3/o/I

DIXON, R. G., Jr. (1968) Democratic Representation: Reapportionment in Law and Politics. New York: Oxford Univ. Press. E/2,4/grs,b,f,e/II,III,IV

——— (1951) "Public power and critical labor disputes." J. of Politics 13 (November): 511–535. H/2/1,s/I,IV

DOLBEARE, K. M. (1967) Trial Courts in Urban Politics. New York: John Wiley. QCS/2,3/o/III

——— and P. HAMMOND (1969) "Local elites, the impact of judicial decisions and the process of change." Presented at the 1969 meeting of the American Political Science Assn. I,CS/2,4/l,s/I,III

——— (1968) "The political party basis of attitudes toward the Supreme Court." Public Opinion Q. 32 (Spring): 16-30. QSR/2,3/l/III

DOLGER, L. and J. GINANDES (1946) "Children's attitudes toward discipline as related to sociometric status." J. of Experimental Education 15 (December): 161–165. QSR,I/1,4/ms/I

DOLLARD, J., N. MILLER, L. DOOB, O. MOWRER, and R. SEARS (1939) Frustration and Aggression. New Haven: Yale Univ. Press. T/1/o/I

DOWNS, A. (1967) An Economic Theory of Democracy. New York: Harper & Row. T/1,6,3/s,b/I

DROR, Y. P. (1970) "Law as a tool of directed social change: a framework for policy-making." Amer. Behavioral Scientist 13 (March-April): 553–559. T/6/sp/I

DWORKIN, R. M. (1967) "The model of rules." Univ. of Chicago Law Rev. 35 (Autumn): 14–46. N/6/grs/IV

DURKHEIM, E. (1964) The Division of Labor in Society. New York: Free Press. T/1,3/grs,l/IV,I

---(1951) Suicide: A Study in Sociology. New York: Free Press. [J. A. Spaulding and G. Simpson, translators] ADA,H/1,3/o/I,III

EASTON, D. (1965) A Systems Analysis of Political Life. New York: John Wiley. T/3/o/I

--- and J. DENNIS (1969) Children in the Political System. New York: McGraw-Hill. QSR/3/ms/I,III

--- and R. HESS (1962) "The child's political world." Midwest J. of Pol. Sci. 6 (August): 229-246. QSR/1/ms/III

--- (1961) "Youth and the political system," pp. 226-251 in S. M. Lipset and L. Lowenthal (eds.) Culture and Social Character: The Work of David Riesman Reviewed. New York: Free Press. T/3/ms/III

ECKHARDT, K. W. (1968) "Deviance, visibility, and legal action: the duty to support." Social Problems 15 (Spring): 470-477. ADA/3/sp/III

ECKSTEIN, H. (1964) Internal War. New York: Free Press. R/3/o/I,III

EDELMAN, M. (1964) The Symbolic Uses of Politics. Urbana: Univ. of Illinois Press. N/1,2,3/o/I,IV

ELDER, G. (1963) "Parental power legitimation and its effects on the adolescent." Sociometry 26 (March): 50-65. QSR/1/l/I

ELLIOT, S. D. (1957–1958) "Court-curbing proposals in Congress." Notre Dame Lawyer 33 (August): 597-616. ADA,H,D/4,3/sp,f/II,III

ELSEN, S. H. and A. ROSETT (1967) "Protections for the suspect under Miranda." Columbia Law Rev. 67 (April): 645-670. CS/1,3,4/f,sp/II

ERIKSON, E. (1969) Gandhi's Truth. New York: Norton. CS/1/m,o/III,IV

--- (1968) Identity, Youth and Crisis. New York: Norton. CL,H/1/m/III,IV

--- (1963) Childhood and Society. New York: Norton. CL,H/1/m/III,IV

--- (1958) Young Man Luther: A Study in Psychoanalysis and History. New York: Norton. CS/1/m/III

ERIKSON, K. T. (1966) The Wayward Puritans. New York: John Wiley. H,T,D/2,3/e,l,s/III,IV

--- (1962) "Notes on the sociology of deviance." Social Problems 9 (Spring): 307-314. T/3/f/I

ETZIONI, A. (1962) Complex Organizations: A Sociological Reader. New York: Holt, Rinehart & Winston. R,T/1,2,3/s,grs,b/I

——— (1961) A Comparative Analysis of Complex Organizations: On Power, Involvement, and Their Correlates. New York: Free Press. T/2,3/o/I

EVAN, W. M. [ed.] (1962) Law and Sociology. New York: Free Press. R/3/o/III

EVERSON, D. H. [ed.] (1968) The Supreme Court as Policy Maker. Carbondale: Southern Illinois University, Public Affairs Research Bureau. R,CS

FAIA, M. A. (1967) "Alienation, structural strain, and political deviancy: a test of Merton's hypothesis." Social Problems 14 (Spring): 389-413. QSR/3/grs/I

FEEST, J. (1968) "Compliance with legal regulations: observation of stop sign behavior." Law and Society Rev. 2 (May): 447-461. PO/1/s,l,sp/I

FEIERABEND, I. and R. FEIERABEND (1966) "Aggressive behaviors within polities, 1948-1962: a cross-national study." J. of Conflict Resolution 10 (September): 249-271. ADA/5/e/I

—————— and B. NESVOLD (1969) "Social change and political violence: cross-national patterns," pp. 497-542 in H. Graham and T. R. Gurr (eds.) Violence in America Report to the National Commission on the Causes and Prevention of Violence. Washington, D. C.: Government Printing Office. ADA,T/5/e/I

FESTINGER, L. (1964) Conflict, Decision and Dissonance. Stanford: Stanford Univ. Press. LG,T/1/l/I

——— (1957) A Theory of Cognitive Dissonance. Stanford: Stanford Univ. Press. T,D,LI/1/l/I

——— (1950) "Informal social communication." Psych. Rev. 57: 271-282. T/2/s/I

——— A. PEPITONE, and T. NEWCOMB (1952) "Some consequences of de-individuation in a group." J. of Abnormal and Social Psychology. 47 (April): 382-389. LG/1,2/1/I

FESTINGER, L., S. SCHACHTER, and K. BACK (1960) "The operation of group standards," pp. 241-259 in D. Cartwright and A. Zander (eds.) Group Dynamics. Evanston, Ill.: Row, Peterson. QCS/2/s/I

——— (1950) Social Pressures in Informal Groups: A Study of a Housing Project. New York: Harper. QSR,PO/2/s/I

FISHBEIN, M. (1965) "A consideration of beliefs, attitudes, and their relationship, " pp. 107-120 in I. Steiner and M. Fishbein (eds.) Current Studies in Social Psychology. New York: Holt, Rinehart & Winston. T/1/o/III,I

FISKE, M. (1959) Book Selection and Censorship. Berkeley: Univ. of California Press. H/1,2,3/s,grs/II

FLANIGAN, W. and E. FOGELMAN (1970) "Patterns of political violence in comparative historical perspective." Comparative Politics 3: 1-20. ADA/5/e,f/I,III

FLAVELL, J. H. (1963) The Developmental Psychology of Jean Piaget. Princeton: D. Van Nostrand. T/1/ms/I,III

FOOTE, C. [ed.] (1966) Studies on Bail. Philadelphia: Univ. of Pennsylvania Law Rev. R,CS/5/o/II,III

FRANK, J. P. (1958) Marble Palace: The Supreme Court in American Life. New York: Alfred A. Knopf. ADA/2,4,1/sp,s,b/III

FRANKFURTER, F. and J. LANDIS (1927) The Business of the Supreme Court. New York: Macmillan. H/4/grs,f/III

FRANKLIN, M. A., R. H. CHANIN, and I. MARK (1961) "Accidents, money, and the law: a study of the economics of personal injury litigation." Columbia Law Rev. 61 (January): 1-39. ADA/3,1/sp/II,III

FRENCH, J. R. and B. H. RAVEN (1959) "The bases of social power," pp. 150-167 in D. Cartwright (ed.) Studies in Social Power. Ann Arbor: Univ. of Michigan Institute for Social Research. T/2,1/s/I

FRIEDELBAUM, S. H. (1952) "Baker v. Carr: the new doctrine of judicial intervention and its implications for American federalism." Univ. of Chicago Law Rev. 29 (Summer): 673-704. CS/3,4/sp,f/II

FRIEDMAN, L. M. (1965) Contract Law in America: A Social and Economic Case Study. Madison: Univ. of Wisconsin Press.

FULLER, L. (1964) Morality of Law. New Haven: Yale Univ. Press.

GAMSON, W. (1968) Power and Discontent. Homewood, Ill.: Dorsey. T/3/s/I

GATES, R. L. (1962–1964) The Making of Massive Resistance: Virginia's Politics of Public School Desegregation, 1954–1956. Chapel Hill: Univ. of North Carolina Press. CS/1,2/o/III

GERARD, H. B. (1953) "The effect of different dimensions of disagreement on the communication process in small groups." Human Relations 6 (May): 249-271. LG/2/s/I

GERSCHENKRON, A. (1964) "Reflections on economic aspects of revolutions," pp. 180-204 in H. Eckstein (ed.) Internal War. New York: Free Press. CS/3/e/III,I

GERTH, H. H. and C. W. MILLS [eds.] (1958) From Max Weber: Essays in Sociology. New York: Oxford Univ. Press. R/7/o/I

GIBBS, J. P. (1968a) "Crime, punishment and deterrence." Southwest Social Sci. Q. 48 (March): 515-530. ADA/4/sp/II

--- (1968b) "Definitions of law and empirical questions." Law and Society Rev. 2 (May): 429–446. T,D/6/sp/I

--- (1966a) "Conceptions of deviant behavior: the old and the new." Pacific Soc. Rev. (Spring): 9-14. T/1,2,3/o/I

--- (1966b) "Crime and the sociology of law." Sociology and Social Research 51 (October): 23-38. T/5/sp/1

--- (1966c) "Sanctions." Social Problems 14 (Fall): 147-159 T/3/s/I

GILLESPIE, J. and B. NESVOLD [eds.] (1970) Macro-Quantitative Analysis: Conflict, Development, and Democratization. Vol. 1. Sage Readers in Cross-National Research. Beverly Hills: Sage Pubns. ADA/3,5/s,f/I,III

GLASER, D. (1960) "Differential association and criminological prediction." Social Problems 8 (Spring): 6-13. T/1/l/I

---(1955) "Criminality theories and behavioral images." Amer. J. of Sociology 61: 433–444.

GOFFMAN, E. (1959) "The moral career of the mental patient." pp. 88-98 in E. Rubington and M. S. Weinberg (eds.) Deviance: The Interactionist Perspective. New York: Macmillan. E/1/o/I,III

GOLDSTEIN, A. S. (1967) The Insanity Defense. New Haven: Yale Univ. Press. T,H/1/sp/II

GOLDSTEIN, J. "Police discretion not to invoke the criminal process: low-visibility decisions in the administration of justice." Yale Law J. 60,4: 543-594. PO,T/2,3/o/II,III

GOSLIN, D. A. (1969) Handbook of Socialization Theory and Research. Chicago: Rand McNally. R/1,2,3,4,5/ms/III

GOTTLIEB, G. (1968) The Logic of Choice: An Investigation of the Concepts of Rule and Rationality. London: George Allen & Unwin. N/6/grs/III

GOULDNER, A. W. (1960) "The norm of reciprocity: a preliminary statement." Amer. Soc. Rev. 25 (April): 161-179. T,D/1,3/s/I

GRAHAM, H. D. (1967) Crisis in Print: Desegregation and the Press in Tennessee. Nashville: Vanderbilt Univ. Press. H/4/o/III

--- and T. R. GURR (1969) Violence in America, Report to the National Commission on the Causes and Prevention of Violence. Washington, D. C.: Government Printing Office. R

GREENBERG, E. S. (1969) "Children and the political community: a comparison across racial lines." Canadian J. of Pol. Sci. 2 (December): 471-492. QSR/1,2/ms/I,III

GREENSTEIN, F. I. (1965) Children and Politics. New Haven: Yale Univ. Press. I,QSR/1,2/ms/I,III

--- (1960) "The benevolent leader: children's images of political authority." Amer. Pol. Sci. Rev. 54 (December): 934-943. I,QSR/1/ms/III

GREY, D. L. (1968) The Supreme Court and the Mass Media. Evanston, Ill.: Northwestern Univ. Press. I/2/o/III

GRIFFITHS, J. and R. E. AYERS (1967) "A postscript to the Miranda project: interrogation of draft protesters." Yale Law J. 77 (December): 300-319. I/1/o/II,III

GRIMSHAW, A. (1960) "Urban racial violence in the U. S." Amer. J. of Sociology 66 (September): 109–120. H,E/3/ms/III

GROSSMAN, J. B. (1970) "The Supreme Court and social change: a preliminary inquiry." Amer. Behavioral Scientist 13 (March–April): 535–551. ADA/1,3/l,sp,f/III

--- and J. TANENHAUS [eds.] (1969) Frontiers of Judicial Research. New York: John Wiley. R

GUETZKOW, H. [ed.] (1951) Groups, Leadership and Men. Pittsburgh: Carnegie Press. R/2,1/s/I

GULICK, L. and L. URWICK [eds.] (1937) Papers on the Science of Administration. New York: Institute of Public Administration. R/2,3/grs/I,III

GURR, T. R. (1970) Why Men Rebel. Princeton: Princeton Univ. Press. ADA,T/5/l,e,f/I

——— (1969) "A comparative study of civil strife," pp. 443-495 in H. Graham and T. Gurr (eds.) Violence in America, Report to the National Commission on the Causes and Prevention of Violence. Washington, D. C.: Government Printing Office. ADA/5,2/s/I

——— (1968) "Causal model of civil strife: a comparative analysis using new indices." Amer. Pol. Sci. Rev. 62 (December): 1104–1124. ADA/5/f,e/I,III

——— (1967) "The conditions of civil violence." Research Monograph 28. Princeton: Center of International Studies. ADA/5/e/I

HART, H. L. A. (1968) Punishment and Responsibility: Essays in the Philosophy of Law. New York: Oxford Univ. Press.

——— (1963) Law, Liberty, and Morality. Stanford: Stanford Univ. Press.

——— (1961) The Concept of Law. Oxford: Oxford Univ. Press. N/1,3/s,grs,sp/IV

Harvard Law Review [Note] (1958) "Congressional reversal of Supreme Court decisions: 1945–1957." 71 (May): 1324–1337. ADA/4/sp,f/III

———[Note] (1958) "Implementation of desegregation by the lower courts." 71 (January): 486–502. *ADA/4/f,sp/II,III

———[Note] (1954) "Evasion of Supreme Court mandates in cases remanded to state courts since 1941." 67 (May): 1251–1259. ADA,D/4/f,sp/II,III

HEIDER, F. (1958) The Psychology of Interpersonal Relations. New York: John Wiley. LG/1,2/s/I

HESS, R. D. (1963) "The socialization of attitudes toward political authority: some cross-national comparisons." International Social Sci. J. 15, 4: 542–559. QSR/5/ms/III

——— and D. EASTON (1962) "The role of the elementary school in political socialization." School Rev. 70 (Autumn): 257–265. T/3/ms/III

——— (1960) "The child's changing image of the president." Public Opinion Q. 24 (Winter): 632–644. QSR/1/ms/III

HESS, R. D. and J. L. TAPP (1969) Authority, Rules and Aggression: A Cross-National Study of the Socialization of Children into Compliance Systems: Part I. Washington, D. C.: U. S. Department of Health, Education and Welfare. QSR/5/ms/I

HESS, R. D. and J. V. TORNEY (1967) The Development of Political Attitudes in Children. Chicago: Aldine. QSR/1,2/ms/III,I

HIRSCH, H. and L. DONOHEW (1968) "A note on Negro-white differences in attitudes toward the Supreme Court." Social Sci. Q. 49 (December): 557–562. QSR/1,2,4/o/III

HOEBEL, E. A. (1954) The Law of Primitive Man. Cambridge: Harvard Univ. Press. T,CS/5/ms/I,III

HOFFERBERT, R. (1966) "The relation between public policy and some structural and environmental variables." Amer. Pol. Sci. Rev. 60: 73-82.

HOGAN, R. (1970) "A dimension of moral judgment." J. of Consulting and Clinical Psychology 35 (October): 205-212. QSR/1/o/I

HOLLANDER, E. P. (1958) "Conformity, status and idiosyncracy credit." Psych. Rev. 65: 117–127. (Reprinted as pp. 465–475 in E. P. Hollander and R. G. Hunt (eds.) Current Perspectives in Social Psychology. New York: Oxford Univ. Press.) LG,T/2/s/I

——— and R. G. HUNT [eds.] (1963) Current Perspectives in Social Psychology. New York: Oxford Univ. Press. R/2/s,o/I

HOLTZ, W. C. and N. H. AZRIN (1961) "Discriminative properties of punishment." J. of Experimental Analysis of Behavior 4 (July): 225–232. LA/1/l,s/I

HONIG, W. K. [ed.] (1966) Operant Behavior: Areas of Research and Application. New York: Appleton-Century-Crofts. LA,R/1/l/I

HORAI, J. and J. T. TEDESCHI (1969) "The effects of credibility and magnitude of punishment on compliance to threats." J. of Personality and Social Psychology 12 (June): 164–169. LI/1/s/I

HOVLAND, C. I., I. L. JANIS, and H. H. KELLEY (1953) Communication and Persuasion. New Haven: Yale Univ. Press. LI/1/s/I,III

HUNTING, R. B. and G. S. NEUWIRTH (1962) Who Sues in New York City? (Joint Committee on Court Calendar Congestion) New York: Columbia Univ. Press. I/1/sp/III

HUNTINGTON, S. (1962) "Patterns of violence in world politics," pp. 17–50 in S. Huntington (ed.) Changing Patterns of Military Politics. Glencoe: Free Press. H,T/4,3/f/III,I

HURST, J. W. (1964) Law and Economic Growth. Cambridge: Harvard Univ. Press. CS/3/s,sp/III

HYMAN, H. H. (1960) "Reflections on reference groups." Public Opinion Q. 24 (Fall): 383–396. T/2/ms/I

——— (1959) Political Socialization. New York: Free Press. D,T/1,2,3,4/ms/I

——— and P. B. SHEATSLEY (1964) "Attitudes toward desegregation." Scientific American 211 (July): 16–23. QSR/1,3,4/l,s/I,III

INKELES, A. (1968) "Society, social structure and child socialization," pp. 73–129 in J. Clausen (ed.) Socialization and Society. Boston: Little, Brown. T/3/ms/III

IRELAND, T. (1967) "The rationale of revolt." Papers on Non-market Decision-making, III. Charlottesville, Va.: University of Virginia Center of Political Economy.

IRWIN, J. and D. R. CRESSEY (1962) "Thieves, convicts, and the inmate culture." Social Problems 10 (Fall): 142–155. CL/1/l/I

JACOB, H. (1969) Debtors in Court: The Consumption of Government Services. Chicago: Rand McNally.

––– [ed.] (1967) Law, Politics and the Federal Courts. Boston: Little, Brown. (Especially articles by McCloskey, Sorauf, and Dolbeare.) R

–––(1965) Justice in America. Boston: Little, Brown. (Especially chapters 2, 3, and 11.) D/3/grs,f/III

JAHODA, G. (1963) "The development of children's ideas about country and nationality. Part I: the conceptual framework." British J. of Educational Psychology 33 (February): 47–60. I/1/ms/III

JAHODA, M. and S. COOK (1952) "Security measures and freedom of thought: an exploratory study of the impact of loyalty and security programs." Yale Law J. 61 (March): 295–333. I,T/2,1,3/s,e,sp,f/IV,II

JAROS, D. (1967) "Children's orientation toward the President: some additional theoretical considerations and data." J. of Politics 29 (May): 368–387. QSR/1/ms/III

––– H. HIRSCH, and F. J. FLERON, Jr. (1968) "The malevolent leader: political socialization in an American subculture." Amer. Pol. Sci. Rev. 62 (June): 564–575. QSR/1,2/ms/III

JEWELL, M. E. (1968) "Effects of redistricting on metropolitan legislative behavior." Presented to the American Political Science Association.

JOHNSON, R. M. (1967) The Dynamics of Compliance: Supreme Court Decision-Making from a New Prespective. Evanston: Northwestern Univ. Press. QCS/1/ms,l/I,III

JONES, E. E. and H. B. GERARD (1967) Foundations of Social Psychology. New York: John Wiley. R/2/l,s/III

JONES, E. M. (1966) "Impact research and sociology of law: some tentative proposals." Wisconsin Law Rev. 1966 (Spring): 331–339. T/6/o/I

JONES. H. W. (1965) The Courts, the Public, and the Law Explosion. Englewood Cliffs, N. J.: Prentice-Hall. R

KADISH, S. H. (1967) "The crisis of over-criminalization." Annals 374 (November): 157–170. N,D/3/f/II

KAHN, H. (1960) On Thermonuclear War. Princeton: Princeton Univ. Press. E,T/1,3/o/I,II

KALVEN, H. and H. ZEISEL (1966) The American Jury. Boston: Little, Brown. QSR/1,2,3/o/II,III

KARLSSON, G. (1962) "Some aspects of power in small groups," pp. 193–202 in J. H. Criswell, H. Solomon, and P. Suppes (eds.) Mathematical Methods in Small Group Processes. Stanford: Stanford Univ. Press. T/2/s,b/I

KATZ, D. (1960) "The functional approach to the study of attitudes." Public Opinion Q. 24 (Summer): 163–204. T/1/o/I

KATZ, E. (1965) "Patterns of compliance with the *Schempp* decision." J. of Public Law 14, 2: 396–408. QSR/1/l/I,III

——— and P. F. LAZARSFELD (1955) Personal Influence. New York: Free Press. QSR,D/1,2/s,l/I

KAUFMAN, H. (1960) The Forest Ranger. Baltimore: Johns Hopkins Univ. Press. CS/3/grs,s/I

KEATING, W. J. (1968) "The Supreme Court interprets the patent statute: a trilogy of cases and their effect today." Dickenson Law Rev. 72 (Winter): 244–268. CS/2/sp,f/II,III

KELMAN, H. C. (1963) "Three processes of social influence," pp. 438–446 in E. P. Hollander and R. G. Hunt (eds.) Current Perspectives in Social Psychology. New York: Oxford Univ. Press. *T/1/s/I

——— (1958) "Compliance, identification and internalization: three processes of attitude change." J. of Conflict Resolution 2 (March): 51–60. *T/1/l,s/I

KELSEN, H. (1967) The Pure Theory of Law. Berkeley: Univ. of California Press. T,N/3,6/sp/IV

——— (1945) General Theory of Law and State. Cambridge: Harvard Univ. Press. T,N/3,4/sp/IV

KERR, C. and A. SIEGEL (1954) "The inter-industry propensity to strike," pp. 189–212 in A. Kornhauser, R. Dubin, and A. Ross (eds.) Industrial Conflict. New York: McGraw–Hill. ADA,T/5,2,3/o/I,II

KESSEL, J. H. (1966) "Public perceptions of the Supreme Court." Midwest J. of Pol. Sci. 10 (May): 167–191. QSR/1/l/I,III

KITUSE, J. I. (1962) "Societal reaction to deviant behavior: problems of theory and method." Social Problems 9 (Winter): 247–256. QCS/1/o/I

KOHLBERG, L. (1969) "Stage and sequence: the cognitive-developmental approach to socialization," pp. 347–481 in D. A. Goslin (ed.) Handbook of Socialization Theory and Research. Chicago: Rand McNally. T/1/ms/I,III

——— (1964) "Development of moral character and moral ideology," pp. 383–431 in M. L. Hoffman and L. W. Hoffman (eds.) Review of Child Development Research, Volume I. New York: Russell Sage Foundation. T/1/ms/I

——— (1963) "The development of children's orientation toward a moral order." Vita Humana 6 (Winter–Spring): 11–33. T/1/ms/I

KRAUSE, M. S. (1968) School Children's Attitudes Toward Public Authority Figures. (unpublished) QSR/1/ms/III

KRISLOV, S. (1968) The Supreme Court and Political Freedom. New York: Free Press. H,T/3/l,grs,sp,f/I,III

——— (1965) The Supreme Court in the Political Process. New York: Macmillan. T/2,3/grs,sp,f/I,III

——— (1959) "Constituency versus constitutionalism: the desegregation issue and tensions and aspirations of southern attorneys general." Midwest J. of Pol. Sci. 3 (February): 75-92. QSR/1/l/I,III

LaFAVE, W. (1965) Arrest: The Decision to Take a Suspect Into Custody. Boston: Little, Brown. PO/3,4/o/II,III

LANDAU, M. (1965) "Baker v. Carr and the ghost of federalism," pp. 241–248 in G. A. Schubert (ed.) Reapportionment. New York: Charles Scribner's. CS,N/3,6/o/IV

LANE, R. E. (1959) Political Life. New York: Free Press. QSR,T/1,2,4/o/I

——— (1953a) "Law and opinion in the business community." Public Opinion Q. 17 (Summer): 239–257. QSR,T/4/e/I

——— (1953b) "Why business men violate the law." J. of Criminal Law, Criminology and Police Sci. 44 (May–June): 151–165. QSR,ADA/1/ms,sp/I,III

LANGTON, K. (1969) Political Socialization. New York: Oxford Univ. Press. QSR/1/ms/III

LARRABEE, E. (1955) "The cultural context of sex censorship." Law and Contemporary Problems 20 (Autumn): 672–688. ADA,D,N/1,3/sp,ms,m/IV,II

LASSWELL, H. D. (1930) Psychopathology and Politics. Chicago: Univ. of Chicago Press. T,CS/1/l/I

LEE, A. M. and N. D. HUMPHREY (1943) Race Riot. New York: Dryden. CS/3/f/II

LEE, S. (1951) "Agrarianism and social upheaval in China." Amer. J. of Sociology 56 (May): 511-518. H/3/f/III

LEFSTEIN, N., V. STAPLETON, and L. TEITELBAUM (1969) "In search of juvenile justice: *Gault* and its implementations." Law and Society Rev. 3 (May): 491–562. PO/4,1/o/II,III

LERNER, M. (1937) "Constitution and court as symbols." Yale Law J. 46 (June): 1290–1319. N,D/1,3/l,e/IV

LEVINE, J. P. (1970) "The Supreme Court and sex censorship: a study of judicial efficacy," in J. Fiszman (ed.) The American Political Arena. Boston: Little, Brown.

———(1967) "The bookseller and the law of obscenity: toward an empirical theory of free expression." Ph.D. dissertation. Northwestern University. QSR/4/grs,sp,e/I

——— and T. L. BECKER (1970) "Toward and beyond a theory of Supreme Court impact." Amer. Behavioral Scientist 13 (March–April): 561–573. T,N/2,3/s,b,f/I,II

LEWIS, A. (1964) Gideon's Trumpet. New York: Random House. CS/3,4/sp/III

LINDESMITH, A. R. and A. L. STRAUSS (1968) Social Psychology. New York: Holt, Rinehart & Winston. R/2/o/III

LIPSET, S. M. (1960) Political Man. Garden City: Doubleday. T,D/1,3/o/I

LITWAK, E. and H. J. MEYER (1966) "A balance theory of coordination between bureaucratic organizations and community primary groups." Administrative Sci. Q. 11 (June): 31–58. T/3/grs/I

LOTT, B. E. and A. J. LOTT (1960) "The formation of positive attitudes toward group members." J. of Abnormal and Social Psychology 61 (September): 297–300. LI/1/l/I

LOWI, T. (1969) The End of Liberalism: Ideology, Policy, and the Crisis of Public Authority. New York: Norton. H,N,D/2,3/grs/II,IV

LUCAS, J. D. (1963) "Legislative apportionment and representative government: the meaning of Baker v. Carr." Michigan Law Rev. 61 (February): 711–804. CS,D/4/sp,f/II,III

LYTLE, C. (1968) The Warren Court and Its Critics. Tucson: Univ. of Arizona Press. H/2/o/III,IV

MACAULEY, S. (1966) Law and the Balance of Power. New York: Russell Sage Foundation CS/2,3/s,sp,b/III

––– (1965) "Changing a continuing relationship between a large corporation and those who deal with it: automobile manufacturers, their dealers, and the legal system." Wisconsin Law Rev. 1965 (Summer–Fall): 483, 740. CS/2,3/s,sp,b/III

McCloskey, R. G. (1960) American Supreme Court, Chicago: Univ. of Chicago Press.

MACCOBY, E. E. (1968) "The development of moral values and behavior in childhood," pp. 227–269 in J. Clausen (ed.) Socialization and Society. Boston: Little, Brown. T,D/3/ms/III

McCORD, W. and J. McCORD (1959) Origins of Crime: A New Evaluation of the Cambridge Summerville Youth Study. New York: Columbia Univ. Press. I,QSR/1/s/III,II

McDOUGAL, M. S. (1962) "The ethics of applying systems of authority: the balanced opposites of a legal system," in H. Lasswell and H. Cleveland (eds.) The Ethics of Powers: The Interplay of Religion, Philosophy, and Politics.

McKAY, H. D. (1960) "Differential association and crime prevention: problems of utilization." Social Problems 8 (Spring): 25–36. T/3/l/I

McKAY, R. B. (1963) "Political thickets and crazy quilts: reapportionment and equal protection." Michigan Law Rev. 61 (February): 645–710. CS,D/4/sp,f/II,III

––– (1957) "With all deliberate speed: legislative reaction and judicial developments, 1956–1957." Virginia Law Rev. 43 (December): 1205–1245. *ADA,D/4,2/sp,f/III,II

MAIER, H. W. (1965) Three Theories of Child Development. New York: Harper & Row. T/1/ms,m/III

MANWARING, D. (1968) "The impact of *Mapp v. Ohio*," pp. 1–43 in D. Everson (ed.) The Supreme Court as Policy-Maker: Three Studies on the Impact of Judicial Decisions. Carbondale, Ill.: Public Affairs Research Bureau, Southern Illinois University. CS/4,2,3/sp,f/II,III

MARCH, J. G. (1966) "The power of power," pp. 39-70 in D. Easton (ed.) Varieties of Political Theory. Englewood Cliffs, N. J.: Prentice-Hall. T,D/1/s/I

--- and H. A. SIMON (1958) Organizations. New York: John Wiley. T/1,2,3/s/I

MASSELL, G. (1968) "Law as an instrument of revolutionary change in a traditional milieu: the case of Soviet Central Asia." Law and Society Rev. 2 (February): 179–228. H,CS/3/s,f,e/I,III

MATTHEWS, V. (1968) "Differential identification: an empirical note." Social Problems 15 (Winter): 376–383. QSR/1/l/I

MAYHEW, L. H. (1968) Law and Equal Opportunity. Cambridge: Harvard Univ. Press. PO,ADA/2,4,3/sp,f,b/II,III,IV

MAYO, L. H. and E. M. JONES (1965) "Legal-policy decision process: alternative thinking and the predictive function." George Washington Law Rev. 33 (October): 318–456. T/3/o/I

MEDALIE, R. J., L. ZEITZ, and P. ALEXANDER (1968) "Custodial police interrogation in our nation's capital." Michigan Law Rev. 66 (May): 1347–1422. QCS/1/o/II,III

MERTON, R. K. (1957a) Social Theory and Social Structure. New York: Free Press. R/3/grs/I

--- (1957b) "Continuities in the theory of reference groups and social structure," pp. 281–386 in R. K. Merton (ed.) Social Theory and Social Structure. New York: Free Press. T/2,3/o,l/I

--- and A. S. ROSSI (1957) "Contributions to the theory of reference group behavior," pp. 225–280 in R. K. Merton (ed.) Social Theory and Social Structure. New York: Free Press. T/1,2,3/o/I

MILGRAM, S. (1965a) "Liberating effects of group pressure." J. of Personality and Social Psychology 1 (February): 127–134. LI,LG/1,2/s,l/I

--- (1965b) "Some conditions of obedience and disobedience to authority," pp. 243–262 in I. D. Steiner and M. Fishbein (eds.) Current Studies in Social Psychology. New York: Holt, Rinehart & Winston. LI/1/s/I

--- (1964) "Issues in the study of obedience: a reply to Baumrind." Amer. Psychologist 19: 848–852. T,N/1/o/I

MILLER, A. S. (1970) "Science challenges the law: some interactions between scientific and legal changes." Amer. Behavioral Scientist 13 (March–April): 585–593. N/3/o/IV

--- (1968) The Supreme Court and American Capitalism. New York: Free Press. H/4/o,sp/III,II

--- (1965) "On the need for 'impact analysis' of Supreme Court decisions." Georgetown Law J. 53 (Winter): 365–401. ADA,T/2,3/f,sp/IV,II

--- and A. W. SCHEFLIN (1967) "The power of the Supreme Court in the age of the positive state: a preliminary excursus." Duke Law J. 1967 (April): 273–320.

MILNER, N. A. (1968) "The impact of the *Miranda* decision on four Wisconsin communities." Ph.D. dissertation. Univ. of Wisconsin.

MINTURN, L. and J. L. TAPP (1970) Authority, Rules and Aggression: A Cross-National Study of the Socialization of Children into Compliance Systems: Part II. Washington, D. C.: U. S. Department of Health, Education and Welfare. *QSR/5/ms/III

MISCHEL, T. (1964) "Personal constructs, rules and the logic of clinical activity." Psych. Rev. 21 (May): 180–192. T/1/o/I

MITAU, G. T. (1967) Decade of Decision: The Supreme Court and the Constitutional Revolution, 1954–1964. New York: Charles Scribner's. CS/2,3/o/III

MOLLAN, R. (1965) "Smith Act prosecutions: the effect of the *Dennis* and *Yates'* decisions." Univ. of Pittsburgh Law Rev. 26 (June): 705–748. CS/3,2/sp,f/II,III

MOORE, B. (1966) Social Origins of Dictatorship and Democracy. Boston: Beacon. H,T/5,3/e,f/III,I

MORRIS, H. (1965) "Punishment for thoughts." Monist 49 (July): 342–376. N/6/s/IV

MUELLER, P. O. (1965) "Right to counsel at police identification proceedings: a problem in effective implementation of an expanding constitution." Univ. of Pittsburgh Law Rev. 29 (October): 65–88.

MUIR, W. K., Jr. (1967) Prayer in the Public Schools: Law and Attitude Change. Chicago: Univ. of Chicago Press. I/1,2/l/I,III

MURPHY, M. J. (1966) "The problem of compliance by police departments." Texas Law Rev. 44 (April): 939–953. *CS,PO,D/4,2/sp,f/III,II

MURPHY, W. F. (1965) Wiretapping on Trial: A Case Study in the Judicial Process. New York: Random House. CS/4,3,2/sp,f/III

––– (1964) Elements of Judicial Strategy. Chicago: Univ. of Chicago Press. H/1,2,3/sp,f/I,III

––– (1962) Congress and the Court. Chicago: Univ. of Chicago Press. CS/2/o/II,III

––– (1959a) "The south counterattacks: the anti-NAACP laws." Western Pol. Q. 12 (June): 371–390. H/2/e/III,II

––– (1959b) "Lower court checks on Supreme Court power." Amer. Pol. Sci. Rev. 53 (December): 1017–1031. H/3/o/III

––– and C. H. PRITCHETT [eds.] (1961) Courts, Judges, and Politics: An Introduction to the Judicial Process. New York: Random House. R

––– and J. TANENHAUS (1968) "Public opinion and the Supreme Court." Law and Society Rev. 2 (May): 357–384. QSR/1,3/msl/I,III

MUSE, B. (1964) Ten Years of Prelude: The Story of Integration Since the Supreme Court's 1954 Decision. New York: Viking. H,D/2,3/sp,f,l,e/III

––– (1961) Virginia's Massive Resistance. Bloomington: Indiana Univ. Press. CS/3,4/sp,s/II,III

NAGEL, S. S. (1970) Overview of law and social change." Amer. Behavioral Scientist 13 (March–April): 485–491. N/2,3/s,sp/III

––– (1969) The Legal Process from a Behavioral Perspective. Homewood, Ill.: Dorsey Press. (Especially chapters 1, 21, 22, 23.) R

––– (1965a) "Testing the effects of excluding illegally seized evidence." Wisconsin Law Rev. 1965 (Spring): 283–310. QSR/2/s/II,III

––– (1965b) "Court-curbing periods in American history." Vanderbilt Law Rev. 18 (June): 925–944. E,H/2,3/o/III

––– and R. ERICKSON (1966–1967) "Editorial reaction to Supreme Court decisions on church and state." Public Opinion Q. 30 (Winter): 647–655. E/3,4/o/III

National Advisory Commission (1968) Report of the National Advisory Commission on Civil Disorders. New York: Bantam. QSR,ADA/3,4/s,sp,f,o/II

National Conference on Bail and Criminal Justice (1964) Bail in the United States. New York: Record Press. ADA/3/sp,s/IV,III

NESVOLD, B. A. (1969) "A scalogram analysis of political violence." Comparative Pol. Studies 2 (July): 172–194. T,ADA/5/e,f/I,III

NEUSTADT, R. (1960) Presidential Power. New York: John Wiley. E,H/1,4/s,b/III

New York University Law Review [Note] (1967) "Amending the rules of civil procedure after *Hanna* v. *Plumer*: rule 3." 42 (December): 1139–1154. CS/3/sp,f/II

NEWCOMB, T. (1957) Personality and Social Change. New York: Holt, Rinehart & Winston. I/1/ms/III

NEWLAND, C. A. (1964) "Press coverage of the U. S. Supreme Court." Western Pol. Q. 17 (March): 15–36. E/3/o/II,III

NEWMAN, D. S. (1966) Conviction: The Determination of Guilt or Innocence without Trial. Boston: Little, Brown. PO/3,4/o/II,III

NIEDERHOFFER, A. (1967) Behind the Shield: The Police in Urban Society. Garden City, N. Y.: Doubleday. PO,I,D/2,4/sp,f/II,III

OAKS, D. H. and W. LEHMAN (1968) A Criminal Justice System and the Indigent. Chicago: Univ. of Chicago Press. QCS,QSR,PO/1,4,3/sp,l/I,II,III

OLSON, M. (1965) The Logic of Collective Action. Cambridge, Mass: Harvard Univ. Press. T/1,2/s/I

––– (1963) "Rapid economic growth as a destabilizing force." J. of Economic History 23 (December): 529–552. H,T/3,4/e,s/II,I

OSBORNE, H. W. (1968) "On crime, punishment and deterrence." Social Sci. Q. 49 (June): 157–160. T/4/o/I

OSGOOD, C. E. and P. H. TANNENBAUM (1955) "The principle of congruity in the prediction of attitude change." Psych. Rev. 62: 42–55. LI/1/l/III,I

PACKER, H. L. (1968) The Limits of the Criminal Sanction. Stanford: Stanford Univ. Press. N,D/1,3,6/s/II,III,IV

PATRIC, G. (1957) "The impact of a court decision: aftermath of the McCollum case." J. of Public Law 6 (Fall): 455–464. *CS/2,3/o,sp,f/II,III

PAULSEN, M. (1950) "The persistence of substantive due process in the states." Minnesota Law Rev. 34 (January): 91–118. H/4/o/II,III

PELTASON, J. W. (1961) Fifty-Eight Lonely Men: Federal Judges and School Desegregation. New York: Harcourt, Brace & World. CS/1,2/e/II,III

––– (1955) The Federal Courts in the Political Process. New York: Doubleday. T,D/2,3/sp,f/I,III

PENNOCK, J. R. and J. W. CHAPMAN [eds.] (1970) Political and Legal Obligation. New York: Atherton.

PETRICK, M. J. (1968) "The Supreme Court and authority acceptance." Western Pol. Q. 21 (March): 5–19. T/3/ms,s,l,sp/I

PIAGET, J. (1965) The Moral Judgment of the Child. New York: Free Press. CL/1/m/III,II

–––(1962) Play, Dreams and Imitation in Childhood. New York: Norton. CL/1/l/III

––– (1955) The Child's Construction of Reality. London: Routledge. CL,T/1/m/I,III

––– (1952) The Origin of Intelligence in Children. New York: International Universities Press. CL,T/1/m/III,I

––– and A. WEIL (1951) "The development in children of the idea of the homeland and of relations with other countries." International Social Sci. Bull. 3 (Autumn): 561–578. I/1/ms/III

PINCOFFS, E. L. (1966) The Rationale of Legal Punishment. New York: Humanities Press. *N,D/1,3,6/s,grs,sp/IV

PLISKOFF, S. S. and C. B. FERSTER (1968) "Learning: reinforcement," pp. 135–143 in International Encyclopedia of the Social Sciences, Volume 9. New York: Macmillan and Free Press. D/1/l/I,III

POTTER, S. (1948) Gamesmanship. New York: Holt, Rinehart & Winston. PO,N/1,6/grs/I,IV

POWELL, T. (1960) The School Bus Law. Middletown, Conn.: Wesleyan Univ. Press. CS/2,3/sp,f/III

President's Commission on Law Enforcement and Administration of Justice (1967) The Challenge of Crime in a Free Society. Washington, D.C.: Government Printing Office. E/1,2,3/o/II,III

PRITCHETT, C. H. (1961) Congress versus the Supreme Court. Minneapolis: Univ. of Minnesota Press. E,H/4/o/III,II

––– and A. WESTIN [eds.] (1963) The Third Branch of Government: Eight Cases in Constitutional Politics. New York: Harcourt, Brace & World. CS,R/4/sp,o/III

QUINNEY, E. R. (1963) "Occupational structures and criminal behavior: prescription violations by retail pharmacists." Social Problems 11 (Fall): 179–185. QCS/3/sp/III

RABIN, R. L. (1967) "Do you believe in a supreme being – the administration of the conscientious objector exemption." Wisconsin Law Rev. 1967 (Summer): 642–684. PO,I/1,3/sp,f,b,e/II,III

RANDALL, R. S. (1968) Censorship of the Movies: The Social and Political Control of a Mass Medium. Madison: Univ. of Wisconsin Press. I/2/sp/III

RAVEN, B. and J. R. P. FRENCH (1958) "Legitimate power, coercive power and observability in social influence." Sociometry 21: 83–97. LG/2/s/I

RAWLS, J. (1963) "The sense of justice." Philosophical Rev. 72 (July): 281–305. N/6/grs/IV

––– (1958) "Justice as fairness." Philosophical Rev. 67 (April): 164–194. N/1,3,6/grs/IV

––– (1955) "Two concepts of rules." Philosophical Rev. 64 (January): 3–32. N/6/grs,ms/IV

REICH, D. (1968) "The impact of judicial decision-making: the school prayer cases," pp. 44–81 in D. Everson (ed.) The Supreme Court as Policy-Maker: Three Studies on the Impact of Judicial Decisions. Carbondale, Ill.: Public Affairs Research Bureau, Southern Illinois University. CS/4/o/III

REISS, A. J., Jr., and D. J. BLACK (1967) "Interrogation and the criminal process." Annals 374 (November): 47–57. PO/3/sp/III

REMPEL, H. D. (1969) "Justice as efficiency." Ethics 79 (January): 150–155. N/6/o/IV

RICHARDSON, L. (1960) Statistics of Deadly Quarrels. Chicago: Quadrangle. ADA/3/s/I

RIDELLA, J. (1967) "*Miranda*: one year later – the effects." Public Management 49 (July): 183–190.

RIKER, W. (1964) "Some ambiguities in the notion of power." Amer. Pol. Sci. Rev. 58 (June): 341–349. T/6/o/I

ROKEACH, M. (1968) Beliefs, Attitudes, and Values: A Theory of Organization and Change. San Francisco: Jossey-Bass. QSR/1/m,grs/I

––– (1960) Open and Closed Mind. New York: Basic Books. QSR,QCS/1/grs/I

ROSE, A. (1965) Sociology: The Study of Human Relations. New York: Alfred A. Knopf. R/1,2,3/o/III

––– (1962) "Some suggestions for research in the sociology of law." Social Problems 9 (Winter): 281–283. D/1,2,3/grs/I

ROSENBERG, M. (1959) "Comparative negligence in Arkansas: a 'before and after' survey." Arkansas Law Rev. 13 (Spring): 89–114. QSR,T,CS/2,3/sp,f/II,I,III

––– (1958) "Sanctions to effectuate pretrial discovery." Columbia Law Rev. 58 (March): 480–497. ADA/3,4/s,sp,f/II,III

––– and R. H. CHANIN (1961) "Auditors in Massachusetts as antidotes for delayed civil courts." Univ. of Pennsylvania Law Rev. 110 (November): 27–56. CS/3,4/sp,f/II,III

ROSENBERG, M. and M. SCHUBIN (1961) "Trial by lawyer: compulsory arbitration of small claims in Pennsylvania." Harvard Law Rev. 74 (January): 448-472. CS/4,3/sp,f/II,III

ROSENBERG, M. and M. I. SOVERN (1959) "Delay and the dynamics of personal injury litigation." Columbia Law Rev. 59 (December): 1115–1170. ADA/2,3/sp,f/III,II

ROSENBERG, M. J., C. I. HOVLAND, W. J. McGUIRE, R. P. ABELSON, and J. W. BREHM (1960) Attitude Organization and Change. New Haven: Yale Univ. Press. LI/1/s,o/III

ROSENTHAL, C. S. (1954) "Deviation and social change in the Jewish community of a small Polish town." Amer. J. of Sociology 60 (September): 177–181. CS/4/s/III

ROSS, H. L. and D. T. CAMPBELL (1968) "The Connecticut speed crackdown," pp. 30–35 in H. Lawrence (ed.) Perspectives on the Social Order. New York: McGraw-Hill.

––– and G. V GLASS (1970) "Determining the social effects of a legal reform: the British 'Breathalyser' crackdown of 1967." Amer. Behavioral Scientist 13 (March): 493–509. QCS/3/sp/II

ROSSITER, C. (1951) The Supreme Court and the Commander in Chief. Ithaca, N. Y.: Cornell Univ. Press. H/3/o/III

ROUCEK, J. S. (1956) Social Control. Princeton: D. Van Nostrand. R/3/o/III

RUBINGTON, E. and M. S. WEINBERG [eds.] (1968) Deviance: the Interactionist Perspective. New York: Macmillan. R/1/l/III

Rutgers Law Review [Note] (1967) "*Dombrowski v. Eastland* – a political compromise and its impact." 22 (Fall): 137-166.

SANDERS, P. H. (1963) "The Warren Court and the lower federal courts," pp. 423–435 in J. Schmidhauser (ed.) Constitutional Law in the Political Process. Skokie, Ill.: Rand McNally. H/4/sp/III

SARRATT, R. (1966) The Ordeal of Desegregation: The First Decade. New York: Harper & Row. H/4/o/III

SARTORIUS, R. (1968) "The justification of the judicial decision." Ethics 78 (April): 171–187. T/2,3/sp/IV

SAVITZ, L D. (1958) "A study in capital punishment." J. of Criminal Law, Criminology and Police Sci. 49 (November): 338–341. ADA/2,3/s,sp,f/I,III

SAYKO, A. F. (1967) "The impact of the Supreme Court Section 103 cases on the standard of patentability in the lower federal courts." George Washington Law Rev. 35 (May): 818–827. CS/3/sp,f/II,III

SCANDURA, J. (1968) "New directions for theory and research on rule learning. I. A set-function language." Acta Psychologica 28 (November): 301–321. T,D/7/o/I

SCHACHTER, S. (1951) "Deviation, rejection and communication." J. of Abnormal and Social Psych. 46 (April): 190–207. LG/2/l,s/I

SCHELLING, T. (1966) Arms and Influence. New Haven: Yale Univ. Press. T/5/b/I

--- (1960) The Strategy of Conflict. Cambridge: Harvard Univ. Press. T,LG/3,6/b,s/I

SCHMIDHAUSER, J. R. (1958) The Supreme Court as Final Arbiter in Federal-State Relations, 1789–1957. Chapel Hill: Univ. of North Carolina Press. H/3/o/III

SCHUBERT, G. [ed] (1965) Reapportionment. New York: Charles Scribner's. R

--- (1957) The Presidency in the Courts. Minneapolis: Univ. of Minnesota Press. E/4/sp/III,II

SCHUESSLER, K. F. (1952) "The deterrent influence of the death penalty." Annals 284 (November): 54–62. ADA/2,3,5/l,sp,f/II,I

SCHUR, E. M. (1968) Law and Society: A Sociological View. New York: Random House. R/3/o/III

--- (1965) Crimes Without Victims. Englewood Cliffs, N. J.: Prentice-Hall.

SCHWARTZ, R. D. (1965) "Introduction to law and society." Social Problems 13 (Summer, special supplement): 1–3. D/1,2,3/grs/III

--- and S. ORLEANS (1967) "On legal sanctions." Univ. of Chicago Law Rev. 34 (Winter): 274–300. *FE,QSR,D/3,2,5,1/s,ms,f/III

SCHWARTZ, R. D. and J. H. SKOLNICK (1963) "Televised communication and income tax compliance," pp. 155–165 in M. Arons and M. Mays (eds.) Television and Human Behavior. New York: Appleton-Century-Crofts. *T/1,3/s,l/I

--- (1962) "Two studies of legal stigma." Social Problems 10 (April): 133–142. FE/2/O/II

SEARS, R. (1961) "The relation of early socialization experiences to aggression in middle childhood." J. of Abnormal and Social Psychology 63 (November): 466–492. T/1/ms/III

--- (1957) "Identification as a form of behavioral development," pp. 149–161 in D. B. Harris (ed.) The Concept of Development. Minneapolis: Univ. of Minnesota Press. T/1/ms,s/I

--- E. E. MACCOBY, and H. LEVIN (1957) Patterns of Child Rearing. Evanston, Ill.: Row, Peterson.

SEEBURGER, R. H. and R. S. WETTICK, Jr. (1967) "*Miranda* in Pittsburgh – a statistical study." Univ. of Pittsburgh Law Rev. 29 (October): 1–26.

SELLIN, T. (1966) "Effect of repeal and reintroduction of the death penalty on homicide rates," pp. 339–351 in H. A. Bedau (ed.) The Death Penalty in America. Chicago: Aldine. R/6,3/sp,f/IV,III

SELZNICK, P. (1949) T.V.A. and the Grass Roots. Berkeley and Los Angeles: Univ. of California Press. CS,T/4/f,l,s,sp,b,e/I,II,III

SHAPIRO, M. (1968) The Supreme Court and the Administrative Agencies. New York: Free Press. D/1,2,3/o/III

--- (1964) Law and Politics in the Supreme Court. New York: Free Press. CS/3/o/I,III

SHIBUTANI, T. (1955) "Reference groups as perspectives." Amer. J. of Sociology 60: 562–570. T,D/2/s/I

SHIPLEY, P. (1961) "Obscene publication prohibition." Nebraska Law Rev. 40 (April): 481–491. CS,D/4,2/sp,f/II,III

SHOEMAKER, D. [ed.] (1957) With All Deliberate Speed: Segregation-Desegregation in Southern Schools. New York: Harper. CS/1,4/sp/II,III

SHORT, J. F., Jr. (1960) "Differential association as a hypothesis: problems of empirical testing." Social Problems 8 (Spring): 14–24. QSR/1/l/I

SIBLEY, M. Q. (1970) The Obligation to Disobey: Conscience and the Law. New York: Council on Religion and International Affairs. N/6/sp/IV

SIEGEL, A. E. and S. SIEGEL (1960) "Reference groups, membership groups, and attitude change," pp. 232–240 in D. Cartwright and A. Zander (eds.) Group Dynamics. New York: Harper & Row. QCS/2/l/I

SIGEL, R. (1969) "Two years after: change and stability in youth's political views." Presented at the Midwest Political Science Association, Ann Arbor, Michigan. QSR/1/ms/III

--- (1968) "Image of a president: some insights into the political views of school children." Amer. Pol. Sci. Rev. 62 (March): 216–226. QSR/1/ms/III

--- (1965) "An exploration into some aspects of political socialization: school children's reaction to the death of a president," pp. 30–61 in M. Wolfenstein and G. Kliman (eds.) Children and the Death of a President. Garden City, N. Y.: Doubleday. QSR/1/ms/III

SIMON, H. A. (1956) Models of Man. New York: John Wiley. T/1/o/I

--- (1947) Administrative Behavior. New York: Macmillan. T/1,2,3/s,l/I

--- and H. GUETZKOW (1955) "The impact of certain communication nets upon organization and performance in task-oriented groups." Management Sci. 1 (April–July): 233–250. LG/2,3/o/I

SIMON, R. J. (1968) The Sociology of Law. San Francisco: Chandler. R/3/grs/III

SKINNER, F. B. (1953) Science and Human Behavior. New York: Macmillan T/1/l/I

--- (1948) "Superstition in the pigeon." J. of Experimental Psychology 38: 168–172. LA/1/l/I

SKOLNICK, J. (1968) Coercion to virtue: the enforcement of morals." Southern California Law Rev. 41: 588–641. , T/3/sp/II
——— (1966) Justice Without Trial: Law Enforcement in Democratic Society. New York: John Wiley. PO/1/ms,sp/I,III
——— (1965) "The sociology of law in America: overview and trends." Social Problems 13 (Summer): 5–39. D/1,2,3/grs/III
SMELSER, N. J. (1964) "Collective behavior and conflict: theoretical issues of scope and problems." Sociological Q. 5 (Spring): 116–122. T/3/s/I
——— (1963) Theory of Collective Behavior. New York: Free Press. T,D/ /ms,f/I
SMITH, A. J. (1957) "Similarity of values and its relation to acceptance and the projection of similarity." J. of Psychology 43 (April): 251–260. LI/1,2/l/I
SMITH, B. (1965) They Closed Their Schools: Prince Edward County, Virginia, 1951–1964. Chapel Hill: Univ. of North Carolina. CS/1,2,4/sp,f/III
SMITH, M. B., J. S. BRUNER, and R. W. WHITE (1956) Opinions and Personality. New York: John Wiley. CL/1/m/III
SOBEL, N. (1966) The New Confession Standards. New York: Gould Pub. CS,D/2,3/sp,f/II,III
——— (1965) "The exclusionary rules in the law of confessions: a legal perspective – a practical perspective." New York Law J. 154. QCS/1/sp,f/II,III
SOLOMON, R. L. (1968) "Learning: avoidance learning," pp. 148–153 in International Encyclopedia of the Social Sciences, Volume 9. New York: Macmillan and Free Press. D/1/l/I,III
——— (1964) "Punishment" Amer. Psychologist 19: 239–253. T/1/l/I
SORAUF, F. J. (1963) "The released time case," pp. 118–148 in C. H. Pritchett and A. F. Westin (eds.) The Third Branch of Government. New York: Harcourt, Brace & World. CS/4/sp/III
——— (1959) "*Zorach v. Clauson*: the impact of a Supreme Court decision." Amer. Pol. Sci. Rev. 53 (September): 777–791. CS/2/o/I,III
SPECTER, A. (1962) "*Mapp v. Ohio*: Pandora's problems for the prosecutor." Univ. of Pennsylvania Law Rev. 111 (November): 4–45. CS/1,2,3/f,sp/III,II
STEPHENS, O. H., Jr. (1965) "Police interrogation and the supreme court: an inquiry into the limits of judicial policy-making." J. of Public Law 17, 2: 241–257. D/1,2/o/II
STEPHENSON, G. M. (1966) The Development of Conscience. London: Routledge & Kegan Paul. QSR/2/s/III
STONE, J. (1966) Social Dimensions of Law and Justice. Stanford: Stanford Univ. Press.
——— (1950) The Province and Function of Law: Law as Logic, Justice and Social Control. Cambridge: Harvard Univ. Press.
STONE, L. (1965) "Theories of revolution." World Politics 18 (January): 159–176. D/3/o/III

STOUFFER, S. (1955) Communism, Conformity and Civil Liberties. New York: Doubleday. QSR/1,2/o/I

STRATTON, J. R. (1967) "Differential identification and attitudes toward the law." Social Forces 46 (December): 256–262. QSR/2/l,sp/I

STUMPF, H. P. (1966) "The political efficacy of judicial symbolism" Western Pol. Q. 19 (June): 293–303. E/2/l/I,III

--- (1965) "Congressional response to Supreme Court rulings: the interaction of law and politics." J. of Public Law 14, 2: 376–395. D/2/o/I,III

--- (1964) "The congressional reversal of Supreme Court decisions, 1957–1961." Ph.D. dissertation. Northwestern University.

SUCHMAN, E., J. P. DEAN, and R. WILLIAMS, Jr. (1958) Desegregation: Some Propositions and Research Suggestions. New York: Anti-Defamation League of B'nai B'rith. T/2,3,1/ms,l,e/I

SUTHERLAND, E. H. (1961) White Collar Crime. New York: Holt. QCS,T/2,3/sp,f,s/I

--- and D. R. CRESSEY (1960) Principles of Criminology. Philadelphia: J. B. Lippincott. R/3,1,2,4/sp,s,ms/III

TEDESCHI, J. T., T. BONOMA, and S. LINDSKOLD (1970) "Threatener's reaction to prior announcement of behavioral compliance or defiance." Behavioral Sci. 15 (March): 171–179. LI/1/s,b/I

TEDESCHI, J. T., J. HORAI, S. LINDSKOLD, and T. FALEY (1970) "The effects of opportunity costs and target compliance on the behavior of a threatening source" J. of Experimental Social Psychology 6 (April): 205–213. LI/1/l/I

THIBAUT, J. W. and H. H. KELLEY (1959) The Social Psychology of Groups. New York: John Wiley. T/1,2/b,s/I

THIBAUT, J. W. and L. H. STRICKLAND (1956) "Psychological set and social conformity." J. of Personality 25 (December): 115–129. LG/1,2/s,1/I

THOMPSON, V. A. (1950) The Regulatory Process in OPA Rationing. New York: King's Point Press. PO,ADA,D/3,1/sp,ms,grs/III,IV

TILLY, C. and J. RULE (1965) Measuring Political Upheaval. Princeton: Center for International Studies, Research Monograph 19. T/3/e/I

TITTLE, C. R. (1969) "Crime rates and legal sanctions." Social Problems 16 (Spring): 409–423.

TOBY, J. (1964) "Is punishment necessary?" J. of Criminal Law, Criminology and Police Sci. 55, 3: 332–337. T/4/s/I,II,III

TREBACH, A. S. (1964) The Rationing of Justice. New Brunswick, N. J.: Rutgers Univ. Press. I,PO/1,2,4/o/II,III

TRUMAN, D. B. (1962) The Governmental Process. New York: Alfred A. Knopf. T,D/2,4/o/I

TUMIN, M. M. and R. ROTBERG (1957) "Leaders, the led, and the law: a case study in social change." Public Opinion Q. 21 (Fall): 355–370. QSR/4/s,ms/I

TUMIN, M. M. et al. (1958) Desegregation: Resistance and Readiness. Princeton: Princeton Univ. Press. QSR,T/1/ms/I

TURNER, L. H. and R. L. SOLOMON (1962) " Human traumatic avoidance learning." Psych. Monographs 76, 40. LI/1/1/I

TURNER, R. (1964) "Collective behavior and conflict: new theoretical frameworks." Sociological Q. 5 (Spring): 122–132. T,D/3,4/o/I

UCLA Law Review [Note] (1966) "The consenting adult homosexual and the law: an empirical study of enforcement and administration in Los Angeles County." 13: 643–832. ADA,D/2,3/sp,f,s/II,IV

VANLANDINGHAM, K. (1957) "Pecuniary interest of justices of the peace in Kentucky: the aftermath of *Tumey v. Ohio*." Kentucky Law J. 45 (Summer): 607–625. CS,D/3,2/sp,f/II

VINES, K. W. (1965) "Southern state Supreme Courts and race relations." Western Pol. Q. 18 (March): 5–18. CS/2/e/III

––– (1964) "Federal district judges and race relations in the south." J. of Politics 26 (May): 337–357. CS/2/e/III

WALD, M., R. AYERS, D. W. HESS, M. SCHANTZ, and C. H. WHITEBREAD II (1967) "Interrogations in New Haven: the impact of *Miranda*." Yale Law J. 76 (July): 1519–1648. QCS/1,2/sp/II,III

WALKER, E. L and R. W. HEYNS (1962) An Anatomy for Conformity. Englewood Cliffs, N. J.: Prentice-Hall.

WALZER, M. (1970) Obligations. Cambridge: Harvard Univ. Press. N/1,2,3/ms,grs/IV

WARREN, C. (1930) "Federal and state court interference." Harvard Law Rev. 43 (January): 345–378. H,D/4,3/sp,f/III

––– (1922) "The early history of the Supreme Court of the United States in connection with modern attacks on the judiciary." Massachusetts Law Q. 8 (December): 1–23. H,D/4/sp,f/III

WASBY, S. L. (1970) The Impact of the United States Supreme Court. Homewood, Ill.: Dorsey Press. D,T/3/o/I

––– (1968) "The pure and the prurient: The Supreme Court, obscenity, and Oregon policy," pp. 82–116 in D. Everson (ed.) The Supreme Court as Policy-Maker: Three studies on the Impact of Judicial Decisions. Carbondale: Public Affairs Research Bureau, Southern Illinois University. CS/3/sp,f/II,III

––– (1965) "Public law, politics and the local courts: obscene literature in Portland." J. of Public Law 14 (Spring): 105–130. CS/4,3/o/II,III

WASSERSTROM, R. A. (1963) "The obligation to obey the law." UCLA Law Rev. 10 (May): 780–807. *N/2,1/grs/IV

WAY, H. F., Jr. (1968) "Survey research on judicial decisions: the prayer and Bible reading cases." Western Pol. Q. 21 (June): 189–205. QSR/1/e/III

WEBER, M. (1947) The Theory of Social and Economic Organization. (A. M. Henderson and T. Parsons, translators; T. Parsons, editor). Glencoe: Free Press. T/3/grs,s,sp/I

WELLS, R. S. and J. B. GROSSMAN (1966) "The concept of judicial policy-making: a critique." J. of Public Law 15, 2: 286–310. T/3,2/sp/I,IV

WHITE, E. S. (1968) "Intelligence and sense of political efficacy in children." J. of Politics 30 (August): 710–731. QSR/2/ms/III

WHITING, B. [ed.] (1963) Six Cultures: Studies of Child Rearing. New York: John Wiley. PO/5,1/ms,m/III

WHITING, J. (1961) "Socialization process and personality," pp. 335–339 in F. L. K. Hsu (ed.) Psychological Anthropology, Approaches to Culture and Personality. Homewood, Ill.: Dorsey. T/5/f/I

---and I. L. CHILD (1953) Child Training and Personality: A Cross–Cultural Study. New Haven: Yale Univ. Press. PO/5/ms/III

WILSON, J. Q. (1968) Varieties of Police Behavior. Cambridge: Harvard Univ. Press. CS/1,2,4/o/II,III

--- (1966) "Police morale, reform, and citizen respect: the Chicago case," pp. 137–162 in D. Bordua (ed.) The Police: Six Sociological Essays. New York: John Wiley. CS,QSR/2,3/ms,l,e/IV,III

WOLFF, R. P. (1965) Article in R. P. Wolff, B. Moore, and H. Marcuse, A Critique of Pure Tolerance. Boston: Beacon. N/3/ms,grs,f/IV

WON, G. and G. YAMAMOTO (1968) "Social structure and deviant behavior." Sociology and Social Research 53 (October): 44–55. QCS/3/s/III

WOOD, A. L. (1969) "Ideal and empirical typologies for research in deviance and control." Sociology and Social Research 53 (January): 227–241. T/3,4/o/II

WOOTTON, B. A. (1963) Crime and the Criminal Law. London: Stevens. N/1,3/s,sp/IV

WOOZLEY, A. D. (1967) "The existence of rules." Nous 1 (March): 63–79. N/6/grs/IV

Yale Law Journal [Note] (1947) "State court evasion of United States Supreme Court mandates." 36 (February): 574–582. CS/1,2/sp/III

YOUNGER, E. (1966) "Interrogation of criminal defendants – some views on Miranda v. Arizona." Fordham Law Rev. 35: 255–262. QSR/2/sp,f/II

ZAJONC, R. (1960) "Concepts of balance, congruity and dissonance." Public Opinion Q. 24 (Summer): 280–296. T/1/o/I

ZEISEL, H., H. KALVEN, and B. BUCHHOLZ (1959) Delay in the Court. Boston: Little, Brown. ADA/4/o/II,III

ZEITZ, L. (1965) "Survey of Negro attitudes toward law." Rutgers Law Rev. 19, 2: 288–316. QSR/1/o/II,III

ZIGLER, E. and I. L. CHILD (1969) "Socialization," pp. 450–589 in G. Lindzey and E. Aronson (eds.) the Handbook of Social Psychology, Volume III. Reading, Mass.: Addison–Wesley. D/5/ms/III

ZIMRING, F. and G. HAWKINS (1968) "Deterrence and marginal groups." J. of Research in Crime and Delinquency 5 (July): 100–114.
*T,QSR/2/s,ms,f/I,II

Index

The Authors

JOSEPH ADELSON *is Professor of Psychology and Co-Director of the Psychological Clinic at the University of Michigan. He is coauthor, with E. Douvan, of* The Adolescent Experience. *Recently, his major area of research has been political socialization in adolescents.*

LYNNETTE BEALL *is a member of the faculty of the University of California's Department of Psychology at Berkeley. She is coauthor with Dr. Joseph Adelson of a forthcoming book entitled* Political Thinking in Adolescents. *Her current research interests include the development of an instrument to measure shame and guilt and a study of therapeutic versus illegal abortions.*

THOMAS V. BONOMA *at the time of writing was Instructor of Social Psychology at U.S. International University and is pursuing his Ph.D. in the same subject area. His areas of academic interest include the study of power and influence, conflict resolution, and international disarmaments. He is presently on the faculty of the State University of New York at Albany.*

WILLIAM J. BOWERS *is currently Visiting Fellow at the National Institute of Law Enforcement and Criminal Justice, on a leave of absence from Northeastern University where he serves as Director of the Russell B. Stearns Study, a center for the study of youth. His academic interests include the sociology of deviant behavior and social control, youth studies, and research methodology. He is presently engaged in research on the sources of youth protest, with Alexander J. Seidler.*

KEITH O. BOYUM *is a graduate student in political science at the University of Minnesota. He has done research applying small group theory to political groups, particularly collegial courts, and is currently studying the phenomenon of delay in trial courts. The judicial process and American political behavior in general are his major interests.*

JERRY N. CLARK *is a Department of Justice graduate research fellow in political science at the University of Minnesota, and formerly was Assistant*

Professor of political science at Heidelberg College. He received a law degree from the University of Chicago and has research interests in the study of organizations in the criminal justice system and in models of law and development.

MALCOLM M. FEELEY *is Assistant Professor in the Department of Politics at New York University. His main research interests focus on the examination of judicial behavior and, more generally, the problems of compliance to law. He is presently coauthor, with Samuel Krislov and Susan White, of* Manual for the Judicial Behavior Laboratory, *written in conjunction with the Political Laboratory Curriculum Project at the University of Minnesota.*

IVO K. FEIERABEND, *Professor of Political Science at San Diego State College, is currently co-directing a research project funded by the National Science Foundation on "Systemic Conditions of Political Aggression." A former consultant to two task forces of the National Commission on the Causes and Prevention of Violence, Professor Feierabend was also a co-recipient of the Socio-Psychological Prize of the American Association for Advancement of Science.*

ROSALIND L. FEIERABEND, *Professor of Psychology, San Diego State College, shared the Socio-Psychological Prize of the American Association for Advancement of Science with I. K. Feierabend. This prize was awarded for their work on cross-national research on conflict. She has also served as a consultant to the National Commission on the Causes and Prevention of Violence.*

ROBERT S. GERSTEIN *is Assistant Professor of Political Science at U. C. L. A. His major interests are in legal philosophy, political philosophy, and constitutional law. He is currently engaged in research on the subject of legal reasoning and the First Amendment.*

NANCY M. HENLEY *is Assistant Professor of Psychology at the University of Maryland, Baltimore County. Her main areas of interest are interpersonal relations, semantic structure, and nomotics. She is currently engaged in research on communication processes (encoding and decoding).*

ROBERT HOGAN *is Assistant Professor in the Department of Psychology at Johns Hopkins University. His major areas of research are moral development, crime and delinquency, and psychological measurement. He has recently completed two studies: one on police effectiveness, which will appear in the*

Journal of Applied Psychology, *and one on moral judgment and perceptions of injustice, which will appear in the* Journal of Consulting and Clinical Psychology.

SHEILAH R. KOEPPEN *is Assistant Professor of Political Science at the University of Minnesota. Her major interests are in political socialization, ethnic politics, and voting behavior in Anglo-American countries. She is currently doing research on children of "new left" parents.*

CHARLES KORTE, *an Assistant Professor of Psychology at Vassar College, is also a Visiting Professor at State University College, New Paltz, N. Y. His academic areas of interest are experimental social psychology and group dynamics. He is involved at the present time in research on the dissolution of pluralistic ignorance through group interaction, as well as social and economic factors in cross-national acquaintenceship networks.*

SAMUEL KRISLOV *is Professor and Chairman of political science and Adjunct Professor of law at the University of Minnesota, and editor of* Law and Society Review. *He is author of several volumes including* The Supreme Court and Political Freedom, *in the Free Press series "The Supreme Court in American Life," of which he is the editor.*

RICHARD O. LEMPERT *is currently Assistant Professor of law at the University of Michigan, where he teaches administrative law and evidence. He is the author, with Kiyoshi Ikeda, of the article "Evictions from Public Housing: Effects of Independent Review" in the October 1970 issue of* ASR. *His major area of academic interest is the sociology of law.*

FELICE J. LEVINE *is presently a Research Associate at the American Bar Foundation in Chicago. Her academic and research interests lie in the areas of compliance, socialization, and related cognitive processes. She has recently been involved in various projects concerning social science and the law.*

JAMES P. LEVINE *is Assistant Professor of Political Science at the University of Oregon. His academic interests are in the areas of civil liberties, judicial behavior, and American politics. He is coauthor with Theodore Becker of the article, "Toward and Beyond a Theory of Supreme Court Impact," in the March 1970 issue of the* American Behavioral Scientist.

NEAL MILNER *is Assistant Professor of Political Science at Grinnell College, where he also serves as Director of its Urban Studies Program. His major interests are in public law, judicial process, and the administration of urban justice. He is a co-editor with Edward Greenberg and David Olson of* Black Politics: The Necessity of Conflict.

BETTY A. NESVOLD, *Associate Professor of Political Science at San Diego State College, serves as co-director of the research project on "Systemic Conditions of Political Aggression" with I. K. and R. L. Feierabend. She has also served as a consultant to the Task Force on Historical and Comparative Perspectives and the Task Force on Assassinations of the National Commission on the Causes and Prevention of Violence.*

SVENN LINDSKOLD *is Assistant Professor of Psychology at Ohio University. His major interest is in social influence, especially verbal communication and its correspondence with behavior.*

ANTHONY R. OBERSCHALL *is Associate Professor of Sociology at Yale University. Interested in methodology and quantitative techniques, he is author of the book* Empirical Social Research in Germany. *Other areas of academic interest include the study of social movements, collective behavior, political sociology, and social change, with special reference to Eastern Africa.*

RICHARD SALEM, *a past Research Associate of the Russell B. Stearns Study, a center for the study of youth, is currently studying for his doctorate in Sociology at Ohio State University. His major academic interests are in deviant behavior, the sociology of law, the sociology of education, and computer methods. He is presently involved in research which is focused on the influence of the formal organizational structure of the college or university upon the development of student subcultures.*

ROGER C. SCHAEFER *is a graduate student in political science at the University of Minnesota. He has done research on the dynamics of police compliance with* Miranda, *and is currently engaged in a longitudinal study of the socialization of police recruits. His major areas of academic interest include judicial process, criminal law, and constitutional law.*

BARRY R. SCHLENKER, *a former Maytag Fellow in the Department of Psychology of the University of Miami, was at the time of writing a Research Assistant to Dr. James T. Tedeschi in the Department of Psychology of United States International University in San Diego. He is presently at the State University of New York at Albany. He is coauthor with T. Bonoma, R. B. Smith, and J. T. Tedeschi of the recent article, "Prestige of Source on Compliance to Threats," in* Psychonomic Science.

JUNE L. TAPP, *Senior Research Social Psychologist and Program Director of the American Bar Foundation, is also Associate Professional Lecturer in the Social Sciences at the University of Chicago. Social Psychology is her major interest, particularly the development of legal and political attitudes through the life cycle in sub- and cross-cultural settings. She is coauthor with F. Krinsly of the book,* Ambivalent America: A Psycho-political Dialogue.

JAMES T. TEDESCHI, *a social psychologist, is currently on the faculty of the State University of New York at Albany. He was previously at United States International University. Interested in social power and influence, he is the editor of the recent book,* The Social Influences Processes. *He is also coauthor with B. R. Schlenker and T. Bonoma of* Experimental Games.

STEPHEN L. WASBY, *an Associate Professor of Government at Southern Illinois University, was a Russell Sage Post-Doctoral Fellow in Law and Social Science at the University of Wisconsin in 1969-70. He is involved in work on the impact of the Supreme Court, particularly on communication of court decisions to affected publics. He is author of the recently published book* Political Science: The Discipline and its Dimensions: An Introduction.